RIGHT TO EQUALITY IN THE INDIAN CONSTITUTION

Gandhian Studies and Peace Research Series

1. Gandhian Model of Development and World Peace / *R.P. Misra.*
2. Conflict Resolution Through Non-Violence : Role of the Universities. Vol-I : Science and Ethics / *K.D. Gangrade* and *R.P. Misra.*
3. Conflict Resolution Through Non-Violence : Role of the Universities. Vol-II : Development without Destruction / *K.D. Gangrade* and *R.P. Misra.*
4. The Social Philosophy of Mahatma Gandhi / *K.S. Bharathi.*
5. Gandhian Humanism / *Mohit Chakraborty.*
6. Gandhian Holistic Economic / *Shashi Prabha Sharma.*
7. Gandhian Spiritualism : A quest for the Essence of Excellence/ *Mohit Chakraborty.*
8. Gandhian Perspective on Population and Development / *A.K. Sharma.*
9. Thoughts of Gandhi and Vinoba : A Comparative Study / *K.S. Bharathi.*
10. Economic Philosophy of Mahatma Gandhi / *Shanti Swarup Gupta.*
11. The Political Thoughts of Mahatma Gandhi / *K.S. Bharathi.*
12. Gandhi and 21st Century / *Janardan Pandey* (Ed.),
13. Gandhian Philosophy of the Spinning Wheel / *Mohit Chakraborty.*
14. Gandhian Satyagraha : An Analytical and Critical Approach / *Ajay Shanker Rai.*
15. Gandhi and His Religion / *P.A. Raju.*
16. Mahatma Gandhi : Vichar Vithika / *S.P. Agarwal.*
17. Poverty of Gandhian Philosophy / *Himansu Roy.*

The Author

Born in the pre-independence days of 1933, the author post-graduated in Economics and Political Science from the University of Bihar. He had a lurking urge to know Gandhi more deeply whom he adores since his adolescence, while he had participated in the public meetings of Gandhi, Nehru and Rajendra Prasad.

He obtained his Ph.D. degree from Bihar University in 1987 and thereby got a chance to peer into the various facets of the Mahatma, resulting in the publication of this book.

Dr. Saraswati was University Professor of Political Science, Lalit Narayan Mithila University, Darbhanga.

Gandhian Studies and Peace Research Series–18

RIGHT TO EQUALITY IN THE INDIAN CONSTITUTION

A Gandhian Perspective

By

DR. SHASHI NATH SARASWATI

CONCEPT PUBLISHING COMPANY, NEW DELHI-110059

ISBN : 81-7022-951-0

First Published 2002

Published and Printed by
Ashok Kumar Mittal
Concept Publishing Company
A/15-16, Commercial Block, Mohan Garden,
New Delhi-110059 (India)

Phones : 5648039, 5649024
Fax : 091-11-5648053
E-mail : publishing@conceptpub.com

PREFACE

This is a study of the right to equality in India, its theory and practice, in the perspective of the Gandhian ideas on the subject, as the very concept of equality in Modern India was born during the course of the freedom struggle. Mahatma Gandhi elaborated this concept and tested it on the anvil of non-violence. He guided the destiny of the nation towards the goal of political freedom and reshaped its social, cultural and economic thoughts in consonance with the ancient Indian traditions. He inspired and electrified the nation to jettison the aberrations of the colonial rule, and adopt a Swadeshi approach towards the solution of all its pressing and painful problems. The concept, thereby, received a strong pragmatic boost during the Gandhian era, and so conceived and dedicated, it fully developed into a Swadeshi spirit enveloping the entire nation.

Though the concept of equality in the modern world was born in the West, Mahatma Gandhi gave a new dimension to it and anointed it with the ethical tenets common to all religions, and in consonance with the spiritual traditions of ancient India, making it capable of universal application.

The right to equality embodied in the Indian Constitution is the product of a multitude of ideas, the Gandhian ideal being its under lying spirit. This study concentrates on an evaluation of the theory and practice of the right to equality, specially under the perspective of the Gandhian thought, and is postulated on the contemporary relevance of Gandhism in the world, in general, and India in particular.

The purpose of the present study is to conceptualize the basic conditions of equality propounded by Mahatma Gandhi in the light of Western and Indian thoughts and in the perspective of the growing national awareness; to put forth the views of the Founding Fathers of the Constitution, vis-a-vis their bestowal within the perimeter of the Constitution of the Indian Republic; and to discern the measures to bring about socio-economic reforms in free India, *pari passu* with the pitfalls, which instead of further strengthening the chord of equality and fraternity that bound the nation during the pre-independence days have only accentuated inequality and rent as under the bond of fraternity. It is meet and proper that the precepts should be correlated to practice so as to assess the nature and extent of deviations and bottlenecks and to formulate the remedy. It may thereby generate a constructive approach to the problems bewildering the nation; a re-appraisal of our policies designed to secure equality; a lessening of the yawning gap between profession and practice; and a reduction of the widening divergence between means and ends. The work is further designed to trace the course of egalitarian revolution under the aegis of the State and observe its crystal form, disembroiled under the judicial focus, to ascertain the seminal meaning to the egalitarian provisions of the Constitution.

The whole life and thought of Gandhi was an experiment with the trinity of "equality, liberty and fraternity" the central idea that dominated the French Revolutionaries. For nearly decades he worked to perfect this idea, and it released an indomitable force that ultimately brought "Swaraj" to a nation steeped in ignorance, drudgery and squalor, but time was not ripe for *swaraj*. It was yet to come. But freedom from foreign yoke was the first essential task, and it was achieved, so that the nation could further proceed on the Gandhian lines towards the achievement of a true "Swaraj". But unfortunately with the liberation of the motherland, the Gandhian era came to a tragic end. The Swadeshi spirit kindled by Bapu was put down by a cruel hand, and the "Videshi" spirit began to raise its ugly head.

The five decades of freedom have silently witnessed the darkness on the horizon stretching its fangs on the nation, penetrating every nook and corner, and the end of the Nehruvian era is marked by a hectic effort to revive and resuscitate the nation sinking in the abyss of despondence. Smt. Indira Gandhi, imbued with the Gandhian spirit and invigorated in the freedom movement, resolutely tried to emancipate the nation drifting and sinking in the whirlpool, deviating from its avowed path, with all her might, but the efforts were only a tinkering with the massive problems and of not much avail. The young Prime Minister of Modern India, Shri Rajiv Gandhi, faced the winds trying to blow up the nation generated by the contradictions of Swadeshi and Videshi rupturing the fabric of the nation. But his life was cut short-before it bloomed. It is high time now that Mahatma Gandhi is remembered and searched out because the writer affirms that only Gandhian prescription can be the panacea for the problems the nation is beset with. It is because the nation has deviated from the right path set by the Father of the Nation and is lured onto the abominable path of the materialistic West which was unequivocally rejected by the pioneers of the national movement, whose zeal, valour and dedication had snatched freedom from the foreign yoke, that an impasse has been created and the nation has reached a blind alley. We have to trace the deviations, select the noble path set out in the constitutional framework and get on to this path unhesitatingly in the national interest.

The main object of the present work is to show that the blind simulation of the Western order and the senseless denunciation of the Gandhian order as archaic, soon after the brutal killing of Gandhi in the post-independence era, by the people at the helm of affairs, have cumulatively acted to produce divisive and chaotic conditions that are bound to lead to decomposing and disintegrating of the nation. It is the resultant of the mistakes and derivatives of the misconceptions which bedeviled the people shaping the destiny of the nation; side tracked from the path of *Swadeshi*; limping on the *Videshi* path; simulating the Western order of devolopment and civilization, forgetting the glorious past of the motherland and deserting the path shown by the Father of the Nation.

For this purpose, we have to examine the main tenets

of Mahatma Gandhi conceived and experimented by him which were prescribed for inherence of equality and fraternity in a society free from foreign yoke, yet rent as under by divisive forces on the social and economic plane. We have further to examine the efforts made by the Founding Fathers of the Constitution towards inculcating the Gandhian prescription of equality and fraternity within the four walls of the Constitution, and to trace, in brevity, the course of the events leading the nation to the brink of disaster. Judicial pronouncements are the surest measure and an accepted yardstick to adjudge whether the hopes and aspirations of the Founding Fathers and the prescriptions of the Constitution have been adhered to by the people at the helm of affairs in the past five decades and whether such prescriptions warranting equality have been followed in practice, in letter and in spirit.

Although there are a number of works on the right to equality, the novelty of the present work lies in presenting a Gandhian perspective in analysis and evaluation of the theory and practice of right to equality under the Indian Constitution. This work has traced the multi-dimensional aspects of the egalitarian revolution in the post-independence era and the judicial pronouncements on disputes related to the equality provisions of the Constitution arising out of State actions. The deadly malignance of the monster of inequality still remains to the scanned. A number of books on the contemporary relevance of the Gandhian views on equality have also been written, but nowhere any diagnosis of the malady permeating the body politic, in the light of the wisdom of the champions of the national struggle been undertaken. The present work is an attempt to show that the Gandhian concept of equality which is the quintessence of the ancient Indian concept, is that notion of equality which was visioned by the eminent leaders of the National Movement as well as the Founding Fathers of the Constitution to pave the way for Swarajya. The Founding Fathers gave a practical shape to this notion as far as the form of a modern democratic constitution and the national perspective permitted. They were all animated with the spirit of equality that had pervaded the whole nation, and this spirit dominates the Constitutional framework.

This study is divided into seven chapters : Chapter One summarizes the notion of equality and presents a gist of its historical development in the modern Western world; compares its philosophic foundation on the paragon of the Indian thoughts on the subject; and proceeds to examine, in brief, the ancient and modern notion of equality in India. As the modern concept of equality in India is directly based on the teachings of Mahatma Gandhi, a synoptic view of the Gandhian concept of equality is also presented. Chapter Two illustrates how the urges towards equality became the driving-wheel of the nation, beginning right from the socio-religious movement which created the embryo of the national movement for liberation from the colonial rule. It puts forth the representative view-points that emanated in the course of the national struggle for freedom including the ideas bequeat-hed by the Founding Fathers of the Constitution, in order to recapitulate how dearly this right was craved for and how deeply our ancestors were spurred with a desire to spray this right in every home in order "to wipe off the tears from every eye". The next four chapters present a crystal clear vision of the equality provisions under Part III and IV of the Indian Constitution disembroiled by the judicial review of the Highest court— Chapter Three contains the meaning and content of the equality of legal Status : Chapter Four succinctly puts forth the provisions of equality of social status; Chapter Five sketches the provisions for equalizing economic opportunities; and Chapter Six deals with the means for ushering in socio-economic revolution enshrined in the Constitution in the form of peremptory directives, not a perfunctory assignment or subterfuge, to the State. These chapters also contain a brief description of the motivating forces behind the adoption of the respective clauses and also a gloomy vista of the governmental policies oriented towards that end.

Chapter Seven visualizes, from the rampart of the fore-going chapters, the conclusion and suggests inter se the long-term panacea which alone can eradicate the dreaded monster of inequality ravaging the nation in spite of the best intent and sound constitutional pharmacopoeia.

In the protracted preparation of this work, the author feels indebted to the following persons and institutions :

(1) All the numberless authors, living or dead, whose books I have desultorily consulted and derived nourishment's from.

(2) My elder brother, Dr. B.N. Saraswati, whose intermittent paternal admonishments was a lively source of inspiration throughout the chequered history of the present work.

(3) My detractors, above all, for making a mountain of the mole-hill that paved the way for my study leave which animated me to address myself to the unfinished task. I am beholden to Dr. Chetakar Jha, Vice-Chancellor, L.N. Mithila University, Darbhanga, for granting the leave.

(4) The Director, ICSSR (Eastern Zone), for the kind grant in November, 1974, which facilitated my studies at the National Library, Calcutta.

(5) The librarian and staff of L. N. Mithila University, Darbhanga Library, National Library, Calcutta, and to my valued colleague, Raj Kumar Jha, for the access to his law library, and to my darling better-half Savitri Rani Saraswati, the luminous light that has guided my destiny, who helped or encouraged in manifold ways in the preparation of this work.

(6) And finally, my mentor and supervisor, Dr. L. P. Sinha, Vice-Chancellor, Himachal Pradesh University, but for whose inspiration and scholarly guidance the present work would not have seen light of the day.

Dahoura-847239 **S. N. SARASWATI**
Darbhanga (Bihar)
The 4th March, 2000

CONTENTS

Preface v

CHAPTER 1

THE CONCEPT OF EQUALITY : WESTERN AND INDIAN **1-81**

(a) Meaning of Equality 1

(b) Evolution of Western Concept 3

(c) Evolution of Indian Concept 18

CHAPTER 2

URGES TOWARDS EQUALITY **82-123**

(a) The Background 82

(b) The Gandhian Era 100

(c) Nehru and Socialism 104

(d) Founding Fathers 114

CHAPTER 3

EQUALITY OF LEGAL STATUS **124-166**

(a) The Background 124

(b) Judicial Interpretation 127

(c) Doctrine of Classification 148

(d) Public Interest Litigation (PIL) 160

CHAPTER 4

EQUALITY OF SOCIAL STATUS **167-215**

(a) Implication and Definition of Terms 167

(b) Judicial Interpretation 169

CHAPTER 5
EQUALITY OF OPPORTUNITY **216-266**
(a) The Background 216
(b) Judicial Interpretation 223
CHAPTER 6
RIGHT TO SOCIO-ECONOMIC JUSTICE **267-300**
(a) The Background 267
(b) Role of Nehru 267
(c) Nature of Directives 274
(d) Role of Indira Gandhi 277
(e) A Resume of the Directives 282
(f) Views of two Founding Fathers 298
(g) Judicial Pronouncements 301
CHAPTER 7
CONCLUSION AND RECOMMENDATION **315-359**
APPENDICES **360-382**
(a) All Parties Conference 1928 360
(b) The Fundamental Rights Resolution 363
(c) Excerpts from advisory Committee Report 368
(d) Fundamental Principles of Governance (Advisory Committee Report) 375
Bibliography 383-390
Index 391-398

CHAPTER 1

CONCEPT OF EQUALITY : Western and Indian

(A) MEANING OF EQUALITY

The notion of equality is, usually, capable of two-fold application. First, it can be used as a moral ideal. We seek equality amongst ourselves, because we think it is just and proper. Not that all men are actually alike, but we think it is just to treat them as such. Secondly, the notion of equality is often related to the notion of sameness, the idea of being alike.

The twin ideas of "equality-as-justice" and "equality-as-sameness" have different connotations, though, ordinarily, one shades into the other. The idea of equality-as-justice first found clear expression in the writings of Aristotle. He firmly believed that equal things should be treated equally and unequal things differently. Yet behind every such argument of equality-as-justice lurks the idea of identical treatment, "of the same measure and proportion for all". When we say "To each his due", we mean that each should have a fair share, and a fair share means that, unless there is justification for acting otherwise, shares should be approximately the same.[1]

The idea of equality-as-sameness was clearly illustrated by Hegel, when he wrote, "equality is the abstract identity of understanding, which means, in plain language, that the levelling and unifying connotation of equality reflects the very pattern of logical thinking, one especially of scientific and mathematical thinking. There is nothing necessarily primitive or ingenuous in thinking of equality as identity. Rather, this notion is another instance of the 'power of reasons', of its ability to reduce the heterogeneous to the homogeneous".[2] Apart from the fact that the idea of justice conveys an idea of sameness, even the scientific thinking of social problems is prone to perceive the sameness of equality much more than equality as just and fair. The point is that the concept of equality in the field of social science proceeds, like natural sciences, by reducing the different to the identical.

The conception of equality is based on the notion of both diversity and identity; whereas equality-as-justice promotes authentic diversity as part of its programme to grant equal opportunity to all, but proscribes privileged differentiation, equality-as-sameness, strictly speaking, stands for uniformity and abhors every diversity. On the operational level, therefore, the principle of equality can be turned into actual operation, into its very opposite; it cuts both ways. We must, therefore, be aware of the import of the word, while using the term "equality", because undue insistence on the notion of equality-as-sameness may lead to its very negation, and it will also be destructive of the notion of justice and fairness, the concept of equality-as-justice. Barring the extremists, therefore, even the modern exponents of equality in the West have positively denied the meaning of equality in terms of equality-as-sameness. Prof. Laski, one of the pioneers of modern socialism, has emphatically repudiated the notion of equality-as-sameness. "Equality does not mean identity of treatment. There can be no ultimate identity of treatment so long as men are different in want and capacity and need. The purpose of society would be frustrated at the outset if the nature of a mathematician met an identical response with that to the nature of a brick-layer. Equality does not even imply identity of reward for effort so long as the difference in reward does not enable me, by its magnitude, to invade the rights of others".[3] Mentioning the conflicting and inter-contradictory role of equality converging on the senses in which we use, Prof. Sartori observes, "The fact that the notion of equality goes back to two irreducible matrices, to two conflicting mental frameworks, helps us to understand why the relationship between equality and liberty is so troublesome. It explains why equality is understood as a way of enhancing individual freedom, but also as a reason for giving up individual freedom : why it can operate as a demand for more respect for each and every individual, but also as a way of repressing individuality and making individuals interchangeable; why it is apprehended as a dynamic ideal intended to promote social, economic and political mobility, but also is denounced as a static and suffocating burden. Actually, in the name of equality, two opposite solutions are favoured : the one which asks for an equality that respects diversity, and the other which sees inequality in every diversity; the one which repudiates privileged differences in order to promote authentic ones, and the other which rejects any difference whatsoever".[4]

It is admitted on all sides that men are evidently unequal as to various characteristics. Apart from the natural differences of capacity and character, sex and colour and other natural endowments, there are also sharp institutional variations as regards citizenship, religion, rank, etc. To claim, in spite of this, that all men are equal, can only mean that the resemblances are more important than the differences. The differences, barring those which are natural, are clearly the result of maladjustments in the society and are created by men. Hence, those differences as are created by men can also be removed by men. On the moral plane also it is admitted that all men are entitled to be treated equally and the moralists, ever since the Stoics, have insisted that men, in spite of their natural differences of character, capacity and intelligence, are of equal dignity as men.

(b) Evolution of the Western Concept

With the fall of the Greek Polis, the idea of equality took leave from that of democracy and, in a space of two thousand years, before the advent of the French Revolution, has grown apart and unconnected with the fate of the sovereign people. The spread of Christianity, the advent of the natural law philosophers, the rise of utilitarians and liberals of the victorian era all have contributed to the growth of the egalitarian notion in the Western thought. They have, however widely differed over the precedence to be given to the various species and have taken equality as the repudiation of certain disparities prevalent in the society, instead of others. Equality before the law, which is based on the principle that every men is equal to the other in his intrinsic worth and dignity, is purely a Christian and ethical conception and though was only a transitory experiment in the Greek Polis, was really affirmed after the fall of the ancient republic. Similarly, the principle that all men have certain basic inalienable and equal rights was based on the nation of natural law, which gained ground in the seventeenth century. John Locke believed "that men by nature are equal,"[5] though he later clarified his statement as referring not to "all sorts of equality since men differ as to age or virtue", but to the equal right that every man hath to his natural freedom".[6] In his essay on human under-standing, he based his idea on the thesis that at birth the soul of man was a tabula rasa, an empty tablet, and everything that developed afterwards was the result of the environment in which he lived, moved and had his being. All his activities, all his conscience and ideas were the result of the happenings around him. "I think I may say", says Locke, "that of all the men we meet with nine parts of ten are what they are, good or evil, useful or not, by their education. It is that which makes the great difference in mankind. The little or almost insensible impressions on our tender infancies have very important and lasting consequences : and there it is as in the fountain of some rivers, where a gentle application of the hand turns the flexible waters into channels that make them take quite contrary courses; and by this little direction given them at first in the source they receive different tendencies, and arrive at last at very remote and distant places. I imagine the minds of children as easily turned this or that way, as water itself".[7]

This notion of Locke that most of the important differences that men had were the result of their own actions shed a new light on the problems of inequality and was a ray of hope to the mankind to check and correct worsening inequalities among them. Locke held that inequalities were not caused by the Divine will nor by Providence, but by something that was done by man himself, and so also can be undone by him.

In 1750, the Academy of Dijon honoured Rousseau for his essay in which he had shown how mankind had degenerated under the civilization. In 1755 he published his work on inequality in which he traced and described the origin and development of inequality among the mankind. Admitting at the outset that there are certain natural and inescapable inequalities based on differences in health, vigour, age, character and intelligence which cannot be made good, he confines his attention to what he calls moral or political inequalities consisting of the "privileges which are enjoyed by some at the expense of others, such as being richer, more honoured, more powerful, or able to make others obey".[8] He maintained that there was perfect equality among the primitive men and it was only with the growth of civilization that inequalities, came to the fore. He concluded, therefore, that all the man-made inequalities, which he called moral and political, all the unhappiness and misery of the human race were growing apace with the growth of civilization". As there is hardly any inequality in the state of nature, all the inequality which now prevails owes its strength and growth to the development of our faculties and the advance of the human mind, and becomes at last permanent and legitimate by the establishment of property and laws. Secondly, it follows that moral inequality, authorized by positive right alone, clashes with natural right, whenever it is not proportionate to physical inequality; a distinction which sufficiently determines what we ought to think of that species of inequality which prevails in all civilized countries; since, it is plainly contrary to the law of nature, however defined, that children should command old men, fools wise men, and that the privileged few should gorge themselves with superfluities, while the starving multitude are in want of the bare necessities of life".[9]

However, Rousseau did not believe in exact economic equality, and held that "political distinctions necessarily produce civil distinctions".[10] In the social contract Rousseau makes several observations about equality. "Everyone should have something, and none too much", "The ideal state is one in which there are neither rich nor poor". "As for equality, it should not mean that all degrees of power and wealth should be exactly the same; rather it should mean that power should never be gained by force or violence, and it should be exercised in an orderly manner and according to law; and as for the wealth, no citizen should be rich enough to be able to buy another, and none so poor as to be forced to sell himself".[11] The message of Rousseau was carried far and wide and the men began to have faith in what he said. He, along with several other thinkers of his time like Helvetins (Det. 'Esprit, Del' Home), Holbach (System de la Nature), Diderot and the Encyclopedists, contended that the universe is essentially materialistic and every phenomenon herein, including those of human miseries, should be adjudged on the materialistic plane. It is not the Divine Power or Providence which has caused human miseries.

If we wish to improve our lot, the remedy lies in our own hands. And thus it was emphatically asserted that man had the power and strength to improve his lot by undoing what had been done blindly. Equality and liberty were within the reach of mankind, if it was not coming it was due to the faults of the erring mankind. Thus, it was ably demonstrated that man possessed tremendous power in his ability to change and form the mind of the young.

The victorian thinkers, like Mathew Arnold as well as the utilitarian, notably J. S. Mill and Jermey Bentham, have all emphasized the desirability of equality, not equality of capacity or attainment, of course, but of circumstances, of opportunities and manners of life. In a discourse on inequality Mathew Arnold had observed that in England inequality was almost a religion. He considered such a situation as an inhuman state of affairs and as incompatible with the dignity of man as a man, which is the hallmark of a civilized nation. "On the one side, in fact, inequality harms by pampering; on the other by vulgarizing and depressing. A system founded on it is against nature, and, in the long run, breaks down".[12] J. S. Mill was a staunch advocate of liberty and was acutely sensitive to the importance of encouraging and maintaining the various diversities of mind and taste in human beings. He urged the direction of social and governmental policy in such a way as to secure increasing equality, though he never meant by his utterances and writings that the varieties of individual genius and character should ever be suppressed by those policies. He firmly held that it was only in a society marked by a large measure of economic equality that such varieties grow and prosper, find their full expression and receive due appreciation. It was in the interest of those diversities of human character and capacity that he argued that "the best state for human nature is that in which, while no one is poor, no one desires to be richer".[13]

Commenting on the Victorian conception of equality, Prof. Tawney, observes : "Perhaps, therefore, the remote Victorian thinkers, like Arnold and Mill...who commended equality to their follow-countrymen as one source of peace and happiness were not speaking so unadvisedly as at first sight might appear. They did not deny that men have unequal gifts... what they were concerned to emphasize is something more elementary and commonplace, that in spite of their varying characters and capacities, men possess in their common humanity a quality which is worth cultivating, and that a community is most likely to make the most of that quality if it takes into account in planning its economic organization and social institutions if it stresses lightly differences of wealth and birth and social position, and establishes on firm foundations institutions, which meet common needs, and are a source of common enlightenment. The individual differences of which so much is made, they would have said, will always survive, and they are to be welcomed, not regretted. But their existence is no reason for not seeking to establish the largest possible measure of equality of environment, and circumstance, and opportunity. On the contrary, it is a reason for redoubling our efforts to establish it, in order to ensure that these diversities of gifts may come to fruition".[14]

The ideal of equality thus marched on and on till the last quarter of the eighteenth century. Sometimes it expressed itself in an open revolt, but more often it smouldered behind the curtain. The writers like Hobbes, Locke and Rousseau gave definite impression to the people that men were unequal because men themselves made them so. Commenting on the startling suddenness with which the ideas of the eighteenth century philosophers were accepted by the people around the world, Prof. Paul Hazard has made the following observation :

> "What a contrast! What a sudden change! The ideas of the seventeenth century were social stratification, discipline, order under authority and a set of beliefs, which firmly ruled life. In contrast, their immediate successors, the men of the eighteenth century hated all constraint, authority and dogma. The former were Christians, the latter anti-Christian; the former believed in Divine Law, the latter in Natural Law; the former lived at ease in a society divided into classes, the latter yearned only for equality. The new generation took delight in criticizing the older; it imagined that it was about to reform a world that had waited all this time for the arrival of this particular new generation at last to progress. Most of the French used to think like Bossuet; all of a sudden they thought like Voltaire. It was a revolution".[15]

Mankind had yearned and fretted about liberty and equality across the ages, and the ideas of the eighteenth century philosophers made them realize that they might be possible of achievement. In France, the champions of liberty, Francis Bacon, Locke, Voltaire, Montesquieu, Diderot had greatly influenced and intoxicated the public mind, while in America their ideas were sponsored in their broader conception, chiefly by men like Benjamin Franklin, Thomas Paine, John Adams, Washington, Hamilton, Dewitt Clinton, Madison, John Marshall and Monroe. In France, the idea of liberty was extended to the field of agriculture, industry and commerce as well by Quesnay, Turgot and later on Adam Smith who developed the idea of laissez-faire. The writings and speeches of these eminent persons in France and America pregnant with the idea of liberty and equality heralded a new age and at last it seemed that men were going to act to get out of the imbroglio created by their own wrongful actions in the past. And far across the seas, it was in the little group of English colonies that they acted first by declaring their Independence. Eulogising the principle of liberty and equality, the declaration of Independence commenced as follows :

"When in the course of human events, it becomes necessary

> for one people to dissolve the political bonds which have connected them with another, and to assume among the Powers of the earth the separate and equal station to which the Laws of Nature and of Nature's God entitle them, a decent respect to the opinions of mankind requires that they should declare the causes which impel them to the separation".
>
> "We hold these truths to be self-evident, that all men are created equal, that they are endowed by their creator with certain unalienable Rights, that among these are Life, Liberty and the pursuit of Happiness".[16]

It is significant that at the time when in Europe there were so many advocates of equality, in America it was only the principle of liberty which concerned most of the thinkers and equality held its sway only on the frontier or in men like Thomas Jefferson. Yet the notion of equality loomed large by 1776 and enjoyed a prime position in the Declaration of Independence. The egalitarians drafted the Declaration of 1776 and also the Ordinance of 1785, but by 1787 the importance of the notion of equality was on the wane. When the constitutional convention was in the process of drafting the constitution, Jefferson was in France, and the liberals held sway for whom liberty was supreme for consideration. The Fathers of the Constitution were stout advocates of liberty and hardly any of the seemed to believe firmly in equality.

In spite of their irreverence to equality, we find that the Fathers of the Constitution were not spiteful of every sort of equality. The American society was a new world inhabited by the "Good old savages" and there was as yet hardly any sharp line of distinction between the rich and the poor. The social classes were not sharply divided nor the class lines sharply drawn. The problem of equality in such a society was not marked by an acute economic or social division. Yet true to the spirit of the Declaration, their actions, in introducing the prohibition of titles of nobility as well as the incorporation of the Bill of Rights which gave to the people equality before the law before the final ratification of the Constitution by the Thirteen States, well exemplify their sentiment, inchoate yet profound, that no matter how unequal men may be in their abilities, which they believed as a fact, in some deeper sense all men are essentially equal by virtue of being rational creatures.

The truth is that in the United States equality to the Fathers of the Constitution meant, above all, an equality of human values. Granting the inevitable differences of character, ability and intelligence in human beings, it was assumed that the new people inhabiting the colonies be given an equal start in the race for success. The race for success could, however, be achieved only when there was liberty to the people. Liberty was, therefore, a more itching problem than equality for this new nation.

The French society, by the age of Louis XVI, was clothed in a multitude of different forms of privileges. The elite of the French society influenced by the writings of Hobbes, Locke, Rousseau, Montesquieu, Voltaire and others, were endowed with a vision of liberty and equality, which embraced the whole world of human effort though its feet were planted on the solid ground of its own generation. The privileges which they attacked were concrete and specific; the equality which they demanded was definite and precise. They resented the special economic privileges guaranteed to the few by the laws of the State; they strived for an equality, which would establish itself in the society when these privileges established by law would cease. The social order against which the attack was launched was bedevilled with an inequality, which was not accidental, but planned and systematized.

The concept of equality in the United States, it seems, was based more on humanistic notion of equality of all mankind, rather an open revolt against the social order. Their faith and belief in equality was based on their conviction that the differences in men were less important than the bond of common humanity that unites them, and, therefore, they were inimical to the capricious divisions between the members of the human race, which were based not on any qualitative distinction, but on external conditions, like birth or wealth, which were the doings of men themselves. The notion of equality to the French was a crying need of the hour and it was symbolic of their revolt against chance, arbitrary and capricious power, and crystallized privileges. It was a revolt against that attitude of the minds of the French people which judges it appropriate and natural that different sections of the community should be sharply divided from each other by the differences of the economic, social and political status, of culture and environment, and regards with approval the institutions and arrangements which perpetuate and emphasize those differences and disparities. The Declaration of Rights of Man only affirmed the principle of equality; and the belief of the liberals, who then held sway in the National Assembly and drafted the Declaration of Rights, in the common bond of humanity that unites every individual, and their determination to eliminate such inequalities as have their source not in individual differences, but in the institutions and organizations established by men themselves. But the liberals were better advocates of liberty and the draft of the Declaration which guaranteed freedom of speech, freedom of worship and freedom of person, and in the economic sphere too adopted the policy of laisez-faire by legislating the Government out of business, bears evidence to it. Then came the National Convention which was dominated by men like Marat and Robespierre with their deep passion and profound zeal for equality. They not only put the government back in the seat of power and made use of its machinery to realize speedily the social changes of their dream, but also guillotined the rich and the well to do, who were against any infringement of individual liberty. Referring to the impact of the French Revolution, Lord Acton has said, "The deepest cause which made the French Revolution so disastrous to liberty was its theory of equality".[17] The champions of equality in the United States were dismayed by what happened to the concept of liberty in France after the National convention where the principle of equality was carried too far; they were, therefore, better advised of moderation and restraint". Most of these same leaders were not enamoured of the idea of equality, beyond a mere equality before the law and an equal voice in government; and undoubtedly the theoretical equalitarians lost some of their enthusiasm in watching the horrors of the French Revolution where liberty was sacrificed at the altar of equality".[18] Where equality in the United States was adopted as a way of life in the New World, the equality to the Revolutionaries in France became a principle of governmental policy and their avowed desire to remove the inequalities enveloping the French society by governmental measures". In the United States equality means, above all, as Bryce remarked, equality of estimation—an equality which goes back to the conviction that men are equal in their 'ultimate value', and which, therefore, resolves itself into equal value which men set upon one another, whatever be the elements that come into this value". For this reason American democracy has been characterized as a social democracy, as a way of life basically expressed in a general levelling of status, in equal treatment and respect for the next man, whoever he may be".[19] The ushering in of democracy in France was of a different order, and it was more like a socialist democracy where the atmosphere remains different than social democracy. "Since, in this case the problem is economic equality (from which, eventually, social equality, will automatically flow), this equality is not felt to be, or practised as, an ethos. The difference lies, then, not only in the dissimilar natures of the respective values of equality, but also in the fact that while social democracy is primarily a way of life, socialist democracy is above all a way of governing, which is tantamount to saying that it is more an enforcement of policy than a spontaneous force in social life, more legislation than custom" [20]

Verily, the political thinkers and theorists expressing themselves on equality may be grouped under three heads : liberals, democrats and socialists. The chief concern of the liberals was to safeguard individual liberty and their moralistic notion of equality-as-justice was understood only as a way of enhancing individual freedom, not in any way hampering it. They did not frown at any such suggestion as equality of treatment, as a mark if ending privileges of the few, by which they meant only an impartial allocation of some benefits or burden. The rules which allocated benefit or burden in equal amounts to everyone were considered egalitarian. The liberals were content with advocating merely the equal allocation of certain basic natural rights, which, they felt, should lead to the equal distribution of opportunities. "If legal privileges are abolished and legal rights protected, no obstacle will stand in the way of anyone's pursuit of happiness".[21]

However, the advent of the Industrial Revolution brought

in its trail an increasing awareness that the equality of opportunity to the mankind cannot be achieved only by the magic wand of equality before the law. Only by giving the least able and the most able an equal start in the race for success, equality of opportunity cannot be achieved. It presupposes not only the equal allotment of certain basic rights, but also the equal satisfaction of certain basic needs of mankind. These needs of mankind can be met with only by following an inegalitarian rule of allotment : privileges for the economically under privileged and socially handicapped. The better endowed will definitely outpace those who are underprivileged and handicapped in the race for success. Wrote Tawney, "Equality of opportunity is not simply a matter of legal equality. Its existence depends not merely on the absence of disabilities, but on the presence of abilities. It obtains in so far as each member of the community whatever his birth or occupation, or social position, possesses, in fact, and not merely in form, equal chances of using to the full his natural endowments of physique, of character, and of intelligence".[22]

The demand for equality started as protest against unjust, arbitrary and man-made inequalities and claimed the adoption of such principles as "the right man in the right place" or "the best man in the highest place". It was a cry against the privileges of the few over the many, and the solution was apprehended in the equal access to opportunities. The classical liberalism held that if only the legal privileges are abolished and legal rights safeguarded, nothing would stand in the way of anyone's opportunity to rise as best as he can. With the advent of Industrial Revolution, however, it was felt that the equality of opportunity cannot be achieved by the "majestic equality of the law which forbids rich and poor alike to steal bread and to sleep under bridges".[23] The rule which confers equally certain basic rights or burdens on everyone deals only with the distribution of access to various positions in the society. But those who are handicapped by the lack of basic physical and educational requirements will naturally lag behind in the race for success where the differences between the haves and the have-nots are wide and agape.

The Industrial Revolution, which brought in its wake the democratic resurgence, led to an increasing realization that the equality of opportunity can be bestowed by the twin principle of equal allotment of basic rights, as well as the equal satisfaction of basic needs. The equal satisfaction of the basic needs, however, required certain levelling process; to give all an equal start in the race for success in achieving the best in one's self. Some must belifted up and others moved down by means of social legislation and by providing social services. It also requires a reduction of extreme in equalities in the distribution of wealth and commodities in order to compensate those with initial disadvantages. This was, probably, the stage where the liberals separated from the democrats in their mission to achieve equality because the panacea smacked of infringement of and interference with the liberties of the people. The liberals were not prepared to yield to the task of denaturalizing the social order and put infringement on the individual liberty in the interest of more equality.

The democrats, therefore, took up the cudgels where the liberals gave way, by seeking precisely that part of the notion of equality as justice, which does not follow spontaneously in the wake of freedom.

The democratic conception about the notion of equality involves three specific points : (i) equal universal suffrage, i.e. equality of opportunity in the exercise of political power as a mark of completion of political freedom; (ii) social equality, i.e. absence of all artificial barriers and discriminations as well as the end of crystallized privileges; and (iii) equality of opportunity, understood not only in the sense of equal allocation of basic rights, but also equal satisfaction of the basic needs. Basically, the democratic movement is concerned with political freedom or political equality and removal of social bondage, yet what separates democracy from the liberalist thought is its doctrine of economic equality as a means of providing equal satisfaction of basic needs to the teeming millions for the ultimate realization of equality of opportunity.

On the other hand, the socialists, like the liberals, are those who are prone to go to the other extreme for the sake of equality. It is not that they do not want liberty, but for the sake of equality they are impelled to propose solutions which may take away some important individual liberties. Thus, the difference between the democrats and the socialists lies primarily in the difference between the values of equality esteemed by them.

The socialists also, like the democrats, seek the goal of equalizing opportunities and towards that end they are staunch advocates of economic equality. Yet the means, the formula of economic equality, propounded by the democrats differs sharply from that of the socialists of the Marxist brand; whereas the former aspire to achieve a synthesis of the different forms to achieve the equilibrium between liberty and equality, the latter devises its own ways and means to achieve economic equality, even to the exclusion of the rest and the negation of liberty. Prof. Sartori has neatly summed up the difference : "The difference between the democratic and the Marxist way of striving for equalization of circumstances can be clearly perceived. This goal can be sought for the sake of mobility or for the sake of sameness, for the sake of freedom or for the sake of levelling. In both cases intervention of political power is required, but this intervention can be employed for entirely different purposes : either with a view to giving to every one enough power to offer him equal opportunities to rise, or with a view to taking away all power from everyone for the sake of equality in itself. And there is an abyss between the approach of granting equal rights, opportunities, and starting points on the basis of the presupposition that the beneficiaries neither are nor must become equal, and the approach of imposing sameness as an *a priori*, definitive solution to the problem of these rights and opportunities".[24] We, therefore, are inclined to hold that the main points of difference between the various systems of thought lie with the ways and means devised to achieve equality as well as their stress on the removal of certain inequalities instead of others.

In their quest for providing equal satisfaction of the basic needs of the people, the democratic socialists' primary emphasis is on a fair and equitable distribution of the means of consumption, while the socialists adhering to the Marxist doctrine decry these solutions as "obsolete verbal rubbish". According to Marx, the basic contradiction of capitalism is the increasingly co-operative nature of production made necessary by the new powers of production and the individual ownership of the means of production. This inherent contradiction in the capitalist system is the cause of all conflict, movement and change. This contradiction shows itself in the existence of two classes, capitalists and workers : the one owning the means of production and the other owning nothing except his labour power. The inevitable antagonism between the incompatible interests of the two classes results in a ceaseless strife. Marx, too, realized that "one man is superior to another physically and mentally" and interpreted equality—at least in the first phase of communism—as the opportunity for each to occupy the position, which corresponds to his ability. Contrary to Neoliberals and socialists, Marx believed that this goal could not be reached through a redistribution of the means of consumption, but only through the abolition of the private control of the means of production. Their "common ownership" would eliminate the possibility of exploitation and class struggle; and "with the abolition of class distinctions all social and political inequality arising from them would automatically disappear by itself".[25]

Marx also refutes the contention of the democratic socialists that the allocation of rewards should roughly correspond with the merit or ability. In view of the inequality of ability, the equal distribution of opportunities will inevitably lead to unequal allocation of rewards. "Marxists believe that the first stage of communism, in which means of consumption are distributed according to the work performed, will inevitably evolve, from formal equality to real equality, i.e. to realizing the rule; 'From each according to his ability, to each according to his need.' Positions would still be correlated to ability, but everyone (so, the Marxists believe) will work spontaneously to the best of his ability even without incentives, and compensations will differ according to need, regardless of the type of work".[26] Marx thus deliberately and ostentatiously has eliminated the moral basis of socialism and its appeal to equality-as-justice. He has shorn the socialist movement of its idealism, and to the utmost of his influence made it sordid. He has deprived the social movement of its universal character and infused into it a leaven of hatred and intolerance. "The principle" from each according to his ability and to each according to his need, is unreal, unscientific, unjust and unjustified. Equal remuneration for unequal ability, for differing labour contribution, are simply new types of injustice. They go against nature, obstruct progress, do nothing to advance productive forces—the material preconditions for equality".[27]

The Marxist resolves the problem of economic equality once and for all by abolishing private ownership of property, thus abolishing one of the strongholds of inequality. Private ownership is substituted by public ownership, which in itself cannot be supposed to bring automatically economic equality as a means of providing adequate economic opportunity to rise. The evidences offered by the communist systems are sufficient to hold that to make everyone a have-not does not satisfy the purposes for which Marx called for the extermination of the haves. "State ownership becomes the foundation of the bureaucratic monopoly of the management of people and all social activities, monopoly over the disposal of all newly created value (surplus) on behalf of society. Although it is not identical with private appropriation on the basis of personal ownership, it nevertheless leads to material privileges and satisfaction of the narrow interests of the bureaucracy. But even if no material privileges were involved, even if the bureaucracy conducted itself with asceticism, it would still hold a great concentration of social power in its hands, and this is a form of inequality. Economic life begins to develop more and more by the logic of political power, subjective decisions, and not on the basis of economic laws and criteria. The outcome is obvious : inefficiency and waste of society's resources".[28]

The State as the sole owner of property and controller of the means of production creates premises for a truly formidable inequality of power. Be property, private or public, it is equally applicable in every case that "power over a man's subsistence is power over his will".[29] In a democratic setup the State keeps an eye on private property owners; but in the socialist system there is no machinery or institution to keep an eye on the property-owning State. The will of the giant State cannot be resisted by the citizens, even if it divests them of their liberty, because they lack the economic self-sufficiency to do so. The result is an arbitrary and unbridled power in the hands of bureaucracy and political bosses.

It is evident, therefore, that the Western concept of equality varies from country to country according to their form of government which they establish and the institutions and organizations which receive their sanction. We are not here concerned with finding out the nature of true equality or finding out the equality in an absolute sense. The differences in the conception of equality chiefly relate to the accentuated emphasis on the removal of particular inequalities on a priority basis or as the repudiation of certain differences amongst the mankind instead of others.

(c) Evolution of the Indian concept

(a) Ancient Concept

The concept of equality in India, however, differs sharply from the Western concept, both in form and content as well as in the ways and means to achieve it. In India it was cultivated as a way of life in the prehistoric age, not as a matter of political expediency as in the West. Though the Indian concept of equality is best epitomized in the Gandhian thoughts because Gandhi, after his deep study of the ancient heritage, ardently believed that if equality is to live, it must be cultivated as way of social life or it would not be alive. The Gandhian concept is only a rephasing of the ancient Indian socio-economic system in the context of modern India. Gandhi puts forth the ancient Indian concept in embryo while formulating his own views on equality. But before we embark on the Gandhian track, it is relevant to trace out some vital differences, between the two streams of thought and some basic tenets of the ancient Indian concept of equality.

(i) Philosophic Foundation

It is meet that in any study of our social customs and ancient traditions we should diligently avoid any blind comparison with those of the West, as they are most likely to lead us to erroneous notions and astounding fallacies, because the basis on which these are founded is the philosophy, the outlook and the way of life, and these, inter se, vary essentially.

The philosophy of the West is essentially materialistic. Everything depends on matter and is the resultant of matter. The Indian philosophy, on the other hand, is a synthesis of matter and spirit. The whole universe is pervaded by these two elements. The matter comes from the spirit, depends on spirit and lives with the spirit. The two are in an inseparable existence.[30] A knowledge of the spirit is essential for the knowledge of the matter. The Indian traditions and systems of thought are, therefore, shaped by this knowledge of spirit and matter, the stress on spirit being accentuated on account of its finality and ultimate reality. To grasp this ultimate knowledge, the window on their civilization was wide open to receive and ponder over the ideas coming from all parts of the world.

The Western traditions and systems of thought are based, primarily, on the knowledge of matter and are shaped and influenced by it. Any comparison of the two social systems must, therefore, reckon with this essential difference underlying them. The Western world has considerably extended our knowledge of worldly materials, but they also owe heavily to the East for an understanding of those phenomena of this worldly life which are not materialistic, but spiritualistic. The concept of equality is not materialistic, because in the material world no two are like. The conception of equality is based on the spiritualistic notion of oneness, and it seems based on the Indian conception of oneness or equality of all beings. The concept of equality has its root in the Indian philosophical thinking, which is admittedly the most archaic in the world, wherefrom, through the migration of men and materials, it has spread to other parts of the globe.

A second characteristic of the Indian system of thought which patently distinguishes it from the Western thinking is the conception and place of individual beings after death. The Western materialistic philosophy, as well as their religion, believes in the automatic evolution of man and that nothing remains or reappears after death. This leads to a longing to enjoy life as best as one can, even to the detriment of others without any apprehension past this life. The Indian conception of life, where the notion of being born again after death and dying repeatedly, is coupled with that of retribution, together with its doctrine of *karma* and transmigration of the soul, is a most powerful deterrent against any evil or inhuman action by the mankind. Even the Buddhist philosophy, which opposed the Brahmanical philosophy of the transmigration of soul admitted that the *karma* (actions) of an individual's past life is carried foreword in the next, though not his soul. Buddha himself remained silent on the question of transmigration.

Another distinguishing trait in the Indian systems of thought is its cosmological conception regarding the place of "being" in nature. "Before the inexorable law of nature every being has equal right to survive through the full course of its cosmic life. Any interference in this law of survival would disturb the harmony in and peace of Nature, and hence regarded undesirable, unnatural and unholy".[31] The value of the individual and his dignity are held in high esteem, as the basic tenet of Hindu philosophy is that there is a speck of divinity in every human being. Thus every human being is essentially the same and is equal participant in the "Universal Self, which is the fullness (Purnam), indivisible and yet divided among creatures".[32] This doctrine of the divinity of man may appear to be merely a metaphysical hypothesis incapable of positive proof. Its validity is not the point at issue. The fact which is of importance to us is that it is accepted as a cardinal article of faith by every Indian, and consequently it has certain social results which are of great import. "The belief that every sentiment being carries within himself a spark of the divine is the origin of the conception of the inalienable worth of the individual and its corollary of the limitation of the absolutism of external force".[33] This basic notion about the individual's cosmic life stands in sharp contradiction to the biological theory of evolution of the individual and the cosmos which has pervaded Western thinking, and in which survival of the fittest is considered to be the law of Nature. This difference in the cosmological thought has shaped the hierarchy of values in life differently in the two systems of thought.

Along with the divergent concept of evolution and creation of cosmic life, the two systems of thought vary sharply on the historical plane as to the evolution of human culture and intellect. It is admitted on all fronts that this universe is transitory, is in a fluid state, a state of transit. But opinions vary whether this transition, this evolution, is a process of growth or decadence. Western thinkers, in the most, believed in historical evolution towards growth and progress, ad finem.

The one step in time is always an advancement over the past, is an important tenet of Western cosmic thought. We, in India, through the days of yore, believe in creation and its decadence through time "Mahakala". With the passing of the age the flow of this world is towards decadence until at last some unforeseen and particular force will again bring this universe back anew on the path of progress and prosperity. This difference of outlook over the nature of this ever-changing universe is consequent to the differences of the ends in view. In one case the emphasis in primarily on spiritual attainments, in the other, on material achievements. The mental and spiritual development is achieved only when Yama (*Ahimsa, Satya, Brahmacharya, Asteya*) and Niyam (*Souch, Santosh, Tap, Ishwar Bhakti*) are fully observed, anger and passion and its fundamental Mamta are kept at the minimum, individual's wants are few and limited, and there is a high sense of unity. Thus with spiritual attainments, no imbalance in society on the material or spiritual fronts occurs, and there is hardly any problem of inequality. A stress on material development, to the exclusion of spiritual one, brings in its tail the problem of inequality. It is a natural phenomenon that the more we have control over our desires, the less we indulge in material pursuits discarding our quest of spiritual knowledge. On the contrary, the more we indulge in material progress, the less we strive for spiritual progress. The Indian way of life was a golden mean between the two and its social arrangement reckoned with the need of progress in either direction. We strived, of course, only for so much of material progress as did not in any way jeopardize our spiritual quest and our humanitarian outlook in life. Our attitude was one which judges the externals of life by their impact on the life of the spirit. Our spiritualism which generates humanism was the very antithesis of materialism. With the passing of the age the harmonious balance between the twin progress, the golden mean, was disturbed resulting in various problems accompany-ing material progress, including the problem of inequality.

The one important element of difference between the Indian and the Western thought is the place of religion in the scientific scheme of thought. In the Western viewpoint, religion and science are taken as contradictory to each other.

Religion is considered dogmatic and superfluous and there are various instances of religious persecution on the altar of science. Jesus Christ was crucified and Socrates was given hemlock to drink. In their religious texts we find the legend that through the effort of Satan, Adam ate the fruit from the tree of knowledge and, therefore, he was castigated and externed from heaven. These and other stories conclusively prove that in that part of the world the religious scriptures have always forbidden the advance of humanity towards knowledge and science and have demanded allegiance and faith in the scriptures blindly. This never happened in India where the tenets of religion have always been tested on the touchstone of wisdom and logic. The great religious preceptor Manu has clearly declared that the advancement of humanity towards knowledge results in a growing taste and liking for the knowledge itself, and he alone can be a devout religious being. Only he who grasps the teachings of religion through the force of logic can be a real knower of *Dharma*. We, in India, have not a single instance of a scientist or a philosopher being at loggerheads with religious preceptors. In India, philosophy is our science, philosophy is the source of knowledge and philosophy is the origin of our *Dharma*. The philosophy is the lighthouse of our religion. Hence, religious scriptures are only a description of knowledge and science. In the Vedas they are depicted in a terse and symbolic language well-knit into *mantras* (hymns), and all other religious scriptures are only an explanation and annotation, sometimes in parables, sometimes in legend and stories to make the pupils and the masses understand the true significance and implications of those Vedic *mantras*. Thus, all religious scriptures really form a series of a process to beget the true import of the Vedic hymns, which epitomize the science of all sciences.

To diagnose the malaise of inequality afflicting India we have to scrutinize the pace of history right from the beginning of Hindu civilization, and survey the chief tenets of Hinduism, which is not only a theology, but also the essentials of social customs and ideals of the Hindus. It is, however, beyond the sphere and scope of the present work and the problem in hand either to attempt a full historical treatment of a subject like this or trace out the philosophical and metaphysical aspect of Hinduism. Our interest will, chiefly, be centered in the socio-historical development of the precepts and practices, of thoughts and habits, which prevailed in India down the ages. We are beset, at the outset, with the non-availability of history of our ancient heritage and the resulting confusion in the ascertainment of historical dates and facts. The history of Hindu civilization begins with the history of the Vedas. The language of the Vedas is symbolic and terse and the symbols used therein are more important than their garb of language. The Vedas are Indian texts. If we have to know them and peep into their secrets, we have to go to the indigenous and Indian view points juxtaposited in abounding texts and literature, which are nothing but an elaboration of the Vedic hymns, and which provide the key to their understanding. We, therefore, feel inclined to reject any foreign interpretation not in consonance with the spirit of the hymns elaborated by eminent Indian scholars and ancillary texts.

(ii) Humanitarian Social Atmosphere

While beginning our quest of equality in the realm of the past, we are at once struck by the humanitarian atmosphere and a rationalized social system of the ancient times. The mark of any age, the amenity and charm of any civilization, depends, mainly, on its power to touch the imagination of those who live in it, and to inspire affection and a sense of fraternity among them. These qualities, and the dignity and mutual appreciation of man inter se are the chief elements that constitute the happiness and wealth of a nation. The search for equality is a means to that end, the happiness and well-being of all. The knowledge deduced from the Vedas is shaped on the humanitarian anvil and is surcharged with a sense of dignity, love and respect for human beings.

Since, time immemorial India has been the cradle of the religion of humanity which has been one of the important tenets of the Vedic sermons. The achievement of true knowledge, the Vedic knowledge, depends on this humanitarian outlook, and the latter depends on the former. The Indian culture spread all over the world, not on the strength of force or violence, but with a message of goodwill and will-being of all.[34] True religion always preaches good feeling and good sense which is another name of humanity.[35] Even the prayers offered to God are for the achievement of good relations and mutual friendship with the entire humanity. Every individual wishers that all be his friends or well wishes; but seldom does any one pray to be the friend of all. Men have prayed to see everybody with the eye of a friend and be seen by everybody with the eye of friend. In the Vedic age man strived to be the friends of all : Brahmins, Kshatriyas, Vaisyas and Sudras and for the friendship of these.[36] By inculcating a sense of common brotherhood mankind grew and prospered.

The riches were never considered as an end in themselves. People, of course, sought wealth, but not to the exclusion of the qualities of mutual affection and appreciation. Honest riches were desired by men in the ancient age for the development of the qualities of humanity which are the wealth of an individual and form part of the wealth of a nation.[37] Men are advised to consider the objects of the world as belonging to God and to enjoy whatever they possess with a sense of renunciation and not to pawn of what others have.[38] The universe itself is conceived as epitomizing the one universal self and every being as part and parcel of that universal self. This knowledge is a key to that spread of humanity and world peace. The whole of humanity has emanated from one Universal Body.[39]

This humanitarian attitude, this trend of mind towards equality of every human being pervades the whole of Vedic philosophy. It has been the corner stone of Indian civilization. Equality is more a way of thinking, a habit of thought. The scourge of inequality arises in the minds of men and, therefore, it should first be banished from there. A civilization a people, which had attained such a state of mental growth, such a height of philosophic attainments cannot but be presumed to possess a deep sense of equality between man and man. the divinity was realized only by dedicated service to humanity. the downtrodden, the weak in body and the weary in soul.

Notwithstanding that it is beyond the purview of our present work to delve deeply into the philosophic foundation of the ancient Indian thinking, it is evident that the problem of equality is, primarily, a problem of self-realization. It is only when men realize the manifestation of the supreme self in all beings that the conception of fundamental equality of all beings can dawn upon them. It is an admitted fact that men essentially differ in character and conduct, but underlying this diversity and manifoldness is the unity of spirit, which pervades them all. Unless the society learns to see this unity underlying the massive manifoldness, it cannot cast off its problem of growing inequality accentuated by ignorance, only by adopting mundane measures aimed at mitigating material causes of inequality which is wont to recur in the absence of the spiritualistic notion of the fundamental oneness. If the society sets a higher value for humanity and humane consideration than material achievements, which are bound to be unequal due to differing human connotations, it not only dispels the darkness of inequality from its horizon, but also makes the society fully enriched by deriving optimum from the differing potentialities of the individual by fitting them to the task most appropriate to each individual without any accompanying sense of inferiority or inequality.

The ancient Indian was firmly grounded in a humane atmosphere pervaded by the knowledge that all beings, even the flora and fauna, are the manifestation of the Supreme Self. "God, who is concealed in all beings is one. He pervades everything. He is the inner soul of every being and the overseer of all activity. He dwells in all forms of life. He is the eternal witness, the conscious Being within, standing apart from that in which He abides and is unqualified".[40] The whole universe is, therefore, a manifestation of that universal Being, who is Himself formless and causeless. The existence of immanent consciousness in even the plants and trees has long back been recognized by the Upanishadic thinkers.[41] The society endowed with a knowledge of this immanence of the Brahma cannot but see all beings with love and affection, and the spirit of humanity must reign supreme in that society. The seers and thinkers of the ancient age had recognized the whole world and worldly beings and epitomizing one's own self, and through their knowledge and self-realization illumined and enlightened the whole society. We can have a fair presumption, therefore, that that society must not have been bedeviled with the problem of inequality.

Humanism or the sense of equality of all beings is closely

related with the ethical standard and spiritual attainments of the society. It can dawn upon the minds of the members of a society only when they have an ingrained disposition of pathos and piety, virtue and knowledge. Only when a man rises above the narrow barriers of self, and the water of humanity washes his mind clear that he can see all beings with a sense of equality. It is not our task to trace in detail the Upanishadic philosophy which gives our heart a humanitarian outlook. Yet, it is relevant to our understanding that the tenets of Upanishadic teachings, propounded in short, a spiritual religion of humanity, which the decadent humanity of the modern age is striving to realize in its social, economic and political systems by enunciating the doctrine of equality. However, in the quest for equality in modern times, it is generally forgotten that the plant of equality must be rooted deep in the heart on the soil of knowledge and lovingly nurtured before the society can hope to reap the fruit thereof Any measure, which does not touch the root of the problem, is only a top-dressing on the social fabric vitiated by the problem of inequality. To achieve real equality, it is essential to realize the truth that there is a secret spirit, a divine reality, which permeates all sentient beings and of which the humanity is the perfect epitome. The sages and seekers of Truth in ancient India not only had realized this eternal Truth in their profession and practice but had also dedicated themselves to the spread of this knowledge for the good of the humanity. There was a growing attempt to even bequeath this knowledge to posterity through the memory culture down the ages so that humanity may progress and prosper and establish a kingdom of divine spirit on earth. The equality of all beings was the leading principle of their lives, practised in their day-to-day activities and their arrangement of the social and economic systems. The individuals had realized, through self-knowledge or the knowledge illumining the society, that the fullness of one's life depended on the lives of his fellow-beings which blossoms only through co-operation and brotherhood achieved with a sense of unity and equality of all beings. They knew the secrets of success of the human race : that only through the achievement of perfect and full life of the individuals could a society extricate itself from the mire of inequality and establish itself in happiness and perfection. This humanitarian outlook was, however, on the wane during the latter part of the ancient age as the conception of the Supreme Self had steadily narrowed down to one's own self. Nevertheless this cannot blind us to the achievements of ancient India when she was at the height of its glory.

(iii) System of Education

The spiritual and human knowledge which pervaded the Vedic thought was grounded in the social and economic fabric of the nation through an educational system devised especially for the purpose.

The pre-eminent position which the ancient India had attained in her contemporary world was due to the success of her educational system she had devised. "Educational institutions unusually mirror the ideals of a nation and enable us to understand the spirit of its civilization".[42] In the Vedic age those who had sought knowledge and had attained it were classed as Brahmins, and every such Brahmin was an institution of education and learning. Every Brahmin, especially during the period of his Vanprasth stage of life, preferred the profession of teaching and thereby illumined the life and mind of his disciples. These disciples, in their turn, penetrated the masses and the knowledge infiltrated through them in the society, shaped the precepts and practices of the age. The education was the beaconlight to the society directing it on the path of wisdom, nourishing it to a healthy growth and invigorating it with delight and comfort. "From the Vedic age downwards the central conception of education of the Indians has been that it is a source of illumination, giving us a correct lead in the various spheres of life".[43]

Knowledge was held in high esteem in the ancient ages. Among the four powers, viz. : knowledge, sword, wealth and service, the first was deemed to be a source of illumination, insight and guidance to the rest. Thus, the other powers tinged with knowledge were neutralized of their evil effects on the society manned by the one Universal Self. If one human being was considered superior to another, it was not due to some superior physical or material properties, but because his self was enlightened and illumined, his mind and intellect were sharpened and rendered more efficient by education.[44] It was believed that though men were born equal, it was through education that they distinguished themselves as possessing higher virtue; it was the environment and training which they received that shaped their character and determined their capacity.[45] Thus, proper education was deemed to be a sine qua non for the development of the individual in any branch of life. The education was not considered a luxury or privilege of the few, but a training to from the essential ingredients of every human being. "Infusion of a spirit of piety and religiousness, formation of character, development of personality, inculcation of civic and social duties, promotion of social efficiency and preservation and spread of national culture may be described as the chief aims and ideals of ancient Indian education".[46]

(iv) Socio-Economic Structure

The humanitarian outlook of the society, if it wants to survive, must be cultivated and practised in the everyday life and activities of the individuals composing it. Otherwise it will decay and die. And this outlook can thrive only in a society where its members acquired the knowledge that the self is other than the changing body and its happiness is conditioned to the happiness of the society at large. Once the immanence of the Supreme Self is realized, the distinction between oneself and others evaporates, and the conception of the equality of all beings, emanating from a Universal Parentage, must dawn upon that society.

The social and economic structure of ancient India revolved round the system of *Varnashrama Dharma*, as propounded in the Vedas. Though the division of classes was not very much accentuated or emphasized in the Satya-Yuga the subsequent ages saw the stratification of classes and a stress on the differentiation of classes. The division of humanity into four classes was based on a scientific analysis of the universe, based on the qualities immanent in man. In the Atharva Veda and other Vedic literature, the four-fold division of classes is applied to the flora and fauna containing medicinal properties, depending on their qualities. The division of humanity into four classes is also based on the organic theory of body as enunciated in the science of biology. There are four departments in the human body—Shiroguha (head), Uroguha (heart), Udarguha (abdomen) and Bastiguha (lower abdomen). In every department or cavity there reside seven lives (Pran) for performance of actions, which are usually termed as Indriya (organ). The centre of these seven lives is one central life, which gives strength to the seven and is called "Indra". Out of these seven lives in every cavity of the body, six reside in pairs of two each, and the seventh resides alone and apart. For example, in Siroguha (head), the six lives—two ears, two eyes, two nostrils—reside in pairs, while the seventh, mouth, remains alone. In it the central life remains centralized in Brahma-randhra, and bestows the strength of knowledge. In the second cavity, Udarguha, there are two hands, two lungs (Fuffus), two breasts (Stan) and the seventh, heart. Its centralized main life is the throat-channel or tongue-gustatory (Kanthakoop), which is the bestower of bravery (Parakram-sakti). The third department Udarguha (abdomen) contains the liver and the spleen, two stomachs (amashya) and colon (Pakwashaya) or intestines, two kidneys (Vrikka) and the seventh, Navi. Its centralized main life is heart, which is the seventh life of the second department, and bestows on it the power of accumulation and distribution of wealth (Anna). The fourth department Bastiguha (lower abdomen) consists of two legs, two holes (kshidra) for passage of urine and semen, two testicles (Anda-kosha) and the seventh guda. Its centralized main life is Navi, which is the seventh life of the third department and bestows on it the power of dedication (Utasarga-sakti) for the maintenance of the physical system.

This, in brief, is the biological structure of the physical body of human beings and on this biological science is based the division of the Universal Self into four parts, narrated in the Purusha-sukti of the Rig-Veda, forming the quintessence of the division of humanity into Chatur-varna, denoting the qualities latent in the beings.

The essential point to note is that this division of class was not based on the birth of an individual, but depended on his quality and conduct. We have already noted that in the Vedic age or Satya-Yuga all the beings performed their actions in accordance with the qualities latent in them and there was no cause of strife. Human beings, who were endowed with Brahmanic virtues, engaged themselves in meditation and the knowledge of the Vedas dawned upon them by the Divine Light. Another section of human beings, who pulsated with vigour and valour, engaged themselves in protection and defence, and was ranked as Kshatriya. The section of humanity who engaged them-selves in the production, accumulation and distribution of riches was ranked as Vaishya, while the fourth category consisted of those human beings who engaged themselves in agriculture and other professions serviceable to humanity as a whole, and ranked as Sudra. Thus, the Chatur-varna system was the axis round which the social organization revolved in a balanced order. It was a system of division of social organization on the basis of the functions of individuals, and not division of individuals on the basis of birth or colour or status in society. This four-fold division of the social organization was also important for maintaining an even balance in the political and social organization of the nation.

(b) The Gandhian Concept

The conception of equality in modern India is marked by the beginning of religious revivalism which successfully generated a sense of national awareness in the people, in the context of the despotic colonial rule of the British Empire wont to plunder and ravage the masses already crushed by grinding poverty, steeped in ignorance and afflicted by many disease, and other vices. The spread of liberal political ideas in the West, which also had their influence on the British administrators, had evolved certain liberal measures in the social, political and economic fields. These ideas and thoughts admixed with a sense of pride in the ancient heritage had a powerful impact on the Indian social thinking in the 19th century and had generated a social challenge. The theme of equality oriented towards social reform was an active response to the challenges of the times.

"Deriving a faith in equality from a rational theistic faith was the outcome of conscious intellectual effort and, with many, part of an active revolt against the hardcore of Indian religious orthodoxy".[47] The century witnessed a deep religious ferment all over India which generated forces that had an important bearing on social reforms and eradication of social inequalities and indignities.

The concept of equality and egalitarianism, like other Western ideas, had been selectively absorbed and had influenced the Indian intellectuals and thinkers of the 19th century, leading to varied interpretations which sometimes involved even contradictions. "The two leading ideas that emerged in the 19th century were : (1) A sharp inequality, both social and economic, was inherent in India's age-old socio-economic structure; (2) the British colonial rule and the colonial economic arrangements on which it rested had not only created a new kind of suppressive and deadening inequality—economic, political and social—but had also compounded and accentuated internal socio-economic inequality which had thus become qualitatively different. The main thrust of this argument was that without political freedom, there was no chance of modern-izing the Indian social system and reducing the sharp economic disparities that had appeared under a colonial regime".[48]

Once the idea that the inequality is inherent in the very social structure of India was accepted, the Indian thinkers and reformers turned their attention to reform in the social structure. And this led to the question of religion and its role in society as a constructive and transforming social force. Swami Vivekanand passed away in 1902, leaving his unfinished task behind, till Mahatma Gandhi after his triumphant return from South Africa in 1915 came on the political scene, vowed to serve his motherland.

The Mahatma had no new recipe for the emancipation of Indian people and resuscitation of their economy. The challenging task before the nation was to bring about a radical change in the ethical, educational and economic status of the teeming millions. Some religious and humanist loaders, before him, had appealed to their countrymen to revive the great virtues of the original Indian culture and people had moved in thousands to join their organizations. But theirs was a movement of religious revival.

The religious revivalism gave rise to a growing sense of national awareness and the nationalism thus generated along with the spread of Western education had led to the formation of political ideologies, moderates and extremists. However, it was not before the advent of Gandhi on the political scene that politics got its mass basis. The glorification of the past was confined not only within the bounds of Hinduism, but was reproduced in the guise of the quintessence of all religions, in the form of truth and non-violence. Basing his conviction on truth and non-violence Gandhi proceeded towards social reforms and stood for an egalitarian society. He believed that human activities are inter-related and they cannot be separated into compartments. The passion for social reform, he said, drew him into politics. But in so doing he gave politics, a mass basis and ethical reorientation in the form of non-violent non-cooperation. He conceived freedom and equality as interdependent and interchangeable, grounded in the solid foundation of humanism.

(i) Swaraj

Describing his conception of Swaraj, Gandhi said : "Let there be no mistake about my conception of Swaraj. It is complete independence from alien control and complete economic independence. So, at the one end you have political independence; at the other, economic. It has two other ends. One of them is moral and the other social, the corresponding end is *Dharma*, i.e. religion in the highest sense of the term. You may recognize it by the name of Truth. Moral and social uplift may be recognized by the term we are used to, i.e. Non-violence. Let us call this the square of Swaraj, which will be out of shape if any of its angle is untrue".[49]

By Political independence, Gandhi never meant the Western democracies. He meant by it what he called Ram Raj, i.e. sovereignty of the people based on pure moral authority. Similarly by economic independence he meant economic uplift of every individual, i.e. Sarvodaya, by their own conscious effort. Thus, Swaraj of Gandhi's dream implies, firstly, attainment of moral authority and is a subject of individual attainment and secondly, external freedom based on individual's self-perfection through acquired virtue. "The outward freedom that we shall attain", says Gandhi, "will be in exact proportion to the inward freedom to which we may have grown at a given moment. And if this is the correct view of freedom, our chief energy must be concentrated upon achieving reform from within".[50] Freedom to Gandhi belongs to the individual only and not to the collectivity of individuals called society or State wherein the sovereignty of individual is denied. Collective freedom exists as a corollary to individual freedom, not in opposition to it. For Gandhi, "The individual is the one Supreme consideration".[51] He insisted that "Swaraj of a people means the sum total of the Swaraj of individuals".[52]

Gandhi was confident that Swaraj of his dream can descend on Mother India only when the brute in man is controlled by the internal freedom achieved by man through the enlightenment of his spirit by means of non-violence. He is more concerned with the "real article," i.e. individual and his training of spirit and mind in the principle of non-violence, than putting in details of future society. Details can be worked out afterwards. What was of real importance was the preparation of individual. And the non-violence order can be established only in the simplicity of village life. The village of Gandhi's dream was not a village of today full of filth, dirt and idleness, but an ideal and self-sufficient entity. Only in villages, as envisaged by him, Swaraj can be brought to fruition. He thus summed up the India of his dreams : "I shall strive for a constitution, which will release India from thraldom and patronage and give her, if need be, the right to sin. I shall work for an India in which the poorest shall feel that it is their country in whose making they have an effective voice; an India in which there shall be no high class and low class of people; an India in which all communities shall live in perfect harmony. There can be no room in such an India for the curse of untouchability or the curse of intoxicating drinks and drugs. Women will enjoy the same rights as men. Since, we shall be at peace with all the rest of the world, neither exploiting nor being exploited, we should have the smallest army imaginable. All interests not in conflict with the interest of the dumb millions will be scrupulously respected, whether foreign or indigenous. Personally. I hate distinction between foreign and indigenous. This is the India of my dreams. I shall be satisfied with nothing else".[53]

Further, the ideal picture of Purna Swaraj or Rama Rajya, as Gandhi called it, envisaged freedom for all or Sarvodaya.

He was not enamoured by the doctrine of the greatest good of the greatest number. "I do not believe in the doctrine of the greatest good of the greatest number. It means in its nakedness that in order to achieve the supposed good of 51 percent, the interest of 49 per cent may be, or rather should be, sacrificed. It is a heartless doctrine and has done harm to humanity. The only real, dignified human doctrine is the greatest good of all and this can be achieved only by utter most self-sacrifice".[54] Again Gandhi said : "I do not believe in the greatest good of the greatest number, nor can I agree that might is right. For human beings, the object in view should be good of all, with the weak being served first. We are two-legged man, but have still to cast away the nature of four-footed beasts".[55] True Swaraj can be ensured in human society only by the greatest good of all. This ideal concept of universal freedom was named Sarvodaya or equal freedom of all. But this freedom cannot be a licence, an unrestricted freedom : In it, each individual will exercise his freedom in such a way as not to jeopardize or interfere with the freedom of others". There is not a single virtue, which aims at, or is consistent with, the welfare of the individual alone, conversely, there is not a single offence, which does not, directly or indirectly, affects many others besides the actual offender. Hence, whether an individual is good or bad is not merely his own concern, but really the concern of the whole community, nay, of the world".[56]

Swaraj, as Gandhi emphasized, can be sustained only by conscious individual effort and vigil. He never regarded India's freedom as synonym with its political freedom. Freedom from alien rule was only a stepping stone and a prelude to the achievement of real freedom to be gained by individuals in an exact proportion to their inward freedom. He made no distinction between British tyranny and actual or potential tyranny by Indians, nor did he make any distinction between an American Rockefeller and a potential Indian Rocke feller. As Gandhi said : "I am not interested in freeing Indiamerely from the English yoke. I am bent upon freeing India from any yoke whatsoever. I have no desire to exchange "King log for King stork".[57] He warned, "Swaraj can be maintained, only where there is a majority of loyal and patriotic people to whom the good of the nation is paramount above all other considerations whatever including their personal profit. Swaraj means government by many. Where the many are immoral or selfish, their government can spell anarchy and nothing else".[58]

Even Swaraj had no meaning for Gandhi, unless it was based on the solid foundation of non-violent and humanitarian social and economic order. His insistence on ameliorating the social and economic conditions of the villages of India was grounded in his realization that India lives in her villages, in her cottages, not in cities and towns. Gandhiji said : "I would say that if the village perishes, India will perish too. It will be no more India. Her own mission in the world will get lost. The revival of the village is possible only when it is no more exploited. Industrialization on a mass scale will necessarily lead to passive or active exploitation of the villagers, as the problems of competition and marketing come in. Therefore, we have to concentrate on the village being self-contained, manufacturing mainly for use. Provided this character of village industry is maintained, there would be no objection to villagers using even the modern machines and tools that they can make and can afford to use. Only they should not be used as a means of exploitation of others".[59] He was confident that the culture, art and education of the nation can survive only if villages are improved on his mental pattern, and a non-violent nation can survive only in villages. His views on these issues were made public long ago in *Hind Swaraj* but even as late as in October, 1945, in a letter to Nehru he maintained the same stand essentially. Gandhi wrote : "I am convinced that if India is to attain true freedom and through India the world also, then sooner or later the fact must be recognized that people will have to live in villages, not in towns, in huts, not in palaces. Crores of people will never be able to live at peace with each other in towns and palaces. They will then have no recourse but to resort to both violence and untruth. I hold that without truth and non-violence there can be nothing but destruction for humanity. We can realize truth and non-violence only in the simplicity of village life and this simplicity can best be found in the *charkha* and all that *charkha* connotes. I must not fear if the world today is going the wrong way. It may be that India too will go that way and like the proverbial moth burning itself eventually in the flame round which it dances more and more furiously. But it is my bounden duty up to my last breath to try to protect India and through India the entire world from such a doom. The essence of what I have said is that man should rest content with what are his real needs and become self-sufficient. If he does not have this control he can not save himself. After all the world is made up of individuals just as it is the drops that constitute the ocean. I have said nothing new. This is a well-known truth.

"But I do not think I have stated this in *Hind Swaraj.* While I admire modern science, I find that it is the old looked at in the true light of modern science, which should be reclothed and refashioned aright. You must not imagine that I am imagining village life as it is today. The village of my dreams is still in my mind. After all every man lives in the world of his dreams. My ideal village will contain intelligent human beings. They will not live in dirt and darkness as animals. Men and women sill be free and able to hold their own against anyone in the world. There will be neither plague, nor cholera nor small pox : no one will be idle, no one will wallow in luxury. Everyone will have to contribute his quota of manual labour in luxury. I do not want to draw a large-scale picture in detail. It is possible to envisage railways, post and telegraph offices, etc. For me it is material to obtain the article and the rest will fit into the picture afterwards. If I let go the real thing, all else goes".[60]

This notion of Swaraj or self-rule, as conceived by Gandhiji, was the dominant political value concept in his framework of future India, as envisaged in his *Hind Swaraj* published in 1909. The concept of Swaraj as envisaged by him had a spiritual content as he visualized India to attain the spiritual height of love, truth and peace. As Shri Devi Prasad has pointed out in an article read in the Budapest seminar on the occasion of the Gandhi Birth Centenary Celebration, "Centralization of power is the opposite of Swaraj in Gandhi's scheme of mass politics". He quoted Gandhi as saying, Self-government means continuous effort to be independent of government control whether it is a foreign government or a national one". Gandhi had the vision to pronounce that unless power reached every home, unless everybody felt that he wielded influence on the decisions made at the centres of power, in fact, unless everybody felt that he was co-responsible for the decisions made, society could never live in peace and prosperity. Devi Prasad made the thought more concrete by quoting Gandhi, who had said "Real freedom will come not by the acquisition of authority by a few, but by the acquisition of the capacity by all to resist authority when abused, in other words, freedom is to be attained by educating the people to a sense of their capacity to regulate and control authority".[61]

(ii) Humanism

One of the values that Gandhiji greatly cherished was humanism, which is the kingpin in the Gandhian value system. The dignity of the human beings must be restored and the social system should permeate with equality between human beings. The humanism of Gandhi had three essential elements : peace, freedom and justice. The whole system of social values propounded by Gandhi was deeply rooted in humanism, aimed at ushering in a harmonious cooperative community of human beings based on peace and brotherhood.

"His overflowing love for humanity revealed his intense humanism. The essence of the humanist spirit is deep love for the people. Gandhiji's sincere love and regard for the people was an expression of his humanism. Even general Smuts testified to his humanism. Smuts wrote : "However, often we may differ from him, we are conscious all the time of his sincerity, his unselfishness, and above all his fundamental and universal humanity. He always acted as a great human, with deep sympathy for men of all classes and all races and especially for the underdog".[62] To a questioner asking Gandhi whether by living in villages and serving villagers, his aim was just humanitarian, he curtly replied : "I am here to serve no one else but myself, to find my own self-realization through the service of these village folk. Man's ultimate aim is the realization of God, and all his activities, social, political, religious have to be guided by the ultimate aim of the vision of God. The immediate service of all human beings becomes a necessary part of the endeavour, simply because the only way to find God is to see Him in His creation and be one with it. This can be done only by service of all. And this cannot be done except through one's country. I am a part and parcel of the whole, and I cannot find Him apart from the rest of humanity. My countrymen are my nearest neighbours. They have become so helpless, so resourceless, so inert that I must concentrate on serving them. If I could persuade myself that I should find Him in a Himalayan cave, I would proceed there immediately. But I know that I cannot find Him apart from humanity".[63]

(iii) Equality

Equality was another value to which Gandhi attached greatest importance. He aspired for equality not only in the field of economic justice but also in a higher social sense. In the social organization in which every individual is but a unit, there shall be no high class and low class of people, leaving no scope of social injustice. Even freedom, to Gandhi, was of no consequence, if it was not built on the solid foundation of equality. Elaborating his conception of equality, Gandhi had said, "we are absolutely equal, but equality is of souls and not bodies. Hence, it is a mental state, We need to think of, and to assert, equality because we see great inequalities in the physical world. We have to realize equality in the midst of this apparent external inequality".[64] In a non-violent society, conditions of equality are necessary for the achievement of higher human values. Describing himself as "social revolutionist"; Gandhi said "violence is bred by inequality, non-violence by equality".[65]

Indeed, freedom and equality are interchangeable terms. Without equality—social, political and economic—there can be no true freedom of the Gandhian dream. Without the elimination of disparities in income and status, between rich and poor, high and low, labour and capital, there can be no real freedom for anyone in society. To Gandhi freedom was an organic whole. As Gandhi said, "I do not divide life into watertight compartments".[66] The entire body of Gandhi's social and political thought sustained by his ultimate values of universal brotherhood, freedom and equality. This integral conception of political, economic, moral and social freedom of man has proceeded from his intense humanism. Political independence without economic, moral and social emancipation is a mockery of democracy. Swaraja meant social, economic, political as well as moral progress of all men. He know full well that any system of political values would remain incomplete until it is given a concrete shape in the socio-economic field, and so he was bent upon eradicating iniquitous inequalities and abysmal disparity between the rich and the poor, the starving masses of India. "The social conditions which Gandhi aimed at creating for man's moral development were not conditions of pleasure or comfort but of love and brotherhood. Any institution or policies which generated competition for power and enmity in competition would hamper man's moral progress and has no place in Gandhi's socio-economic model. He certainly considered it essential that there should be a new society, free of colonial rule, so decentralized in its decision-making structures that all individuals may participate in its processes, endowed with socio-economic equality, largely rural in its patterns of economic organization, in which moral criteria would predominate".[67]

(iv) Non-Violence

Thus, the goal of equality, liberty and fraternity is the *summum bonum* of the Gandhian conception of Swaraj and none can be achieved in isolation. Indeed, freedom cannot be achieved in the face of oppressive social and economic inequality, and equality cannot be had without creating the invaluable treasure of fraternity in the hearts of men. Fraternity or universal brotherhood shall be clearly an attribute of a non-violent social order. Talking about the lofty French ideal of liberty, equality and fraternity, Gandhi had said that it was only when the revolutionaries forgot about fraternity that they flew at the throats of each other. Fraternity is the fountainhead of freedom and equality. It is an attribute of humanity born out of the non-violent human instinct; violence is a baser animal attribute in man. Therefore, fraternity can be cultivated and developed only in a non-violent socio-economic order, and so Swaraj and equality which are the fruits of fraternity can thrive only to the extent the society is based on non-violence.

There can be neither freedom nor equality without non-violence. The former are inseparably interwoven with the latter. If freedom and equality or justice in every walk of life is sought for, the only means for obtaining them is non-violence, Indeed, Gandhi's belief in non-violence stemmed from this inseparability of ends and means in human life. He scoffed at the futility of endeavour to create a non-violent social order by violent means. Jayaprakash Narayan adroitly argues : "The most important characteristic of this (non-violent) method is that its means must be in harmony with its ends. If the end is a non-violent society, the means also must be non-violent : if human freedom is the end, coercive means (except moral coercion) are ruled out; if man is an end in himself, he cannot be used as a means; if truth is to be the basis of the new life, untruthful means are inadmissible; if the end is the dispersal of power, the means cannot be centralized power".[68]

The noble Marxist ideal of a non-violent society with the State having withered away after achievement of the voluntary way of life, from each according to his capacity and to each according to his needs, failed to come into existence because the means employed were not in harmony with the end in view. Jayaprakash reiterates his unshakable faith in the efficacy of non-violence as the only weapon of the brave. He says : "Power to the people has been the slogan of so many of the modern revolutions of history. Yet, because they were all born in violence, it happened invariably that those who succeeded in taking hold of the means of organized violence usurped power for themselves, professing, no doubt, that they were doing so in the name of the people and for the good of the people. Not that these revolutionary leaders were frauds or charlatans. They were only working out the logic of violence. It is nearly two centuries since the Great French Revolution, yet the French revolutionaries of the present-day are still crying for power at the lovel of the work-place whether these workers be students, academics, industrial labourers or even peasants. Lenin marched to power on the crest of the slogan, all power to the soviets. Soviet-Russia is a super power today, but the soviet of workers, peasants, and soldiers deputies have no power, if they exist at all".[69]

The futility of the violent means and the power of non-violence have not only been praised by Mahatma Gandhi, but is equally accepted by the votaries of violence in their chastened mood. Napoleon, towards the end of his career, admitted this superiority of love or *ahimsa* thus : "Alexander, Charle Magne, and I founded great empires. We founded them on force. Where are they today? Jesus Christ founded his on love, today millions would gladly die for him".[70] Even the great General Douglas MacArthur, while describing Gandhi as a prophet who lived far ahead of his time, said : "In the evolution of civilization, if it is to survive, all men cannot fail eventually to adopt his belief that the process of mass application of force to resolve contentious issues is fundamentally not only wrong but contains within itself the germs of self-destruction.[71] The Gandhian concept of non-violence is not based on the negative value of abstinence from inflicting injury or harming other, but connotes a positive value of pure love for all living beings, i.e. a sense of universal brotherhood. Thus *ahimsa*, love and fraternity are inter-changeable terms. In its positive form, *ahimsa* means the largest love, greatest charity".[72] Eulogizing its infinite power, Gandhi said, "Non-violence is a power which can be wielded equally by all—children, young men and women or grown-up people—provided they have a living faith in the God of love and have therefore equal love for all mankind".[73]

In fact, the ultimate goal of freedom, equality and brotherhood is interconnected and inseparably linked to each other as ends and means to one another. They are bound together in a reciprocal end-means relationship. None can exist without the other.

"Equality and non-violence are inseparably inter-related. There cannot be any non-violence without equality, and there can be no equality without non-violence. The political equality follows inevitably from Gandhi's emphasis on individual freedom and his suspicion of all collective authority including the authority of the State. Freedom and equality are also thus inextricably inter-connected. Without social and political equality, there cannot be any freedom, and without universal freedom three can be no social and political equality".[74]

Thus, non-violence or love is the basic tenet of Gandhian

conception of a social order based on equality and freedom, and these taken together constitute his synthetic ideal of justice. He firmly held the view that "social justice, even to the least and lowliest, is impossible of attainment by force".[75]

However, Gandhi held that complete non-violence is only an ideal, always to be kept in mind, always to be strived for. What was realizable was only relative non-violence, which is only an approximation of the ultimate absolute value. "Perfect non-violence is impossible so long as we exist physically, for we would want some space at least to occupy. Perfect non-violence whilst you are inhabiting the body is only a theory like Euclid's point or straight line, but we have to endeavour every moment of our lives".[76]

It is not within the reach of the present endeavour to trace in detail the Gandhian idea on freedom and fraternity, as we have to keep within our bounds to the subject matter of equality and the ways and means which Gandhi devised to rid the Indian masses of the glaring inequality in social and economic fields with an intent to fructify equality in the realm of politics and with an ultimate aim of a just social order, or Rama Rajya, as he called it.

(v) Swadeshi

Mahatma Gandhi laid great stress on the fact that colonialism had not only subjugated a country but also dehumanized man. His programme of action, therefore, envisaged complete replacement of the political, social, cultural, economic and educational values inherited from the alien rule and also the institutions thriving on it by a system of Swadeshi which would make Swaraj of his dreams possible in all its manifestations. The colonial rule had contaminated the totality of society and, therefore, he held a comprehensive view of Swadeshi. He explained his views thus : "Swadeshi is that spirit in us which restricts us to the use and service of our immediate surroundings to the exclusion of the more remote. Thus, as for religion, I must restrict myself to my ancestral religion. That is the use of my immediate religious surroundings. If I find it defective, I should serve it by purging it of its defects. In the domain of politics, I should make use of the indigenous institutions and serve them by curing them of their proved defects. In that of economics, I should use only things that are produced by my immediate neighbours and serve those industries by making them efficient and complete where they might be found wanting".[78]

Gandhi considered Swadeshi spirit as the rule of life and consistent with the law of humility and love. He said, "A true votary of Swadeshi will never harbour ill-will towards the foreigner, he will not be actuated by antagonism towards anybody on earth. Swadeshism is not a cult of hatred. It is a doctrine of selfless service that has its roots in the purest ahimsa, i.e. love".[79]

Gandhi evolved Swadeshi as a most potent weapon, not only in the national struggle for independence, but also as a panacea for the removal of pauperization of the Indian masses and for forging the bond of spiritual unity. The concept of Swaraj and Swadeshi flow form each other and together they lay the foundation of Gandhian economy. He however, held the view that Swadeshi spirit cannot be attained all at once, it had to be cherished and attained in successive stages. "Swadeshi, after all, is a goal to be reached by steady effort. And we would be making for the goal even if we confined Swadeshi to a given set of articles, allowing ourselves as a temporary measure to use such things as might not be procurable in the country".[80] Thus, Swadeshi was a living spirit to kindle the flames of Swaraj and a means to achieve a high degree of self-reliance at the economic, political and social levels with a view to resuscitating the village economy, rejuvenating the Indian society and reconstructing the political structure on non-violent lines. The most significant concept that is relevant to revalidating Gandhi is that which went by the name "Swadeshi". A modern name for it would be "self-reliance" or "economic independence". The new spirit of Swadeshi, not in form. such as khadi, but in essence, implies a positive force to fight neo-colonialism which is having an increasingly tightening grip over the Indian economy and society. Swadeshi is not merely an economic concept, it is also a political concept. The cultural onslaught from the West during the past fifty years has brought about a kind of social fragmentation in this country to which there seems no other answer except the revival of Swadeshi all over again. The

British were able to exploit this country, take away its treasures and resources and subjugate our physical selves, but they were not able to buy our minds. Today we find that the cultural and technological imperialism of the West, as also of the East, has completely enslaved the Indian mind. There is very little left of the pride in Indianness, not to speak of Indian civilization. Swedeshi was the first and last message of Gandhi, everything else was secondary.[81]

(vi) Satyagrah

If non-violence was the backbone of Gandhian social order, Swadeshi was the flame to be kindled in every soul for its sustenance and Satyagrah was a legitimate method of right struggle to keep the social order in a state of equipoise. To arrest the degeneration of the ultimate values of liberty, equality and fraternity and to avoid stagnation, poverty and alienation, Satyagrah was devised as the only remedy, in lieu of the method of class struggle of the Marxists. It is based on the unswerving faith in the truth that man is not matter only, he is not body only. Man is the spirit immanent in the body, as God is immanent in the world. "This fundamental truth links religion and politics in Gandhi : because man is not brute, freedom and equality are not merely political concepts to be guaranteed by constitutions and juridical systems of law. Gandhi did not, therefore, seek political solutions to political problems. It is a lesson which the Gandhian philosophy teaches to the contemporary world, that political problems will not be solved by political policies or pacts, or through a political reconciliation of political differences".[82] Every problem, political or otherwise, can be solved only on the basis of truth and non-violence. Thus, Satyagrah was the non-violent weapon for the achievement of Swaraj and equality. The very purpose for which it was to designed was to create a social ferment in support of truth and justice, and thus to change the existing conditions.

Gandhi considered Satyagrah effective and relevant for all times and in all contexts. This non-violent struggle forms part of the life of individuals and a society infested with grinding poverty and cancerous alienation must give it a proper shape and a revolutionary bent so that it does not degenerate into hienous violence, pervasive hatred, entrenched corruption and unethical politics. Gandhi had made it abundantly clear that Satyagrah would be required even after securing independence.

The realization of truth and justice through Satyagrah and non-violence is all the more relevant and the only recourse today when the alternative to non-violence is non-existence, in a world full of horrors of amazing scientific invention of weapons of co-destruction. Typical of the times was a comment by Mrs. Indira Gandhi who said : "I hesitate to speak of the other great teaching left us by Gandhi, non-violence. I hesitate not because I find any justification for violence. But mankind has accumulated such a fearful store of weapons of destruction that I sometimes wonder whether we have any right to hope. Wars still erupt here and there but even more distressing and alarming is the growth in all parts of the world of hatred in thought and violence in action, and the reckless recourse to the agitation approach".[83] Satyagrah is a non-violent corrective to the aberrations in the social order.

(vii) Bread Labour

Non-violence is the master key to the Swaraj of Gandhi's dream, and hence also to the ultimate justice of liberty, equality and fraternity. A society cannot exist if it does not eschew violence as its policy. No society ever existed on the earth having violence as its creed. In fact, the very creation of society pre-saged a non-violent order. But lasting peace and justice in every field can spring only from a right education of spirit in the habits of non-violence. The laws of Satyagrah or soul-force, as also of bread-labour were steps in the direction of training of spirit in the habits of non-violence. "The bread-labour, according to Gandhi, will establish the bond of love through common voluntary labour among all members of society. It will also reduce our wants, simplify our lives and thus promote the virtues of renunciation which is one of the essential elements of non-violence".[84] Bread-labour, as defined by Gandhi, is "The divine law that man must earn his bread by labouring with his own hand".[85] When nine-tenths of the humanity live by tilling the soil, the world would be much happier if the remaining one-tenth followed them. It would surely obliterate the invidious distinction of rank and usher in the moral and social atmosphere for the realization of full equality. Gandhi was confident that if the society accepts this principle, all men would be equal and none would starve. It will bring about a silent revolution in the structure of society and the struggle for existence shall be replaced by the struggle for mutual service. The distinction of rank shall disappear and it would also eliminate the distinction between social classes. Thus, bread-labour is the sole antidote to rampant exploitation and invidious distinction between human beings. It is "an important means for the removal of all inequalities, economic as well as social. Non-exploitation is the essence of bread-labour since everyone earns his minimum requirements through bread-labour and contributes the rest of his labour, whether physical or intellectual, to society, instead of using it for the accumulation of personal wealth; there is an end of all exploitation, and, hence, all disparity of wealth".[86]

Thus, by emphasizing bread-labour, Gandhi was not belittling the importance and significance of the other form, i.e. intellectual labour, as it had an undoubted place in the scheme of life. What he really meant was to create an atmosphere of equality and permeate the social outlook with love, the corner-stone of the edifice of equality, in a world of manifest inequality.

"The implications of this concept are far-reaching for any society but much more so for the modern world. In all modern societies communist, capitalist, developed, developing, etc., one notices great disparities of one kind or another between a small ruling minority, that is the elite, and the masses, Socialism, welfarism, collectivism, which made claims to reduce these inequalities, have by the very process of reducing one kind of inequality, in fact, produced another kind. Though the present day Communist countries may have reduced income inequalities—recent trends show that income inequalities have started increasing again—they have reached unprecedented and monstrous proportions in political and status inequalities. Gandhi, like many others, wanted to obliterate this distinction between the elite and the masses. But unlike others he suggested the central operational concept of bread-labour in the absence of which these distinctions could not eliminated, no matter what system was adopted. It is tragic that in the land of Gandhi, physical labour should be looked down upon".[87]

(viii) Education

The scourge of inequality arises in the mind of men, and it is, therefore, from the minds of men that it should be banished. The scheme of Swaraj and equality with the resultant scheme of social order clearly envisaged a complete change in the educational order as well. The existing educational system, which was designed to feed back the order of the society based on violence, could not be fitted in a non-violent social order with freedom, equality and love. The prevalent educational system had not only isolated the educated from the people, but, what was worse, made their education of no consequence whatsoever to the people. Gandhi considered the existing system of education defective on three counts :

1. It is based upon foreign culture to the almost complete ignorance of indigenous culture. The child is never taught to have any pride in his surroundings. "The higher he goes, the farther he is removed from his home, so that at the end of his education he becomes completely estranged from his surroundings. He feels no poetry about his home life. The village scenes are all a sealed book to him. His own civilization is presented to him as imbecile, barbarous, superstitious, and useless for all practical purposes. His education is calculated to wean him from his traditional culture. And if the mass of educated youths are not entirely denationalized, it is because the ancient culture is too deeply embedded in them to be altogether uprooted even by an education adverse to its growth".[88]

2. It confines itself simply to the head, ignoring the culture of the heart and the hand. In India, where eighty percent population is agricultural, only literary education renders the students unfit for manual work in after-life. The education of the heart cannot be imparted through books. It can be done only through the living and affectionate touch of the teacher. As Gandhi said : "Literacy is not the end of education nor even the beginning. It is only one of the means whereby men and women can be educated. Literacy in itself is no education".[89]

3. Real education is not possible through the medium of a foreign language. "The foreign medium has caused brain fag, put an undue strain upon the nerves of our children, made them crammers and imitators, unfitted them for original work and thought, and disabled them from being the vehicles of learning for their family or the masses. The foreign medium has made our children practically foreigners in their own land".[90]

Thus, the existing educational order had lost sight of the vital relationship between education and life. Unless education was given an entirely new orientation aimed at the removal of defects as pointed out by Gandhi, it was not possible to build up a social order, which he cherished. He firmly held the view that what was needed to make democracy function and sustain it, is not the knowledge of facts, but right education. "What goes by the name of education in our schools and colleges in the cities today is in reality only intellectual dissipation. Intellectual, training is there looked upon as something altogether unrelated to manual or physical work. The young man who emerges from this system can in no way compete with physical endurance with an ordinary labourer. The slightest physical exertion gives him a headache; a mild exposure to the sun is enough to cause him giddiness. And what is more, all this is looked upon as quite natural. As for the faculties of the heart, they are simply allowed to run to seed or to grow anyhow in a wild undisciplined manner. The result is moral and spiritual anarchy. And it is regarded as something laudable".[91]

Gandhi was emphatic in his assertion that the present education was not only unadaptable to the Swaraj of India but ran counter to it. It enslaved the mentality and bedevilled the soul. The educated youth ran after government white-collar jobs or sought and outlet for their frustration by fermenting trouble and unrest. They were not even ashamed to beg or sponge upon others or their families. It was a sad plight and led to his realization that mere academic training and intellectual refinement is not of much avail, because the existing education fails to impart that solidity of character which makes a man withstand vicissitudes and temptations. Education which ignores the purification of character and salvation of the soul is no education. The moral education along the non-violent lines was essential for the sustenance of the social order contemplated by Gandhi. If the individuals succeeded in building their character, society could take care of itself.

Enunciating his views on what constitutes real or true education, Gandhi said : "I hold that true education of the intellect can come only through a proper exercise and training of the bodily organs, e.g. hands, feet, eyes, ears, nose, etc. In other words, an intelligent use of the bodily organs in a child provides the best and quickest way of developing his intellect. But unless the development of mind and body goes hand in hand, with a corresponding awakening of the soul, the former alone would prove to be a poor lop-sided affair. By spiritual training I mean education of the heart. A proper and all round development of the mind, therefore, can take place only when it proceeds *pari passu* with the education of the physical and spiritual faculties of the child".[92]

Gandhi devised his system of education, which attached the highest value to the all round education of the child through activities, creative and productive, instilling in him the spiritual element of self-confidence, dignity of labour, and universal brotherhood basically required in a non-exploitable social order. Claiming originality for the system of education devised by him Gandhi said : "I have given many things to India. But this system of education together with its technique is, I feel, the best of them. I do not think I will have anything better to offer the country".[93] Indeed, the theory of trusteeship and system of basic education, as devised by Gandhi, were the two best gifts to the nation. Let us briefly trace the fundamentals of his educational system. He enumerated them as follows :

1. All education to be true must be self-supporting, that is to say, in the end it will pay its expenses excepting the capital which will remain intact.
2. In it the cunning of the had will be utilized even up to the final stage, that is to say, hands of the pupils will be skilfully working at some industry for some period during the day.
3. All education must be imparted through the medium

of the provincial language.

4. In it there is no room for giving sectional religious training. Fundamental universal ethics will have full scope.
5. This education, whether it is confined to children or adults, male or female, will find its way to the homes of the pupils.
6. Since millions of students receiving this education will consider themselves as of the whole of India, they must learn an inter-provincial language".[94]

It is apparent that the Gandhian concept of education is revolutionary and is aimed at inculcating moral, cultural and economic values in the individuals with a view to promoting creative values of life. In formulating his plan of education, Gandhi had a clear vision of the social purpose behind. "My plan", he said, "to impart primary education through the village handicrafts like spinning and carding is thus conceived as the spearhead of a silent social revolution fraught with the most far-reaching consequences. It will provide a healthy and moral basis for relationship between the city and the village, and thus, go a long way towards eradicating some of the worst evils of the present social insecurity and poisoned relationship between the classes. It will check the progressive decay of our villages and lay the foundation of a just social order, in which there is no unnatural division between the 'haves' and the 'have-nots' and everybody is assured of a living wage and the right to freedom".[95]

The doctrine of self-reliance and value of spiritual humanism was inherent in his system of education. It was also aimed at the enforcement of his principle of bread-labour. He certainly wanted to improve the standards of living of the Indian masses by making them more hard-working and industrious, but he was also anxious to infuse in them the spirit of a true humanism. It is one of the great proofs of his moral and intellectual greatness that to him these two objectives were not separate but fused into a unity. In his system of thought even the smallest act and word was related to these eternal values which give life, depth and significance. He was himself an indefatigable worker and wanted to teach children as well as adults through work, because it was only through this approach that people could learn intellectual and practical integrity, sincerity and honesty of purpose without being caught in the illusion of words. He wanted to propagate the principles of peace and non-violence through education and to abolish the differences and discriminations which have become established in human society".[96]

The educational scheme formulated by Gandhi was aimed at the development of the spiritual content in man dedicated to truth and non-violence. He stressed the need for an educational system making possible the development of body mind and soul together. But the educational system propounded by Gandhi is often distorted by laying undue emphasis on what were only instruments in his scheme and by forgetting its essential elements. "Only a couple of month before his death, that is, in December, 1947, Gandhi said : "Basic education is generally interpreted as education through craft. This is true to a certain extent, but this is not the whole truth. The roots of *Nayee Talim* go deeper. It is based on truth and non-violence in individual and collective life. Education is that which gives true freedom. Untruth and violence lead to bondage and can have no place in education".[97] On another occasion, while warning the members of the Talimi Sangh against the danger of any tendency to lean on the government for funds which would spell the end of *Nayee Talim*, Gandhi explained the features of basic education thus : "Our system of basic education leads to the development of body, mind and soul. The ordinary system of education cared only for the mind. *Nayee Talim* was not confined to teaching a little spinning and a little sweeping. However, indispensable these were, they were valueless, unless they promoted the harmonious development referred to".[98]

"It there ever was a tragedy as poignant and real as the assassination of Mahatma Gandhi, it was the killing of his ideas on education at the hands of the political and intellectual elite, who inherited or claimed to have inherited his legacy. Gandhi gave a clarion call not merely for the formal independence of India from the British but also for the freeing and regenerating of Indian civilization and the universalization of its value system. Now, that Gandhi's relevance is again being talked about quite mutedly though, we might as well have a second look at his ideas on education and see in that context what road we have followed, at what crossroads we stand, and which turning we must take".[99]

Even nearly fifty years after political independence, we find that our educational system is modelled on the same values that prevailed during the alien rule, and instead of creating a really educated man we have created only a class of parasites. It generates superficial elitism and is the most concentrated form of alienation. Prof. Shriman Narayan has sounded a note of caution at the prevailing conditions : "If our educational pattern continues to be 'bookish' and academic, divorced from the realities of life, and does not become work-oriented, creating an atmosphere of productivity all along the line, I am convinced that all our aspirations of achieving an accelerated rate of economic growth, social justice and full employment would remain only idle dreams. In the absence of such a development-oriented system of education, we shall be faced with the very difficult problem of educated unemployment, which would endanger and imperil the very foundations of democracy by creating conditions of violent disorders".[100]

The new educational system as enunciated by Gandhi was closely linked to the economy of the nation, and he firmly believed that the education of the individual cannot serve the social purpose if it was imparted in a rarefied atmosphere. He said : "The educational system has been planned to supply the needs of this lop-sided economy. If now, we wanted to create a new India, then our outlook must be changed altogether. Democracy had to be built inch by inch in the economic, social and political life. Considering the magnitude of the task, it naturally would require a very stout heart to grapple with the problem".[101] On another occasion, Gandhi exhorted the workers to steel their hearts to get out of the state of simulation and despondence. He said : "One year's work was not enough. We have to sweep aside the accumulated debris of centuries of subjugation. Even a lifetime might not prove enough. If our education had been otherwise, we might not have yielded so rapidly to despondence. We have to steel our hearts and look forward to the bright future to enable us to get out of the slough of despondence. So long as we persevere, the struggle itself is victory. It was only courage of this kind which could lead India to the new age".[102]

Verily, the education system devised by Gandhi, is the only system, which can establish a non-violent social order. It is the system calculated to bring to fruition all other Gandhian conceptions of society and state rolled into one.

(ix) Untouchability and Constructive Programme

For the cherished goals of liberty, equality and fraternity ushering in "Poorna Swaraj" of Gandhi's dream, a spiritual base was sought to be maintained and sustained by devising ways and means of cultivating a social outlook ingrained in mutual love and universal brotherhood, i.e. a spiritual equality of all beings. It was sought to be established by a new educational system aimed at the development of body, mind and soul together in a child. Yet, Gandhi was not oblivious to the actual state of inequality in the social and economic order of the nation. The greatest impediment towards social equality amongst the Hindus was the practice of Untouchability. Gandhi considered it a blot on Hinduism. In fact, he started his non-violent revolution in the social field, after his realization that the unity needed to drive out the alien rule was not possible unless this practice of untouchability is eliminated He considered untouchables as a bleeding wound of the Hindu society and the practice of untouchability as a hydra-headed monster and warned the nation that unless the wound is healed and the practice discontinued, Swaraj would remain a mirage. He proclaimed that untouchability was not only against the true spirit of religion, but was also a challenge to our honour, and humanity and to all that was noble and worthy of human character. It perpetuates injustice and inequality, it sets man against man, and divides humanity and human relationships into watertight compartments. Gandhi bound the material of emotion with the cement of reason and succeeded at last in building a solid edifice of political independence. He stated categorically : "So long as the Hindus wilfully regard untouchability as part of their religion, so long as the mass of Hindus consider it a sin to touch a section of their brethren, Swaraj is impossible of attainment".[103]

Untouchability was supposed to have the sanction of religion and, therefore, Gandhi tackled it at its root. It was necessary to impress on the people's mind that this inequality in the social field was a part of religious orthodoxy. His movement for the removal of untouchability gained momentum because it was led by a man who himself lived his life in accordance with the highest ideals of Hinduism, and who even laid down his life singing its praises. It was his unswerving faith in religion and truth that could wipe out in essence even during hid life-time, the curse of untouchability from the horizon of the nation. Once he remarked : "Two of the strongest desires that keep me in flesh and bone are the emancipation of the untouchables and the protection of the cow. When these two desires are fulfilled, there is Swaraj, and there in lies my own *Moksha*".[104]

Gandhi had emphatically states that there should be no untouchability not only between Hindus, but also between Hindus, Christians, Muslims and the rest. He exhorted Indians to live as one people trusting each other and making a common cause for the attainment of Poorna Swaraj, for making his dream a reality. He pointed out : "It is untouchability with all its subtle forms that separates us from one another and makes life itself unlovely and difficult to live".[105] Untouchabiltiy was incompatible with the principle of non-violence, and if the social fabric was to be woven by the threads of non-violence, it was imperative that the practice should be abandoned. "His fight against the curse of untouchability and the success he achieved, resulting in the burial of the monster, will go down in history as one of the greatest efforts ever made for the purification of Hinduism, and for the elevation of suppressed humanity".[106]

Paying glowing tributes to this achievement of the Mahatma, Henry Brailsford says : "The campaign of this mystic, who cleaned latrines one day and opened temples the next, is one of the strangest chapters in history and one of the noblest. Has any saint in human memory done more to lighten the misery of the oppressed and restore their self-respect? He had broken a cruel institution that dated from the night of time, based on superstition, buttressed by religion, sanctioned by many conquests and maintained not merely by prejudice, but by physical shrinking. India honours Gandhiji today chiefly because he led the fight for independence. Humanity owes him an even heavier debt because he opened the road of the untouchables to freedom".[107]

Gandhi treated life as a compact whole and felt that the problems related to it cannot be placed in watertight compartments. He, therefore, adopted an integrated approach to the various problems of the masses. The goal of equality and justice could be attained only if the monster of inequality was subjected to an all-pronged attack. This was sought to be achieved by launching a programme of constructive works including the scheme of education and removal of untouchability. The constructive programme of Gandhi was aimed not only at weaving a strong national fabric and win Poorna Swaraj, but was also designed to shape the character of the people, and this could be considered as a movement of self-reform or self-purification, as Gandhi called it. He devised the following as his constructive programmes : 1. Communal unity, 2. Removal of untouchability, 3. Prohibition, 4. Khadi, 5. Other village industries, 6. Village sanitation, 7. Basic education, 8. Adult education, 9. Women, 10. Education in health and hygiene, 11. Provincial languages, 12. National language, 13. Economic equity, 14. Kisans, 15. Labour, 16. Adivasis, 17. Lepers, 18. Students, and 19. Cow service (Goseva). The list was only illustrative and designed to a truthful and non-violent way of Swaraj for winning Poorna Swaraj. In spite of the genuine apprehension in some circles that forty crore people could not possibly participate in a programme of such a magnitude, Gandhi pinned the hope of its success on the dedicated band of workers, and this reflects the impact of Gokhale's thoughts on him. "According to him, political emancipation means the rise of mass consciousness. This cannot come without affecting all the branches of national activity. A truly awakened nation will not be satisfied with reform in only one department of life. Therefore, all movements of reform should proceed simultaneously. The struggle for Swaraj is an all-round awakening—social, educational, moral, economic and political".[108]

The awakening of the mass consciousness was an imperative necessity for any social reform because, ultimately, it was the individual that mattered in every scheme of reform. The constructive programme was designed to fulfillthis task of awakening the mass consciousness and seeking an end to the era of despondence. Yet we have to remember that "for Gandhi all constructive activity, however good in itself, was a political instrument. Indeed, constructive work was necessary to prevent the national movement from degenerating into destructive populism of which we have had a taste in recent years. Masses can be easily exploited by high-sounding slogans by all kinds of demagogues and charlatans. Constructive work was the winnowing-machine which separated the wheat from chaff, good leaders from the bad".[109] It may be very difficult for the political leaders today, but there is no escape from it if we have to remodel India on the non-violent lines in our efforts to seek equality. As Gandhi himself stated : "India is within an ace of achieving the end, if only Congressmen will be true to their creed of non-violence and live upto it. The working of the constructive programme is the test... Thirty-four years of continuous experience and experimenting in truth and non-violence cannot be sustained, unless it is linked to conscious body-labour and finds expression in our daily contact with our neighbours. This is constructive programme. It is not an end, it is an indispensable means and, therefore, is almost convertible with the end. The power of non-violent resistance can come only from honest working of the constructive programme".[110] The constructive programme was a practical programme of enchaining the individuals with the treble chain of liberty, equality and love in order to hasten the pace of India's greatness come to reality in not too distant a future.

It was an acid test and the political machinery devised by Gandhi, unfortunately, did not come up to the expectation. The constructive work programme came to be adopted by the Congress as a part of the non-cooperation programme. There was mass upheaval and even intelligentsia joined in. But with the achievement of political independence, the interest in the constructive programme waned and the scramble for power politics heralded the birth of an undreamt of India, shattering Gandhi's vision of Rama Rajya. Addressing the constructive workers, Gandhi lamented : "The Congress lent the constructive worker's *sangh* its name. It gave them the charter to function. But the Congressmen failed to come up to scratch and shoulder the burden. Such is our bankruptey".[111] Indeed, the constructive workers were worried and felt dejected at the paradox which the free India government presented. "The Congress had sworn adherence to the constructive programme for years, while it was in the wilderness. But having come to power it showed the signs of giving it the go-by".[112] Further, pointing out the objective of constructive work he warned them to keep aloof from politics, "The objective of the constructive work organization is to generate political power. But if we say that political power having come, it must be ours as a prize for our labours, it would degrade us and spell our ruin. Today politics has become corrupt. Anybody who goes into it is contaminated. Let us keep out of it altogether, our influence will grow thereby. The greater our internal purity, the greater shall be our hold on the people, without any effort on our part".[113]

The constructive programme was an integrated approach to the socio-economic maladies inflicting the nation and on its success depended the Swaraj of the Gandhi dream heralding an ear of liberty, equality and fraternity. The various items in the constructive programme were selected to usher in the new era of a non-violent social order, and its achievement was dependent on the sincerity of the band of workers. It could be worked only by men who had adopted it by heart as well as by intellect. It was an uphill and difficult task. The Congress collected various constructive workers into different *Sanghs*, but soon after the assumption of power, scant attention was paid to constructive work. The digestion of power has been found to be difficult and still goes on taking time. As Gandhi said : "The Congress created the Hindustani Talimi Sangh, but never took any interest in it. Similarly, the Charkha Sangh is the progeny of the Congress, but it never made it its own. Who cares for these institutions today? When the Congressmen had only a little money and a little experience, they paid some attention to constructive work. Today, however, the entire government has come into our hands, They have not yet digested the power it has brought. They will take time to do so.[114]

Apart from the constructive devices on the social plane, the item in the constructive programme affecting the economic life of the nation, about which we are most concerned, is the economic equality, including, of course, Khadi and other village industries. Of its importance, Gandhi said : "This last is the master key to non-violent independence. Working for economic equality means abolishing the eternal conflict between capital and labour. It means the levelling down of the few rich in whose hands is concentrated the bulk of the nation's wealth on the one hand, and the levelling up of the semi-starved millions on the other. A non-violent system of government is clearly an impossibility so long as the wide gulf between the rich and the hungry million persists".[115] Let us examine more closely how Gandhi formulated his plan to usher in a non-violent economic order in the Swaraj of his contemplation.

(x) Economic Equality

The Gandhian economic policies, unlike his policies in the social field, are not directly derivable from his principle of non-violence. Though it is true that these cannot be derived without assuming the principle of non-violence, non-violence is not the basic determinant of these policies. "The principle of non-violence does not appear as a principle determining the goals of his economic policies but simply as a basic constraint on the types of policies which might be used to achieve these goals. The simplest proof of this is that non-violent policies may be directed to policy goals quite different from the typical Gandhian ones".[116] To mitigate the misery and suffering of the masses and banish unemployment, creation of conditions of equality among all individuals, high and low, is the basic proposition underlying the Gandhian economic thought. Non-violence oriented economic policies are prescribed and advocated only because policies based on violence have so far failed to achieve these human objectives. And if violence is practical, non-violence cannot be dubbed as impractical or ideal. Gandhi held the view "that social justice even to the least and lowliest is impossible of attainment by force".[117] These policies are based on the practical economic reality prevailing in India, and are based on a clear vision about the working of colonial economy in British India. To fight the miseries propelled by the working of the colonial economy Gandhi had thought out certain ideals for economic policies in such areas. These ideals themselves are such that they are unattainable by the use of violent policies. The meaning and consistency of the Gandhian economic policy lay hidden in his analytic vision of the operations of colonial economics. After examining the working of the colonial economy, Gandhi firmly held the view that the introduction of Western capitalism and industrialization in the environment of Indian agrarian economy and the parasitic role of the cities were solely responsible for the creation of mass poverty and unemployment. Four-fifth of the population of India depended, directly or indirectly, on agriculture. It was the main industry, the main source of subsistence for the people. With the destruction of the ancient system of village self-government flourishing for thousands of years in India, the ancient land system withered away. The village industries could not withstand the onslaught of the Empire. Thus, both agriculture and industry perished under the heavy weight of centralized administration and industry copied from the West. With the uncertain state of agriculture and the decay of domestic handicraft industries in villages resulting in loss of occupations, the impoverization of masses became all the more acute. The villagers had but one occupation left to them. In this process of village decay, what was clear to Gandhi was that the city sector of the colonized areas played the same role as did the manufacturing industries of the colonizing country. The Western capitalists as well as the domestic capitalists treated the villages as their markets of free trade, and together they completed the economic ruin of the village. As India lived in her villages, it spelt total economic ruination of the nation. The Gandhian diagnosis of the economic malaise of the nation remains superb and unbeaten.

No body did more to bring home the accuracy of Gandhi's diagnosis of the malaise of modern industrialized societies than Dr. E. F. Schumakar, before his premature death in September, 1977. He visited India in 1962 to study rural development for the Planning Commission and made a second visit to this country in 1973. Delivering the fourth Gandhi Memorial lectures at Varanasi, he explained the logical nature of

Gandhi's people-oriented economic thinking thus : "Gandhi insisted that modern mass production industry depends on exploitation. If India adopted it, whom would she exploit? I confess that this argument puzzled me for a long time. Why exploitation? Why could mass production industry not be efficient enough to pay decent wages and also pay decent prices for materials purchased from other producers? This, surely, was simply a question of attaining the requisite level of productivity. The answer is : of course, such an industry, if well equipped and efficiently run can pay decent wages and prices : but its output must be sold, and by selling its output it will deprive other people of their livelihood. What greater exploitation could there be than robbing other people of their livelihood, robbing them thereby of their very basis of existence".[118]

He added : "We normally call it exploitation if an employer pays a man less then what he is worth, thereby robbing him of part of his livelihood. Gandhi, however, looked beyond the factory gates and considered the people whose living is destroyed by the introduction of mass production : they, not the employed workers, are the victims of the grossest exploitation".[119]

All protagonists of equality, in East and West, are persons enamoured by the humanitarian considerations and as such economic equality cannot be viewed except as an ethical ideal in economics. While pleading for economic equality Gandhi stresses the adoption of "a system in which the economic needs of the individual in society are regarded as limited in principle and the objective of the economic system is seen to be the provision of this basic minimum for all".[120] However, this self-imposed limitation of economic needs of an individual is not conceived as a permanent phenomenon, but is conditioned with the achievement of this minimal needs to all, rich and poor alike. "If by abundance you mean everyone having plenty to eat and to drink and to clothe himself, enough to keep his mind trained and educated, I should be satisfied. But I should not like to pack more stuff into my belly than I can digest and more things than I can ever usefully use. But neither do I want poverty, penury, misery, dirt and dust in India".[121] After the satisfaction of the necessities of all, minimum for human living, there can, of course, be no objection if individual needs are further augmented and satisfied. But, essentially, Gandhi believed that human happiness lies in the curtailment of wants. The materialistic cravings of an unsatiated man kill his manhood and make him synonym with his machine. Material things are of real importance up to a point. For the removal of the economic conditions of misery, a certain check on the augmentation of individual needs—a minimization of wants—was inevitable. But economic progress up to the point of sufficiency was not tabooed in Gandhian economic thinking.

"The contrast between the rich and the poor, as it exists today, is a painful sight. The poor villagers are exploited by the foreign government and also by their own countrymen, the city dwellers. They produce food and they go hungry. They produce milk and their children have to go without it. It is disgraceful. Everyone must have a balanced diet, a decent house to live in, facilities for education of one's children and adequate medical relief. This constitutes my picture of economic equality. I do not want to taboo everything above and beyond the bare necessaries, but they must come after the essential needs of the poor are satisfied. First things must come first".[122] Gandhi was, however, emphatic in his assertion that equality—economic, social or religious—must mean the equality of all human beings. "If mankind was to progress and to realize the ideal of equality and brotherhood, it must adopt and act on the principle of *Unto this Fast* (Ruskin) : it must take along with it even the dumb, the hale and the lame".[123]

Expressing his opinion on what constitutes the basis of India's future economic constitution, Gandhi said : "The economic constitution of India, and for that matter of that of the world, should be such that no one under it should suffer from want of food and clothing. In other words, everybody should be able to get sufficient work to enable him to make two ends meet. And this ideal can be universally realised only if the means of production of elementary necessaries of life remain under the control of the masses".[124]

Economic equality of Gandhi's conception did not literally mean the same amount for everyone. It only means that everybody should have enough for his or her needs. The real meaning of economic equality was "to each according to his need". As Gandhi said : "Economic equality must never be supposed to mean possession of an equal amount of worldly goods by everyone. It does mean, however, that everyone will have a proper house to live in, sufficient and balanced food to eat, and sufficient Khadi with which to cover himself. It also means that the cruel inequality that obtains today will be removed by purely non-violent means".[125]

Gandhi confidently believed that the real cause of India's grinding poverty lay at the door of imperialism and colonialism of the alien rule. "A starving human being", says Gandhi, "thinks only of food. Such is the situation for millions of people in India. To them freedom, God and all such words are mere words without the slightest meaning. They are jarring notes in their ears.[126] It was one of the great ingenious efforts of Gandhi that the Khadi movement was launched with a view to inculcating in individuals a feeling of self-respect and a belief in him that he was worth worrying about. Talking about the efficacy of the Khadi movement, he said : "If we want to give these people a feeling of freedom, we must provide them with employment of a kind which they can easily carry out in their dreary homes, and which will, at any rate, give them the barest means of existence. This can only be done by the spinning wheel. And when they begin to trust themselves and to be able to stand on their own, then it will be possible for us to speak to them about freedom, about Congress, etc. And so, those who provide them with work and a means of existence will be their deliverers, and also those who will make them hunger for freedom. This is the political value of the spinning wheel quite apart from the fact that it can replace foreign fabrics and material".[127]

To Gandhi, the spinning wheel was a national necessity. It denoted the beginning of economic freedom and equality of all in the country. It was a dynamic means for resuscitation of the village economy and its re-introduction was aimed at supplementing their slender resources. He was convinced that the revival of Khadi would usher in the economic and moral regeneration of India. It was not only a supplementary source of income for the starving millions, but was also the symbol of the unity of India. It was the practice of Swadeshi in the field of economics in order to establish a self-sufficient village republic. As Gandhi said : "In hand spinning is hidden the protection of women's virtue, the insurance against famine, and the cheapening of prices. In it is hidden the secret of Swaraj".[128]

Swaraj had no meaning for Gandhi in the midst of hunger and idleness. The love of foreign cloth had ousted the wheel from its position and created penury and hunger amongst the starving millions. It was, therefore, a sacred duty of all to popularize the spinning wheel for the sake of dumb millions. Said Gandhi : "Hunger is the argument that is driving India to the spinning wheel. We must think of the millions who are today less than animals, who are almost in a dying state. The spinning wheel is the reviving draught for the millions of our dying countrymen and the country women".[129]

Charkha was a remedy for India's poverty, about which Gandhi was deeply concerned. It was the only ready means of driving out penury and forced unemployment. Gandhi was, for the sake of people famished and idle, even ready to "favour the use of the most elaborate machinery, if thereby India's pauperism and resulting idleness be avoided".[130] So, intense was his desire to drive out penury and unemployment of the Indian agricultural masses that in 1939 he had clearly stated that if these could be eradicated through more advanced technology, he would have no objection to its use, provided they did not cause exploitation and inequality. The pragmatic character of his approach to the immediate economic problems facing the country was evident when on a report of the National Planning Committee set up by the Congress in 1939, a controversy had arisen. "When the dispute was finally referred to Gandhi, he is referred to have advised the preparation of two separate and alternative plans by the two wings on the basis of the assumptions that there would be no dependence on foreign loans, that all the available money, whether lying with private organizations or public, would be fully utilized for national development, and that a definite standard of living would be accepted as the given objective. He is reported to have added that if it were discovered that Kumarappa Das Gupta plan involved an inordinately long time or expense in comparison with the other plan, then before he retired, he would love to save all the wood used fore manufacturing spinning-wheels, at least for use as domestic fuel".[131]

Gandhi also viewed *Charkha* as a symbol of protect against machine civilization exposing the villages to penury and destitution. He was not against machinery as such, but it was his intense desire that no one should suffer from want of food and clothing, i.e. everybody should get sufficient work so that they can earn their bread by the sweat of their brow, which had led to his opposition to industrialism.

He was quite opposed to giving doles to the able-bodied and he was going about with the message of *Charkha* in order to wipe out that shame. Work was worship. It was the harbinger of *Ahimsa* or non-violence. In fact, it was against the idleness of the village-folk created by industrialism that had led him to strive for the revival of the village economy where means of production of the elementary necessaries of life will remain in the control of the masses, i.e. decentralization of production and distribution of the elementary needs of the masses. He expressed his view thus : "My Ahimsa would not tolerate the idea of giving a free meal to a healthy person who has not worked for it in some honest way, and if I had the power, I would stop every Sadavrata where free meals are given. It has degraded the nation and it has encouraged laziness, idleness, hypocrisy and even crime".[132] The spinning wheel was found to be the answer to these evils permeating the Indian masses. It was an effective device for a break through in the state of idleness, sloth and simulation to which the masses had fallen a prey, because it was capable of universal application by all persons of any age group at any time and place. It was not only a solution to the problem of penury and unemployment, it was an attempt at the basic reconstruction of the Indian economy and a symbol of revival of village industries. It was Gandhi's great genius that realized far ahead of others that even after the British left India, the essence of the problem would remain very much unchanged, however much we try to industrialize India on the pattern set forth by the colonial economy.

Gandhi had explained his central idea of village production giving rise to a self-sufficient village republic so far as the basic needs of the masses are concerned, i.e. Swadeshi, as follows: "The central idea is not no much to carry on a commercial war against foreign countries as to utilize the idle hours of the nation and thus by natural processes to help it get rid of her growing pauperism".[133] Justifying the introduction of the spinning wheel, he stated : "The entire foundation of the spinning wheel rests on the fact that there are crores of semi-employed people in India. And I should admit that if there were none such, there would be no room for the spinning wheel".[134]

He further says : "I would welcome every improvement in the cottage machine, but I know it is criminal to displace hand-labour by the introduction of power-driven spindles unless one is at the same time ready to give millions of farmers some other occupation in their homes".[135]

Indeed, Gandhi's insistence on village industries stems from his deep-rooted conviction that the machine civilization was set to displace hand-labour, create unemployment, drudgery, sloth and idleness amongst the masses, and thereby making them prone to exploitation in the colonial economy designed by the capitalists. The policy of Khadi and his insistence on rehabilitation of village and village industries were insistence to serve his immediate goal of making the colonial economy unworkable.

In his *Small is Beautiful* Schumakar had shown how the Keynesian emphasis on exploiting the human weakness of selfishness for economic development in the purely material sense inevitably led to expansionism and conflict. In this context, he recalled what Gandhi said, that "earth provides enough to satisfy every man's need, but not for every man's greed." In his Gandhi Memorial lecture at Varanasi he saw non-violence as one of the goals that provide guidelines for a manageable society. Here, again, it is hard to improve on his own language :

> "It seems to me incontrovertible that, to work himself out of misery and to lead a becoming life, man needs to use his intellect, and this means, in present day terms, to employ science and technology. As this is precisely what we have been doing during the last few centuries—and it has led us into a worldwide crisis—it appears that we

are called upon to consider the direction in which science and technology have hitherto been utilized and to study the possibility of a change of direction. In the economic field, we have been moving at ever-increasing speed into large-scale immense complexity : high capital intensity to 'eliminate the human factor' and if I may use the term, violence".

"If this road is leading us into a crisis of survival, we may consider whether new guidelines may be called for, which would point in the opposite direction : towards smallness rather than giantism; towards simplification rather than growing complexity; towards capital-saving rather than labour-saving; and towards non-violence, in a rather generalized sense".[136]

Gandhi's insistence on providing an economic system based on Khadi and what it means was the result of his faith that industrial civilization was a disease and an evil for mankind. He wanted to balance the materialism of the West with the humanism, which it had abandoned in the process of inevitable changeover from the economy of need to an economy of acquisition. To a question that the material resources of the West had far advanced its moral resources and something was required to balance them Gandhi replied, "That is precisely what the *Charkha* is intended to do".[137] Thus, the *Charkha* was also conceived and forged as a weapon for moral regeneration to set right the imbalance between the material and spiritual welfare and the lop-sided development in man. He firmly believed that the one fundamental cause of inequality was the desire in human beings to excel each other in the matter of acquisition of goods and services. He had, therefore, enunciated a need-based economic policy and had thoroughly disapproved what is called consumerism.

Contriving for the breakdown of the colonial economy based on exploitation and consumerism, Gandhi had also strived for its replacement by Swaraj economics paving the way for true economic independence and equality. The basic principle on which Swaraj economics of Gandhi thrived was decentralization of Industries and production and distribution of goods in the economic field and devolution of power in the political field. As Gandhi succinctly put it : "I suggest that, if India is to evolve along non-violent lines, it will have to decentralize many things. Centralization cannot be sustained and defended without adequate force. Simple homes, from which there is nothing to take away, require no policing, the palaces of the rich must have strong guards to protect them against dacoity. So must huge factories. Rurally organized India will run less risk of foreign invasion than urbanized India".[138] Gandhi realized that without economic independence, which was the very basis of equality, political independence becomes a mockery and democracy a mere form. The concentration of wealth in a few hands, i.e. the private accumulation of capital not only undermined the economic independence of the individuals but also caused a sharp division between the classes and the masses, the haves and the have-nots. This was further accentuated by the lure of industrialism and the factors of large-scale production. The horrors of capitalism advancing menacingly in India due to the working of the colonial economy were sought to be checkmated by a dispersal and decentralization of industries along with the means of production and distribution and efforts to meet the essential needs of the masses.

The dangers of industrialism become manifest through its craze for machinery. The large-scale factory production had led to mass-production and the craze for improvement in machinery and technology intensified day by day. It is this craze which has made machine the master of man. The concentration of wealth in the hands of a ever-narrowing group of capitalists has created a class war leading to bloody revolutions. Gandhi quoted the following comments of a correspondent of the *Manchester Guardian* : "Unless unemployment is abolished within a reasonable time, even by means that appear novel and unorthodox, the machinery age will disappear in revolutions and wars will destroy us all. So, long as machinery promotes the happiness and the prosperity of the masses as well as the classes, it is a beneficent agent. But when it leads to the unemployment and starvation of millions, as is happening in the highly industrialized countries of the West, it becomes a curse. Machinery exists for man, and not vice-versa, and must be made subservient to the well-being the people and should not be allowed to become their master".[139] Gandhi did not consider machine and scientific inventions harmful in themselves. Its useful application will surely lead to an increase in the common wealth and prosperity of the nation. What was, however, obvious that the colonial economy had abused the machines and technological inventions for the benefit of a few at the cost of many rendering a vast mass of people unemployed, destitute and exploited. Gandhi's repugnance to machine was directed towards such debasement which makes man a cog in the machine.

He was not averse to the use of machine and was positively disposed towards the role of science in the making of free India. He wrote : "I would prize every invention of science made for the benefit of all. I am not aiming at the eradication of all machinery, but limitation, because the supreme consideration is man. The machine should not tend to make strophied the limbs of man".[140] He further elaborated : "What I object to is the craze for machinery, not machinery as such. The craze is for what they call labour-saving machinery Men go on "saving labour" till thousands are without work and are thrown on the open streets to die of starvation. I want to save time and labour, not for a fraction of mankind, but for all. I want the concentration of wealth, not in the hands of a few, but in the hands of all. Today machinery merely helps a few to ride on the backs of millions. The impetus behind it all is not the philanthropy to save labour, but greed. It is against this constitution of things that I am fighting with all my might".[141]

This makes it absolutely clear that Gandhi was not opposed to the use of machinery as such, but was of the opinion that the use of machinery and scientific inventions should not be based on greed and actuated by the motive of exploitation, its use must be restricted by conditions aimed at the improvement of the condition of the masses. When a socialist asked Gandhi if the village industry movement was not meant to oust all machinery, he relied : "Who said so? If we could have electricity in every village home. I should not mind villagers plying their implements and tools with the help of electricity. But then the village communities or the State would own power-houses, just as they have their grazing pastures. I would prize every invention of science made for the benefit of all. There is a difference between invention and invention.

I should not care for the asphyxiating gases capable of killing masses of men at time. The heavy machinery for work of public utility which cannot be undertaken by human labour has its inevitable place, but all that would be owned by the State and used entirely for the benefit of the people. I can have no consideration for machinery which is meant either to enrich the few at the expense of the many, or without cause to displace the useful labour of many".[142]

He, thus, made it quite clear that heavy machinery and large-scale industries are not baneful if they are kept in the public sector. But it was not the public sector of his conception that we find today in India or in the socialist countries. He was of the view that scientific discoveries should be directed towards ameliorating the miserable conditions of the masses and should cease to be mere instrument of greed. In fact, he approved of any machine "which does not deprive the masses of men of the opportunity to labour but which helps the individual and adds to his efficiency and which a man can handle at will without being its slave".[143]

"When some one posed the straightforward question to Gandhiji : Are you against large-scale production? he unequivocally replied, 'I never said that. The belief is one of the many superstitions about me. Your question is based upon loose newspaper reports. What I am against is large-scale production of things which the villagers can produce without difficulty".[144]

He further said : "I do visualize electricity, ship-building, iron-works and machine-making and the like existing side by side with village craft. But my order of precedence will be reversed. Hitherto, industrialization has been so planned as to destroy the villagers and the village handicrafts. In the State of the future, it will subserve the villages and their craft. I do not believe in the socialist belief that the nationalization of the necessities of life will conduce to common welfare when nationalized industries are planned and owned by the State".[145] He also said that while the capitalist has a soul, the State is a soul less machine.

In fact, he was opposed to capitalist industrialization, but was agreeable to industrialization in those fields where it was required, i.e. in the public sector. He was of the opinion that the Soviet system of industrialization, while apparently free from exploitation, had elements of violence and use of coercive power as another sort of exploitation. The industrialization that he approved was designed to shed the evils of capitalist or socialist industrialism. As he put it : "But I am socialist enough to say that such factories should be nationalized, or State-controlled. They ought to be working under the most attractive and ideal conditions, not for profit, but for the benefit of humanity, love taking the place of greed as the motive. It is an alteration in the conditions of labour that I want. This mad rush for wealth must cease, and the labourer must be assured not only of a living wage, but a daily task that is not mere drudgery. The machine will, under these conditions, be as much a help to the man working it as to the State, or the man who owns it. The present mad rush will cease, and the labourers will work under attractive and ideal conditions".[146]

Gandhi was, of course, opposed to technological determinism. He did not view technology outside the realm of economics, social justice and its impact on humen values. He was of the view that science should regulate all the activities of man. Analyzing the scientific approach of Gandhi, Mr. Pyarelal writes : "Modern science has two aspects—educative or fundamental and economic or technological. In its fundamental aspect, science has been an educative and liberating force, which has set free truth from the shackles of dogma. This aspect of science Gandhi personified as perhaps no other living person. None strives harder than he to cultivate that intellectual integrity, that habit of dispassionate inquiry into and search for objective truth as against a fanatical assertion of the truth of one's own dogma which the discipline of science demands, or the inculcate in the people at large the habit of scientific approach to everything in life".[147]

(xi) Trusteeship

Apart from devising ways and means for obliterating the differences between the classes and the masses, created by the working of the colonial economy. Gandhi had also turned his inquisitive eyes to the problem of labour-capital friction which was a by-product of industrialism and colonial economic order. Like the solutions of other maladies in the socio-economic fields, the solution which Gandhi finally pronounced for the termination of this eternal conflict was not the class conflict of the socialists, but class-cooperation; and if the latter was not forthcoming, non-violent non-cooperation. He was in favour of cooperation between labour and capital, between the poor and the rich, so that a non-violent order based on equality can be established. He held the view that all land belonged to the State. He insisted that the capital of the capitalists and the riches of the few rich should be shared with the poor; the fruits of capital, which were really those of labour and a result of exploitation of labour by the capitalists, should be utilized in the interests of the poor and the rich men should act as the trustee of those ill-gotten fruit, to be utilized in the interest of the poor. Thus collaboration and cooperation, not class-conflict, was the essential method of Gandhi through which he had planned to establish Swaraj.

The Western countries infatuated by industrialism, made a clear-cut division between the employer and the employee. Gandhi was of the view that this relation ought to be one of father and children. Addressing mill-owners, Gandhi said :

> "What I expect of you, therefore, is that you should hold all your riches as a trust to be used solely in the interest of those who sweat for you, and to whose industry and labour you owe all your position and prosperity. I want you to make your labourers co-partners of your wealth. From the moment your men come to realize that the mills are theirs no less than yours they will begin to feel towards you as blood brothers, there would be no question of their acting against the common interest and the need of having a heavy supervisory establishment over them".[148]

Gandhi was of the view that the workers can obtain justice without their having recourse to violence. The reason why labour has so often failed is that instead of sterilizing capital, labour wants to seize that capital and become capitalist itself in the worst sense of the term. He was trying to get rid of this law of the jungle which is ill-suited to man by formulating his law of trusteeship.

Explaining the contents of his statutory trusteeship, which

shall be made applicable on all forms of riches, Gandhi said :

> "As for the present owners of wealth, they would have to make their choice between the class war and voluntary converting themselves into trustees of their wealth. They would be allowed to retain the stewardship of their possessions and to use their talent to increase the wealth, not for their own sakes, but for the sake of the nation and, therefore, without exploitation. The State would regulate the rate of commission which they would get commensurate with the services rendered and its value to society. Their children would inherit the stewardship, only if they proved their fitness for it. He maintained that along with the fixation of the rate of commission by the State, the commission itself shall be slashed down on a graduated scale at the higher level of income. He also insisted that the State should have control over the selection of heirs of the trustees, whose right of nomination should not be taken away entirely.
>
> "Choice should be given to the original owner who became the first trustee, but the chioce must be finalized by the State. Such arrangement puts a check on the State as well as the individual".[150]

Gandhi visualized that the law of trusteeship shall evolve from the village level itself and the conceived village Panchayat as a self-governing village republic. And he sounded a note of caution to the rich : "If they do not become trustees of their own accord, force of circumstances will compel the reform, unless they court utter destruction. When Panchayat Raj is established, public opinion will do what violence can never do. The present power of the zamindars, the capitalists and the Rajas can hold sway only so long as the common people do not realize their own strength. If people non-cooperate with the evil of zamindari, it must die of inanition. In the Panchayat Raj only the Panchayat will be obeyed and the Panchayat can work only through the law of their making".[151] Gandhi held the view that the trusteeship would have a statutory though voluntary basis. "When the people understand the implications of trusteeship and the atmosphere is ripe for it, the people themselves, beginning with Gram Panchayats, will begin to introduce such statutes. Such a thing coming from below is easy to swallow, coming from above, it is liable to prove a dead-weight".[152]

Gandhi believed that there was nothing like inevitability of class conflict, and trusteeship was devised as a marriage between labour and capital which was reckoned to foster co-operation and co-ordination between them. Asked to comment on the justification of carrying on a class war by peasants and workers, Gandhi replied that he was himself carrying on a revolution on their behalf. In fact, he declared himself carrying on a revolution on their behalf. In fact, he declared himself a revolutionary—albeit a non-violent revolutionary. Indeed, trusteeship was a revolutionary idea grounded in non-violence and based on class cooperation, because Gandhi firmly believed that what was gained by violence was destined to be lost in violence.

Trusteeship lies at the root of the doctrine of equal distribution, which is the fountainhead of economic equality and economic freedom. For Gandhi, trusteeship was the only means for the achievement of economic equality of all beings. The doctrine underlines his differences with the socialists who look towards the end in view and are prepared to adopt any means to achieve it. Gandhi believed that we can control only the means, the end result is not in our hands, and if we preserve the purity of the means, the end result must be the happiness and well-being of all. Trusteeship is the non-violent path through which economic transformation will take place in a non-violent society. Honesty on the part of trustees is an imperative condition for the successful implementation of the trusteeship formula. Ruling out dispossession of the wealthy or confiscation of their wealth as tantamount to violence, Gandhi pleaded :

> "The rich man will be left in possession of his wealth, of which he will use what he reasonably requires for his personal needs and will act as trustee for the remainder to be used for society. In this argument, honesty on the part of the trustee is assumed".[153]

This assumption of honesty on the part of trustees can

take place only in the Gandhian social order. It, therefore, follows that unless such a social order comes into being, the doctrine of trusteeship remains unattainable.

Gandhi held the view that if the rich men accepted the trusteeship formula, their will be no need of philanthropy in the society, their commission shall be regulated by law, and they shall have no heir but the public. A simple, practical trusteeship formula which has had the approval of Gandhi was quoted by Pyarelal thus :

1. "Trusteeship provides a means of transforming the present capitalist order of society into an egalitarian one. It gives no quarter to capitalism, but gives the present owning class a chance of reforming itself. It is based on the faith that human nature is never beyond redemption.
2. It does not recognize any right of private ownership of property, except in as much as it may be permitted by society for its own welfare.
3. It does not exclude legislative regulation of the ownership and use of wealth.
4. Thus, under State-regulated trusteeship, an individual will not be free to hold or use his wealth for selfish satisfaction in disregard of the interest of society.
5. Just as it is proposed to fix a decent minimum living wage, even so a limit should be fixed for the maximum income that could be allowed to any person in society. The difference between such minimum and maximum incomes should be reasonable and equitable and variable from time to time, so much so that the tendency should be towards obliteration of the difference.
6. Under the Gandhian economic order, the character of production will be determined by social necessity and not by personal whim or greed".[154]

And if the rich men do not accept their duty of helping their poor brethren in the true sense of the term, the only solution to this riddle prescribed was the non-violent non-cooperation and civil disobedience. If the knowledge of the strength of Ahimsa entered into the soul of the poor, they would become strong and free themselves by means of non-violent, non-cooperation with the rich from the crushing inequality, which has brought them to the verge of starvation.

Indeed, trusteeship was conceived as device to weed out capitalism and eliminate bureaucratic statism in the non-violent economic order. Gandhi categorically stated : "there is no other choice than between voluntary surrender on the part of the capitalists of super-fluities and consequent acquisition of the real happiness of all on the one hand and, on the other, the impending chaos into which, if the capitalist does not wake up betimes, awakened but ignorant famishing millions will plunge the country and which not even the armed forced that a powerful government can bring into play can avert".[155]

Gandhi was not in favour of the bureaucracy taking over from the capitalist class the reins of the economy to solve the problem of economic exploitation as was being done in the socialist countries, mainly, Russia. But he was not totally averse to it either. He was reconciled to accept it to a limited extent as a step towards the cherished form of economic organization. He said : "I would be very happy if the people concerned behave as trustees, but if they fail I believe we shall have to deprive them of their possession through the State with the minimum exercise of violence. That is why I said at the Round Table conference that every vested interest must be subject to scrutiny and confiscation ordered where necessary—with or without compensation, as the case demanded".[156]

Gandhi perceived that the non-violent experiment was still in the making, and the method had begun to work though ever so slowly in the direction of equality and asked the Congress workers to lead the way. As he said : "And since non-violence is a process of conversion, the conversion if achieved, must be permanent. A society or a nation constructed non-violently must be able to withstand attacks upon the structure from without and within. We have moneyed Congressmen in the organization. They have to lead the way. This fight provides an opportunity for the closest heart-searching on the part of every individual Congressman. If ever we are to achieve equality, the foundation has to be laid now. Those who think that the major reforms will come after the advent of Swaraj are deceiving themselves as to the elementary working of non-violent Swaraj. It will not drop from the heaven all of a sudden one fine morning. But it has to be built up brick by brick by corporate self-effort. Every Congressman has to ask himself what he has done towards the attainment of economic equality".[157]

Of all the Gandhian ideas and concepts, the theory of trusteeship was the most original and dynamic. But like his other concepts, it was also interrelated with other concepts, and was not absolute but relative to space and time. Gandhi wrote : "Absolute trusteeship is an abstraction like Euclid's definition of a piont, and is equally unattainable. But if we strive for it, we shall be able to go farther in realizing a State of equality on earth than by any other method".[158] The concept of trusteeship which envisages economic transformation on non-violent lines is a completely dynamic concept. That is why Gandhi claimed himself a better Communist. He said : "The Socialists and Communists say that they can do nothing to bring about economic equality today. They will just carry on propaganda in its favour and to that end they believe in generating and accentuating hatred. They say, when they get control over the State they will enforce equality. Under my plan the State will be there to carry out the will of the people, not to dictate to them or force then to do its will. I shall bring about economic equality through non-violence, by converting the people to my point of view by harnessing the forces of love as against hatred. I will not wait till I have converted the whole society to my view but will straightway make a beginning with myself".[159] Thus, trusteeship was not a matter of statecraft. Its implementation, like the coercive laws of the State, cannot be left to the State. In fact, the non-violent economic, social and political order envisages the awakening of the masses and their scientific search of truth passionately. The idea of trusteeship presupposes a beginner, a leader endowed with a fiery zeal to translate the principle into action and to adopt those in his own life and habits before persuading others to fall line with him. It is a principle of persuasion, not a method of coercion, though Gandhi accepted the use of State machinery to a very limited extent of its regularization. The idea could not gain much headway, firstly, because the first convert having departed for his heavenly abode, the rest left were only zeros; and secondly, its successful implementation depended on the application of other principles in the social and educational field which he had enunciated. The principle of non-violence, equality, Swaraj and trusteeship are so interlinked that it is not possible to have one without having the other three. As Gandhi succinctly put it : "In order to reach this state, we may not look at things philoso-phically and say that we need not make a move until all are converted to socialism. Without changing our life we may go on giving addresses, forming parties and hawk-like seize the game when it comes our way. This is no socialism. The more we treat it as game to be seized, the farther it must recede from us.

Socialism begins with the first convert. It there is one such, you can add zeros to the one and the first zero will account for ten and every addition will account for ten times the previous number. If, however, the beginner is a zero, in other words, no one makes the beginning, multiplicity of zeros will also produce zero value".[160]

REFERENCES

1. Democratic Theory, Sartori, p. 330.
2. *Ibid* : p. 331.
3. A Grammer of Politics : Harold Laski, pp. 152-53.
4. Sartori, *op. cit.*, p. 332.
5. The Political Philosophers : Commins and Linscott (Ed.); p. 111.
6. *Ibid.*
7. Some thoughts concerning education John Lock, (1880) London, p. 60.
8. Liberty *vs.* Equality, William F. Russel (1936); (quoted) p. 46.
9. The Political Philosophers : ed., Commins and Linscott (New York), p. 298.
10. *Ibid.*, p. 291.
11. Russel, *op. cit.*, (quoted) : p. 47.
12. Equality, Tawney (1936), quoted (ch. II) p. 24.
13. *Ibid.*, p. 49.
14. *Ibid.*, p. 61.
15. Russel *op cit.* (quoted at) p. 37.
16. Political Writings of Thomas Jefferson : Ed. E. Dumbauld (1966); p. 43.
17. Russel, *op. cit.*, (quoted at) p. 11.
18. *Ibid.*, p. 74.
19. Sartori, *op. cit.*, p. 337.

20. *Ibid.*
21. *Encyclopaedia of Social Sciences* Vol. 5. (1968), p. 105.
22. Tawney, *op. cit.,* : pp. 103-4.
23. Encyclopaedia : *op. cit.,* quoted Anatole France; p. 105.
24. Sartori : *op. cit.*, p. 352.
25. Encyelopaedia : *op. cit.*, p. 106.
26. *Ibid.*
27. Socialist Thought and Practice (No. 34)–*A Yogoslav Journal*, Dr. Miroslav Pecujlic.
28. *Ibid.*
29. The Federalist (No. 79); Ed. Hamilton.
30. Taittriya Upanishad, "From whom all the material elements have their being, are having existence and in whom it inheres in the last, that is Braham Search Him".
31. A Proposal for Indian Classification of Cultures : An Article—Dr. B. B. Saraswati p. 5.
32. The Indian Scheme of life : R. K. M. (Ram Krishna Mission) p. 33.
33. Essential features of Indian Culture K. M. Panikkar; p. 11.
34. *See* Atharva. 5/19/1 (Mankind exhorted to remain with love and affection among themselves as do cows love their calves.
35. *See Ibid.*, 1/24/9 (True religion always preaches good feeling and good sense, which is another name of humanity).
36. *See* Shukla Yajur. 36/18 (i) (To see everybody with the eye of a friend and to be seen by every body with the eye of a friend).

    (ii) Atharv. 19/5/6.

    (iii) *Ibid.* 19/14/1.

    (iv) *Ibid.*12/1/18.

    "Expect kindness for yourself when it is flowered in your own heart".
37. *See* (i) Atharva 7/115/2 (The Riches which are ill got are proscribed as never an item of desire, only those riches are desired which are derived through religion, ethical conduct and labour).

    (ii) *Ibid.*, 7/115/3.

    (iii) *Ibid.*, 7/115/4.

    (iv) *Ibid.*, 7/120/1.

    ("Riches through Sacred means have been the object of desire, but riches through evil means have been cursed and asked to go to devil".)
38. *See* Ishopanishad 01 (Men are advised to consider the whole worldly objects as belonging to God and hence to enjoy whatever belongs to them with a sense of renunciation.)
39. *See* Rig Veda 10/90/1 (The whole world is a figure of one Universal self and every being is part and parcel of that Univercal self, everyone emanating from an organ of that Great Body.)
40. Upanishads—C. Rajgopalachari, Bharti Vidya Bhawan, Bombay, p. 41.
41. Chandogya Upanishad., (6/11/1-2).

42. Education in Ancient India, Altekar, p.1.
43. *Ibid.*, p. 4.
44. *See* Rig Veda. X.7.7.
45. *See* Atharva Veda 5.1.19.
46. Altekar : *op.cit.,* pp. 8-9
47. Concept of Equality., B.N. Ganguli (1975), p.17.
48. *Ibid.*, p. 19.
49. Socialism of My Conception : M.K. Gandhi (1966), p. 115.
50. *Young India*, Nov. 1, 1928.
51. *Ibid.*, Nov. 13, 1924.
52. *Harijan* : March 25, 1939.
53. Good bye. Mr. Gandhi : Kanwarlal (1969), p. 124.
54. The Diary of Mahadeva Desai, June 4, 1932. p. 149.
55. *Ibid.*, July 10. 1932; p. 221.
56. Truth is God, M.K. Gandhi, pp. 123-24.
57. *Young India*, June 12, 1924.
58. Democracy, Real and Deceptive; M.K. Gandhi (1961), p. 3.
59. *Harijan,* Aug. 29, 1936.
60. Kanwar Lal : *op.cit;* pp. 125-26.
61. The Sage in Revolt, Pran Chopra (ed) (1972), pp. 54-55.
62. The Political Philosophy of Mahatma Gandhi : V.P. Verma (1965), pp.71-72.
63. *Harijan*, Aug. 29, 1936.
64. Chopra, *op. cit.*, p. 53.
65. *Ibid.*
66. *Harijan*, Feb. 20, 1937.
67. Chopra, *op.cit.*, pp. 68-69.
68. Contemporary Relevance of Gandhi, M.P. Sinha (1970), Int. p. XII.
69. *Ibid.*, Int. p. XIII.
70. Gandhi's view to life : C. Shukla (1968, p.79).
71. Mahatma Gandhi, The Last Phase, Pyarelal; Vol. II.
72. Selections from Gandhi, N.K. Bose (1957); p. 157.
73. *Ibid.,* p.154.
74. Social and Political thought of Gandhi : J. Bandyopadhyaya (1969), p. 86.
75. *Harijan*, Mar., 20, 1940.
76. *Ibid.*, July 21, 1940.
77. To the Students, M.K. Gandhi (1966), p. 292.
78. Socialism : M.K. Gandhi, *op.cit.*, p. 67.
79. *Ibid.*, p. 79.
80. *Ibid.*, p. 69.
81. Gandhi To-day : J.D. Sethi (1979) p. 15.
82. Gandhi's Discovery of Religion : N.A. Nikam (1963), p. 13.

83. Chopra, *op.cit.*, p. 111.
84. Bandyopadhyaya, *op.cit.,* p. 51.
85. Bose, *op.cit.,* p. 50.
86. Bandyopadhyaya, *op.cit.,* p. 90.
87. Sethi, *op.cit.*, pp. 36-37.
88. Changing India, Raja Rao and Iquabal Singh (1939), pp. 144-45.
89. Basic Education, M.K. Gandhi (1951)., p. 31.
90. Rao and Singh, *op.cit.*, p, 146
91. Basic Education, *op.cit.*, p. 11.
92. *Ibid.*, p. 10.
93. The Problem of Education, M.K. Gandhi; (1941), Int. p. V.
94. Basic Education, *op.cit.,* p. 53.
95. Ahluvalia, *op.cit.,* pp. 106-7.
96. *Ibid.*, p. 144.
97. Tendulkar, *op.cit.,* Vol.VII, p. 449.
98. Ahluwalia, *op.cit.,* p. 135.
99. India Needs Gandhi, Shriman Narayan (1976), pp. 89-90.
100. Tendulkar, *op.cit.*, Vol.VIII, p. 104.
101. *Ibid.*
102. Dimensions of Peace and Violence, Anima Bose (1987); p. 55.
103. The Bleeding Wound, M.K.Gandhi (1932), p. 10.
104. *Ibid.*, p. 17.
105. *Harijan*, Jan. 26, 1934.
106. Shukla, *op.cit.*, p. 142.
107. *Ibid.*, p. 143.
108. Ahluwalia, *op.cit.*, p. 137.
109. Sethi, *op.cit.,* p. 16.
110. *Harijan,* Jan. 27, 1940.
111. Tendulkar, *op.cit.,* Vol. VIII, p. 280.
112. *Ibid.*, p. 276.
113. *Ibid.*, p. 280.
114. *Ibid.*, Vol.VII. p. 451.
115. Constructive Programme, M.K. Gandhi (1948), p. 20.
116. M. P. Sinha, *op.cit.,* p. 59.
117. *Harijan,* Apr. 20, 1940.
118. A Manageable Future Article by Ajit Bhattacharjea, The Indian Express, Feb. 13, 1978.
119. *Ibid.*
120. M.P. Sinha, *op.cit.,* p. 75.
121. *Harijan,* 1938, p. 1.
122. Socialism, M.K. Gandhi, *op.cit.*, p. 279.
123. Tendulkar, *op.cit.,* Vol. VII, p. 215.
124. *Young India*, Nov. 15, 1928.

125. *Harijan,* Aug. 18, 1940.
126. *Young India*, March 18, 1926.
127. *Ibid.*
128. Socialism : Gandhi; *op.cit.,* p. 81.
129. *Ibid.*, p. 84.
130. *Ibid.*, p. 90.
131. Bandyopadhyaya, *op.cit.*, p. 154.
132. Selections, Bose; *op.cit.,* p. 47.
133. *Young India*, Dec. 8, 1921.
134. All Men are Brothers, M.K. Gandhi (1957), p. 127.
135. *Ibid.*, p. 126.
136. Bhattacharjea, *op.cit.,* The Indian Express, Feb.13, 1978.
137. *Young India,* 1927; p. 276.
138. *Harijan*, Dec. 30, 1939.
139. *Harijan,* Oct. 27, 1933.
140. Tendulkar, *op.cit.,* Vol. IV, p. 34.
141. *Young India,* Nov. 13, 1924.
142. *Ibid.*, June 22, 1935.
143. New Technology—A Gandhian Concept, Ram. K. Vepa (1975), p. 99.
144. Mahatma—the Revolutionary : Article J.B. Kriplani; The Indian Express; Oct. 2, 1977.
145. *Ibid.*
146. *Young India,* Nov. 13, 1924.
147. Pyarelal, *op. cit.*, Vol. II, p. 586.
148. Socialism : Gandhi, *op.cit.,* pp. 207-8.
149. *Ibid.* p. 53.
150. Studies in Gandhism, N.K. Bose (1959), p. 55.
151. Tendulkar, *op.cit.*, Vol.VII, p. 476.
152. *Harijan,* March 31, 1946.
153. Socialism : Gandhi, *op.cit.,* p. 274.
154. *Harijan,* Oct. 25, 1952.
155. *Ibid.*, Feb. 6, 1931.
156. Towards Trusteeship : (quoted) Bandna Sarkar (1974); p. XXIV.
157. Constructive Programme Gandhi, *op.cit.,* p. 20.
158. *Young India,* Dec. 5, 1929.
159. *Harijan,* March 31, 1946.
160. Socialism : Gandhi, *op. cit.,* pp.1-2.

CHAPTER 2

URGES TOWARDS EQUALITY

(a) The Background

An important landmark in the history of the British rule in India was the defeat of the Marhattas in the early nineteenth century which made the East India Company a paramount power. A new responsibility devolved on the British administrators, which began to take some interest in the welfare of the Indian people. Enamoured with a liberal political thought, some British administrator began to introduce measures for urgent social reforms, whose nature and character were mostly shaped by the liberal political philosophy that was influencing the United Kingdom at the time. The abolition of *sati*, introduction of Western educational system in 1835, withdrawal of the restrictions on the Press and steps for the codification of Indian laws were all a pointer to the fact that liberalism had entered the Indian scene. The sum total of all those social and administrative reform measures was the release of liberal and progressive forces, for the first time, in the country. The attitude of Englishmen to India during this period has been succinctly put by Eric Stokes thus :

> "The missionaries of English civilization in India stood openly for a policy of "assimilation". Britain was to stamp her image upon India. The physical and mental distance

> separating East and West was to be annihilated by the discoveries of science, by commercial intercourse, and by transplanting the genius of English laws and English education. It was the attitude of English liberalism in its clear, untroubled dawn, and its most representative figure in both England and India was Macaulay."[1]

However, not withstanding the liberal forces at work, an uninterrupted policy of expansionism and gain of territorial power for the Company was at work. A reorganization of the administrative machinery and reform of public service during the rule of Lord Cornwallis effected a policy of systematic exclusion of the natives from any share in the administrative decision-making. Several insurmountable legal difficulties were put in the way of the employment of the Indians in the higher ranks. When Lord Hastings arrived in India in October, 1813, he found himself confronted with many problems, notably the question of the control of the Press, which had assumed great importance. The Government of India was quite opposed to a free and unregulated Press as it believed that it might corrupt and disaffect the army and work for the overthrow of the Empire. It was held that "it must spread among the people the principle of liberty, and stimulate them to expel the strangers who rule over them and to establish a national government. A free Press and the dominion of strangers are things which are quite incompatible and cannot long exist together."[2]

The new regulations of 1823 envisaged submission of all papers and books to the Government for inspection, and inspite of a petition signed by Raja Ram Mohun Roy and Babu Dwarka Nath Tagore, it cam into force as law in August, 1823. Thus the challenges of the foreign rule and the discriminations, exploitations and iniquities meted out to the Indians were taken as an affront to their self-respect, and prominent individual thinkers of the time, like Mr. Roy, came out singing the glory of the ancient Indian heritage with a view to arousing national consciousness and foster a constructive social and cultural synthesis. The deep humanism and reformist zeal in Mr. Roy was highly appreciated by Jermey Bentham, who was his personal friend and admirer. Ram Mohun Roy was an ardent crusader for social legislation to ensure social equality and his enthusiasm for equalitarian ideas can be traced to his faith in theistic religion as the basis of a just and equitable social order. He had a penetrating insight into the subtle social distortions created by the working of the colonial economy, which had begun to create a gulf between the urban classes and rural peasants. He attributed these distortions to the impact of the rising social and economic disparities generated by a peculiar combination of trade and administration during the rule of the East India Company.

Ram Mohun Roy had served as a Revenue Collector from 1803 to 1813 in the East India Company. This had given him a first-hand knowledge of the increasing inequality of agrarian relations, characteristic of a colonial economy and the resulting extraction of maximum economic surplus from a low-level economy. He was deeply moved by the sad plight of agricultural labourers. His clear exposition of the extraction of maximum economic surplus and its complicated mechanism of transfer to the metropolitan country became the rock-bottom of the famous "Drain Theory" of Dadabhai Naoroji. He was greatly influenced by Lord Bentinck's progressive and liberal ideas, and his ideas reflect a clear synthesis of Western liberalism and humanitarian tenets of the Indian cultural heritage. He was also the foremost champion of the new Western learning, which was introduced by Lord Bentinck in 1835. "Ram Mohun Roy's vision of a true renaissance and a synthesis of the Indian and Western cultures appealed to the intelligentsia. It was no good discarding the essence of Hindu religion and culture along with the caste system and the superstitions and social tyranny inherent in an outmoded social system. The social reform movement thus became embedded in Protestant religious movement all over India, the object of which was to humanize society by means of a humanistic religious faith, to purge society of its inequalities and indignities to which the vast masses were subjected. There was no desire to give up the essence of true religion or the Indian way of life or the Indian worldview."[3] Roy stood for a harmonious adaptation of the Western concept of equality with the ancient heritage of humanitarianism and was against all forms of social inequality and other evils, rampant in the Indian society.

Ram Mohun Roy and the other thinkers of his time were

deeply influenced by their personal contact with the West and indoctrinated by the social and political philosophy of the French egalitarians which explains their moral fervour and their avowed faith in equality. Their profound faith in equality derived from national theistic faiths was the outcome of a conscious intellectual effort, which led them to revolt against the religious orthodoxy prevalent during the period. This revolt was led by Ram Mohun Roy, in the early nineteenth century, when he accepted the challenge of Christianity with its equalitarian ethics. The new religious response of Mr. Roy described as Neo-Vedantism provides unique illustration of the power of Indian religious synthesis in one of its highest forms of expression. His thoughts reveal serious attempts at reconciling Western social thoughts and culture with the Hindu cultural traditions. "His anxiety was to avoid a clash of two cultures and yet give Hinduism a modern orientation and a modern world outlook. The religious movement that he thus initiated condemned the inequalities of a caste-bound society. It emphasized the dignity of human beings their 'natural rights'—the right to life, liberty and property, the right of free speech and association—tempered by the principle to Loke-Sreys (People's Welfare). This explains much of Ram Mohun Roy's reformism in the wider sense. His new religion was designed to be an instrument of national renewal and 'modernization' in the best sense of the word—a universal religion designed to create a universal man and a rational and humane socio-economic order, the polar opposite man of rational and humane socio-economic order, the polar opposite of a closed society fissured by inequalities and narrow privileges."[4]

The spread of the liberal ideas in the social and educational field, which had given rise to a deep religious, social and political ferment leading to the birth of a national movement, received a serious jolt when the era of liberalism gave way to a new age of imperialism, a facet of the capitalist economy, as an aftermath of the Industrial Revolution. The Great Rising of 1857, acclaimed as the First War of Indian Independence and which coincided with the New Age, is another turning point in the history of British India. Though the Rising which began on January 23, 1857, at Dumdum, near Calcutta was quelled and peace was restored soon, it presaged the end of the Company Rule as on April 30, 1858 an Act for the Better Government of India was enacted by the British Parliament transferring the Government of India from the Company to the Crown. The transfer of power was announced by a Royal Proclamation issued on November 1, 1858. "The proclamation was couched in a beautiful and dignified language and breathed a spirit of magnanimity, clemency, friendliness and justice and assured to the Princes their rights, dignity, honour and privileges, and to the people freedom of religion and equal protection of law, admission to offices, irrespective of their race or creed, on the basis of education, ability and integrity."[5]

Thus began, the era of representative institutions in India. The introduction of a modern State apparatus and an efficient administrative machinery along with the spread of Western education and improvement in the means of transport and communication served a very useful purpose in the promotion of political unity among the people of far-off places, which became germane to the growth of national consciousness. The manifestation of the national consciousness was to be, inevitably, in the form of social and religious reform movements, in a predominantly agricultural country like India. Most importantly, the part played by Western education in the national awakening was no less significant. It had brought Indians in touch with the best European thoughts of the time. The works of Jermey Benthem, J.S. Mill, Edmund Burke, Thomas Carlyle, Auguste Comte, Herbert Spencer and others "instilled in them the life-giving conceptions of liberty, nationality and self-government and made them discontented with the political conditions as they existed in the country and the demand self-governing institutions and a better place in the services."[5(a)] It had opened for them a new vista for inter communion, a common programme of action, instilled by a common desire for the betterment of their worsening conditions.

The impact of economic, political and cultural transition that was rapidly being undertaken under the British regime during the nineteenth century had generated a social challenge. A restructuring of the social order with a view to developing a sense of national unity, consequent to the rise of a new national awakening, became the call of the time. The social thinkers and reformists were broadly influenced by two currents of thought : one led to the social regeneration on the basis of Western ideas and the other wanted the social reconstruction based on ancient traditions, which spelt national unity and a humanitarian outlook. The deteriorating economic condition of the country, stoked by the planned destruction of its traditional industries, in order to colonize the country and made it a market for finished British goods and a hunting ground for raw materials, had sharpened the problem of inequality and worsened the conditions of the downtrodden, aggravated by recurring famines. The introduction of Christianity as a proselytizing religion in India, which looked particularly attractive to the depressed and the downtrodden for its avowed principles of equality and equalitarian ethics, had thrown an open challenge to the religious sentiments of the Indians.

These events made a political impact and goaded the thinkers to strive for reform in the prevailing conditions. To meet this social and religious challenge, leaders of thought and zealots of reform began to make a fervent appeal to the religious instinct and sentiments of the people in order to instil in them a sense of national unity by recalling the humanitarian and equalitarian tenets of the eternal religion of India. The theme of equality that was oriented towards social action was thus, an active response to the challenges posed by the socio-economic onslaught of the British. The challenges of Christianity and the influence of Western civilization were sought to be countermanded by what may be called Protestant religious movements. The most important of the new religious movements, which were the primary expression of national consciousness, were the Brahmo Samaj, Arya Samaj, Theosophical Society, Ramakrishna Mission and others.

Brahmo Samaj was a regional movement in the East, which condemned ritualism, idol worship and the caste-system of the Hindus and acted as a potent instrument of meeting the challenge to the Hindu society of the proselytizing religions and containing the growing discontent and disillusionment with the iniquitous social order. The Arya Samaj movement started from Punjab as a rebellion against medievalism with all its superstitions, idol worship and the caste system. It believed that so long as the superstitions and the caste system enchained the Hindu society, it could not defend itself against alien religions. Its main features were Puritanism, militancy and emphasis on patriotism and equality. Both these movements were pioneers in the renovation of the Hindu faith, in active response to the alien challenges in the social and cultural field. The theosophical movement was neither a Protestant religious movement nor one that sought inspiration from a particular faith. It held the view that the ancient religious scriptures of India, which contained the universal spiritual wisdom, were the fountain-head of the eternal truths emanating from different religions which were only the different manifestations of it. It was Western in origin and its fountain of inspiration was the ancient wisdom. It was not necessarily against the caste system or idol worship and was wedded to Western education and culture, which it held to be essential for the flowering of the ancient wisdom. "Theosophy appealed to those Indians who did not like the Brahmo Samaj for cutting itself adrift from the Hindu society and religion and the Arya Samaj for isolating itself from Western education and learning. Theosophy thus became a rallying point for an isolated section of the educated elite who had absorbed the best elements of Western culture and Western learning. They were no doubt patriotic men with deep social sympathies and moral fervour. Some the them, like, Annie Besant, were social and political activists, but they relied more on education and the liberation of the human spirit as the means to our social and economic transformation."[6]

However, these movements were essentially a socio-religious movement to eradicate the Hindu social order of its age-old stupor, superstition and caste base. Even though they made a political impact in the sense that the focused attention on the inter-relation between politics and religion, they had, of course, not enunciated any political ideology. Religion was sought as an instrument of social regeneration and reform and the protagonists of these movements equally believed in the philosophic notion that basically it is the humanitarian aspect of religion which alone can ensure social justice and give rise to the formation of humane and equalitarian society, in response to the needs of the time. Lala Lajpat Rai, a prominent political leader and social reformer of this period, summed up the basic difference in the two approaches—one reformist and the other revivalist—of the various shades of the religious leaders and reformists of the nineteenth century, in the following words :

> "The former are bent on relying more upon reason and the experience of European society, while the latter are disposed to primarily look at their shastras, and the past history, and the traditions of their people and the ancient institutions of the land which were in vogue when the nation was at the zenith of its glory."[7]

While the reformist, like the Brahmo Samaj and others, played no part in the political field, the revivalist movement created self-confidence and national awakening in the country as also a deep religious ferment all over India. It generated forces that had an important bearing on the political aspirations and socio-economic reform in the form of eradication of all inequalities and indignities inflicted under the British rule and medieval religious orthodoxy. The last quarter of the nineteenth century was swept by a tidal wave of Hindu revival in the form of neovedantism, which found a powerful exponent in Swami Vivekananda. "He interpreted it as a faith dynamic enough to generate a social revolution through the removal of the archaic caste system and its attendant inequalities and indignities, a social ethics of fraternity and many-sided development of national strength and energy, with the ultimate aim of fulfilling India's mission as a nation."[8] Swami Vivekananda was of the view that freedom is meaningless unless it is based on the edifice of equality. According to him, equality "was the way to freedom : inequality the way to bondage. No man and no nation can attempt to gain physical freedom without physical equality, nor mental freedom without mental equality."[9]

Delving into the causes of human misery, he found the trio of ignorance, inequality and desire as its begetter. "Each follows the other in inevitable union. Inequality is the bane of human nature, the curse upon mankind, the root of all misery. This is a source of all bondage—physcial, mental and spiritual."[10]

Vivekananda was a radical reformer aiming at a revolutionary change in the Indian social order. He firmly believed that India's only hope was her masses, and the higher classes were unresponsive and inert. He derived the principle of human equality from the scriptures and the spiritual inspiration underlying his quest for social equality remained unmistakably pronounced. He conceived equality as an ideal for constant striving; everyone should persevere in it and should hope to attain it sometime, and gradually the ideas of universal brotherhood by pulling down the wall of inequality shall be achieved. He warned the higher classes of the predicament that lay in store for them. He said : "The peasant, the shoe-maker, the sweeper, and such other lower classes of India have much greater capacity for work and self-reliance than you. They have been silently working through long ages, and producing the entire wealth of the land, without a word of complaint. Very soon they will get above you in position. Gradually capital is drifting into their hands and they are not so much troubled with wants as your are. Modern education has changed your fashion, but new avenues of wealth lie yet undiscovered for want of the inventive genius. You have so long oppressed these forbearing masses : now is the time for their retribution. And you will become extinct in your vain search for employment, making it the be-all and end-all of your life."[11]

He was a staunch advocate of socialism and held the view that nation lives in the cottage. He pleaded for equality of opportunity to all the members of the society. His radical thought on redistribution of pains and pleasures could clearly brand him as precursor of Indian social revolution. He admitted :

"I am a socialist not because I think it is a perfect system, but half a leaf is better than no bread. The other systems have been tried and found wanting. Let this one be tried—if nothing else, for the novelty of the thing. A redistribution of pain and pleasure is better than always the same persons having pains and pleasure. Let every dog have his day in this miserable world."[12] He was a vehement critic of Hindu caste system and held the view that the caste system is opposed to the religion of the Vedanta. But he was not in favour of a class struggle, and had strongly advocated to shun the path of strife. He believed that the only way to bring about the levelling of castes was to appropriate for the downtrodden the education and inculcate in them, the culture which was the strength of the higher caste. He felt that the modern caste distinction was a barrier to India's progress, but hoped that it will crumble before the advance of ideas. He exhorted the higher classes that their well-being depended on helping the lower classes to get their legitimate rights. Addressing the higher classes in his colourful words, he presented the following vision of a new India :

> "Merge yourself in the void and disappear and let New India arise in your place—out of the peasant's cottage grasping the plough, out of the huts of fishermen and cobblers and sweepers. Let her spring from the grocer's shop, from beside the oven of the fritter-seller. Let her emerge from the factories and marts and markets, from the groves and hills and mountains."[13]

However, the socialism that he advocated had a humanitarian base and a spiritual inspiration as its beacon-light. He was not enamoured of a mere economic equality, rather, for a cultural and spiritual fraternity in which there would not be only economic equality and political freedom, but also a moral and intellectual kinship. He conceived of an India where diversity of ability and capacity would remain, but privileges to the few would vanish. His motto seems to have been "from caste to socialism through culture."[14]

It was during the viceregalship of Lord Bentinck in 1835 that English education was introduced in India. Raja Ram Mohun Roy had been an untiring crusader of English education in India. Before the advent of English education, only a few at the top of the social hierarchy, who could afford education in Europe, were reckoned to be the leaders of the society. The spread of English education in the country had led to the ascendancy of the middle class in the society, which had begun receiving it in large number even under the stresses and strains of their economic conditions. In areas where English education had spread considerably, committees were formed whose chief aim was to submit petitions to the government for the redressal of their grievances. In 1851 British Indian Association was formed at Calcutta and two years hence. Bombay Association and Madras Association also came into being. In 1875, the initiative of Surendra Nath Banerjee and Anand Mohun Bose bore fruit and an "Indian Association" was formed at Calcutta. The object of the latter association was not restricted to petitions, prayers and protests only, but was enlarged to include educating public opinion, with an ultimate aim of achievement of self-government within the British Empire by all legislative means. Thus, the establishment of the Indian Association was the first overt attempt of the intellectuals set to improve the socio-economic conditions in the yet unexplored field of politics, and it twinkled the twilight of nationalism in a purely secular sense. "There is no doubt that the Indian intellectuals had realized the need for nation-building, so that nationalism could release the integrating cultural and social forces operating hitherto in narrow, exclusive confines and getting perversely articulated through the difference of castes and communities. Nation-building in this sense was urgent, not merely for the sake of freedom from foreign domination, but for the more fundamental task of national or political solidarity on the foundation of social and economic equality."[15]

The establishment of the "Indian Association" is a landmark in the political history of India. Its founder, Surendra Nath Banerjee, began his political debut as the great champion of national unity, travelled for and wide and made earnest efforts to popularize the concept of the Indian Nation. He became the symbol of moderation in Indian politics, reposed his faith in the providential character of the British rule, and hoped for social and economic reform, equality and justice, under the British Raj. Addressing a meeting of the students Association at Calcutta in 1878, he said :

> "It is England's mission in the East to save, regenerate, emancipate from the chains of ignorance, error and superstition, 250 million of human beings, to heal the wounds that have been inflicted on them by the rapacity of their former rulers, to develop in them a self-reliant, mainly, energetic character, to spread through the land the great blessings of peace, contentment and happiness, but above

> all it is England's noble mission in the East to help towards the consummation of Indian unity, to reconcile the jarring conflicts of the diverse Indian nationalities, to bring them nearer together, to evoke in them a sentiment of brotherhood and make them feel that they have to make common cause for the redress of common grievances."[16]

The situation in the last two decades of the nineteenth century was explosive, particularly after the famine of 1877, and the discontent was mounting. It was in such a situation, keeping in view the well-being of the Indian people and the safety of the British Raj from mounting dissatisfaction, that Mr. Allan Octavian Hume laid the foundation of the Indian National Congress with the support of the contemporary liberal leaders, irrespective of caste, creed, colour, community, sect or religion, at Bombay in December, 1885. About 89 elites of the country attended the foundation ceremony. It is not within the ambit of the present work to trace the historical development of the Indian National Congress which emerged as the singular political party under whose banner the political movement for self-government, and later Poorna Swaraj, was launched. The formation of the Indian National Congress, thus, heralded the dawn of the freedom movement, though at the outset it was dominated by moderates who had drawn their inspiration largely from rationalism, liberalism and enlightenment of the West and wanted the reconstruction of the Indian society on modern and Western lines.

The concept of equality, though crystallized on the political forum only after the advent of Gandhi, finds clear expression in the views of some prominent moderates of the time. Before the Gandhi era, the moderates were chiefly concerned with the attainment of progressive self-government within the British Empire, and their thoughts mainly veered round the process of achieving political equality; they held the view, by and large, that the attainment of self-government would itself accelerate the pace of social reform. Nonetheless, we find that the main strands of ideas on the theme of equality, which entered into social thought in the early twentieth century, find a clear enunciation in the speeches and writings of some moderate intellectuals and religious reformists of the nineteenth century.

Bankim Chandra Chatterjee's *Samya*, a collection of his essays, was published in 1879. It is a fairly comprehensive essay, which mirrors the process of thinking of the intellectuals of his time. In his essay, he has illustrated the social structural character of the age-old problem of inequality, when he says :

> "To the extent to which workers become more miserable the disparity between them and other social classes increases, first, the disparity of wealth, resulting, secondly, in the disparity of rights and privileges, Because the workers were depressed in the social scale, the power of the brain workers increased correspondingly. The greater their power, the greater their oppressiveness."[17] This sociological analysis of inequality led him to conclude that the perditions of the lower orders affect the entire social order.

Bipin Chandra Pal was a notable exception among the extremist leaders who visualized the interlink of the social reform and the political movement and tried to make a synthesis. In 1889, he expressed his views :

> "Drinking or poverty or other evils of the same nature do not war against the fundamental principles of democracy, but caste and the train of monstrous customs connected with it do so in this country. Our religious customs proclaim not equality of men but their inequality. Our society recognizes not the virtues of merit, but the virtues of birth. The social evils under which we groan are based upon a synthesis of life in which inequality, caste, moral servitude and spiritual slavery form the flesh, the marrow and the bones."[18]
>
> He recognized the priority of social reform when he said : "The growth of ideas, which proceeds and accompanies the growth of reformed political institutions, embraces all the departments of nation's life."[19]

Another intellectual, Ramesh Chandra Dutt, a civil servant-turned historian, was deeply moved by the penury of the masses and the discriminating treatment meted out to Indians even in higher brackets. He pleaded for Swadeshi movement and village Panchayats. "Forecasting the impact of Swadeshi movement he stated that it would increase industries; relieve millions of weavers and artisans from semi-starvation; minimize the effects of famine and bring about a state of import substitution. Thus, he stood for Swadeshi as a means to Indian moral and material progress."[20] Dutt inquired into the nature and causes of Indian poverty and the impact of the British rule with a missionary zeal and came to this conclusion : "Verily, the moisture of India blesses and fertilizes other lands."[21]

Along with Dutt, there are three other economists of his time who deserve mention because they all shared in common a social philosophy. They were all votaries of nationalism with its slogans of Swaraj and Swadeshi.

Dadabhai Naoroji's views on Swaraj are best reflected in his presidential address to the Congress session held in Calcutta in 1906, when he was passed 81. The great political sage expressed his last will to the Nation, as follows :

"Freedom is the very breath of our life. We stand for liberty. The whole of the administration, in every department, must be in the hands of the people. If this had been in Indian hands, there should have been no poverty, wretchedness and dissatisfaction, of the Indian people. These are my last words. Be united, persevere, and achieve self-government, so that the people now perishing by poverty, famine and plague, and the scores of millions that are starving now on scanty subsistence, may be saved, and India may once more occupy her proud position of rare amongst the greatest and most civilized nations of the world."[22] Naoroji enunciated his drain theory which clearly throw light on the mechanism invented by the British for syphoning off the wealth from India and which demonstrates that the real cause of the poverty of the masses was this drain. He also stood for protection against free trade and mixed economy.

Paying glowing tributes, Dr. Schchidananda Sinha, wrote of him :

> "As one who had successfully carried his countrymen through the early stages of political advancement, as one

who amidst despair refused to be less hopeful of the future, as one who proclaimed from the Congress presidential chair, for the first time, the message of 'Swaraj', as one to whom patriotism and service of his people was the very breath of his existence till the last, in short as one whose seventy two years of public life was all consecrated at the altar of the mother country, Dadabhai Naoroji's public carrier was one long chapter to point a moral in the field of patriotism, and to adornatale in the domain of sound and healthy public activities in the cause of one's country."[23]

Mahadeva Govind Ranade, while accepting the premises of Naoroji, endeavoured to demonstrate the distinction between the colonial economy of India and the colonizing economy of Great Britain. He emphasized the growth of domestic economy and resort to industrialization.

Gopal Krishna Gokhale was a great advocate of British liberalism. The goal of the country was well defined by him in the course of a speech at Allahabad in 1907. "And here at the outset," said he, "let me say that I recognize no limits to my aspiration for our Motherland. I want our people to be in their own country what other people are in theirs. I want our men and women, without distinction of caste or creed, to have opportunities to grow to the full height of their stature, unhampered by cramping and unnatural restrictions. I want India to take her place among the great nations of the world, politically, industrially, in religion, in literature, in science and in arts. I want all this."[24] He stood for self-government, free and compulsory primary education and eradication of social inequality, including untouchability. Gokhale was the first Indian social thinker who conceived that without creating an organization of social missionaries, socio-economic reform could not be implemented.[25] He, therefore founded the Servants of India Society in 1905.

The Servants of India Society, during the short span of ten years, achieved an appreciable measure of success in the various fields of national activity. "It was thus as a faithful, unwearied, and unselfish servant of India that he lived, and as a servant of India that he died, and it was this aspect of his life which inspired in his countermen the deepest feelings of reverence and love, a reverence so deep and a love so strong that in their presence, the voice of even the most captious criticism stand hushed."[26]

However, the various moderates and extremists holding different political ideologies and having different action plans perched on the Congress forum, which, in its early phase, was an assembly of eminent intellectuals with discordant views on the socio-economic front and without any mass-based politics.

The Indian National Congrees was dominated by the moderates like Surendra Nath Banerjee, Madan Mohan Malviya, Dadabhai Naoroji, Gopal Krishna Gokhale and others until 1905. Their economic and political demands were based on the interest of the new social classes of elites and their approach was more pragmatic than ideological. "In the political sphere, the interest of the new social classes demanded the Indianization of the service, expansion of the Legislative Council, and laying of the foundation for self-government in India. Such political and administrative reforms would have given great opportunities to the educated classes to express themselves in the administrative and legislative fields. All these demands were based on the liberal political concepts of the West. But the economic aspirations of the new classes were primarily the industrialization of the country and the freeing of India from the economic domination of Great Britain. The leaders of the new social classes believed that for the fulfillment of these economic aspirations, the government should give protection to indigenous industries and assist in various ways in the economic development of the country. Although some of them had a vague sense of social justice and the concept of the equitable distribution of income among all the sections of the people, they were not in any sense socialists."[27] However, the political activities of the moderates strengthened political democracy and the rule of law in India and made the economic problems of the country conspicuous.

At its Lucknow session in 1899, the Indian National Congress adopted its first Constitution proclaiming its object : to promote by constitutional means the interests and well-being of the people of the Indian Empire. Mahadeva Govind Ranade, a prominent moderate, summed up the creed of the Congress as follows :

> "Liberalism and moderation will be the watchwords of the Association. The spirit of liberalism implies freedom from race and creed prejudices and steady devotion to all that seeks to do justice between man and man, giving to the rulers their loyalty due to the law that they are bound to administer, but secure at the same time to the people the equality which is their right under the law. Moderation implies the conditions of never vainly aspiring after the impossible or after the remote ideals, but striving each day to take the next step in the order of the national growth that lies nearest to our hands in a spirit of compromise and friendship."[28]

The division of Bengal, during the period of Lord Curzon, in 1905, was a turning point in the history of the Indian National Congress. It sparked a wave of protest throughout the country and gave rise to political radicalism of the extremist leaders. The next phase of the Indian National Movement was dominated by extremist leaders who, like the religious revivalists, apparently stood for the rejection of the Western ideas, an their notion of socio-economic changes was based on the glorious heritage of ancient India. Their new political spirit was in unison with the traditions and sentiments of the past, and commensurate with their belief that political emancipation should precede social reforms. The partition of Bengal gave them a platform for mass contact and their policies were designed to serve as a effective instrument of political regeneration and social reconstruction. They forced a split in the Congress at Surat in 1907 and impelled the Congress to make suitable amends in its object. The goal of the political aspirations of the Indian National Congress, for the first time, became the attainment by India of self-government similar to that enjoyed by the self-governing Dominions of the British Empire and participation by her in the rights and respons-ibilities of the Empire on equal terms with those Dominions. These objects were sought to be achieved by "constitutional means by bringing about a steady reform of the existing system of administration and by promoting national unity, fostering public spirit, and developing and organizing the intellectual, moral economic and industrial resources of the country."[29]

The extremist also enunciated the policy of Swadeshi and boycott of foreign goods and added into their political armoury the novel, but powerful, weapon of passive resistance. The prominent exponents of such political redicalism were Bal Gangadhar Tilak, Lala Lajpat Rai, Bipin Chandra Pal and Aurobindo Ghose. Of all the extremists of the time, Lokmanya Tilak deserves special mention because of his mass approach to buttress political agitation and spiritual orientation to the nationalist impulse. "In those early days he envisaged a Constituent Assembly to frame a Constitution for the country; universal adult franchise; division of Indian Provinces on the basis of language; introduction of nation-wide prohibition; protection of labour through a guaranteed minimum wage; and development of public sector for key industries. Here indeed was gigantic intellect unafraid of looking decades ahead and discerning the imperatives of freedom."[30] His method of agitation bid fare-well to the era of arm-chair politics, and he declared, for the first time, the political mantra "Home-Rule is my birth right and I will have it." Gandhi paid an eloquent tribute to him : "No man of our times had the hold on the masses that Tilak had. No man preached the gospel of Swaraj with the consistencey and insistence of Lokmanya."[31]

The concept of socio-economic equality covered the planks of the Indian National Congress only when its policy became mass-oriented, whose rock-bottom was laid down by Tilak—Lokmanya, as popularly called in a spontaneous surge of affection and reverence. The Congress continued to be virtually an intellectual gymnasium of people belonging to the upper strata of the society until Gandhi became a potent force in the party; and the Congress, which was to some extent circumscribed in its range of interests and activities, now under the leadership of Gandhi sought to give this movement a mass basis and widened its base by opening its gates to the masses whose will became the sanction behind the whole organization. The Nagpur session of the Congress in 1920 became landmark in the history of freedom movement when the Congress, for the first time, in its new Constitution proclaimed as its objective "attainment of Swarajya by the people of India by all legitimate and peaceful means."[31a] Thus "Swaraj", a word coined by Lokmanya Tilak, now became the objective of the freedom movement launched by the Indian National Congress.

(b) The Gandhian Era

Gandhi's emergence on the political scene marks another epoch in the history of the Indian National Movement. Beginning with his leadership of a nation-wide agitation against the Rowlatt Act in 1919, he dominated the Indian political scene, remaining as the Pole Star to guide the nation during crises, shaping its present and planning for the future. "His political ideas do not yield to any traditional method of analysis. In one sense they were a synthesis of the earlier trends of thought, which had influenced the Hindus and the Muslims towards the close of the nineteenth century and the beginning of the twentieth; but in another sense they were unique because he gave a new philosophic interpretation to them and also because he placed before the country a new economic and political programme."[32]

Gandhi was inspired by Gokhale to endow the principle, which became cardinal to his faith, that morality must govern not only private life but public activity as well.

He was the greatest of the great thinkers of modern India who have drawn inspiration largely from the intellectual, cultural and religious traditions of India and tried to co-relate them with the social and political realities of the time. He gave a new dimension to the freedom struggle by drawing the common people into political action in large numbers. The upsurge of the masses was the resultant of the non-cooperation movement launched by Gandhi and the mass participation came into Indian politics as a new phenomenon in the task of national political education. His austerity and simplicity and his ideal of plain living and high thinking brought him closer to the masses and annihilated the distance between him and the suffering humanity of India. He became the standard-bearer of the down trodden identifying himself with the "least, lowliest and the lost." Political and moral liberation of the people, forming a fifth of the entire human race, was his supreme goal. It was really this concern for the ordinary mass that inspired his political activities. Yet he differed from preceding prophets in that he developed the weapon of non-violence into a technique for mass mobilization and its practical application for achieving concrete ends in political and socio-economic fields.

Gandhi was born at a time when the magnificence of the British Empire and the novelty of the Western civilization had dazzled the elites of India. The industrial revolution had taken place and the fruits of scientific investigations were creating a revolutionary change in outlook and thought. Unprecedented developments in technology were taking place on the material plane, and on the economic plane capitalism and rationalism were holding ground. Liberal democracy had manifested itself on the political plane and on the social plane buoyancy and faith in reason were driving out the various superstitions accompanying the social behaviour. Thus, it was an era of endless progress, opening new vistas on the horizon of science and democracy. European civilization had held its sway over the Indian intellectuals. The masses, however, did not feel that way. They had an innate sense of value of their own national culture and attempts to create an Anglo-Indian culture were frawned at by them, though passively. The intellectuals and the distinguished Indians who even before Gandhi championed the causes of the downtrodden, could not win over the masses and their activities centered round the middle and upper classes mainly. It was Gandhi's singular genius that foresaw this division of interest between the classes and the masses. He like Vivekananda held the truth that India lives in cottages not in towns. As a astute politician, he transmuted the inertia and inaction of the masses into a source of strength by evolving a spirit of Swadeshi in thought and deed and out of this Swadeshi he invented weapons of unprecedented and unforeseen power to drive out the various malaises afflicting the society and the nation. But it was not an easy task. The first step towards its achievement was to identify oneself with the masses. So, he identified himself with the masses in the mode of conduct and life, thought and action, clothing and food. He adopted their language, ate their food, wore their clothes and slept in their hovels. It proved the genius of the man, as Gandhi, and no one else, had felt the pulse of India, and his life pulsated with the lives of the masses. He shared their pleasures and pains personally and not only commiserated with them put worked out the weapons of proven temper, not unknown to them, of truth and non-violence, and put those weapons into use by a whole nation dazed into inertia and degradation. This complete identification with the masses was the real secret of his hold over the Indian people.

Gandhi gave a new dimension to politics—the dimension of mass approach. The concept of equality became the drill-sergeant of the masses drawn up to achieve the cherished goal of "Swarajya". The Indian National Movement was distinctly marked by the two specific contributions of the Mahatma—mass basis of politics and non-violent non-cooperation. The concept of equality came to the fore of the national movement only after the mass-oriented politics of Gandhi who inhered to his view that equality was a necessary adjunct to "Swarajya". Equality thus became the *summum bonum*, which was bound to emerge out of "Swarajya" of the Gandhian conception.

Gandhi, undismayed by the initial setbacks in his experiments in passive resistance and non-cooperation movement as a protest against the Rowlatt Act, started his campaign for social reform and removal of untouchability, which as the Report of the Director. C.B.I indicates, "Produced the utmost bitterness between the upper castes, jealous of their age-long prerogatives, and the lower, who began to proclaim their right to equal treatment in all social matters."[33] In a special session of the Indian National Congress at Bombay in 1918, it was, for the first time, resolved that the statute to be passed by Parliament should include Declaration of the rights of the people of India as British citizens and that all Indian subjects of His Majesty should be equal before the law. Thus the concept of equality became the kernel of political philosophy behind the freedom movement under the leadership of Gandhi.

His views on equality have already been traced in the previous chapter, and before outlining the views of other prominent persons of his time, it would be appropriate to trace, briefly, the part played by the political organization which fought for "Swarajya" under his unrivalled leadership, in enunciating and giving a precise shape to the concept of equality and devising a concerted action plan to drive away inequality. The cherished goal of equality is reflected not only in the objectives of the Indian National Congress, but it also finds its proper place in the First Draft of Fundamental Rights contained in the Report of the Motilal Nehru Committee appointed by the All Parties Conference held in Bombay on 19 May, 1928, as a sequel to the Madras Congress Resolution of the previous year which, *inter alia*, had resolved that "having regard to the general desire of all political parties in the country to unite together in settling a Swaraj Constitution authorizes the Working Committee to draft Swaraj Constitution for India on the basis of the a Declaration of Rights."[34] Thus, it was, for the first time, proposed that the basis of a constitution of free India must be a Declaration of Fundamental Rights. The various articles of the Constitution of "Irish Free State influenced the members of the committee" because the conditions obtaining in Ireland before the treaty were the nearest approach to those in India. The recommendation on Fundamental Rights contained in the said Report is given in Appendix A. A perusal of the whole gamut of rights aspired by men who had dedicated themselves to free the motherland from the foreign yoke leads us to visualize the picture of an egalitarian society that they cherished, and compare them with the progress and achievements made subsequently.

Before the revival of the Civil Disobedience Movement in 1932, an event of profound and far-reaching importance took place. The Congress session in March, 1931, met at Karachi and adopted a Resolution on Fundamental Rights and Economic Programme. It was reviewed by the All India Congress Committee at its meeting held in Bombay in August 1931. The resolution of the Congress ran as follows :

"The Congress is of the opinion that to enable the masses to appreciate what "Swaraj", as conceived by the Congress, will mean to them, it is desirable to state the position of the Congress in a manner easily understood by them. In order to end the exploitation of the masses, political freedom must include real economic freedom of the starving millions. The Congress, therefore, declares that any constitution which may be agreed to on its behalf should provide, or enable the Swaraj Government to provide,"[35] Fundamental Rights to the people. The Karachi and Bombay Congress Resolutions are contained in Appendix B.

The Lucknow congress in 1936 stressed upon the agrarian

reform to drive out unemployment, inequality and penury, and expressed its opinion that "The most important and urgent problem of the country is the appalling poverty, unemployment and indebtedness of the peasantry, fundamentally due to antiquated and repressive land tenure and revenue systems, and intensified in recent years by the great slump in the prices of agricultural produce."[36]

On the eve of election of provincial legislatures, the All India Congress Committee (AICC) met at Bombay on August 22, 1936, and adopted its election manifesto, which, *inter alia*, declared : "The poverty stricken masses are today in the grip of an even more abject poverty and destitution, and this growing disease urgently and insistently demands a radical remedy. Poverty and unemployment have long been the lot of our peasantry and industrial workers; today they cover and crush other classes also—the artisan, the trader, the small merchant, the middle-class intelligentsia. For the vast millions of our countrymen the problem of achieving national independence has become an urgent one, for only independence can give us the power to solve our economic and social problems and end the exploitation of our masses."[37]

(c) Nehru and Socialism

The AICC meeting, under the presidentship of Jawaharlal Nehru, which met in Delhi in March, 1937, adopted the following resolution on Fundamental Rights :

(i) Every citizen of India has right of free expression of opinion, the right of free association and combination, and the right to assemble peacefully and without arms, for a purpose not opposed to law or morality.

(ii) Every citizen shall enjoy freedom of conscience and the right freely to profess and practise his religion, subject to public order and morality.

(iii) The culture, language and script of the minorities and of the different linguistic areas shall be protected.

(iv) All citizens are equal before law, irrespective of religion, caste, creed or sex.

(v) No disability attaches to any citizen by reason of his

or her religion, caste, creed or sex, in regard to public employment, office of power or honour, and in the exercise of any trade or calling.

(vi) All citizens have equal rights and duties in regard to wells, tanks, roads, schools and places of public resort, maintained out of state or local funds, or dedicated by private persons for the use of the general public.

(vii) The State shall observe neutrality in regard to all religions.

(viii) The franchise shall be on the basis of universal adult suffrage.

(ix) Every citizen is free to move throughout India and to stay and settle in any part thereof, to acquire property and to follow any trade or calling, and to be treated equally with regard to legal prosecution or protection an all parts of India."[38]

This resolution is an improvement on the Nehru Committee Report in the sense that non-interference in matters of conscience, religion or culture and non-intervention in the personal law of minorities have been made manifest. Secondly, the ideas of a cooperative commonwealth seem to have been abandoned. So far as the rights pertaining to equality are concerned, we note the growing concern about the equality of womenfolk and prohibition of discrimination on the ground of sex in the 1937 resolution, while the other rights of equality resemble almost equally.

The Congress High Command issued an election manifesto in October, 1945. The relevant highlights of the manifesto were :

(1) The Congress stands for equal rights and opportunities for every citizen of India.

(2) It stands for the unity of all communities and religious groups and for tolerance and goodwill between them.

(3) It stands for full opportunities for the people, as a whole, to grow and to develop according to their own wishes and genius.

(4) It stands for freedom of each group and territorial area to develop its own life and culture within the larger framework.

(5) It stands for the regrouping of the provinces on linguistic and cultural basis.

(6) It stands for rights of all those suffering from social tyranny and injustice, and for the removal for them of all the barriers to equality.

(7) The Congress envisages a true democratic State with the fundamental rights and liberties of all its citizens, guaranteed in its constitution.

(8) The Congress stands for a federal constitution having a great deal of autonomy for its constituent units.

(9) The Congress will tackle the most urgent and vital problem of India, namely, the removal of the curse of poverty and the raising of the standard of life of the masses.

(10) The Congress stands for the modernization of industry and agriculture and social control of all sources of wealth, methods of production and of distribution, so that India may grow into a cooperative commonwealth."[39]

In our quest to discern the urges towards equality and equalitarianism during the course of the national movement for freedom, and the ideas, forces and factors enveloping those urges, we have to bear in mind the difference of approach, notwithstanding the identity of thoughts, between stalwarts—Mahatma Gandhi and Jawahar Lal Nehru—on the fundamental question of its attainment, and the break with the moderates under the leadership of Nehru on the question of dominion status was the turning point in the history of the national movement surging towards the cherished goal of Swaraj and equality. In the Lahore session of the Congress in 1929, under the presidentship of Nehru, "Swaraj" as the objective of the Congress was enunciated to mean "Puran Swarajya"—complete independence, meaning severance of all connection with the British Empire. Nehru said : "Many people still think that Dominion Status is something next door to independence. As a matter of fact they are two different types entirely, two roads going in opposite directions. It is not a question of fourteen annas and sixteen annas but of different species of coins which are not interchangeable".[40] He held the view that unless complete independence is granted, we cannot solve economic problems and have freedom to decide about our own social structure and relieve the masses of their crushing burdens of inequity, ignorance and disease.

Nehru firmly believed that the whole basis and urge of the national movement came from a desire to come out of the economic morass and to end the exploitation of the masses. Tracing out the goal of the freedom movement he discerned the ending of all exploitations of the people as the immediate goal. He conceived equality as the *summon bonum* of the freedom movement. Complete independence was required because equality cannot be had without it. He defined the immediate goal as : "Politically, it must mean independence and the severance of the British connection, which means imperialist dominion; economically and socially it must mean the ending of all special class privileges and vested interests."[41] He was confident that India was treading its way to "the great human goal of social and economic equality, to the ending of all exploitation of nation by nation and class by class, to national freedom within the framework of an international cooperative socialist world federation."[42]

After his deep study of Western thoughts and conditions he was confident that capitalism was no remedy to India's miseries. He held the view that the European civilization of the nineteenth century was based on the French ideology with its slogan of liberty, equality and fraternity but with the growth of industrial capitalism it became outmoded. Political liberty carried no meaning in the face of growing economic inequality. Economic equality can be had only by a control of the means of production and a rigorous restriction on private property. Capitalism as a remedy, in the nature of things, is worse than the disease, it cannot provide such equality. He believed that the real independence must mean divesting of the vested interests and he became the leader of the socialist group within the Congress fold. Nehru wrote in 1936 :

> "As the Congress became more radical and dependent on mass support, the Indian vested interests that were represented in it, became frightened and some of them dropped out. It was out of these leavings that the small

and ineffective Moderate or Liberal group was formed. Association with the masses forced economic issues to the front in the Congress and a socialist ideology began to develop. A number of vaguely socialist resolutions were passed from time to time and in 1931 the Congress took a more definite step in this direction by adopting an economic programme at Karachi."

"The direct action struggle of the Congress during the last four years and the slump and rapid march of economic events in the world during this period have resulted in influencing the Congress powerfully in a socialist direction, and the struggle for independence has come more and more to mean a radical change in the social order to bring relief to the suffering masses."[43] Nehru, thus, optimized the struggle for a radical change of the social structure and cessation of all exploitation of the people of India. At the Lucknow congress in 1936 in his presidential address, he clearly emphasized his view that freedom cannot be complete without socialism. He said :

"I have no desire to force the issue in the Congress and thereby create difficulties in the way of Independence. I imagine that every country will fashion it (socialism) after its own way and fit it with its national genius."[44]

Nehru became the messiah of the youth during the "Quit India" movement of 1942, chiefly due to his socialistic leanings and the innate sense of social justice, which had made him endearing to the masses during all these years. Social justice to Nehru meant the removal of economic injustice meted out to individuals in a capitalist society. As Nehru has written in his autobiography, the greatest sufferer was "the agricultural proletariat, the large number of landless labourers in rural areas who were drawn to the national movement of liberation because of the growing pauperization of both the petty landholders and the tenants."[45] He, therefore, held that only a solution to the basic problem of land can avoid inevitability of class conflict.

Nehru had developed a deep faith in the ultimate success of socialism in the whole world. He believed that the socialism was the only way out to drive out human miseries and put an end to degradation and deprivation. He, therefore, concluded : "Inevitably we are led to the only possible solution—the establishment of a socialist order, first within national boundaries and eventually in the world as a whole, with controlled production and distribution of wealth for public good."[46] Again on another occasion, he wrote to his daughter, Indira Priyadarshini, in 1933 : "Socialism, I have told you, is of many kinds. There is general agreement, however, that it aims at the control by the State of the means of production, that is, land and mines and factories and the like, and the means of distribution, like railways, etc., and also banks and similar institutions. The idea is that individuals should not be allowed to exploit any of these methods or institutions, or the labour of others, to their own personal advantage."[47]

Nehru firmly held the view that the very basis and foundation of the capitalist system, with its inherent acquisition of wealth and property, was violence. Though violence, he felt, was common in both capitalism and socialism, its nature was different in each case; while it was inherent in the former, in the latter it was a transitional phase in the process of the formation of a new social order based on equality, peace, progress and freedom. He had realized that "a measure of political liberty meant little indeed when the fear of starvation was always compelling the vast majority of people everywhere to submit to the will of the few to the greater glory and advantage of the latter."[48] These convictions in him led him to a firm belief in the ultimate success of socialism. He declared in 1936 :

> "I am convinced that only key to the solution of the world's problems and of India's problems lies in socialism, and when I use this word I do so not in a vague humanitarian way but in the scientific, economic sense. Socialism is, however, something even more than an economic doctrine : it is a philosophy of life and as such also it appeals to me."[49] Thus, Nehru was fully convinced that changes in the political, economic and social structure of a nation aimed at ending of all exploitations and vested interests in land and industry can be possible only through socialism. With the march of time, as he progressed with his aim of nation building, the dimension of the socialistic pattern

widened in his thoughts. He began to look upon it "as a growing, dynamic conception, as something which is not rigid, as something which must fit in with the changing conditions of human life and activity in every country."[50]

It was Gandhi who gave the Congress a socialist orientation and he had declared Nehru as his political heir. Nehru was the architect of modern India and had a pivotal role in the Constitution—making with its built in mechanism for the realization of equality in the free India. He had learnt the primary lessons of socialism at the feet of the Mahatma, but held no orthodox attitude towards the notion of equivalence of the ends and means, with regard to the goal of equality, and his socialist ideas, unlike Gandhi's were permeated with the glowing achievements of communism in the Soviet Union. Before we proceed to probe into the hopes and aspirations of the Founding Fathers of the Constitution and examine the constitutional device to untwine the treasure of equality, it would be relevant to scan the differences which cropped up between the two leaders as to the means for the achievement of their common goal. Both agreed that poverty, unemployment, deprivation and other kindred ills that have afflicted the nation must be banished, and with it must go the capitalistic order. Gandhi's vision of self-sufficient village republic with a decentralization of industries and devolution of power was not fully shared by his heir apparent, Jawaher Lal Nehru, the first Prime Minister of free India. To question whether his economic policies differed with Nehru, Gandhi replied : "Yes, we seem to differ in our ideas of village uplift and reconstruction. The difference is of emphasis. He does not mind the village uplift movement. He believes in industrialization; I have grave doubts about its usefulness in India. He believes in the ultimate inevitability of class conflict, though, he would avoid it, if he could."[51] Gandhi held the view that socialization of important industries is no remedy for the evils of industrialism. Referring to his differences with the socialist Nehru, Gandhi said : "Nehru wants industrialization, because he thinks that if it is socialized, it would be free from the evils of capitalism. My own view is that the evils are inherent in industrialism, and no amount of socialization can eradicate them."[52]

Gandhi unswervingly held that non-violence was the only effective way to true socialism, Nehru had been equivocal and evasive on this point and did not rule out violence and coercion; rather, as we have seen, Nehru was convinced of the inevitable transitional phase of violence in communism, after his study of socialism in the Soviet Union, but held that it was in order to herald an age of peace, prosperity and cooperation. Gandhi, on the other hand firmly ruled out violence, and was not enamoured of the socialist revolution in the Soviet Union because it was based on violence; neither was he inquisitive about the conditions obtaining under the system which was grounded in violence and, therefore, repelled him. He was an uncompromising opponent of violent methods, even to serve the noblest of causes. Gandhi had himself put this difference, compendiously, in the following words : "He perhaps puts an emphasis on the result, whereas I put on the means. Perhaps, according to him, I am putting an over-emphasis on non-violence, whereas he, though he believes in non-violence, would want to have socialism by other means, if it was impossible to have it by non-violence. Of course, my emphasis on non-violence becomes one of principle. Even if I was assured that we could have independence by means of violence, I should refuse to have it. It won't be real independence."[53]

In 1947, talking to a journalist, Gandhi had again described his difference with Nehru : "Jawahar Lal Nehru wants Englishmen to go but Angreziat (English ways and culture) to stay. I want Angreziat to go Englishmen to stay as friends."[54] Indeed, "Gandhi wanted to rid India of the Western culture which had been imposed on the country and had stifled the order and more natural Indian cultural and social traditions. Nehru, although the idol of the masses, was aloof from them mentally. He was an Englishman in Indian skin."[55]

Nehru became the first Prime Minister of free India and the architect of India's destiny. His role in the constitution-making speaks eloquently of his deep-seated conviction towards socialism and his bubbling spirit for devising a machinery to realize the cherished goal of equality, of course, according to his own light. The Nehruvian spirit is reflected in the Objective

Resolution regarding aims and objects, moved in the Constituent Assembly on 13 December, 1946. Before the Assembly set to the task, Dr. Radhakrishnan, in his sonorous note, while felicitating Dr. Rajendra Prasad on being elected its Chairman, expressed his profound hope that the ideals, which guided and sustained us during the freedom struggle, shall continue to guide our efforts in framing the constitution of free India. Dr. Rajendra Prasad, welcoming the Members, hoped that in spite of limitations, the Assembly shall successfully "place before the world a model of a constitution that will satisfy all our people, all groups, all communities, all religions inhabiting this vast land, and which will ensure to every one freedom of action, freedom of thought, freedom of belief and freedom of worship, which will guarantee to everyone opportunities for rising to his highest, and which guarantee to everyone freedom in all respects". And concluding he said "above all, what we need is freedom and as someone has said 'nothing is more valuable than the freedom to befree."[56] The objective Resolution was moved by Pandit Nehru, which contained fundamentals which were commonly held and accepted by the people, and showed whither India shall go. As Nehru explained : "The Resolution does not go into details. It only seeks to show how we shall lead India to gain the objectives laid down in it. You will take into consideration its words and I hope you will accept them; but the main thing is the spirit behind it. Laws are made of words but this Resolution is something higher than the law. It is not a law; but it is something that breathes life into human minds."[57]

During the various stages of consideration of the Resolution, Nehru made forcefully clear his conception of democracy. When some members objected to the exclusion of the word 'democracy' and 'socialism' in the Resolution, Nehru retorted :

> "Obviously we are aiming at democracy and nothing less than democracy. In any event, whatever system of government we may establish here must fit in with the temper of our people and be acceptable to them. Although we have not used the word democratic, we have done something much more than using the word. We have given the content of democracy in this Resolution and not only the

content of democracy but the content, if I may say so, of the economic democracy in this Resolution."[58]

When V. D. Tripathi expressed apprehension that the high-sounding phraseology of the Resolution might be interpreted in their own way by the persons in power and, therefore, advised a categorical provision in the Constitution itself that it shall not be established on a capitalistic basis and urged upon the addition of the word "socialism", in the Resolution, Nehru said :

> "Well, I stand for socialism and, I hope, India will stand for socialism and that India will go towards the constitution of a Socialist State and I do believe that the world will have to go that way. What form of socialism again is another matter for your consideration. But the main thing is that such a Resolution, if, in accordance with my own desire, I had put in that we wanted a socialist State, we would have put in something which might be agreeable to many and might not be agreable to some and we wanted this Resolution not to be controversial in regard to such matters. Therefore, we have laid down not theoretical words and formulas, but rather the content of the thing we desire."[59]

Purushottam Das Tandon, while seconding the objective Resolution moved by Nehru, stressed that the equality was the underlying theme of the Resolution, and said :

> "We have to reach the point where we may place the ideal of equality not only before our own country but before the world at large. We aim at giving equality to each and every inhabitant of our mother land "[60]

While concluding the debate, Nehru hoped that "While India will no doubt play a great part in all the material spheres, she will always lay stress on that spirit of humanity instilled by the Father of the Nation."[61] The objective Resolution became the corner-stone of the Constitution, which was not an end in itself but, as Nehru hoped, would be only the basis for further work. And the greatest and most important work, as Nehru underlined, was to solve the problem of the poor and the starving. He warned : "If India goes down all will go down : if India thrives all will thrive and if India lives all will live including the parties, communities and groups."[62]

(d) Founding Fathers

In the debates that followed, the Founding Fathers expressed their deep-seated emotions and long-cherished ambitions, which reflect their hopes and aspiration. D.N. Samanta emphasized that as the Constituent Assembly was the outcome of untold sufferings and unfathomable sacrifices of the people, the Constitution should be so framed as to promote the needs and interests of the masses and benefit the country as a whole.

Speaking on the provisions pertaining to the Fundamental Rights, Prof. N.G. Ranga hoped that in order to see that these are actually enforced, the masses will be enabled to demand from the State necessary financial assistance to seek the protection of their rights as is provided in criminal cases, while V.R. Muniswamy Pillai felt proud of the fact that the Fundamental Rights should cause no discrimination to any man who is considered to be lower in the rank and file of the nation and guarantee equal opportunity to employment to all.

Evaluating the provisions made as Directive Principles of Governance, Dr. P.S. Deshmukh expressed his total dissatisfaction, and lamented that it could have been more useful had it provided for the State ownership of all mineral resources and industries and that no person shall be let to be exploited by another. Sardar Hukum Singh stated that though a perusal of the principles engrafted in Part IV leads one to a make-belief that ours is going to be a Socialist State, there was nothing in the rest of the Constitution to support this pious platitude. However, Mrs. Purnima Banerjee opined that Articles 38 and 39 provided the means to change the social infrastructure and these two articles were the corner-stone of the Constitution, and B.K. Das expressed that the Directive Principles aimed at the paramount task of nation-building. M. Ananthasayanam Ayangar viewed that the force of public opinion was the real sanction behind the Directive Principles; that it was open to the electorate not to vote the very same person who remained insensitive to public opinion. Prof. S.L. Saxena hoped its inclusion in the Constitution itself was sufficient to show that every legislature will be bound to respect these principles; any act which offended the Directive Principles shall be ultra vires; it would be open to the President of every Assembly to declare so; and hoped that the principles enunciated therein, as the ideal to be striven for in free India, will be given effect to and incorporated in the laws of the country at no distant date Dr. B.R. Ambedkar was quite convinced of it utility and refuted the allegation that they had no binding force in law. Justifying its inclusion in the Constitution, he said : "The Draft Constitution as framed only provides a machinery for the government of the country. It is not a contrivance to install any particular party in power as has been done in some countries. Who should be in power is left to be determined by the people as it must be, if the system is to satisfy the tests of democracy. But whoever captures power will not be free to do whatever he likes with it. In the exercise of it, he will have to respect these instruments of instructions, which are called Directive Principles. He cannot ignore them. He may not have to answer for their breach in court of law. But he will certainly have to answer for them before the electorate at election time".[63]

In the Constituent Assembly there was a wide divergence of opinion as to whether the Constitution was drafted to serve as a vehicle to bring to fruition the Gandhian ends. Some members complained that the Constitution had made no provision for the decentralization of political power and industries, for the self-contained village republic, which was the rock bottom of the Gandhian scheme of a free India. H.V. Kamath said that the goal that Mahatma Gandhi had in view had not been achieved by a mere political freedom and it was the bounden duty of the Assembly to lead India to that goal. He lamented that the immutable principles of Justice, Liberty, Equality and Fraternity in the Preamble have been watered down to a considerable extent in the contents of the Constitution; and hoped that a time would come when we will come out of the transition period and India would become stabilized and strong, that Gandhi's plan of decentralized democracy or Panchayat Raj, with village units self-sufficient in food, clothing and shelter and interdependent as regards other matters, will be given a fair trial. Expressing faith in the future and an urge to proceed towards the goal, he said :

> "A Constitution will live or die in so far as it cares for or hinders the happiness, the life and liberty of the ordinary man, the common man. It is in his name that we have framed this Constitution; it is in his name that we have struggled for freedom, achieved it and assembled here. Let us work this Constitution in his name, let us go ahead in his name under the blessings of the Almighty and under His guidance, and with the full cooperation of the people of India. Let us strive to reach the goal envisaged by Mahatma Gandhi, and all our prophets, sages and seers, the goal I would simply call Panchayat Raj. We who are assemble here, let us resolve that we shall not rest till we have achieved that goal which has animated the whole nation for the last sixty years or more, and which I hope would continue to inspire us during the difficult days to come."[64]

T. Prakasham, evaluating the Constitution, said that Gandhi had planned out the Panchayat Raj and had recommended it to the nation; but, he lamented, the basis on which this country had been educated by him has been discarded. Pointing to the unsuitability of the Draft Constitution. K. Hanumanthaiya said : "We wanted the music of veena or sitar, but here we have the music of an English band."[65] He viewed the Draft Constitution as complete abnegation of the principle of constitution-making as envisaged by the Father of the Nation, and said :

> "We were, during the days of freedom struggle, wedded to certain principles and ideologies as taught to us and as propounded to us by Mahatma Gandhi. The first and foremost advice which he gave in his picturesque language was that the constitutional structure of this country ought to be broad-based and pyramid-like. It should be built from the bottom and should taper right up to the top. What has been done is just the reverse. The pyramid has been reversed. The initiative from the provinces and the States

and from the people has been taken away and all power has been concentrated in the Centre. That is exactly the kind of Constitution Mahatma Gandhi did not want and did not ensvisage."[66] He hoped that though it was too soon to pass any judgment on the rationale for adoption of a contradictory principle, "the future will judge for itself."[67]

R. K. Sidhva was sorry that no effort had been made to realize the ideal of "real Swaraj" and hoped that, notwithstanding the Constitution, the State governments will see that villages are made self-sufficient, because unless there was village self-sufficiency there will not be peace and happiness and prosperity for the common man. Prof. N. G. Ranga looked forward to the day when it would be possible to achieve a cooperative commonwealth through the experience, wisdom and statesmanship of the people; he hoped it would be so possible as envisaged by Bapu, only through "the Kisan-Mazdoor-Buddhijivi-Kalakar Raj, that is, the Raj of the toilers of this country, not the Raj of the idlers or exploiters, but the Raj of the people who lived by their own toil, who made their contribution to the society in an honest and progressive manner; the Raj of the people who lived, worked and died for democracy and democracy alone and never countenanced dictatorship."[68]

Seth Govind Das expressed the hope that the civilization and culture which is our proud heritage, and the continuity and vitality of which in all spheres of life and social order, for the maintenance of which Mahatma Gandhi sought to promote in many a way, shall be retained along with the advantages of the modern age. He also hoped that the Preamble, which contains the gist of the Constitution, shall serve as a beacon-light to the ship of the State, and the country shall be ruled in accordance with the cannons of justice and the spirit of the preamble.

Pandit Lakshmi Kant Maitra, while defending the Constitution, solemnly warned of the dangers inherent in the implementation of the Constitution in its true spirit by all those required to give a concrete shape to it. He counselled :

"Unless those who are in charge of putting this democracy into action could fully make the people understand it and act up to it, this Constitution will be little worse than useless. The success of democracy in a country depends upon the joint, collective endeavour of all concerned. The provisions you have embodied in the Constitution must be implemented in letter and in spirit, more in spirit than in letter. The success or failure of this Constitution would lie in the hands of people who work it. We have to see that if we want to implement whatever we have provided in this Constitution, if all that we want to achieve is to be achieved, then we must start here and now to create an atmosphere for it; we must without delay bring about the conditions necessary for the proper evolution of a secular democracy in this country. You have given adult suffrage to your people. If you do not set about with all earnestness to completely remove illiteracy from the people, then this grant adult suffrage instead of being a boon would be a boomerang."

"The future legislators, the future parliamentarians, the future ministers, the people who would be called upon to operate this Constitution, to administer the government of this land —they should be the first to set an example to the rest of the country by their selfless devotion, by their hard and earnest endeavour to implement the spirit of the provisions of this Constitution. If that is done, I have every reason to hope that we shall be able to make this country worthy of its great past."[69]

Similarly, while N.V. Gadgil opined that the Draft Constitution was really calculated to secure these social and economic aims for which the Preamble stood, M. Ananthasayanam Ayangar saw the imprint of the teachings of Mahatma Gandhi on the Preamble of the Constitution. Shankar Rao Deo hoped that the Constitution would serve as an effective instrument to realize our ideal. He, however, admitted :

"We have not faithfully followed our Master. But constitutions are not only made but they also grow. I may say in conclusion that this Constitution gives us sufficient scope, if we remain true to our aspirations and to our ideals, to slowly bring about a social change, a vital and fundamental change, without any violent change in the Constitution. This will enable us to realize our ideal, which is a non-violent and non-exploitative society where all men will be equal and will have equal opportunity for their self-development."[70] In a similar vein, K. Santhanam pinned his hope on the efficacy of the Constitution in bringing about the desired chage. He said :

> "I think we are assured of the fullest democracy that any Constitution can give. How that democracy will work, to what extent it will be utilized to convert it into not only political democracy, but into industrial democracy, into social democracy, that depends upon those who will work that Constitution; upon the general will of the people of India and the leaders who will be produced by the people of India. No Constitution can provide such things."[71]

Rebutting the contention that the Constitution is un-Gandhian and un-Indian, Jaspat Ray Kapoor pleaded that the Draft Constitution epitomizes all the principles that Gandhiji inhered. He pointed out that Parts III and IV of the Constitution gave a direct lie to such criticism that by taking a decision in favour of adult suffrage in deference to the wishes of Mahatmaji, political power in the hands of the masses, the peasants and labourers has been assured; that persons professing different religions have been granted absolute equality in law and in the eyes of the state, commensurate with the Gandhian ideal of a secular State; that his idea of Village Panchayats as a self-sufficient unit of local government has found a place in Article 50 and provision has been made for the spread of cottage industries by a specific provision in Article 43; that prohibition, which was an important plank in the Gandhiji's programme has been contemplated under Article 47; and that the ingestion of the Gandhian principle of truth and non-violence also appreas in Article 51, wherein it has been provided that the State shall endeavour to promote international peace and security, maintain just and honourable relations between nations and encourage settlement of international disputes by arbitration, and not by having recourse to force or war. Thus, he refuted the contention of the critics that the Constitution was not inspired by Gandhism.

The immediate goal of political freedom having been attained, the makers of the Constitution were deeply concerned with the establishment of an economic democracy in the country on which the fate of the political democracy is bound to depend and which will hasten the realization of a just and egalitarian socio-economic order. In the debates of the Constituent Assembly, we find different shades of opinion on the question whether the Draft Constitution could be a potent instrument for the establishment of the coveted socio-economic order. Domodar Swarup Seth complained that the Constitution does not give any indication of the socio-economic order in view. He said :

> "We all know that the society in which we now live is of capitalistic order or character an in this society we see exploiter and the exploited classes, both existing side by side; and the exploiting class is naturally the top-dog, and the exploited class the under-dog. In such a society we clearly see that the real welfare of the masses, of the toiling millions, can neither be secured nor protected, unless the society in made clear of the exploiter class, and that can be possible only when we establish a socialist democratic order, and transfer to public ownership the important means of production, communication, credit and exchange, mineral resources and the resources of natural power and such other large economic enterprises as are matured for socialism; bring about the municipalization of public utilities; and the encouragement of the organization of agriculture, credit and industries on a cooperative basis."[72]

Similarly, Brajeshwar Prasad maintained that the Constitution was a harmonious blending of the best Indian traditions. He believed that the State which would emerge out of the Draft Constitution shall be based on *Dharma*; and a State based on *Dharma*, the concept which includes all that is noble and good and rejects the evils that have crept in it, will never tolerate economic inequality or social injustice. He warned, "as long as there is economic inequality, the goal of decentralization will elude our grasp."[73]

H.V. Kamath expressed his opinion that parliamentary democracy which has been secured by this Constitution is not enough; it has to be translated into life of the common man in economic and social terms. Expressing satisfaction over the provisions under Articles 31 to 34 of the Draft Constitution, he expressed confidence that if the provisions of these articles are going to be implemented in right earnest, they shall open the charter of a new life for the exploited, disinherited and the bracketed sector of humanity in India and will provide a blue-print of a socio-economic order. However, he forewarned of the dangers if the attempts to establish a socio-economic order fail or are foiled. He said : "When democracy is opposed or resisted, it gives rise to a totalitarian form of government. Even today we see the world is half-slave half-free. In Asia and Africa vast tracts of land are under colonial rule. That is why this movement of communism is growing space. You may call them Communist bandits or Communist follow-travellers. It is no use dubbing them and calling them names. Unless you change your exploiting social order into a freer order, this movement of violently ending the social order will continue. Therefore, we should take heed betimes and try to establish in our country economic and social democracy."[74]

In the midst of surging emotions, enchanting hopes and lucid observations made by the Fathers of the Constitution and the viewpoints of the Father of the Nation, let us now take our inquest into the various facets to equality provided under the Constitution for heralding the desired socio-economic order and the role of the State in the attainment of the goal that still eludes us and the bottlenecks that lie beneath such attempts.

REFERENCES

1. The English Utilitarians and India—Eric Stokes (1959) pp. XIII-XIV.
2. Land marks in Indian Constitutional : Gurumukh Nihal Singh (1959) and National Development (quoted Vol. I. p. 50 from *Modern Review* Aug. 1913).
3. *Concept of Equality*, B.N Ganguli, (1975). p. 44.
4. *Ibid.* p. 112.
5. G.N. Singh, *op.cit.* p.73.

5a. *Ibid.*, p. 109.

6. Ganguli, *op.cit.*, pp. 15-16.
7. Modern Indian Political Tradition, Ed. K.P. Karunakaran (1962), p. 8.
8. Ganguli, *op.cit.*, p. 17.
9. Vivekanand, Swami, *The Complete Works* (1966), Vol. IV, p. 328.

10. *Ibid.*, pp. 328-29.
11. *Caste, Culture and Socialism*, Vivekanand (1947), p. 93.
12. Vivekanand, *op.cit.,* vol. VI. pp. 342-43.
13. Ganguli, *op.cit.,* (quoted), p. 121.
14. *Vivekanand, Caste, Cultural Socialism* : Int. IV.
15. Ganguli, *op.cit.,* p. 11.
16. Karunakaran, *op.cit.,* p. 34.
17. Ganguli, *op.cit.,* p. 90.
18. *Ibid.*, p. 55.
19. *Ibid.,* p. 56.
20. From Naoroji to Nehru : V.B. Singh (1975) p.98.
21. *Ibid.,* pp. X. 117.
22. Some Eminent Indian Contemporaries, Dr. Sachchidanand Sinha (1976) p. 199.
23. *Ibid.*
24. *Ibid.*, 216.
25. V.B. Singh, *op.cit.,* p. 9.
26. Dr. Sachehidanand, *op.cit.,* 213.
27. Karunakaran : *op.cit.,* pp. 13-14.
28. *Ibid.,* p.10.
29. Development in th Congress Constitution, Dr. N.V. Raj Kumar, pp. 14-15.
30. India, from Curzon to Nehru and After, Durga Das, pp. 62-63 (1969).
31. *Ibid.* p. 61.

31(a) N.V. Raj Kumar, *op.cit.,* p. 47.

32. Karunakaran *op.cit.* p. 21.
33. India in 1921-22, Report of L.F. Rush Brook Williams, Director, C.B.I. Govt. of India, p. 68.
34. All Parties Conference, 1928, Report of the Motilal Nehru Committee appointed by the conference to determine the Principles of Constitution of India, p. 19.
35. A.Call to the Nation : Congress Education Manifesto, p. 7, 1936.
36. *Ibid.,* p.10.
37. *Ibid.,* p.1.
38. Report of the General Secretary I.N.C., J.B. Kriplani, Feb.12, 1938, p. 29.
39. *Mahatma*, Tendulkar, D.G., Vol.VII, p. 17.
40. Recent Essays and Writings : J.L. Nehru, p. 78 (1937).
41. *Ibid.,* p. 22.
42. *Ibid.,* p. 25
43. *Ibid.,* pp. 119-20.
44. Nehru—A political biography, Brecher, Michael (1959), p. 144.
45. *Autobiography* : J.L. Nehru, p. 281.
46. *Ibid.,* p. 523.
47. *The Political Philosophy of J.L. Nehru*, M.N. Das (1961), p. 159.
48. *Autobiography* : J.L. Nehru, p. 361.

49. M.N. Das, *op.cit.,* p. 139.
50. J.L. Nehru's Speeches, Govt. of India, Pub. Div. (1958) Vol. III, p. 52.
51. *Socialism,* M.K. Gandhi p. 248.
52. Tendulkar, *op.cit.,* Vol. V, p. 336.
53. *Socialism,* M.K. Gandhi, p. 263.
54. Durga Das, *op.cit.* p. 261.
55. *Ibid.*
56. C.A.D. Vol. I, No. 3, p. 51.
57. *Ibid.*, I.5. 13. Dec., 46
58. Nehru, The First Sixty Years, Ed. Dorothy Norman (1965), Vol. II, p. 283.
59. *Ibid.*
60. C.A.D.I.5. 13 Dec., 46.
61. *Ibid.,* II. 3. 22 Jan., 47.
62. *Ibid.*
63. *Ibid.,* VII.I. 4 Nov., 48.
64. *Ibid.,* XI.6.19. Nov., 49.
65. *Ibid.,* XI.4.17. Nov., 49.
66. *Ibid.*
67. *Ibid.*
68. *Ibid.,* XI,5.18 Nov., 49
69. *Ibid.*
70. *Ibid.,* XI.7.21. Nov., 49.
71. *Ibid.,* XI.6.19 Nov., 49.
72. *Ibid.,* VII.p. 19 Nov., 48.
73. *Ibid.,* XI. 10.24 Nov., 49.
74. *Ibid.* VII. 9. 19. Nov., 48.

CHAPTER 3

EQUALITY OF LEGAL STATUS

(a) The Background

During the various phases of the national movement for liberation under the leadership of Mahatma Gandhi, the progressive development of the urge towards equality has been surveyed in Chapter 2. The fortunes of World War II along with American pressure made the British respond favourably to the Congress demand for the grant of independence. When Lord Wavell, the Viceroy, invited the Congress President to lead the Government, Nehru inherited the responsibility of office and an interim government took office on September 2, 1946. After the attainment of political independence, when a new Congress constitution had become the need of the hour, Gandhi handed over a draft of his suggestions, as required by the Constitution Committee, on January 30, 1948, a few hours before his death, which advocated the disbanding of the existing Congress with a view to "flower into a Lok Sevak Sangh" for attaining the social, moral and economic independence of the country. The Working Committee dissented from this basic approach and in the Bombay session in April, 1948, a new Constitution was shaped and adopted. However, even the new Constitution of Congress adopted as its objective, "the well-being and advancement of the people of India by peaceful and legitimate means of a cooperative commonwealth based on equality of opportunity and of political, economic and social rights and aiming at world peace and followship".[1] Thus, the Congress continued as a political party to shape the social, moral and economic independence of the nation from the pedestal of power.

With the formation of Constituent Assembly to frame a Constitution for free India when the dawn of freedom appeared on the firmament of the Nation, the Congress, kindled by the spirit of freedom struggle, set itself to the task of drafting a Constitution as a machinery for the realization of the cherished goal of equality. Jawahar Lal Nehru, on Friday, December 13, 1946 moved a resolution regarding the aims and objects, which contained, *inter alia*, that "This Constituent Assembly declares its firm and solemn resolve to proclaim India as an Independent Sovereign Republic and to draw up for her future governance a Constitution, wherein shall be guaranteed and secured to all the people of India justice, social, economic and political; equality of status and of opportunity, and before the law; freedom of thought, expression, belief, faith, worship, vocation, association and action, subject to law and public morality; and wherein adequate safeguards shall be provided for minorities, backward and tribal areas, and depressed and other backward classess".[2]

The Constituent Assembly, through its Resolution of January 24, 1947, appointed an Advisory Committee on Minorities, Fundamental Rights, etc., under the chairmanship of Sardar Vallabhabhai Patel. After the Indian tricolour replaced the Union Jack and was hoisted from the ramparts of the Red Fort heralding the new age of Swarajya, the Constituent Assembly, on August 29, 1947, appointed a Drafting Committee with Dr. B.R. Ambedkar as chairman, to prepare a draft of the new Constitution. The Report of the Advisory Committee was submitted in two parts. The. part containing justiciablè Fundamental Rights was submitted to the Assembly on the April 20, 1947, and the other part containing non-justiciable Rights was submitted on the August 30, 1947. The Drafting Committee submitted the draft on February 21, 1948. The Fundamental Rights to equality contained in the Interin Report of the Advisory Committee, the corresponding Rights enumerated in Part III of the Draft Constitution and also as it finally emerged are given in Appendix C. The Draft contains only five broad categories of Fundamental Rights, viz. Rights of Equality, Right relating to Religion, Cultural and Educational Rights, Right to Property and Right to Constitutional Remedies. In fact, the Rights of Equality contained in Articles 9 to 18 contain the rights specified under the Right to Equality, Right to Freedom and Right against Exploitation in the present Constitution, as finally adopted by the Constituent Assembly on November 26, 1949. In the context of our present study, we shall be adducing the relevant rights, at the appropriate place, for an easy comparison with those that finally emerged. There was no exclusive Article on Equality before law. However, Article 15 contained this Right as "protection of life and personal liberty and equality before law." Which read as follow :

> "15. No person shall be deprived of his life or personal liberty except according to procedure established by law, nor shall any person be denied equality before the law or the equal protection of the laws within the territory of India."[3]

Article 15 of the Draft Constitution was finally split into two parts and Article 14 of the new Constitution emanates from the second part. However, the Fundamental Rights in the new Constitution begin with Article 14 thus giving it a place of pride in the galaxy of Rights enunciated in Part III of the Constitution which was finally adopted and enacted by the Constituent Assembly. It serves as a beacon-light of justice, social, economic and political, aspired by the Founding Fathers and is the harbinger of the Rule of Law in Independent India as against the Imperialist Rule of a country in bondage.

The framers of the Constitution foresaw that the right to equality was the pivot round which other rights revolved and without it the guarantees of other rights would be futile and meaningless. As such the right to equality is the harbinger of a better future for the country. But equality cannot be delivered to a society only by adopting this right in the Constitution; the limitations of the law can be attributable to the fact that, as Gandhi said, equality is of souls and it is from the realm of individual's mental framework that inequality should be banished; the law cannot stir the soul. Morality cannot be legislated, yet the social behavior can be regulated and the habits, if not the hearts, can be altered, by recourse to egalitarian laws. It is precisely in this sense and in adherence to the humanitarian accent of Gandhi that the fundamental law of free India has incorporated the human approach to equality by embodying Article 14 as the first item in the Fundamental Rights enumerated in Chapter III of the Constitution. Whereas, the other Rights of this part are hedged with certain restrictions and limitations the right to equality adumbrated in Article 14 proclaiming that all human beings are fundamentally equal in the eyes of the State is without any ostensible reservation or restriction and compares favourably well with the Gandhian concept.

(b) Judicial Interpretation

It ought to be remembered that the concept of justice conceived by Gandhi did not divide life into watertight compartments; and it laid emphasis on individual justice, on the interest of social well-being, which was the sum total of individual well-being. This conception of justice finds reflection in the Fundamental Right to Equality in the sense that all the fundamental rights conferred in Part III form an indivisible whole. They all constitute the fabric of justice, woven round the "supreme" individual as protective fortification of his political freedom and for his fullest development as a citizen of the free country . As Gandhi said : " The individual is the one supreme consideration."[4] This concern for individual lies at the root of all progress and, therefore, the fundamental rights are justiciable and are guaranteed rights of each individual citizen for his all-round progress. The Supreme Court has been specifically mandated under Article 32 of the Constitution to act as a bulwark and watch-dog against any invasion by the State in the domain of individual's fundamental rights as adumbrated in Part III of the Constitution. Referring to this protective umbrella for the safeguard of the fundamental rights, the chairman of the Drafting Committee Dr. Ambedkar, said in the Constituent Assembly :

> "If I was asked to name any particular article of the Constitution as the most important —an article without

which the Constitution would be a nullity—I would not refer to any other article except this one. It is the very soul of the Constitution and the very heart of it."[5]

The different threads constituting the whole fabric are woven together to render a sense of invincibility and to make State intrusion into the domain of individual's rights difficult; the highest court in the land has been endowed with the responsibility to protect those precious rights and has been equipped with an armory of writs under Clause (2) of the said Article. The different threads weaving the net of Fundamental Rights are not severable or isolated but interpenetrable and interposing. They are an indivisible part of a great scheme to secure justice and the whole structure rests on the in-built foundation of justice—economic, social and political. Especially is this true of the rights to equality with which we are here concerned. Justice is the resultant of their free interplay in the portals of a independent judiciary ensured by the provisions of the Constitution. Each Article is designed to expand but never to curtail the rights, which the other connotes. Indeed, as we shall see, the various rights under Articles 14 to 18 are not only interwoven and form a code of equality in unison, but also overlap each other and intertwine with other fundamental rights to prevent injustice against any individual. Thus, an impugned State action satisfying the requirements of Article 15 or 16 will also be tested on the touch stone of Article 14, and similarly a law meeting the requirements of Article 21 would still have to meet the challenge of Article 14 and Article 19 of the Constitution. Verily, it can be said that the position occupied by Article 14 as the very First Right in the firmament of Fundamental Rights enshrined in the Constitution is justified by the fact that it not only focussed on the universal brotherhood, in consonance with our cultural tradition and Bapu's dream, and is of universal application to ward off any injustice, but also acts like a pole star, navigating justice in the turbulent sea to reach its destination, the supreme individual. It is rather the steering wheel of the ship of justice, a constitutional amulet fastened to the individual; or it is, as Lord Harcourt had put it with reference to the British Prime Minister, not "Primus inter pares" nor even "inter stella luna minores"; it is the sun round which the planets revolve in relation to all other rights enshrined in the Indian Constitution.

Article 14 reads : "The state shall not deny to any person equality before the law or the equal protection of the laws within the territory of India."[6]

This right to equality before law enunciated in Article 14, contains two different clauses : "equality before the law and "equal protection of the laws". Though the two expressions seem identical, they mean differently, having been borrowed from two different constitutional frameworks providing different form of governance. The former owes its origin to the British Common Law, while the latter is a phrase used in the XIVth amendment of the U.S. Constitution. The twin phrase conjointly provides equal subjection of all to the laws of the land and confutes special privileges to any individual on grounds which are not rational. Explaining, what constitutes equality before law, Dicey has said :

> "Equality before the law does not mean absolute equality of men, which is a physical impossibility, but the denial of any special privilege by reason of birth, creed or the like in favour of any individual and also the equal subjection of all individuals and classes to the ordinary law of the land administered by the ordinary law courts."[7] It implies that every human being shall be subjected to the same law of the land by the State, notwithstanding differences in caste, creed colour, religion, wealth, social status and the like. It is based on the principle of natural justice that all persons should be treated likewise and the law which violates this principle is a negation of this fundamental right and attracts to provision of constitutional remedy. "With us every official, from the Prime Minister to a constable or a collector of taxes, is under the same responsibility for every act done without legal justification as any other citizen."[8]

The Right to Equality connotes the noble ideal, cherished on humanitarian grounds, that all men are essentially equal, and thus, ensures the dignity of all individuals alike. It is an expression of the realization that ultimately equality must partake of the character of universal brotherhood. In this sense of universal brotherhood, equality must be viewed as similarity of all beings. Nevertheless, the concept of equality does not denote that individuals should be treated alike in all circumstances, irrespective of ability or capacity, and it was to denote this feature of equality before the law that the second clause of "equal protection of the laws" was added signifying subjection to equal laws of all in a similar circumstance. It does not provide equality under unequal circumstances or amongst unequal persons or a group of individuals. Thus, whereas equality before the law denotes a negative concept of equality subjecting all persons in the land to equal laws, the equal protection of the laws is a more positive concept implying equality of treatment in equal circumstances; the former prevents discrimination, the latter ensures that like shall be treated alike. Both the expressions enjoin equality of treatment under the law and the object of both is basically the same. The one is a denial of special privilege, the other is an affirmation of equal treatment to equals. In fact, absolute equality is inconceivable and what is really meant by equality is that the laws should be equal and be equally administered. It is in this sense what Jennings has observed :

> "Equality before the law means that among equals the law should be equal and should be equally administered, that like should be treated alike; the right to sue and be sued or to prosecute and be prosecuted, for the same kind of action should be the same for all citizens of full age and understanding and without discrimination of race, religion, wealth, social status or political influence."[9]

In the context of social sciences, "The concept of equality refers, sometimes, to certain properties which men are held to have in common, but more often, to certain treatment which men either receive or ought to receive. Equality must be constructed in the sense of similarity."[10] Even the Greek thinker, Aristotle, considered a law inegalitarian "when either equals are awarded unequal shares or unequal equal shares."[11] Thus, impartiality is the basic consideration for a person to have equal treatment. In fact, equality before the law emphasizes the impartial application of the law which is possible only if an individual gets an impartial treatment envisaged by the law of the State.

The Supreme Court and the different High Courts of India have as occasions arose, interpreted and elaborated the twin phrase under Article 14 while disposing of various cases of infringement of this Fundamental Right and while so doing have given a meaning and content to it. In order to have a better view of this precious right it is imperative to look into the interpretations given to it enlarging or restricting its meaning, as the development and vastness of this vital clause conferring equality of treatment on all can be gauged only through these pronouncements at the highest pedestal of justice, making the Constitution appear what it really is.

In the case Shivashankar *vs.* State of Madhya Pradesh, Mangal Murti and Mudholkar, J.J., observed as follows :

> While both the expressions aim at establishing what may be regarded as equality of legal status for all, there is some difference between these expressions. The former expression is some what negative concept implying the absence of any special privilege in favour of an individual, while the latter is a more positive concept implying equality of treatment in equal circumstances.[12]

Similarly, in the Supreme Court of India, in the State of U.P. *vs.* Deomon, Justice Subba Rao, in his dissenting judgement, has perceived this distinction between the two expressions, while declaring that all persons are equal before the law is a fundamental tenet of every civilized constitution, "The concepts are inherent in this guarantee : one of 'equality before the law', a negative one and the other...'Equal protection of law', a positive one..... The negative aspect is in the prohibition against discrimination and the positive content is the equal protection under the law to all who are situated similarly and are in like circumstances."[13]

Justice Patanjali Shastri of the Supreme Court of India has made the following observations :

> "The first part of the article, which appears to have been adopted from the Irish Constitution, is a declaration of the equality of civil rights of all persons within the territory of India and thus enshrines what American judges regard as the basic principle of republicanism."[14] The views of the Supreme Court in the above case have been put as follows :

"1. Article 14 is designed to protect all persons in similar circumstances against legislative discrimination and if the legislature takes care to reasonably classify persons for legislative purpose and if it deals equally with all persons belonging to a well-defined class, it is not open to the charge of denial of equal protection on the ground that the law does not apply to other persons.
2. Laws must operate alike on all persons under like circumstances.
3. Equality of right is a principle of republicanism and Article 14 enunciates this equality principle in the administration of justice... the same rule must exist for all in similar circumstances.

   The principle, however, does not mean that every law must have universal application for all persons who are not, by nature, attainment or circumstances, in the same position.
4. The protection afforded by the article is not a mere eyewash but it is a real one and unless a just cause for discrimination on the basis of a reasonable classification is put forth as defence, the Statute (in question) has to be declared unconstitutional.
5. Article 14 only means that all persons similarly circumstanced shall be treated alike both in privileges conferred and liabilities imposed."[15]

In the Reference of Special Courts Bill, 1978, under advisory jurisdiction, Chief Justice Y. V. Chandrachud described the two parts of Article 14 as follows :

> "The first part of Article 14 which was adopted from the Irish Constitution is a declaration of the equality of civil rights of all persons within the territory of India. It enshrines a basic principle of republicanism. The second part, which is a corrolary of the first and is based on the last clause of the first section of the Fourteenth Amendment of the American Constitution, enjoins that equal protection shall be secured to all such persons in the enjoyment or their rights and liberties without discrimination of favouritism. It is a pledge for the protection of equal laws, that is, laws that operated alike on all persons under like circum-stences."[16]

It may be noted that Article 14 by its terms applies to all including artificial persons or corporations : but it is a safety valve against discrimination only in the sphere of State activity and has nothing to do against discrimination by private individuals. Moreover, under the Constitution, certain privileges and immunities are provided to heads of foreign states and ambassadors thereof, enforced as law of nations, and certain protections to presidents and governors and of publication of legislative proceedings are stipulated under Article 361. Similarly, Articles 105 and 106 guarantee certain parliamentary privileges to the members of Parliament and similar provision has been made with regard to the members of the State Legislature in Articles 194 and 196. The members in judicial service also enjoy certain immunities and privileges with respect to their official function, Section 197 Cr. P. C. provides immunity from prosecution, without governmental sanction, for offences by Government servants in relation to their official acts. The intention behind this provision is that no public official should be unduly harassed by private prosecution unless, in the opinion of the government, there were reasonable ground for prosecution, Such different procedure for prosecution of public officials is warranted by the nature and scope of their duties and is in no way a negation of the equality principle placing the officials above the Constitution. The Supreme Court has on several occasions upheld the contention that a rule of procedure attracts the provision of Article 14 as much as the rule of substantive law. In Meenakshi Mille Ltd. *vs.* A.V.V. Shastri and Budhan Chaudhary and others *vs.* State of Bihar the Supreme Court has viewed discrimination not only by a substantive law but by rule of procedure also as violative of Article 14. In the case of State of West Bengal *vs.* Anwar Ali Sarkar it expressed itself on the point thus : "A rule of procedure laid down by law come as much within the purview of Article 14 of the Constitution as any rule of substantive law and it is necessary that all litigants, who are similarly situated, are able to avail themselves of the same procedural rights for relief and for defence with like protection and without discrimination."[17] Even Section 197 Cr. P.C., which provides certain immunity to a public servant on official duty from prosecution for acts in performance of his official duty, has been interpreted as not intending to create by the law a privileged class of persons. "It is a matter for the judicial consideration of a court of law at the trial to judge for itself the circumstance in which the accused was placed owing to his official position and duties. It is not the function of the executive or the legislature to determine the acquittal without prosecution."[18]

The Supreme Court has also held that subordinate legislation cannot escape the protective umbrella of Article 14 of the Constitution. In the case of Indian Express Newspaper Ltd. and others *vs.* Union of India, the court while clarifying the distinction between subordinate legislation and the Act observed : "A piece of subordinate legislation does not carry the same degree of immunity which is enjoyed by a statute passed by a competent legislature. Subordinate legislation may be questioned on any of the grounds on which plenary legislation in questioned. In addition, it may also be questioned on the ground that it does not conform to the statute under which it is made. It may, further, be questioned on the ground that it is contrary to some other statute. That is because the subordinate legislation must yield to plenary legislation. It may also be questioned on the ground that it is unreasonable, not in the sense of not being reasonable, but in the sense that it is manifestly arbitrary.

A distinction must be made between delegation of a legislative function in the case of which the question of reasonableness cannot be inquired into, and the investment by the statute to exercise a particular discretionary power. In the latter case the question may be considered on all grounds on which administrative action may be questioned, such as non-application of mind, taking irrelevant matters into consideration, failure to take relevant matters into consideration, etc. On the facts and circumstances of a case, subordinate legislation may be struck down as arbitrary or contrary to the statute, if it fails to take into account very vital facts which either expressly or by necessary implication are required to be taken into consideration, by the statute or say, the Constitution. This can be done only on the ground that it does not conform to the statutory or constitutional requirement or that it offends Article 14 or Article 19 (1) (a) of the Constitution. It cannot, no doubt, be done merely on the ground that it is not reasonable or that it has not taken into account relevant circumstances which the court considers relevant. The power to grant exemption should be exercised in a reasonable way."[19]

Similarly the court has held that violation of natural justice by the State shall be an arbitrary action which will attract the provisions of Article 14.

In Union of India *vs.* Tulsi Ram Patel (1985) the Supreme Court opined, "Violation of rule of natural justice results in arbitrariness which is the same as discrimination and where discrimination is the result of State action : it is violation of Article 14. Therefore, a violation of the principle of natural justice by a State action is violation of Article 14."[20]

In Satyavir Singh *vs.* Union of India, while dealing with the relation between natural justice and Article 14, the Supreme Court significantly observed : "The principles of natural justice are not the creation of Article 14 of the Constitution. Article 14 is not the begetter of the principles of natural justice but is their constitutional guardian."

> "Article 14 applies not only to discriminatory class legislation but also to arbitrary and discriminatory State action. Violation of rule of natural justice results in arbitrariness which is the same as discrimination, and when discrimination is the result of State action, it is a violation of Article 14."

Elaborating the point further, the court held that "The principles of natural justice apply both to quasi-judicial as well as administrative inquiries entailing civil consequences."[21]

The literal meaning of the clause "equal protection of the laws" is subjection to equal laws applying alike to all in a like situation. It forbids any arbitrary discrimination by the legislature in framing the laws or by the executive while implementing them. No one should receive undue favour and none should be subjected to arbitrary discrimination or disadvantage in the circumstances that do not warrant a different treatment. It implies that the laws shall confer its equal protection to all persons situated in like circumstances. It provides security positively to all under law of the land

and prohibits special privileges or distinction on grounds, which are not rational.

In Francis Coralie Mullin *vs.* Union Territory of Delhi (1981) the Supreme Court struck down an order based on special discrimination on grounds which were not rational, and held :

> "If any prison regulation or procedure laid down is regulating the right to have interview with members of the family or friend, say, once a month, it is definitely arbitrary and hits Article 14."[22]

Even administrative orders, in exercise of the executive power without making of laws, are within the purview of the Constitution and attract the provisions of Article 14. Any action or administrative order that smacks of unreasonability or arbitrariness are bound to be declared void as violative of Article 14. In Brij Bhusan *vs.* State of Jammu and Kashmir (1986), an administrative order of the State Government sanctioning supply of crude oleoresin to three entrepreneurs for running their factories established in the State for manufacturing resin and turpentine derivatives was challenged in the Supreme Court. It was contended on behalf of the petitioners that the State Government had acted arbitrarily in selecting respondents for setting up factories within the State without affording any opportunity to the petitioners and others for obtaining such a contract and this action of the State Government was not based on any rational or relevant principles and was, therefore, violative of Article 14. The court held the claim untenable, and while dismissing the petition held :

> "If the State were giving tapping contract simpliciter, there can be no doubt that State would have to auction or invite tenders for securing the highest price, subject, of course, to any other relevant overriding considerations of public weal or interest, but in a case like this where the State is allocating resources such as water, power, raw materials, etc., for the purpose of encouraging setting up of industries within the State, we do not think the State is bound to advertise and tell the people that it wants a particular industry to be set up within the State and

invite those interested to come up with proposals for the purpose. The State may choose to do so if it thinks fit and in a given situation it even may turn out to be advantageous for the State to do so, but if any private party comes before the State and efforts to set up an industry, the State would not be committing breach of any constitutional or legal obligation if it negotiates with such party and agrees to provide resources and other facilities for the purpose of setting up the industry. The contact cannot be assailed as invalid so long as the State has acted bonafide, reasonably and in public interest. There is nothing at all to show that the State acted malafide or out of improper or corrupt motive or in order to promote the private interest of someone at the cost of the State. We are, clearly, of the view that the three impugned orders do not suffer from any infirmity and they cannot be assailed as invalid."[23]

But in Express Newspapers Pvt. Ltd. *vs.* Union of India (1986), the Supreme Court struck down the administrative order on the ground of arbitrariness. Justice E.S. Venkatramiah in his concurring judgement observed : "I agree that Shri Jagmohan Lt. Governor of Delhi, the second respondent herein, has taken undue interest in getting the impugned notices issued to the first petitioner and his action which has come up for consideration in this case is not consistent with the normal standard of administration. I am satisfied that the said notices were issued by the authorities concerned under the pressure of the second respondent. The material available in this case is sufficient to hold that the impugned notices suffer from arbitrariness and non-application of mind. They are violative of Article 14 of the Constitution. Hence, they are liable to be quashed."[24]

Again, in Central Inland Water Transport Corpn. Ltd. *vs.* Tarun Kanti Sengupta (1986), the Supreme Court struck down the Rule empowering the Government corporation to terminate services of its permanent employees by giving notice or pay in lieu of notice as opposed to public policy and violative of Article 14. The court ruled :

"Clause I of Rule 9 of of C.I.W.T. Corp. Ltd. Service

(Discipline and Appeal) Rules (1979) is void under Section 23 of the Contract Act as being opposed to public policy, and is also ultra vires of Article 14 of the Constitution to the extent that it confers upon the corporation the right to terminate the employee by giving him three months, notice in writing or by paying him the equivalent of three months basic pay and dearness allowance in lieu of such notice, which besides being arbitrary and unreasonable, wholly ignores audi alteram partem (hear the other side) rule. It is also violative of directive principles contained in Articles 39 (a) and 41". It cannot be supported on the basis of mutuality on the ground that similar right is conferred on employees also. The right conferred on the employees to resign is, however, not void.[25]

> "Equal protection of the laws means the protection of equal laws. It forbids all invidious discrimination but does not require identical treatment for all persons without recognition of differences in relevant circumstances."[26] It is a positive guarantee of the dearly cherished right to equality under the law and ensures against irrational discrimination, hostile cessation or mala fide circumvention by the State. As Prof. D.D. Basu has observed, it postulates "the right to equal treatment in similar circumstances both in the privileges conferred and in the liabilities imposed by the law. There should be no discrimination between one person and another if as regards the subject matter of legislation their position is the same."[27]

The Supreme Court has reiterated the above principle while delivering judgement in a case A.D. Shetty *vs.* International Airport Authority of India (1979). It observed :

> "It is now well settled that Article 14 strikes at arbitrariness in State action and ensures fairness and equality of treatment. It requires that the State action must not be arbitrary but must be based on some rational relevant principle which is non-discriminatory; it must not be guided by any extraneous or irrelevant considerations, because that would be denial of equality. The principle of reasonableness and rationality which is legally as well as philosophically an essential element of equality

or non-arbitrariness is projected by Article 14 and it must characterise every State action whether it be under authority of law or in exercise of executive power without making of law."[28]

Similarly, in an earlier case Maneka Gandhi *vs.* Union of India (1978), the Supreme Court expressed an identical view. It observed :

"Article 14 strikes at arbitrariness in State action and ensures fairness and equality of treatment. The principle of reasonableness, which legally as well as philosophically, is an essential element of equality or non-arbitrariness pervades Article 14 like a brooding omnipresence."[29]

In E.P. Royappa *vs.* State of Tamil Nadu (1974) the Supreme Court made a significant observation :

"Equality is a dynamic concept with many aspects and dimensions and it cannot be 'cribbed, cabined and confined' within traditional and doctrinaire limits. From a positivistic point of view, equality is antithetic to arbitrariness. In fact equality and arbitrariness are sworn enemies : one belongs to the rule of law in a republic while the other, to the whim and caprice of an absolute monarch. Where an act is arbitrary, it is implicit in it that it is unequal both according to political logic and constitutional law."[30]

In Union of India *vs.* Tulsi Ram Patel (1985) the Supreme Court observed : "Article 14 contains a guarantee of equality before the law to all persons and a protection to them against discrimination by any law. It prohibits hostile classification by law and is directed against discriminating class legislation, i.e. treating equals as unequals and unequals as equals. To treat one person differently from another when there was no rational basis for doing so would be arbitrary and thus discriminatory. Arbitrariness can take many forms and shapes, but whatever form or shape it takes, it is nonetheless discrimination forbidden by Article 14."[31]

Similarly in State of Andhra Pradesh *vs.* Nalla Raja Reddy (1967) the Supreme Court observed : "Official arbitrariness is more subversive of the doctrine of equality than statutory discrimination. In respect of a statutory discrimination one knows where he stands, but the wand of official arbitrariness can be waved in all directions indiscriminately."[32]

Likewise, on a habeas corpus petition filed by a Tihar Jail prisoner, the Supreme Court hold that the Punjab Police Manual, in so far as it puts the ordinary Indian beneath the better classbreed is untenable and arbitrary and directed that the Indian humans shall not be dichotomized and commoner discriminated against regarding handcuffs. The rule of prisoners in transit between the prison and the court is "freedom handcuffs", declared the Supreme Court.[33]

Yet, the equal protection clause is not absolute. The doctrine of classification has been formulated to permit a rational classification between unequals. The Supreme Court has iterated in various decisions that while Article 14 prohibits class legislation, it does not preclude reasonable classification for the purpose of legislation. "Legislation which is based on a rational classification is permissible."[33(a)] It does not visualize the universal application of all laws and is not repugnant to separate treatment for different classes of persons on a rational basis. This does not mean that all laws shall be equal in their application to all persons. As Prof. Wills has compendiously put it :

> "The guarantee of equal protection of the laws means protection of equal laws. It forbids class legislation, which rests upon unreasonable grounds of distinction. It does not prohibit legislation, which is limited either in the objects to which it is directed or by the territory within which it is to operate. It merely requires that all persons subjected to such legislation shall be treated alike, under like circumstances and conditions both in the privileges conferred and in the liabilities imposed. Similarity, and not identity of treatment, is enough. The fact that only one person or one business or one locality is affected is not a proof of denial of equal protection of the laws."[34] It only means, "there should be no discrimination between one person and another if as regards the subject matter of the legislation their position is the same."[35] Thus, the whole problem under the equal protection clause is one

of classification or drawing lines and the rule of classific-ation was enunciated for the first time by the Supreme Court of India to uphold the government decision in taking over the Sholapur Spinning and Weaving Mills Ltd., in the judgement of the case noted above. The court observed that the rule of equality did not mean that all laws should be identically applied to all persons in spite of differences in circumstances and conditions, and held that "the rule of equality did not take away from the State the power of classifying persons for legitimate purposes; however, such classification could not be made arbitrary and without any substantial basis."[36]

Justice Dey has observed : "While reasonable classification is permitted without doing violence to the equal protection of the laws, such classification must be based upon some real and substantial distinction bearing a reasonable and just relation to the things in respect of which such classification is imposed, and classification cannot be arbitrarily made without any substantial basis. Arbitrary selection, it has been said, cannot be justified by calling it a classification."[37]

Upholding the doctrine of classification in the case, State of Bombay *vs.* Bulsara, the Supreme Court of India analysed its meaning and scope, which may be summed up as follows :

"1. The presumption should always be in favour of the constitutionality of an act since it must be assumed that the legislature rightly understands and correctly appreciates the needs of its own people : that the laws are enacted to deal with the problems manifested by experience and discriminations are based on reasonable grounds.

2. This presumption can be rebutted in certain cases where it can be shown that there is no classification at all and no difference peculiar to any individual or class, yet the law hits only a particular individual or class.

3. The principle of equality does not take away from the State the power of classifying persons for legitimate purposes, as the varying needs of different classes of persons often require separate treatment.

4. Every classification in some way or the other produces inequality, but mere production of inequality is not enough to strike down classification.
5. If a law deals equally with members of a well-defined class, it cannot be deemed to deny equal protection on the ground that it does not apply to other persons of a different class.
6. The classification must be based on some real and substantial distinction bearing a reasonable and just relation to the object sought to be attained."[38]

Again, in V. N. Syed Mohammad and Co. *vs.* State of Madras, the Supreme Court, in its judgement, laid down the scope of equal protection clause as follows :

"(i) The guarantee of equal protection of laws does not require that the same law should be made applicable to all persons or that the law should have the same operation on all persons. It taboos only an application of different laws to persons who are in similar circumstances.

(ii) The necessities as to equal protection of laws do not forbid legislative classifications, provided such classifications rest on some differences related to the purpose of the statute.

(iii) That a classification cannot be upheld on purely imaginative grounds.

(iv) That with reference to financial enactment, the legislature has considerable latitude in making classifications. It can select such persons or things as it chooses for purposes of taxation.

(v) The financial legislation must also satisfy the test of equal protection, and are liable to be struck down, if otherwise.

(vi) That there is a strong presumption in favour of the vitality of legislative classification and it is for those who challenge it as arbitrary or unconstitutional to establish it beyond all doubts.

(vii) That the power to make classification could be excised not only by the legislature but also by administrative bodies under the Act."[39]

Justice Gajendragadkar, while commenting on the Prevention of Corruption Act, 1947, opined :

> "Article 14 does not forbid reasonable classification for the purposes of legislation : but if it appears that the impugned legislation is based on a reasonable classification founded on intelligible differentia and that the said differentia have a rational relation to the object sought to be achieved by it, its validity cannot be successfully challenged under Article 14."[40]

In Kathi Ranning Rawat *vs.* State of Saurashtra, Justice Mukherjee, observed :

> "A legislature for the purpose of dealing with the complex problems that arise out of an infinite variety of human relations cannot but proceed on some sort of selection or classification of persons upon whom the legislation is to operate."[41]

Likewise, in D.D. Joshi *vs.* Union of India (1983) the Supreme Court observed :

> "It is well settled that Article 14 forbids class legislation but does not forbid classification for the purpose of legislation. It is equally well settled that in order to meet the test of Article 14 (i) classification must be based on intelligible differentia which distinguishes persons or things that are grouped together from those that are left out of the group and (ii) the differentia must have a rational nexus to the objects sought to be achieved by the executive or legislative action under challenge."[42]

Article 14 contains a guarantee of equality before law to all persons and protection to them against discrimination by law. It forbids class legislation or hostile classification. This view has been reiterated by the Supreme Court in the Union of India *vs.* Tulsi Ram Patel (1985), thus :

> "What Article 14 forbids is discrimination by law, that is, treating persons similarly circumstanced differently and treating those not similarly circumstanced in the same way or, as has been pithily put, treating equals as unequals

and unequals as equals. Article 14 prohibits hostile classification by law and is directed against discriminatory class legislation."[43]

Thus, the meaning and content given to Article 14 in the various decisions of the Supreme Court make it manifest that equality, in the eyes of law, connotes equal protection of all persons who are socially and economically equal, otherwise its universal application may pepetuate the curse of age-old inequalities rampant in the social and economic fabric of the nation and frustrate the very purpose of this Right.

There may be an enactment relating to a single individual or object, if it is proved that on account of some specific reasons applicable to him and in applicable to others, that single individual is a class in himself. In this connection the Supreme Court has observed : "A law may be constitutional even though it relates to a single individual; if, on account of some special circumstances for reasons applicable to him and not applicable to others, that single individual may be treated as a class by himself."[44]

The Commission of Inquiry Act, 1952, which empowered the government to inquire into any definite matter of public importance, was challenged in the case Ram Krishna Dalmia *vs.* Justice S.R Tandolkar, when a commission headed by Justice Tandolkar was constituted to enquire into the affairs of Dalmia concern, on the ground that the Act violated the equality clause and was discriminatory. The Supreme Court upheld the Act and maintained that the discretion conferred by the Act was not unguided as the Act explicitly laid down the policy of inquiring into matters of public importance. The fact that the Act could be used against a particular individual or concern did not, by itself, make it discriminatory.

Similarly, Article 14 is not designed to prevent legislatures from passing law introducing reforms in some of the institutions only or objects having common characteristics or to particular areas only.

In Atam Prakash *vs.* State of Haryana, pre-emption right guaranteed to the tenants and co-sharers under Section 15 of the Punjab Pre-emption Act. (as applicable to the State of Haryana) was impugned on the ground of irrational classification. The Constitution Bench of the Supreme Court presided over by Chief Justice P.N. Bhagwati held that the impugned section did not infringe either Article 14 or 15 of the Constitution, and observed :

> "The right of pre-emption given to co-sharers is justified as the classification of co-sharers as a class by themselves for the purpose of vesting in them the right of pre-emption is reasonable. The right of pre-emption in favour of a tenant granted by the Act is only another instance of legislation aimed at protecting the tenant. There can be no denial that the tenants form a distinct class by themselves and the right of pre-emption granted in their favour is reasonable and in the public interest."[45]

An Act of the legislature cannot be declared violative of Article 14, only if after selecting certain areas and objects to which the law would apply in the first instance empowers the executive to add the similar areas or objects according to its own judgement. "If the policy and object of the Act can be found out within the four corners of that Act including the preamble, and discretion is vested in the government to make a selection in furtherance of that policy and object for the application of the Act, then the provision conferring such powers is not void as violating Article 14. If such power is arbitrarily exercised in a particular case which is not in furtherance of the policy and object of the Act, then the court can strike down the exercise of such power on such occasion."[46]

It, however, implies that the Supreme Court is bound to strike down any arbitrary power vested by the legislature in the executive branch of the government to do whatever it likes unrestrained by any directive, principle or guidelines as to the exercise of those vested powers. As Chief Justice Patanjali Shastri has observed :

> "If the impugned legislation indicates the policy which inspired it and the object which it seeks to attain, the mere fact that the legislation does not itself make a complete and precise classification of the persons or things to which it is to be applied, but leaves the selective application of the law to be made by the executive

authority in accordance with the standard indicated or the underlying policy and object disclosed, is not sufficient ground for condemning it as arbitrary and, therefore, obnoxious to Article 14."[47]

Similarly, the Banking Companies (Acquisition and Transfer of Undertakings) Act, which was proclaimed as enhancing the general welfare, was declared as "flagrantly hostile discrimination." The Supreme Court observed : "The fourteen named banks are prohibited from carrying on banking business.... disability for which there is no rational explanation. Banks other than the named banks may carry on banking business in India and abroad, new banks may be floated for carrying on banking business.... Section 15 (2) of the Act, which by the clearest implication prohibits the named banks from carrying on banking business is, therefore, liable to be struck down."[48]

But when the Prize Chits and Money Circulating Schemes (Banning) Act (43 of 1978) was challenged in a case Shrinivasa Enterprises *vs.* Union of India (1981), the Supreme Court upheld the Act. It observed :

> "When a general evil is sought to be suppressed some martyrs may have to suffer, for the legislature cannot easily make meticulous exceptions and has to proceed on broad categorization, not singular individualizations".
>
> "It cannot be said that conventional chits and prize chits are substantially similar... conventional chits and prize chits are different categories with different financial features and different damaging effects. Hence there is no violation of Article 14..."
>
> "There are enough arguments to justify the different classification of these items and their exemption cannot be called in question, on the ground of violation of Article 14. Reasonable classification wins absolution from the charge of discrimination, if the differentia has a nexus with statutory object."[49]

On the question of nationalization, the Supreme Court has clearly held that the extent and range of any scheme of nationalization are essentially matters to be decided by the

State, and in the domain of policy-making the judiciary should not normally intervene. "The distribution between public-private and joint sectors and the extent and range of any scheme of nationalization are essentially matters of State policy which are inherently inappropriate subjects for judicial review. Scales of justice are not designed to weigh competing social and economic factors. In such matters legislative wisdom must prevail and judicial review must abstain."

Declaring the impugned Coking Coal Mines (Nationalization) Act (36 of 1972) as not violative of Article 14 and intra vires, the Supreme Court made a significant observation on the process of nationalization.

> "The process of nationalization of the coal industry is, of course, not complete yet. Nationalization of any industry or means of production may not be and need not be effected all at once. It may be achieved in stages. If in the process of nationalization, some units are left out in the earlier stages, either because it is so planned or because of some mistake, it cannot be said that there has been a violation of Article 14".
>
> A law regarding prohibition, making a difference between a civil and military personnel and between foreign visitors and Indian citizens, the Bombay Prohibition Act, 1949, was declared valid and the Supreme Court Observed : "There was an understandable basis for exemption granted and, therefore, there was nothing wrong in the legislation according special treatment to persons who form a class by themselves in many respects."[50]
>
> The Supreme Court upheld the classification provided by the Hindu Religions Trust Act (Bihar) for separate trust boards for Hindu and Jain Religious Trusts, on the ground that Hindus, Jains and Sikhs differed in the religious faith, practices, etc, hence could be treated differently in this respect."[51]

Thus, it is manifest from the various judicial pronouncements made from the apex court that while rational classification is permissible, the classification must have as its basis a real and substantial distinction bearing a reasonable and just relation to the object expressed in the Act. "In making the classification, the legislature cannot certainly be expected to provide abstract symmetery. It can make and set apart the classes according to the need and exigencies of society and as suggested by experience... but the classification should never be arbitrary. It must always rest upon real and substantial distinction bearing a reasonable and just relation to that thing in respect of which the classification is made."[52]

(c) Doctrine of Classification

Though a common formula or criterion cannot be laid down as the basis of such rational classification, because the time, circumstance and attitude are prone to change with the passing of time, certain common factors may form the basis of classification. A variety of grounds can be conceived on which a classification may be justly made :

(i) Classification Based on Police Power

"The police power, a phrase used by Marshall, C. J. in 1827, is the plenary power inherent in every Sovereign State. It comprehends all things touching the common welfare, e.g. Peace, safety, health, comfort, education, and good order of the people, and the welfare of society. Legislation may be made in pursuance of the valid exercise of the police power but whether the limit to the valid exercise has been exceeded or not, is a question of substituting the judgement of the court for that of the legislature."[53]

The doctrine of police power, however, has not received much encouragement from the judiciary in India. In the State of West Bengal *vs.* Subodh Gopal Bose, Chief Justice Patanjali Shastri observed :

> "The American doctrine of police power as a distinct and specific legislative power is not recognized in our Constitution."[54]

Similarly, in the State of Bombay *vs.* Bombay Education Society the Supreme Court held :

> "Such being the fundamental right, the police power of the State to determine the medium of instruction must yield to this fundamental right to the extent it is necessary to give effect to it and cannot be permitted to run counter to it."[55]

(ii) Classification Based on Taxation

"The power to tax is an incident of Sovereignty. All persons, to which the sovereign power of a State extends, are objects of taxation. The power is co-extensive with that to which it is incident. In the field of taxation, the rule of reasonable classification has been liberally applied."[56] Provision of the Indian Income Tax Act, which provides for collection of arrears of Income Tax as arear of land revenue, has been a subject matter of litigations in a number of cases before the Supreme Court. The law regarding collection of land revenue being different in different States, income tax used to be recovered differently in different States. The Supreme Court held :

> "This difference in the recovery machinery was not hit by Article 14 because defaulters are grouped Statewise and in each State all defaulter are treated alike."[57]

The Madras General Sales Tax Act, which singled out certain commodities as liable to sales tax, was held to be valid in the case V.M. Syed Mohammad Ali *vs.* State of Madras (1952). Thus, the legislature has been allowed enough powers to determine the manner and rate of taxation and freedom to choose the articles to be taxed. Similarly, for the purpose of tariff, the classification of tobacco according to the uses to which it may be put has been upheld by the Supreme Court in the case Jagannath *vs.* Union of India (1962). Through a liberal interpretation of the provisions of law in matters connected with taxation, "the State is allowed to pick and choose districts, objects, persons, methods, and even rates for taxation, if does so reasonably."[58]

"But where the tax clearly results in flagrant and palpable inequality between the burden imposed and benefit received so as to amount to an arbitrary taking away of property or where the basis of classification is fanciful, the tax has been held to contravene equal protection clause..... In Suraj Mal Mehta and Co. *vs.* A.N. Vishwanatha Shastri (1954) S.C. A. (C. W. N.) 743, Section 5 (4) of the Taxation of Income (Investigation Commission) Act, 1947, which equally applies to the same categories of income-tax evaders as are referred to in Section 34 of the Income Tax Act, was held to be discriminatory, because the decision of the Income Tax

Investigation Commission is final on a question of fact but whereas the decision of the Income Tax authorities in similar cases is not final on a similar question of fact."[59]

In Aryodaya and Wvg. Mills Co. Ltd. *vs.* Municipal Corporation, Ahmedabed, the provision of the Bombay Provincial Municipal Corporations Act providing for the assessment of properties for levying property tax was challenged and the method of levy of tax on the basis of floor area was held to be against provisions of the Act and the rules made thereunder. However, while deciding this case, the court iterated the rationale of classification :

> "Article 14 did not forbid classification. But permissible classification must be based on an intelligible differentia which distinguished persons or things that were grouped together from others left out of the group, and the differentia must have a rational relation to the effect sought to be achieved by the statute in question. In permissible classification mathematical nicety and perfect equality were not required. Like-wise, identity of treatment was not essential. If there was equality and uniformity within each group, the law would not be condemned as discriminative, though due to some unforeseen circumstances arising out of a peculiar situation some included in a class got an advantage over others, so long as they were not singled out for special treatment. Taxation law was not an exception to this doctrine. However, with regard to application of principles, the legislature should have wide discretion in the matter of classification owing to the inherent complexity of fiscal adjustment of diverse elements. But such a classification must be based on the fundamental principles of the said doctrine. The power of the legislature to make classification was not only of wide range but also flexible so that it could adjust its system of taxation in all proper and reasonable ways."[60]

Similarly, in the State Karnataka *vs.* M/s. Hansa Corporation (1981), in which Section 3 of the Karnataka Tax on Entry of goods into Local Areas for Consumption Act (27 of 1979) was challenged, a question arose as to whether the State Government had a choice in the matter of selecting local areas? The Supreme Court declared :

"Choice to select local areas is a necessary concomitant of a choice to select, rates, which power is admittedly conferred on the State Government. The impugned measure is a taxing statute and in the matter of the taxing statute the legislature enjoys a larger discretion in the matter of classification so long as it adheres to the fundamental principle underlying the doctrine of classification. The power of the legislature to classify is of wide range and flexibility, so that it can adjust its taxation in all proper and reasonable ways. It would therefore, be idle to contend that a State must tax everything in order to tax something. It cannot be said that if a State Government is granted a choice in the matter of selection of local area, ipso facto, the statute would be unconstitutional as violative of Article 14."[61]

Again, in M/s. Vrajlal Manilal and Co. *vs.* State of Madhya Pradesh (1986), the Supreme Court held :

"Mere non-mention of Tendu leaves in any entries of Schedule would not absolve it from levy of tax under Section 6 read with residuary entry No. 1 in Part (b) of Schedule 2. Thus, levy of sales-tax on the sales and purchase of Tendu leaves at a rate different from that on the sales and purchase of other goods would not be violative of Article 14 of the Constitution."[62]

Likewise, in the Malwa Bus Service Pvt. Ltd. *vs.* State of Punjab (1988), the Supreme Court observed :

"Even a fiscal legislation is subject to Article 14 of the Constitution. But it is well settled that a legislature in order to tax some need not tax all. It can adopt a reasonable classification of persons and things in imposing tax liabilities. A law of taxation cannot be termed as being discriminatory because different rates of taxation are prescribed in respect of different items, provided it is possible to hold that the said item belongs to distinct and separate groups and that there is a reasonable nexus between the classification and the object to be achieved by the imposition of different rates of taxation. The mere fact that a tax falls more heavily on certain goods or persons may not result in its invalidity." It ruled :

"The levy of different rates of tax on State carriages and public carriers does not suffer from the vice of hostile discrimination."[63]

(iii) Classification Based on Geographical Situation

In a modern Welfare State, a classification based on the geographical situation can be justified on a rational ground to enable the State to confer special benefits, privileges or liabilities on the bona fide residents of that special area through a suitable legislation, provided there is a nexus between the basis of classification and the object sought to be achieved. In a vast country like India, with different religions and cultures embodying the haves and have-nots, local conditions are apt to vary in different localities. Hence a law prescribes different rules for different areas is not held to contravene the equality clause for that reason alone. It is not essential for a law to be operative throughout the territory of the State. The State may adopt particular laws for particular areas, and for a particular class of subjects, provided there is a rational basis for such classification. Thus Section 269 of Cr. P.C. enabling the State to introduce a system of trial by jury in different localities by a notification was held to be intra vires in Badri Parasad *vs.* State of Bengal (AIR, 1953). But when the State Government singled out a particular case in the Burdwan Text Relief case as not to be tried by a jury, the trial was held to be illegal. (D.K. Mandal *vs.* Legal Remembrancer 1954 S.C.A. (C.W.N.) 588).

In Shrikrishna Singh and others *vs.* The State of Rajasthan where in the revenue Act of the State was impugned on the ground that as it applied only to a particular area, it was discriminatory, the Supreme Court held :

"It being shown that special legislation had to be enacted for certain areas to meet the special situation there the impugned Act cannot be held to be discriminatory."[64]

Indeed, the permissible classification on the basis of geographical situation would stand vitiated if it is proved to intend to discriminate against a particular race or class of people residing in that particular area. The important condition is that the law enacted on the basis of a geographical situation should be equally administered in the particular area carved out by the law.

(iv) Classification Based on Special Legal Procedure

"Procedural law comes as much within the purview of Article 14 as a rule of substantive law. Thus a piece of legislation, which confers on the government or its officers an unfettered discretion to pick out certain cases for trial by a special procedure which takes away from the person affected a right to resort to a more liberal procedure, comes within the mischief of Article 14. On the above principle, Section 5(1) of the West Bengal Special Courts Act (10 of 1950) which empowers a court of special jurisdiction set up by the Act to try such offences or class of offences, cases or class of cases, as the State Government may by general or special order, in writing direct, was held by the majority of the Supreme Court to be discriminatory, and as such void, the necessity for a speedier trial mentioned in the preamble being held to afford no reasonable basis of classification [State of West Bengal *vs.* Anwar Ali Sarkar (1952) S.C.A (C.W.N.) 148]."[65] In a later decision, however, the court reversed its earlier stand. [Kedarnath Bajoria *vs.* State of West Bengal (1953) S.C.A. (C.W.N.) 838]. The Supreme Court has thus given its sanction to the practices of providing for trial of certain offences by special courts and under a special procedure contrary to the provisions stipulated by the ordinary law. "If there is a reasonable basis of class-ification, special treatments may be created for the trial of cases of special nature."[66]

According to Section 11 of the Saurashtra State Public Safety Measures Ordinace, the Government was authorized to select only such offences or class of offences for trial by the special court in accordance with the special procedure which were calculated to public safety, maintenance of public order and preservation of peace. According to Section 9 of the ordinance the use of the special procedure must essentially be confined to only disturbed areas or those areas where adoption of public safety measures was essential. The Supreme Court, upholding the classification made by the Ordinance, observed :

"It will be going too far to say that in no case and under no circumstances can a legislature lay down a special procedure for the trial of a particular class of offences and the recourse to a simplified and less cumberous procedure for the trial of those offences even when abnormal conditions prevail will amount to a violation of Article 14."[67]

In fact, the Supreme Court has given divergent verdicts in various cases pertaining to special procedures and special tribunals. As it has opined, the question "should be determined in each case as it arises, for, no general rule applicable to all cases can safely be laid down."[68]

Thus an Act laying down special procedure for determining the compensation of land has been held valid by the Supreme Court. In Prakash Amirchand Sah *vs.* State of Gujarat (1986), the Supreme Court declared :

"The acquisition of land under the Town Planning Scheme by the local authority under Section 53 cannot be said to be discriminatory or offending the equality clause on the ground that local Authority has an option to acquire land under the Land Acquisition Act, 1894, which is a more favourable method of acquisition as regard the landowner. The local Authority has no such an option. On the final Town Planning Scheme coming into force under Section 53 of the Act there is an automatic vesting of all lands required by the local authority, unless otherwise provided, in the local authority. This statutory vesting operates as acquisition.

If in the above context the Act has made a special provision under Sections 67 to 71 of the Act for determining compensation payable to the owners of the original plots it cannot be said that there has been any violation of Article 14 of the Constitution."[69]

(v) Classification on the Basis of Difference in Time Age and Sex

It is the discretion of the legislature to determine the date from which the enactment shall be enforced. Such law cannot be invalidated merely because it does not affect prior transaction. Likewise an Act can be made effective with prospective or retrospective effect. "It is a matter exclusively for the legislature to decide form what date a (civil) law should be given operation and the law cannot be challenged as discriminatory in not affecting prior transaction, if it applies generally to all persons coming within its ambit as from the date on which it becomes operative."[70]

In D.D. Joshi *vs.* Union of India (1983), the Supreme Court held :

> "The choice of a date as basis of classification cannot always be dubbed as arbitrary even if no particular reason is forthcoming for the choice unless it is shown to be capricious or whimsical in the circumstances or the case." The court, therefore, in the present case ruled : "There is no division of a homogeneous class by the choice of the date. The object underlying the benefit extended to the new entrants determines the choice of the date. Inducement for attracting fresh recruits from the market must come into force by a certain date. In such a situation choice of date is not wholly arbitrary and has no tendency to divide a homogeneous class. We see no classification amongst those who enter AMC (Auxiliary Medical Corps) after acquiring a postgraduate qualification determined by the length of ante-dating benefits because each one at the relevant time obtained the advantage of ante-dating as it was then in force. There is no differential treatment. There is no division of a homogeneous class. The distinct possibility is that if petitioner's contention is accepted there would be vertical splitting of a homogeneous class. It is, therefore, difficult to accept the contention that the note under the impugned Army Instruction is violative of Article 14 or 16."[71]

Similarly, in L.P. Appelwar *vs.* State of Maharashtra (1985), The Supreme Court observed :

> "It is permissible for the legislature to make a classification on the basis of time for a law to operate provided there is a reasonable nexus between the basis of classification as to time and the object sought to be achieved."[72]

Similarly, special treatment to lunatics, minors, ladies, etc., under the Indian Contract Act is intra vires of the Constitution. The classification can also be based on the nature of persons, trade, calling or occupation, which is sought to be regulated by the legislation. As a matter of fact, "It is not possible to exhaust the circumstances or criteria which may afford a reasonable basis for classification in all cases. It depends on the objects of legislation in view and whatever has a reasonable relation to the object or purpose of the legislation is a reasonable basis for classification of the objects coming under the purview of the enactment."[73]

Article 14 provides equality to all before the law and for its enforcement has provided in the very Article, the Equal Protection clause safeguarding every person against discrimination resulting from State action, not only in the matter of substantive law put also from procedural laws. The State has been permitted to make classified legislation by enunciating the doctrine of classification, provided the same is founded on rational differentia. Though every classification is bound to produce some inequality, yet the mere production of inequality is not by itself a ground to condemn the classification made by the impugned legislation. The person who is aggrieved by the given piece of legislation has to challenge the classification as being discriminatory and irrational and prove that the difference created by the classification has no nexus with the object sought to be achieved by such a classification. As such the court has to probe the question "whether there is some difference which bears a just and reasonable relation to the object of the legislation and not to see if it has resulted in inequality."[74] Instead of entering into legal subtleties, the court has to determine it commonsensically. In ascertaining the policy behind the Act and the object sought to be achieved by it, it has to look into the title, preamble and provisions of the Act. An impugned Act has to pass the test of arbitrariness, and as Justice S.R. Das in the case of State of West Bengal *vs.* Anwar Ali Sarkar, remarked :

> "The classification must not be arbitrary but must be rational; that is to say, it must not only be based on some

qualities or characteristics which are to be found in all persons grouped together and not in others who are left out but these equalities and characteristics must have a reasonable relation to the object of the legislation. In order to pass the test, two conditions must be fulfilled, viz. (i) that the classification must be founded on an intelligent differentia which distinguished those that are grouped together from others, and (ii) that the differentia must have a rational relation to the object sought to be achieved by the Act. The differentia which is the basis of classification and the object of the Act are distinct things and what is necessary is that there must be some nexus between them."[75]

Thus, the difference which warrants a reasonable classification must be real and substantial and must bear some just and rational relation to the object sought to be achieved by the Act. In another case the Supreme Court has reiterated the test of permissible classification to the following effect :

"(1) That the classification must be founded on an intelligible differentia which distinguishes persons or objects grouped together from others outside the group;

(2) That the differentia must have a reasonable relation to the object sought to be achieved by the Act. The classification may be founded on different bases, namely, geographical or according to objects or occupations or the like, but the essential thing is that there must be a nexus between the basis of classification and the object of the Act."[76]

Likewise in K. Rajendran *vs.* State of Tamil Nadu (1982) S/2 of Tamil Nadu Abolition of Posts of Part-time Villages Officer's Act (3 of 1981) providing abolition of postes of such village officials appointed after December 16, 1970, was challenged. The Supreme Court ruled :

"The grouping together of the part-time posts mentioned in Section 2 (c) is not unconstitutional. Any classification should satisfy two tests : (1) that there exists an intelligible

> differentia between those who are grouped together and those who are not included in the group, and (2) that there exists as reasonable nexus between the differentia and the object for which classification is made."

Elaborating the Court further held : "The aspect of the case has to be examined from two angles : (1) whether the step taken by the legislature to abolish the village officers in question is so arbitrary as to conflict with Article 14 of the Constitution, and (2) whether unequals have been treated as equals by the legislature.

> "The object of the impugned legislation is to abolish posts which were part-time in nature and which had come into existence under laws, which were feudalistic in character and to replace them by posts held by new incumbents who are recruited under it. The posts were not even governed by regular service rules applicable generally to all officials in the State. Rightly, therefore, the Administrative Reform Commission recommended their abolition an reorganization of Village Service. Even though the village officers appointed after 16-12-70 are in a way different from the village officials appointed prior to that date, they too cannot be equated with the new village administrative officers who will be appointed under the Act and the rules made thereunder. It cannot, therefore, be said that Article 14 of the Constitution has been violated in abolishing the posts held by those appointed after 16.12.70."[77]

The enactment may relate to single individual, family or object or to a body corporate. The real test is whether the law arbitrarily selects the one and visits penalty on them which is not inflicted upon others guilty of a like delinquency. However, too much reliance on the doctrine of classification is fraught with the danger of surrendering the very Right into the hands of legislature and forging a weapon of oppression in the armoury of the executive. A note of caution has been sounded by Justice Bose who observed : "Even those who propound this theory (or classification) are driven to making classifications. Thus, it is not enough merely to classify but the classification must not be discriminatory, it must not amount to 'hostile action', and there must be 'reasonable grounds for distinction, it must be rational and there must be no 'substantive discrimination'. Judges must look straight into the heart of the things and regard the facts of each case correctly much as a jury would do; and yet not quite as a jury, for we are considering here as a matter of law and not just one of fact."

"Do these laws which have been called in question offend a still greater law before which even they must bow?"[78]

> As Justice Subha Rao has observed : "It shall also be remembered that a citizen is entitled to a fundamental right of equality before the law and that the doctrine of classification is only a subsidiary rule evolved by courts to give a practical content to the said doctrine. Over-emphasis on the doctrine of classification or an anxious and sustained attempt to discover some basis for classification may gradually and imperceptibly deprive the article of its glorious content. That process would inevitably end in substituting the doctrine of classification for the doctrine of equality, the fundamental right to equality before the law and equal protection of the laws may be replaced by the doctrine of classification."[79]

The right to equality before the laws emanates from the principle of equal justice. It signifies, therefore, equal justice to all. Equality before the law also denotes, as Sir Jennings has observed, "The right to sue and be sued : or to prosecute and be prosecuted, for the same kind of action, should be the same for all citizens of full age and understanding and without discrimination of race, religion, wealth, social status or political influence."[80] Thus, equal access to courts, signifying the right to sue and be sued, is a natural corollary to the equal protection clause. The Right to Equality will surely lose much of its vitality if citizens fail to enjoy equal facilities of access to the courts for the protection of their basic rights due to circumstances beyond their control. Hence, for the equal availability of the right to equal access to courts, it is the bounden duty of the State to provide for legal aid to the poor and the downtrodden, whose rights remain circumvented by the paucity of wealth or stark inequality in social status. It is only when this right is assured to the famishing millions that the right to equality will be endowed with a reality. In England this necessity has been served by passing the Aid and Advice Act 1949, providing legal aid to the poor. Article 14 of our Constitution has provided an implied guarantee of equal access to the courts and if any person is deprived of this access to the courts, "for the vindication of this legal right which others have got, there is a denial of the right to sue and be sued in the same way for the same kind of action."[81] "The meanest of citizens has a right of access to a court of law for the redress of his just grievances."[82]

Not only violation of natural justice has been held to contravene Article 14, but even all actions or laws creating injustice have been held to be violative of Article 14. In Sheel Barse *vs.* State of Maharashtra (1983), Justice P.N. Bhagwati, delivering judgement on behalf of the Supreme Court, declared :

> "Legal assistance to a poor or indigent accused who is arrested and put in jeopardy of his life or personal liberty is a constitutional imperative mandated not only by Article 39 (A) but also by Articles 14 and 21 of the Constitution. It is a necessary *sin qua non* of justice and where it is not provided, injustice is likely to result and undeniably every act of injustice corrodes the foundations of democracy and rule of law, because nothing rankles more in human heart than a feeling of injustice and those who suffer and cannot get justice because they are priced out of the legal system, lose faith in the legal process and feeling begins to overtake them that democracy and rule of law are mere slogans or myths intended to perpetuate the domination of the rich and the powerful and to protect the establishment of the vested interest."[83]

(d) Public Interest Litigation (PIL)

As the Law Commission has suggested : "If the law is to be open to everyone on the same terms, the law must be the guardian of its own gates."[84] Apart from the fact that legal assistance to the poor in a criminal trial by the State is assured under the law, it is heartening that laudable efforts have been made by the Supreme Court, during the time of

Chief Justice P.N. Bhagwati, to allay the sufferings of the poor on this count by devising a system of "Public Interest Litigation" (PIL), which tried to relate legality to justice. Indicating an inevitability in the reform of the judicial system, Justice Krishna Iyer, on behalf of the Supreme Court, had observed in Municipal Council, Ratlam *vs.* Vardichan (1980) thus :

> "Admirable though it may be (it) is at once slow and costly. It is a finished product of great beauty, but entails an immense sacrifice of time, money and talent."[85]

Again, in Fertilizer Corporation Karmachari Union *vs.* Union of India (1981), the Supreme Court observed on our judicial system :

> "This 'beautiful' system is frequently a luxury, it tends to give a high quality of justice only when, for one reason or another, parties can surmount the substantial barriers which it erects to most people and to many types of claim."[86] In another case, the court observed :
>
> "We have no doubt that in a competition between courts and streets as dispenser of justice, the rule of law must win the aggrieved persons for the law court and wean him from the lawless street. In simple terms, locus standi must be liberalized to meet the challenges of the time, ubi-jusibi-remedium must be enlarged to embrace all interests of public-minded citizens or organizations with serious concern for conservation of public resources and the direction and correction of public power so as to promote justice in its truite facets."[87]

In S. P. Gupta *vs.* Union of India (1981), the Supreme Court pithily put the reason for the relaxation of rules :

> "It is true that there are rules made by this court prescribing the procedure for moving this court for relief under Article 32 and they require various formalities to be gone through by a person seeking to approach this court. But it must not be forgotten that procedure is but a handmaiden of justice and the cause of justice can never be allowed to be thwarted by any procedural technicalities. The court would, therefore, unhesitatingly and without the slightest qualms of conscience cast aside the technical

rules of procedure in the exercise of its dispensing power and treat the letter of the public-minded individuals as a writ petition and act upon it."[88]

Again, on another occasion, Justice P.N. Bhagwati, speaking on behalf of the Supreme Court, made a significant observation on the liberalization of the rule :

> "This broadening of the rule of locus standi has been largely responsible for the development of public interest litigation, because it is only the availability of judicial remedy for enforcement which invests law with meaning and purpose or else the law would remain merely a paper parchment, a teasing illusion and a promise of unreality. It is only by liberalizing the rule of locus standi that it is possible to effectively police the corridors of power and prevent violations of law.
>
> There is also another reason why the rule of locus standi needs to be liberalized. Today we find that the law is being increasingly used as a device of organized social action for the purpose of bringing about a socio-economic change. The task of national reconstruction upon which we are engaged has brought about enormous increase in developmental activities and law is being utilized for the purpose of development—social and economic. It is creating more and more a new category of rights in favour of large sections of people and imposing a new category of duties on the State and the public officials with a view to reaching social justice to the common man. Individual rights and duties are giving place to meta-individual collective social rights and duties of classes or groups of persons."[89]

This has opened the gate of the temple of justice for the legal redress of bonded labourers, abused women, children in jails or protection homes, undertrials or prisoners who are victims of torture, starving employees of closed down factories, the afflicted millions of environmental poisoning for private greed and the victims of State atrocities like blinding, by merely posting a letter to the judge or the court on the ground of being economically or physically handicapped. "Almost the whole of public interest litigation in the Supreme Court has been initiated on the basis of a newspaper report tagged to a letter or a bare bones petition."[90] The object and purpose of public interest litigation have been lucidly depicted in the judgement of a PIL case, peoples Union for Democratic Rights *vs.* Union of India (1982), by the Supreme Court, thus :

> "Public interest litigation which is a strategic arm of the legal aid movement, and which is intended to bring justice within the reach of the poor masses, who constitute the low visibility area of humanity, is a totally different kind of litigation from the ordinary traditional litigation which is essentially of an adversary character where there is a dispute between two litigating parties. Public interest litigation is brought before the court not for the purpose of enforcing the right of one individual against another as happens in the case of ordinary litigation, but it is intended to promote and vindicate public interest which demands that violation of constitutional or legal rights of large numbers of people who are poor, ignorant or in a socially or economically disadvantaged position should not go unnoticed and unredressed. That would be destructive of the rule of law, which forms one of the essential elements of public interest in any democratic form of government. The rule of law does not mean that the protection of the law must be available only to a fortunate few or that the law should be allowed to be prostituted by vested interests for protecting and upholding the status quo under the guise of enforcement of their civil and political rights. The poor too have their civil and political rights and the rule of law is meant for them also, though to day it exists only on paper and not in reality."

After an analysis of the facts and the law relevant to the instant case, the court ruled :

> "The petitioners are employees of contractors, but the Union of India, Delhi Administration and Delhi Development Authority which have entrusted the construction work of Asiad projects to the contractors cannot escape their obligation for the observance of the various labour laws by the contractors" as per Section 16, 17, 18 of the Contract Labour (Regulation and Abolition) Act, 1970.

"It is the principle of equality embodied in Equal Remuneration Act, 1976, and if the Union of India, Delhi Administration or Delhi Development Authority at any time finds that the provisions of the Equal Remuneration Act, 1976, are not observed and the principle of euqlity before the law enshrined in Article 14 is violated by its own contractors, it cannot ignore such violation and sit quiet by adopting a non-interfering attitude and taking shelter under the executive that the violation is being committed by the contractors and not by it."[91]

REFERENCES

1. Constitution of the Indian Natonal Congress 1948 (Art.1) N.V. Raj Kumar, *op.cit.*
2. C.A.D., Vol. I, No. 5, Dec. 13, 46.
3. Draft Constitution of India (1948) : Govt. of India Press, p. 8.
4. *Young India,* Nov. 13, 1924.
5. C.A.D., Vol.VII, p. 953.
6. The Constitution of India (1986); p. 5.
7. Law of the Constituion, A.V. Dicey, p. 193.
8. *Ibid.,* p. 202.
9. The Law and the Constitution, Ivor Jennings (1955), p. 49.
10. *International Encyclopedia of the Social Sciences,* F. Oppenhein Vol. V, p. 102.
11. *International Encyclopeadia of Social Scionce* : Ed. Sills David (1968), Vol.V, p. 103.
12. Shiv Shankar *vs.* State of Madhya Pradesh; AIR 1951, Nag. 58.
13. State of U.P. *vs.* Deoman : (1961) I.S.C.R.14
14. AIR 1952. Sc.75.
15. (1952) 3. SCR. 294.
16. 1979 2. SCC. 476.
17. AIR 1952 Sc. 82.
18. AIR 1952 Sc. 284.
19. AIR 1986 Sc. 515.
20. (1985) 3 SCC. 398.
21. AIR 1986. Sc. 555.
22. AIR 1981 Sc. 746.
23. AIR 1986 Sc. 1003.
24. AIR 1986. Sc. 872.
25. AIR 1986 Sc. 1571.
26. The Constitution of U.S.A, Corwin (1953); p. 1144.
27. Shorter Constitution of India; D.D. Basu (1970) p. 27.
28. AIR 1979 Sc. 1628.

29. AIR 1978, Sc. 597.
30. (1974) 2 SCR. 348.
31. (1985) 3 SCR. 398.
32. (1967) 3. SCR. 28.
33. *The Times of India*, May 1, 1980.
33(a) Harnam Singh *vs.* R.T.A. Calcutta Region, AIR 1954.
34. Constitutional Limitations : Prof. Wills, pp. 579-80.
35. Chiranjit Lal *vs.* Union of India, (1950)-2, SCR-869.
36. *Ibid.*
37. The Constitution of India, T.K. Tope (1971) (quoted), p. 47.
38. State of Bombay *vs.* Bulsara (1951) 2. SCR. 708.
39. AIR. 1954. Sc. 314.
40. C.I. Emdon *vs.* State of U.P., AIR. 1960 Sc. 548.
41. AIR 1952 Sc. 123.
42. AIR 1983 420.
43. (1985) 3 SCC 398.
44. Ramkrishna Dalmia *vs.* Justice S.R. Tandolkar, (1959), 3 SCR. 279.
45. AIR 1986. Sc. 859.
46. Globe Theatres Ltd. *vs.* State of Madras, AIR, 1954 Sc. 691.
47. Kathi Ranning Rawat. *vs.* State of Saurashtra, AIR, 1952 Sc.123.
48. AIR 1970 Sc. 564.
49. Srinivasa Enterprises Vs. Union of India : AIR. 1981, Sc. 504.
50. Yusuf *vs* .State of Bombay : AIR 1951 Sc. 470
51. Moti Das *vs.* Sahi, AIR 1959 Sc. 942
52. G.N.Das : *op.cit.* p. 18.
53. *Ibid* : p.19.
54. State of West Bengal *vs.* Subodh Gopal Ghose, (1954) 5 SCR. 606.
55. State of Bombay *vs.* Bombay Education Society, (1955) 2 SCR. 568
56. G.N. Das, *op.cit.*, p. 20.
57. Purushottam *vs.* Desai, AIR 1956 Sc 20.
58. Khyerbani Tea Co. *vs.* State of Assam, AIR 1964, Sc. 925.
59. G.N. Das, *op.cit.* p. 21.
60. AIR 1975, Sc. 1234
61. AIR 1981, Sc. 463
62. AIR 1986, Sc. 1085.
63. AIR 1983, Sc. 634.
64. AIR 1955, Sc. 951.
65. G.N. Das., *op.cit.*, p. 22.
66. Lachman *vs.* State of Punjab, AIR 1963, Sc. 222
67. AIR 1952, Sc. 123.
68. Kangasari *vs.* State of West Bengal, AIR 1960 Sc. 457.
69. AIR 1986 Sc. 468.
70. D.D. Basu : *op.cit.* p.31.
71. AIR 1983 Sc. 420.
72. (1985) I.SCC. 479.

73. D.D. Basu : *op. cit.,* p. 31.
74. Suraj Mall *vs.* I.T.I. Commissioner, AIR 1954 Sc. 545.
75. (1952) 3 SCR. 284.
76. Bidi Supply Co. *vs.* Union of India, AIR 1956 Sc.479.
77. AIR 1982 Sc. 1107.
78. (1952) 3 SCR. 359 .
79. Lachman Das. *vs.* State of Punjab (1963) 2 SCR. 353.
80. Ivor. Jennings, *op.cit.,* p. 49.
81. D.D. Basu, *op.cit.,* p. 468.
82. Ram Pd. *vs.* State of Bihar, AIR 1953 Sc. 578.
83. (1983) BBCJ. (SC) 73.
84. Law Commission Roport, July 1972, Vol. I, para 27.
85. (1980) 4 SCC. 162.
86. (1981) I. SSC. 568.
87. (1981) I. SCC. 584.
88. (1981) Supp. Sc. 87.
89. (1981) Supp. Sc. 213.
90. *The Hindustan Times* : Dec. 22, 1986.
91. AIR 1982 Sc. 1473.

CHAPTER 4

EQUALITY OF SOCIAL STATUS

(a) Implication and Definition of Terms

The founding fathers of the Constitution knew fully well that freedom in the political sphere was meaningless for the common man, reared in the midst of deprivation and discrimination, unless it is backed by freedom in the social and economic sphere. It was, therefore, that while proclaiming justice, as one of their cherished goals, in the Preamble to the Constitution, they had enumerated the social, economic and political sphere in their order of importance. Discrimination in the Indian society was rampant chiefly because of social and economic inequality. As Rabindranath Tagore had warned : "The narrowness of sympathy which makes it possible for us to impose upon a considerable portion of humanity the galling yoke of inferiority will assert itself in our politics in creating the tyranny of injustice".[1] A Caste-ridden society, where not only the few thrived on the exploitation of the teeming millions, but where one-sixth of the population was bedeviled by the curse of untouchability, cannot enjoy the fruits of its political freedom unless the maladies in the social and economic fields are retrieved soon. As Laski has succinctly put it : "A community divided into rich and poor is, when the latter are numerous, built upon foundation of sand."[2] The constitution-makers were entrusted with the task of overcoming this oddity in the social and economic field, in so far as it can be done away by any fundamental law, and to establish a rule of law which envisages a uniform body of laws to regulate all human conduct in the State which is a manifestation of a well-organized society. A social fabric, reeking with the vice of graded inequality on the social plane and reeling in deprivation and simulation, was embalmed with the heating touch of Articles 15 and 16 providing non-discrimination in the social and economic fields as justiciable Rights of the citizen. The prevailing disabilities in the Indian society prompted the framers of the Constitution to provide prohibition of discrimination in the social plane and in the matters of public employment under the State. Gandhi had taught that life is a coherent whole and the political, social and economic life of the nation cannot be divided into water-tight compartments and the problems of the life of the nation, like those of individuals, must be dealt with as a compact whole. It was to put this Gandhian vision to practice that Nehru desired for free India a constitution which ensures, "to bring freedom and opportunity to the common man...and to create social, economic and political institutions which will ensure justice and fullness of life to every man and women."[3]

The Draft Constitution, which was considered by the Constituent Assembly before the adoption of the final form, contained provisions in respect of social equality in Articles 9, 11 and 12 of the Draft, Article 9 of the Draft Constitution was accepted and adopted as Article 15 of the Constitution in its final form. Article 15 provides social justice and guarantee against discrimination to the citizens of India in the matter of rights, privileges and immunities pertaining to him as a human being. Article 14 also prohibits the State to make discrimination against any person within the territory of India under the "equal protection" clause. But it is a general provision for all, whereas Article 15 is a specific application of Article 14 for protecting citizens only against discrimination on specific grounds of religion, race, caste, sex, place of birth or any of them. Clause 1 of the Article provides safety against discrimination by the State on the above grounds, it is to be noted that the prohibited discrimination in Article 15 is limited to specific grounds of religion, race, caste, sex, place of birth or any of them. Any discrimination to citizens on other than these grounds has to be viewed under Article 14 which provides a guarantee, in general, to all persons, against discrimination on any ground whatsoever, if it is irrational, inconsistent or unbridled. A provision, entailing prohibition for employment of children below a certain age which may impair their health or of women in mines and factories, ruinous to their health and unsuited to their strength, may not be declared void under Article 14 or challenged successfully under Article 15. However, the specific prohibitory grounds mentioned in Article 15 extend to political, civil as well as other rights of the citizen and have a wide scope.

A reading of Article 15 reveals that whereas the first clause specifies various prohibitory grounds for the State only on which it cannot discriminate between citizens for any purpose whatsoever, the second clause restrains both the State and the individual from discriminating against citizens on those grounds for the specific purpose of access to or use of public places or properties as enumerated in the clause, whosoever may be in control thereof. The third and fourth clauses enable the State to make laws enumerating special provision for women and children, and special provision for advancement of socially and educationally backward classes of citizens or for the Scheduled Castes and Scheduled Tribes notwithstanding the prohibitions stipulated in the first two clauses of Article 15. The enabling clause (3) had formed a part of the Constitution during its enactment by the Constituent Assembly. The clause (4) was added to the Constitution by the First Amendment Act, 1951.

(b) Judicial Interpretation

Article 15 (1)

Clause (1) of Article 15 provides safety against discrimination by the State. Any action of the State, discriminating on one or more of these grounds would be null and void. However, it does not prohibit the State from making discrimination on other rational grounds, apart from the exceptions enumerated in Clauses (3) and (4), such as residence, health, morality and the like, if they are in consonance with the other provisions of the Constitution.

The dictionary meaning of the word "discrimination" in clause (1) is to "make an adverse distinction with regard to or distinguish unfavourably from others". It denotes differential treatment. Thus the clause forbids discrimination or differential treatment based solely on the ground that the individual in question professes a particular religion, or comes of a particular race or caste, or is of a particular sex or is born in a particular State. The State is absolutely barred under this clause to treat any citizen unfavourably only on these various grounds. However, this bar is imposed on the State for citizens only and foreigners or resident aliens do not come within its scope. Thus, no foreigner can claim like treatment under this clause from the State and, as in India only affected person can move the Supreme Court under Article 32, cannot seek judicial protection.

The word "only" occurring in Clauses (1) and (2) is of wide import and needs clarification. It implies that no discrimination can be made on the grounds of religion, race, caste, sex, place of birth, but does not mean that no discrimination can be made on other grounds say, of residence, health, general welfare, and the like. It also means that the discrimination which attracts the provision of this clause is that which is solely based on the enumerated grounds and in no case in conjunction with other grounds. The principal of a college, for example, may certainly refuse admission to a student if he or she does not possess the requisite qualification for entrance. Similarly, the proprietor or manager of a hotel, theatre or a cinema may refuse admission to a person suffering from a contagious disease or found indulging in some disorderly conduct. Besides, if the discriminating on one or more of the enumerated grounds is made in combination with some other ground or grounds not enumerated in the Article, the impugned discrimination, not having been based solely on the enumerated grounds, cannot be invalidated under the Article. The Bombay Beggars Act, 1945 was challenged on the ground that it provided differential treatment to beggars by providing for detention of beggars in a Beggars' Home, if they were born and domiciled in the State of Bombay, and the externment of such beggars not so born and domiciled. The High Court, while dismissing the petition, stated :

"The discrimination was not based only on place of birth,

but also on another factor, domicile, and, therefore, it was not hit by Article 15."[4]

Similarly, in Giridhar Gopal *vs.* State of Madhya Bharat it was held by the High Court that Section 354 IPC envisaging penal provision for outraging the modesty of women is not within the scope of Article 15. "For in addition to the consideration of sex, there were other considerations e.g. proprietary, public morals, decency, decorum and rectitude".[5]

The word "Religion" implies that no special privilege can be accorded by the State to any individual citizen nor can it be so claimed by the latter, on the ground of religion. Our Constitution establishes a Secular State guaranteeing freedom of conscience and freedom to profess, practice and propagate any religion to all persons in Articles 25 to 28 of the Constitution. Article 15(1) and 15 (2), therefore, enjoin upon the State not to make any discrimination in any public matter concerning a citizen, except as otherwise provided under the Constitution. Religion, therefore, will not be a sole ground of restriction or limitation in a citizen's access to any shop, restaurant, hotel or places of public entertainment, or their use of wells, tanks and places of public resort maintained, wholly or partly, out of the State fund, or dedicated to the use of the general public.

The word "race" signifies an assurance to the different races of the world that India shall be a free country wherein no racial prejudice can be sustained, not only by the State in the public matter, but also by private individuals at public places or places of public resort. There shall be no racial discrimination, which has been a patent source of litigation in America, and the policy of apartheid of South Africa where Indians and native Africans have undergone untold sufferings. Article 14 does away, once for all, with any such discrimination for all persons and Article 15 and 15(2) specifically prohibits such discrimination for citizens. A citizen, be he of any race or colour, will be protected against all discriminations arising out of race in the matter of his access to shops, hotels, public restaurants and places of public entertainment and also of his use of wells, tanks, roads and places of public resort, either maintained, wholly or partly, out of State fund, or dedicated to the use of the general public.

The inclusion of the word "caste" heralds an era of unification and integration of the Hindu society, which was ravaged by the curse of untouchability. It had also dwarfed one-sixth of the nation, by casting them away from the mainstream of the Hindu social fabric. Any act of the State based solely on caste consideration shall be void. Similarly, caste cannot be a sole ground of discrimination with citizens with regard to his access to or his use of public place or property as enumerated in Clause (2) even by private individuals managing or owning a public place or property.

The inclusion of word "sex" denotes an era of liberation of women along with men in free India and sounds a death-knell to all differential treatment with the womenfolk causing humiliation and hardship. The State cannot frame laws differentiating disadvantageously the womenfolk from men, and further, in getting access to public places or properties women cannot be differentiated to their disadvantage or to the extent detrimental to their interest. They are assured equal treatment, equal political and civil rights, like suffrage, employment, etc. Not only are they guaranteed equality of treatment, to be treated on par with men, but are granted protective discrimination with men where, on account of the fraility of their physique or the compulsions of motherhood, it so required. Clause (3) of the Article provides that the State can make special provision for them. Thus, on the one hand, women are assured of equal treatment, and on the other, they are specially provided for protective discrimination where their interest so warrants.

The insertion of the words "place of birth" in Clauses 1 and 2 of Article 15 is intended to do away with the disruptive forces and provincialism that may set in, bringing disaster to the unity of India. The provision is designed to strengthen national unity and solidarity of the nation. It may, however, be mentioned that the term "place of birth" did not find place in Article 9 of the Draft Constitution prepared by the Drafting Committee of the Constituent Assembly of India. It was interested in Article 9 by way of amendment, on the motion of Syed Abdul Rout in the Constituent Assembly on November 29, 1948. Speaking in favour of his motion, he said : "I am afraid, Sir, the evil elements who might attempt to make discrimination against citizens will do so not on the ground of religion, race, caste or sex...In my opinion attempts may be made to make discrimination against citizens on the ground of place of birth and under the guise of local patriotism. To guard against this possibility I have brought this amendment and I hope it will be accepted."[6] The amendment was finally included in the grounds prohibited, under Clauses (1) and (2) of Article 15 of the Constitution of India.

The mention of "place of birth" as probihited ground of discrimination should not be confused to mean that no discrimination can be made on the ground of "residence" or "domicile". If a State grants its residents free education up to the higher secondary level, it shall be acting within the constitutional bound, for the Constitution prohibits is only "place of birth" and the State is free to discriminate on the ground of "residence" or domicile. In fact, the States of the Union can be empowered under a parliamentary legislation, in regard to a particular class or classes of employment or appointment, to impose a requirement as to residence within that State or Union Territory for a particular period prior to such employment or appointment, as provided by Article 16(3). But, unless Parliament so prescribes, the State is bound under Article 14 and is not entitled to disqualify a candidate seeking employment or appointment to an office under the State solely on the ground of "residence".

The technical terms occurring in Article 15 (1) having been defined, it is desirable to compendiously put forth the judicial interpretations of Clause (1) of Article 15, in order to get a clear view of the matter.

In Indra Narayan *vs.* State of West Bengal, Article 15(1) came up for special consideration. The West Bengal Foodgrains (Movement Control) Order, 1951 was objected to in this case on the ground that it sought to discriminate on the ground of place of birth. The order restricted free movement of foodgrains not only from one State to another but also from a blockaded area to a place outside the blockade area within the State, except on a permit. It was contended that persons born within a blockaded area were put under special disability, for they were restrained from moving foodgrains from their place of birth to any place outside. However, it was held by the High Court that the prohibition did not arise from the fact that the citizen concerned was born at a particular place but it was in the interest of the general public of that particular area that foodgrains should be made available to them sufficiently and in time during lean seasons or period of sacrcity."[7]

Similarly, the Bombay Prevention of Hindu Bigamous Marriages Act 25 of 1945 was upheld on the ground that introduction of social reform by stages, territorywise or communitywise, was not an unreasonable basis of classification and does not amount to discrimination [State of Bombay *vs.* Noresu Appu Mali-AIR (1952) Bombay]. Likewise, the Madras Hindu (Bigamy Prevention and Divorce) Act VI of 1949 was impugned as violating Article 15 as it sought to discriminate between citizens professing different religions, punishing only the Hindus for bigamy, while others were left out. It was held that the alleged differentiation did not occur as a result of discrimination on the ground of religion by a law of the State, but was the result of an enactment made under Item 5 of List III in the Seventh Schedule of the Constitution of India codifying the personal law of the Hindus. If polygamy was considered a present social evil among the Hindus, legislation to end it was not ultra vires. It was further held that the State may decide to bring about reform either on a territorial basis or communitywise. The Muslims have easy divorce laws, and polygamy is legitimate according to their personal law, while a Hindu marriage is indissoluble in its pious form, according to the personal law applicable to them. Therefore, if the law with regard to bigamous marriages is not uniform the difference cannot be said to be arbitrary but based on a valid ground (AIR 1952, Madras, p. 198).

In the Lakshmindra Teertha Swamiar *vs.* The Commissioner, Hindu Religious Endowments case, the Madras High Court held that the classification of institutions, based on religion—Hindu, Muslum, Christian—was neither arbitrary nor unreasonable having regard to the object of the Act, viz. better management of such institutions (AIR, 1952, Madras, p. 613).

A famous case came up for decision in the Supreme Court whose judgement moved the Union Government to amend the Constitution and insert Clause (4) in Article 15 for protecting the interest of the Backward Classes and Scheduled

Castes and Scheduled Tribes. In the case, Champakam Dareirajan *vs.* State of Madras, "The Madras Communal Government Order" was challenged by the petitioner, Smt. Champakam, as violating Article 15(1). This order controlled admission to colleges on the basis of an arbitrary ratio which provided that for every fourteen seats, the candidates should be selected communitywise in the ratio as stipulated in the order. The Madras High Court declared the order as violative of Article 15(1). The Chief Justice. P.V. Rajmannar, while delivering the judgement, observed :

> "The Communal Government order states that a limited number of seats are allowed to members of a particular caste, namely, Brahmins. The qualifications which enable a Brahmin candidate to secure a seat in a college would necessarily be higher than the qualifications which would enable a person of another caste or religion to secure admission. There is thus clear discrimination."[8]

The above decision of the Madras High Court was upheld in appeal by the Supreme Court, which observed :

> "Though the Government could prescribe qualifications and standards for admission of students, these should be reasonably relevant and must be the same for all citizens seeking admission to educational institutions."[9]

Again, in Yusuf Abdul Aziz *vs.* State of Bombay the apparent discrimination on the ground of sex under Section 497 of the IPC was legally justified as not contravening Article 15(1). The Court held that while Article 15(1) provides a general protection against discrimination, Article 15(3) ensures an exception to this general principle and authorizes special provision for women. The conditions of women in India justifies such a safeguard to them and this is what explains when "men" alone are penalized under Section 497 IPC. In appeal, the Supreme Court upheld the contention of the High Court. It observed : "Article 14 is general and must be read with the other provisions which set out the ambit of the Fundamental Rights. Sex is a second basis of classification, and although there can be no discrimination in general on that ground, the Constitution itself provides for special provisions in the case of women and children."[10] It is thus obvious that for the protection and upliftment of women, any constitutional or legal bottlenecks can be removed by the State under the special provision of Article 15(3) of the Constitution and it cannot be challenged on the ground of reasonable classification under Article 14 of the Constitution.

In public matters, no discrimination can be made merely on the ground that a citizen is born in a particular place in India. In this connection, a famous case, State of Bombay *vs.* Shaik Husain may be cited. Section 27 (2A) of the City of Bombay Police Act provided that a person once convicted of certain offence could be externed from Greater Bombay if he was a person born outside Greater Bombay, while a similar person born in Greater Bombay could not be so externed. The impugned section was struck down as violative of Article 15(1) as there was clear discrimination on the ground of place of birth.[11]

In Jagwant Kaur *vs.* State of Bombay, the Maharashtra Government had initiated the construction of a Harijan Colony exclusively for Harijans. This was challenged on the ground of discrimination on the basis of caste. It was held in this case that although Section 5 of the Bombay Land Acquisition Act, 1948, was discriminatory since it allowed the construction of a colony soley for Harijans, but after insertion of Clause (4) in Article 15 which postulstes special provision for the Scheduled Castes the statutes was intra vires (AIR 1952, Bombay 461).

Similarly, in Dattatraya Motiram More *vs.* State of Bombay it was held by the High Court that the provision in Section 10(1) of the Bombay Municipal Boroughs Act for reservation of seats for women and the rules made by the Government there under were intra vires of Articles 14 to 16.[12]

The U.P. Court of Words Act 1912 empowering the Government to declare a lady incompetent to manage her property merely on the ground of sex was declared void, in Mrs. Cracknell *vs.* State of U.P. (AIR 1952 All. 746). It was held that the provision that a female proprietor could be disqualified at the will of the government while a male proprietor could be so declared on a specific grounds and only after giving an opportunity to be heard was a clear violation of Articles 14 and 15 on the ground of sex.

But in Pratap Singh *vs.* Union of India (1985), the Supreme Court held Section 14(1) of the Hindu Succession Act, 1956, neither vague nor uncertain nor violative of Articles 14 and 15 (1), being a beneficent provision enacted to remedy the plight of Hindu women. It observed :

> "The petitioner in this case over-looks the benign constitutional provision in Clause (3) of Article 15 of the Constitution which provides that nothing in Article 15 shall prevent the State from making any special provision for women and children. The said provision overrides Article 15(1)...Section 14(1) of the Act was enacted to remedy to some extent the plight of a Hindu women who could not claim absolute interest in the properties inherited by her from her husband but who could only enjoy them with all the restrictions attached to a widow's estate under the Hindu law. There is now hardly any justification for the males belonging to the Hindu community to raise any objection to the beneficent provision contained in Section 14 (1) of the Act on the ground of hostile discrimination. The above provision is further protected by the express provision contained in Clause 3 of Article 15, since it is a special provision enacted for the benefit of Hindu women."[13]

In Nainsukh Das *vs.* State of U.P., the Supreme Court explicity laid down the principle that any law making provision for election on the basis of separate electorate for members of different religious communities was void as being discriminative on the ground of religion, according to Article 15(1). Any election held in pursuance of such a law, after the enforcement of the Constitution, shall be void.[14]

In University of Madras *vs.* Shanta Bai, the High Court observed that the question of refusal to admit a lady student into a college under its rules really comes within Article 29(2) and not under Article 15(1) and the university is under no obligation to admit a lady student beyond the provisions of its rules. It further held that the case would have attracted the provision of Article 15(1), if the university was being maintained by the State, not otherwise. Thus the University of Madras, being a State-aided institution, was under no constitutional obligation to admit a lady student beyond the number of seats for women fixed after consideration of hostel accommodation available for them.[15] In an earlier decision of the Punjab High Court in Omprakash *vs.* State of Punjab, the court ruled that where, however, the rules for admission do not contravene the rights conferred by Articles 14, 15 and 29 (2) and are otherwise reasonable, it is open to the college authorities to refuse admission under their rules of admission.[16] Likewise, in Jaichand *vs.* State of Punjab, Rule 6 of the Punjab University calendar was declared intra vires. The rule providing a list of compulsory subjects in a classical language stipulated that Urdu can be offered only by Europeans, Anglo-Indians and women. The court held that the classification was not arbitrary and did not offend Article 15 in that it was not based only on sex, religion or place of birth but on other considerations also. It was further held that Punjab University being state aided and not State maintained, their regulations could not come within the scope of Article 15(1).[17]

In O.P. Joshi *vs.* State of Madhya Bharat, capitation fee for admission from Non-Madhya Bharat students and exemption from it to the residents of the State was not held discriminatory under Article 15(1) since the discrimination was not based on the ground of place of birth but on residential qualification.[18]

But in Dr. Pradeep Jain *vs.* Union of India (1984) the wholesale reservation of seats by some States in the medical colleges on the ground of residence, etc. was held void and in contravention of Article 15(1). The Supreme Court ruled :

> "Wholesale reservation made by some of the State Governments on the basis of "domicile" or residence requirements within the States or on the basis of the institutional preference for students who have passed the qualifying examination held by the University of the State, excluding all students not satisfying this requirement, regardless of "merit" was unconstitutional and void as offending the equality clauses of the Constitution".

The court after condemning such wholesale reservation, proceeded to observe that viewed in the perspective of social justice, some type of reservation based on residential requirement or institutional preference for students passing the qualifying examination held by the University or State may be justified to an extent. As to the extent of such reservation, the court observed : "Such reservation could in no event exceed the outer limit of 70% of the total member of 'open seats' after taking into account other kinds of reservation. We are laying down this outer limit or reservation in an attempt to reconcile the apparently conflicting claims of equality and excellence."[19]

A year after in Dr. Dinesh Kumar *vs.* Motilal Nahru Medical College, Allahabed (1985), the Supreme Court clarified the rule laid down by it in the above case, as the above judgement was misinterpreted to mean that 30 per cent of the total number of seats available for admission to the M.B.B.S. course in medical colleges should be kept free from reservation on the basis of residential requirement or institutional preference. "That is total misreading of our judgement. What we have said in our judgement is that after providing for reservation validly made, whatever seats remain available for non-reserved categories, 30 per cent of such seats at the least, should be left free for open competition and admission to such 30 per cent open seats should not be based on residential requirement or institutional preference, but students from all over the country should be able to compete for admission to such 30 per cent open seats".[20] And for postgraduate courses, M.D. and M.S. such percentage of "open seats" was fixed at 50 per cent on the basis of an all-India competitive test for admission to those seats, like that of the "open seats" in the M.B.B.S. course.

Thus, excessive reservation in the matter of admission in medical courses on the ground of residential requirement or institutional preference was struck down :

> "In the case of State of Rajasthan *vs.* Thakur Pratap Singh, which came up before the Supreme Court, Section 15(5) of the Police Act was impugned as violative of Article 15(1) of the Constitution, which sought to impose a levy on the villages, where an additional police force was required to be stationed, to meet the cost of the additional force, while exempting Harijans and Muslims from the incidence of the tax on the ground that they were peaceful. The court held the tax to be invalid, as there was no reasonable basis for the classification, peacefulness being an individual not a communal featurs."[21]

An analysis of some judicial decisions cited above leads to the following conclusions with regard to the ambit of Article 15(1) :

1. The impugned discrimination must be based solely on the ground of religion, race, caste, sex, place of birth or any of them, which are prohibited under Article 15 but discrimination on one or more of these grounds in conjunction with some other grounds may attract the provision of Article 14, not of Article 15 (1).
2. The Clause (1) of Article 15 relates to State only and the other clause (2), attracts both State and individual's actions.
3. Thus discrimination made even on the ground of place of birth can be upheld in the public interest or if it is purported to serve the general welfare.
4. The provisions of Clause (1) are applicable only to State-maintained institutions and not to State-aided or affiliated institutions.
5. Discrimination on the ground of personal law of the two religions cannot be invalidated.
6. Discrimination on the ground of social reform, territorywise or communitywise, can be upheld.
7. Classification of institutions and endowments based on religion and legislation for their separate and more efficient administration are not discriminatory under Article 15(1).
8. Separate electorates for different religious communities are barred under Clause (1) of Article 15.
9. Article 15 (1) is applicable to all legal rights, privileges and immunities of a citizen.
10. Residential qualification for admission in institution cannot be held discriminatory.
11. Special provision for protection and upliftment of women, in view of the conditions of women in India, cannot be held discriminatory.
12. Discrimination with women on the ground of sex is not permissible.

Article 15(2)

At the outset, it is noteworthy to add that, though the prohibited grounds of discrimination mentioned under clauses (1) and (2) are similar, yet they differ in that while the former prohibits discrimination by the State only, the latter restrains both the State and private individuals from providing or effecting any discrimination with citizens. Thus, Clause (2) is meant to establish social equality without any discrimination. The Constitution lays the gravestone of an old unjust order and the cornerstone of the new humane order. The prohibition of racial discrimination under Clause (2) is a novelty of the Indian Constitution. "Prohibition against discrimination on grounds of race even in public places managed by private individuals places the Indian Constitution in advance of any other leading constitution of the world."[22]

Thus, Clause (2) prohibit racial segregation and discrimination on the basis of colour, even on the part of private individuals, along with the State. In the USA, in Shelly *vs.* Kramer, the Supreme Court held that the "equal protection clause" of the 14th Amendment merely restricts discriminatory State action and not discriminations by private individuals. It is, therefore, that racial segregation and discrimination by private individuals even at public places is prevalent in America. In South Africa, Indians and native Africans have no access to these public restaurants, waiting rooms, hotels and places of public entertainment which are exclusively meant for whites.

Sub-clause (a) of Clause 2 of Article 15 postulates that no citizen shall be subjected to any disability, liability, resriction or condition with regard to access to shops, public restaurants, hotels and places of public entertainment, on grounds only of sex, religion, race, caste, place of birth or any of them. Here the word "disability" connotes a burden or pecuniary punishment or otherwise : a "restriction" signifies curtailment of the qualification : and a "condition" postulates essential requirement, which will enforce the exercise of the right to access. However, the owners of these public places cannot be deemed to transgress constitutional limitation if some extra fee for extra comfort or separate accommodation is charged or restrict entry of persons on other grounds beyond the pale of the constitutional prohibitions say, health, public order and the like. But private places or concerns where the general public has no right of access, e.g. religious and social functions of a family, private burial ghats, etc. do not come under the purview of this clause.

It may be mentioned here that the word "shop" in Sub-clause (a) has been used in a broad sense of a place where people purchase services or objects or both. The word was explained by Dr. Ambedkar in the Constituent Assembly as :

> "The word "shop" does include laundry and shaving places. To define the word "shop" in the most generic term one can think of, is to state that 'shop' is a place where the owner is prepared to offer his service to anybody who is prepared to go there seeking his service."[23] Similarly, to a query whether the word included the offices of a doctor or lawyer, Dr. Ambedkar answered : "Certainly, it will include anybody who offers his services, I am using it in a generic sense. I should like to point out, therefore, that the word 'shop' used here is not used in the limited sense of permitting entry. It is used in the larger sense of requiring the services if the terms of services are agreed to."[24]

Though the Constitution does not itself defines technical words, which are left to interpretation in the judicial domain, the Untouchability (Offences) Act, 1955, lays down definition of certain terms. Section 2(E) of the Act explains a "shop" appearing in Article 15 as :

Shop "means any premises where goods are sold either wholesale or by retail or both wholesale and by retail and includes a laundry, a hair-cutting saloon and any other place where services are rendered to customers."[25]

Section 2(a) of the Act defines "places of public entertainment" as follows :

"Any place to which the public are admitted and in which an entertainment is provided or held.

Explanation : Entertainment includes any exhibition, performance, game, sport and any other form of amusement."[26]

Thus, Sub-clause (a) of Clause 2 provides a wides scope to the public to have access to even those places which are under the ownership of private persons, and where member of the public may not generally have a legal right to enter, if any public entertainment is arranged there.

Similarly, Sub-clause (b) of Clause 2 of Article 15 provides that citizens shall not be subjected to any disability, liability, restriction or condition on grounds only of religion, race, caste, sex, place of birth or any of them, with regard to their use of wells, tanks, bathing ghats, roads and places of public resort which are either wholly or partly maintained by State funds or which are dedicated to the use of the general public. It implies, first, that the citizens have a right to the use of even those wells, tanks, bathing ghats, roads and places of public resort which, though not mantained, partly or wholly, by the State fund are merely dedicated to the use of the general public and, second, all wells, tanks, bathing ghats, roads, and places of public resort which are either State-maintained or State-aided, are open to the use of all citizens, without any discrimination solely on the prohibited grounds mentioned in the Article. Even a customary right of use can be subjected to a test of reasonableness, if that right is sought to be restricted. In the case Arumugha Kumar *vs.* Narayan Asari, the Madras High Court after testing the validity of a custom with reference to Article 15 (2b) held it to be invalid as it restricted the use of a village well to certain families. The court ruled :

> "If a section of the public puts forward an exclusive right to the use of a public well, it must establish that the well was not dedicated to the use of the general public but was dedicated to the exclusive use of the particular section of the public."[27]

The technical word "place of public resort" or public place requires to be explained in view of the divergent views regarding its definition. D.D. Basu defines it as :

> "A place is one of public resort, if members of the public are, in fact, allowed access and where they habitually resort to, irrespective of any legal right to be there."[28]

Section 4 of the Untouchability (Offences) Act, 1955 provides the implication :

> "(iv) The use of, or access to, any river, stream, spring, well, tank, cistern water-tap or other watering place, or any bathing ghat, burial or cremation ground, any sanitary convenience, any road, or passage, or any other place of public resort which other members of the public or persons professing the same religion or belonging to the same religious denomination or any section thereof. As such person, have a right to use or have access to;[29]
>
> (v) The use of, or access to, any place used for a charitable or a public purpose maintained wholly or partly out of State funds or dedicated to the use of the general public, or persons professing the same religion, or belonging to the same religious denomination or any section thereof, as such person."[30]

Section 2(d) of the Act, further defines place of public worship as follows :

> "Place of public worship means a place by whatever name known, which is used as a place of public religious worship or which is dedicated generally to, or used generally by, persons professing any religion, or belonging to any religious denomination or any section thereof, for the performance of any religious service or for offering prayers therein and includes all lands and subsidiary shrines or apartment attached to any such place."[31]

The above three sub-sections of the Untouchability (Offences) Act, 1955, throw ample light on the words used in Sub-clause (b) of Clause 2 of Article 15. Further, the "place of public resort" as included in the Sub-clause (b) lays down that the particular place should be one either (i) wholly maintained by State fund, or (ii) partly aided by State fund, or (iii) dedicated to the use of the general public. Either of the three conditions must be fulfilled so that a place may be deemed to be "a place of public resort". Also, the dedication of a place to the use of the general public may either be complete or partial—"a complete dedication, when the owner of the property completely divests himself of ownership and vest the property in some religious, charitable or social institution or object"[32] and partial "if the owner retains the property himself but grants to the community an "easement" over it for certain specified purpose."[33]

Explaining the word "places of public resort" Dr. Ambedkar said in the Constituent Assembly :

> "The term "places of public resort" would include a burial ground, subject to the fact that such a burial ground was maintained wholly or partly out of public funds"[34] and, he said :
>
> "Where there are no burial grounds maintained by a municipality, local board or taluk board or provincial government or village Panchayat, no body of course has any right, because there is no public place about which anybody can make a claim for entry. But if there is a burial ground maintained by the State out of State funds, then obviously every person would have every right to have his body buried or cremated therein...the word 'public' is used here in a special sense. A place is a place of public resort provided it is maintained wholly or partly out of State funds. It has nothing to do with the definition (of the word 'public') given in the Indian Penal Code."[35]

In this connection, "a case Deane *vs.* Commissioner of Police came up before the Calcutta High Court, in which the court observed :

> "The Calcutta Maidan, an extensive open space, maintained by the Government of India, is a place of public resort within the meaning of Article 15 (2) (b)."[36]

Article 15 (3)

The enumeration of Clause (3) of Article 15 is a device of protective discrimination in the interest of woman and children granted to the State as an exception to the principle of equality enunciated in Articles 14 to 16 of the Constitution, to enable it to make special provision for them in consonance with their interest and also to secure the Directive Principle of State Policy on the subject under Part IV of the Constitution.

Thus, Clause (3) is an exception to the rule against discrimination, subject to the rider that the provision is not arbitrary or irrational out-turning the object of the Rule itself. Especially, after the verdict of the Supreme Court in Keshavanand Bharati *vs.* State of Kerala case (AIR 1973, Sc. 1461) when the Directive Principles of State Policy has been given an edge over the Fundamental Rights, the State is now under no constitutional restraints generally to fulfil the cherished aspiration of the Farther of the Constitution and Father of the Nation to usher in a social and ceonomic domocracy and bring a fundamental change in the structure of the Indian society. Concessions to women and children like maternity relief to women workers, special provision at public place for women and children, limited hours of work and reservation of seats in institutions and of posts in employment for women can be fairly initiated under this clause, apart from protection against any disadvantageous discrimination of women against men accruing to them under Articles 14 to 16. In Anjali Roy *vs.* State of West Bengal, the order of the Director of Public Instruction was impugned on the ground that it directed the transfer of admitted girl student of one college having co-education to a newly-started women's college. It was held by the High Court that it was in the interest of promoting development of a new college for women and, therefore, did not violate Article 15 (3). The special provision for women and children in Article 15 (3) was in favour and not against the interest of women.[37] In Dattatraya *vs.* State of Bombay, the High Court observed that "the State may discriminate in favour of women against man, not vice-versa" and held that "reservation of seats for women in a college"[38] was not violative of Article 15.

Similarly, in Yusuf Abdul Aziz *vs.* State of Bombay, the Supreme Court held Section 497 IPC which exempted women from punishment as an abetter of the offence of adultery, as intra vires on the basis that the discrimination was not based on the ground of sex alone.[39] However, with significant changes in our social life after independence, this section has been amended by enacting the Indian Penal Code (Amendment) Act 1972 which has placed women on a equal footing with men for seeking redress against crime of adultery since the amended section now provides that a women who acts as an "abetter" and consents to or encourages a married man to commit adultery would be liable for prosecution by the wife of the adulterous man.

In Binay Bhusan Chakravarty *vs.* Govind Chandra Sharma, the court upheld Rule 3 of the Election Rules under the Assam Municipal Act of 1923 which provided some special voting facilities to women. This discrimination was held valid under Article 15(3) of the Constitution.[40]

Again, in a far-reaching significant judgement in the case Mohd. Ahmed Khan *vs.* Shah Banu Begum, the Supreme Court held that a divorced Muslim wife was entitled to maintenance from her former husband under Section 125 Cr. P.C. so long as she does not marry, and declared that "there is no conflict between the provisions of Section 125 Cr. P.C. and those of the Muslim personal law on the question of the Muslim husband's obligation to provide maintenance for a divorced wife who is unable to maintain herself."[41] The judges observed that the religion professed by a spouse had no place in the scheme of these provisions. "Whether the spouses are Hindus, or Muslims, Christians or Parsees, Pagans or heathens, is wholly irrelevant in the application of these provisions."[42] it was held that Section 125 Cr. P.C. is truly secular in character and "overrides the personal law, if there is any conflict between the two".[43] The judges regretted that "Article 44 of the Constitution which said the State shall endeavour to secure for the citizens a uniform civil code throughout the territory of India had remained a dead letter."[44]

Article 15 (4)

The Clause (4) of Article 15 was not originally provided for in the Constitution but was inserted by way of amendment according to Section 2 of the Constitution (First Amendment) Act, 1951 which received the assent of the President on June 18, 1951. The Government of the day had brought this amendment before the Parliament soon after the adverse judgements in Champakam Dorai Rajan and C.R. Shrinivasan cases delivered by the Supreme Court of India [AIR (1951) SC 226 and (1951) S.C.R. (525)]. Wherein a full bench of the

Supreme Court held that the order of the Madras Government enforcing certain rules regarding admission to the medical and engineering colleges of the states, communitywise and also districtwise, Constitutes a clear violation of Article 29 (2) of the Constitution. Justice S.R. Das. while delivering the judgement, interpreted Clauses (1) and (2) of Article 29 as follows :

> "It will be noticed that while Clause (1) protects the language, script or culture of a section of the citizens, Clause (2) guarantees the fundamental right of an individual citizen. The right to get admission into any educational institution of the kind mentioned in Clause (2) is a right which an individual citizen has as a citizen and not as a member of any community or class of citizens. This right is not to be denied to the citizen on grounds only of religion, race, caste, language or any of them. If a citizen who seeks admission in any such educational institution has not the requisite academic qualifications and is denied admission on that ground he certainly cannot be heard to complain of an infraction of his fundamental right under this article. But, on the other hand, if he has the academic qualifications but is refused admission only on grounds of religion, race, cast, language or any of them, then there is a clear breach of his fundamental right."[45] Thus, the purpose of Clause (4) is to bring Article 15 and 29 in conformity with Articles 16 (4), 46 and 340 so as to make it constitutional for the State to reserve seats in educational institutions for the advancement of socially and educationally backward classes of citizens and Scheduled Castes and Scheduled Tribes. It harmonizes the fundamental right of citizens with the claim of social good. In fact, the amendment has completed the code of equality into a triangle, concordating Articles 14 to 16, which embody the essence of classless egalitarianism envisaged by the Father of the Nation. Apart from serving the fundamental needs of the common man it is designed to bring about a structural change in the Indian social order. But as has been rightly observed by justice Reddy in Keshavanand Bharati *vs.* State of Kerala case, with reference to the provisions of the first Amendment Act,

that "these provisions do not in any way abrogate the right in Article 14."[46]

In Gurumukh Singh *vs.* Union of India case, the Constitution Scheduled Castes Order, 1953 issued by the President of India under Article 341 (1) was impugned as discriminatory. The said order notified 34 different castes of Punjab as Scheduled Caste in that State. Para 3 of the order stated that no person who professes a religion other than Hinduism should be deemed to be a member of the Scheduled Caste. He was a Bawara Sikh not included in the list and contended that discrimination on the ground of religion rendered the order unconstitutional. The Supreme Court observed that Clause 4 of the Article 15 and Article 341 were exceptions to the general rule laid down in clause 1 of Article 15. The power of the President under Article 341 of the Constitution in selecting a caste or even a group within a caste for special treatment is within his competence. Thus, if the President selected four castes and further selected groups within thirty castes in Punjab for their inclusion in the list of Scheduled Castes, it was within the scope of this power and this right of pick and choose was not contrary to the provision of Clause 1 of the Article 15 as regulated by Clause 4 of the same Article. The Court has no authority to go into the question whether a group within a caste is actually backward or not.[47]

In Thomas *vs.* State of Madras, the court held that concessions cannot be demanded as a matter of right and if under Article 15 (4) special encouragement was given to the Backward Classes and the government sought to include among them only a particular category of Harijan convert boys and not other, the court cannot question it. If the government made some allowance to recent converts only, the petitioner could not claim the same. He could not be treated as a recent convert since his grandfather was converted to Christianity and thus a case of discrimination could not be made out.[48]

A similar question arose before the Supreme Court in the case of Principal, Medical College, Guntur *vs.* V. Mohan Rai. The Supreme Court was of the opinion that a person whose parents belonged to a Scheduled Caste before their conversion to Christianity, can, on conversion or reconversion to Hinduism, be regarded as a member of the Scheduled Caste only if he is accepted as a member of that caste by the other members of the caste. On such acceptance he would be eligible for the benefit of reservation of seats for Scheduled Castes in the matter of admission to a medical college. In the words of Justice P.N. Bhagwati "It will, therefore, be seen that on conversion to Hinduism, a person born of Christian converts would not become a member of the caste to which his parents belonged prior to their conversion to Christianity, automatically or as a matter of course, but he would become such a member, if the other members of the caste accept him as a member and admit him within the fold it is for the member of the caste to decide whether or not to admit a person within the caste. Since, the caste is a social combination of persons governed by its rules and regulations, it may, if its rules and regulations so provide, admit a new member just as it may expel an existing member."[49]

In Ramkrishna Singh *vs.* State of Mysore, a government notification, providing reservation of seats for admission to medical colleges containing a list of Backward Classes composed of 95 per cent of the total population of the State leaving only a few castes and communities, was challenged. The High Court was of the opinion that determination of Backward Classes was not based on an intelligible principle since it deprived only a few castes and communities from the benefit of reservation of seats in medical colleges, and held that it was more a discrimination against those castes and communities who were left out in the list than a provision for the backward classes. Moreover, it was a provision not for the socially and educationally backward classes, but for the classes who were comparatively backward to the most forward classes. The court, therefore, held the notification void under Article 15(4).[50]

In State of Uttar Pradesh *vs.* Pradeep Tandon, the main question for consideration was whether the instructions framed by the state in making reservations for admission of students to medical colleges of the State in favour of candidates from rural areas, hill areas and Uttarakhand were constitutionally valid. It was held by the Supreme Court that the reservation for rural area could not be sustained on the basis that the rural area represented socially and educationally backward classes of citizens. This reservation was made for the majority population of the State. Eighty percent of the population in the State of U.P. in rural area cannot be a "homogeneous class" by itself. Their occupation and standard were different. Population cannot be a class by itself. Rural element does not make it a class. "Poverty in rural areas cannot also be the basis of classification to support reservation for rural area."

Poverty is found in all parts of India."[51] The Supreme Court further maintained that the reservation on the ground of place of birth violates Article 15. So, the reservation of seats for candidates from rural area was unconstitutional on this ground also because the incidence of birth in rural areas was made the basic qualification. The Supreme Court finally held that "the reservation of seats in favour of candidates from rural area is unconstitutional. The reservation for the Hill and Uttarakhand is severable and these are valid."[52] Further, as Chief Justice A.N. Roy ruled :

> "The reservation for rural areas cannot be sustained on the ground that the rural areas represent socially and educat-ionally backward classes of citizens. This reservation appears to be made for the majority population of the State. Eighty-six per cent of the population of the State cannot be a homogeneous class. Poverty in rural areas cannot be the basis of classification to support reservation for rural area."[53]

Similarly, in Miss Arti Sapru *vs.* State of Jammu and Kashmir (1981), the Government order classifying more than 95 per cent of the villages as socially and educationally backward calling for reserve quotas in the matter of admission to medical colleges was challenged under Article 15(4) of the Constitution. The Supreme Court ruled :

> "The classification attempted by the State Government by its order dated 24 September, 1980 suffers from the vice of arbitrariness and must be declared invalid. There is no intelligible differentia is before us to sustain the classification. No doubt the State Government had acted in its own wisdom, but the material to which the wisdom was applied has not been disclosed at all. The fact by itself that some hundreds of villages have been brought

within the classification is of no assistance whatever...We are not satisfied that the State Government has succeeded in bringing the case within Article 15(4) of the Constitution."[54]

The judgement of the Supreme Court in M.R. Balaji *vs.* State of Mysore was a landmark in the history of judicial interpretation of Clause (4) of Article 15. The Mysore Government by an order reserved twenty-eight per cent, twenty-two per cent, fifteen per cent and three per cent of the total seats in medical and engineering colleges of the State for Backward Classes, more Backward Classes, Scheduled Castes and Scheduled Tribes respectively. The Supreme Court held that the impugned order was a fraud on the Constitutional power conferred on the State, and quashed the order. While interpreting Article 15(4), the judgement of the court has hammered home the following points :

(a) The backwardness relevant to Article 15(4) must be social and educational.

(b) The social backwardness is concomitant of the poverty of the downtrodden people. Hence, "the basis of annual income of families below a prescribed minimum can be a rational, broad and scientific approach because backwardness, social or educational, is ultimately and primarily due to poverty."[55]

(c) In assessing whether any class of citizens is socially backward or not, it may not be irrelevant to consider the caste factor. But caste cannot be the only relevant factor in determining the backwardness of a class of citizens or a group of citizens within that class and the relevance of caste should not be too much stressed.

(d) The sub-classification into backward and more backward classes does not appear to be justified under Article 15(4).

(e) Article 15(4) does not empower the State to obliterate the fundamental rights under Article 15(1). Therefore, it would not enable "the State to extend the reservation to such an extent as to nullify the guarantee of equality under Article 15(1) altogether."[56] It is authorized to make only special provision for the advancement of any socially and educationally backward classes of citizens, as an exception to the general rule, i.e. it is authorized to do what would otherwise have been unconstitutional.

The Supreme Court also maintained that in laying down principles for the determination of backwardness not only the measures for the advancement of backward classes but also measures for the removal of the causes accelerating the backwardness should be taken into account. Indeed, Article 340(1) makes for the same. The Article stipulates a commission "to investigate the conditions of socially and educationally backward classes within the territory of India and the difficulties under which they labour and to make recommendations as to the steps that should be taken by the Union or any State to remove such difficulties and to improve their condition..."[57]

The court further held that, "the appointment or recommendation of the commission under Article 340 is not a condition precedent for the State to make special provisions for backward classes under Article 15(4)".[58] The State is fully competent to frame its own test of classification for determining the socially and educationally backward classes of citizens within its own territory by executive or legislative action till it is not determined by the commission constituted by the President under Article 340. Hence, the court authorized the State "to give assistance to the backward classes according to the tests prepared by the State Governments themselves".[59] But when validity of the provision made by the State is questioned, and if it is found that classes other than the socially and educationally backward classes have been benefited or classes who are socially and educationally backward have not been benefited, then the notification or order making such classification will amount to a fraud on the Constitution.

According to the court, social backwardness was the direct resultant of poverty, occupations of citizens, place of habitation of a community of persons in the society, and the like. The problems of rural India are such that certain classes of citizens in rural areas are really socially backward and would fall within the purview of Article 15(4).

In determining the educational backwardness, the court observed, the State average of the student population should be taken as a test for determining the educational backwardness of a community, group or caste which may constitute that particular class whose educational backwardness is to be ascertained. A community or caste which conforms to such an average cannot be regarded as a educationally backward class of citizens. The Supreme Court further held that a caste or community whose average student population is less than fifty percent of the State average should be included in the list of educationally backward classes.

Lastly, the Supreme Court made certain lucid comment in the judgment of this case which is germane to out understanding of Article 15(4). It held that the special provision made under Article 15(4) must essentially be within reasonable limits and not at the cost of the interest of the community as a whole. To quote :

> "It must not be ignored that the provision which is authorized to be made is a special provision, it is not a provision which is exclusive in character, so that in looking after the advancement of those classes the State would not be justified in ignoring altogether the advancement of the rest of the society. It is because the interests of the society at large would be served by promoting the advancement of the weaker elements in the society that Article 15(4) authorizes special provision to be made... But if a provision, which is in the nature of an exception completely excludes the rest of the society, that clearly is outside the scope of Article 15(4). It would be extremely unreasonable to assume that where the advancement of the backward classes or the Scheduled Castes and Tribes was concerned the fundamental rights of the rest of the society were to be completely and absolutely ignored."[60]

In considering the proportion of reserved quota in the context of admission in educational institutions, the court laid down that broadly a special provision providing for reservation should be less than fifty percent and how much less than fifty percent would depend on the relevant prevailing circumstances in each case. Justice Gajendra Gadker, speaking for the court, observed :

"When the State makes a special provision for the advancement of the weaker sections of society specified in Article 15(4), it has to approach its task objectively and in a rational manner. Undoubtedly, it has to take reasonable and even generous steps to help the advancement of weaker elements : the extent of the problem must be weighed, the requirements of the community at large must be borne in mind and a formula must be evolved which would strike a reasonable balance between the several relevant considerations."[61]

In Chitralekha *vs.* State of Mysore case, the Supreme Court did not lay down any new proposition, but only explained the earlier decision in Balaji *vs.* State of Mysore. The Court, however, held that the special provision made under Article 15(4) would stand valid even if the caste factor has not been taken into consideration along with other relevant factors while determining the backwardness of a class. "If the group has been classified as backward on other relevant consideration, that classification cannot be challenged as invalid on the ground of omission to take caste into consideration."[62]

In P. Rajendran *vs.* State of Madras and State of Andhra Pradesh *vs.* P. Sagar cases, the Supreme Court laid down new propostions as to how a list of backward classes could be prepared in consistency with the provision of Article 15. "In both the cases the Court took the view that a list of socially and educationally backward classes could be specified by castes provided that it was not based on caste alone. It expressed the view that when a question arose whether a law which prima facie infringed a guaranteed Fundamental Right is within an exception, the court could call for materials to satisfy itself that the law was validly made and was within the ambit of the exception provided under Clause (4) of Article 15."[63]

However, in A. Peerianaruppan *vs.* State of Tamilnadu, : Reservation of 41 per cent of seats in the medical colleges for students coming from socially and educationally backward classes was upheld. The Supreme Court observed :

"There is no basis for the contention that the reservation

made for the backward classes is excessive. Undoubtedly we should not forget that it is against the immediate interest of the Nation to exclude from the portals of our medical colleges qualified and competent students but then the immediate advantages of the nation have to be harmonized with its long-range interests. It cannot be denied that, unaided, many sections of the people in this country cannot compete with the advanced sections of the nation. Advantages secured due to historical reasons should not be considered as fundamental rights. Nation's interest will be best served—taking a long-range view—if the backward classes are helped to march forward and take their place in line with the advanced sections of the people."[64]

The principles enunciated in the above cases leave some questions unanswered. Strict adherence to this principle will lead to a situation where persons, who are socially and educationally backward but do not belong to any such caste or community whose members as a whole are socially and educationally backward and also where individuals who are socially and educationally backward but do not belong to any particular caste or community, will be left out of the protective umbrella under Article 15(4). Moreover, it should not be forgotten that if a list of socially and educationally backward class of citizens is drawn castewise or communitywise for giving protection under Article 15(4), it will only perpetuate the caste system and will transform the movement towards an egalitarian society into a mirage, frustrating the preambled objective of the Fathers of the Constitution. It was only in this spirit that Prof. K.T. Shah brought an amendment to Clause (2) of Article 9 purporting to add "or for Scheduled Castes or Scheduled Tribes" for their advantage, safeguard or betterment. Dr. B.R. Ambedkar had opposed the amendment in the Constituent Assembly, claiming that it might have just the opposite effect. He said, "The object which all of us have in mind is that the Scheduled Castes and Scheduled Tribes should not be segregated from the general public. For instance, none of us, I think, would like that a separate school should be established for the Scheduled Castes when there is a general school in the village open to the children of the entire community. If these words are added, it probably will give a handle to a State to say : 'Well, we are making special provision for the Scheduled Castes. To my mind they can safely say so by taking shelter under the article if it is amended in the manner the professor wants it. I, therefore, think that it is not a desirable amendment."[65] The vision of Dr. Ambedkar was prophetically true, as we see today a growing attempt to raise the politically advantageous caste bogey by the politician that be, in a hot race to win the favour of a particular caste by devising measures exclusively for them and thus segregating them from the general citizenry.

Thus, an exclusive arrangement for Harijan Hostels and colonies is oriented towards segregation and not towards integration leading to a classless egalitarian society.

However, in the Kumari Jayashree *vs.* State of Kerala case, the Supreme Court held that "economic backwardness plays a part in social and educational backwardness. Poverty or economic standard is a relevant factor. Economic backwardness contributes to social backwardness".[66]

The court opined that "in ascertaining social backwardness of a class of citizens it may not be irrelevant to consider the caste of the group of citizens. Caste cannot, however, be made the sole or dominant test. Social backwardness is in ultimate analysis the result of poverty to a large extent. Social backwardness which results from poverty is likely to be aggravated by considerations of their caste. This shows the relevance of both caste and poverty in determining the backwardness of citizens. Poverty by itself is not the determining factor of social backwardness. Poverty is relevant in the context of social backwardness".[67] The Court further held that "the problem of determining who are socially and educationally backward classes is undoubtedly not simple. Sociological and economic consideration come into play in evolving critera for its determination. This is the function of the State. The Court's jurisdiction is to decide whether the tests applied are valid. If it appears that the tests applied are proper and valid, the classification of socially and educationally backward classes based on the tests will have to be consistent with the requirements of Article 15(4)".[68]

The Constitution does nowhere define the term "backward

classes" except that under Article 340(1) the President is empowered to constitute a commission to investigate into the condition of backward classes and suggest remedies. Soon after the Constitution of the first elected Parliament, a commission under the chairmanship of Kaka Sahab Kalelkar was constituted in 1953 to determine, amongst others, the test by which any particular class or group of people can be called backward. The commission submitted its report in March, 1955, but failed to overcome the practical difficulty in finding criteria to determine the "backwardness" of a class or group of people. As a result, the State Governments were authorized to evolve their own basis of classification till it is not determined by a central commission. Thus the State Governments have been acting under the above-said decision. The State Governments have formulated their own tests for classification, even by appointing a commission at their end to specify the test or basis of classification of backwardness. The Kalelkar Commission had listed 2099 communities as backward classes, including women. The Government did not accept the view that women should be classified as a backward class. The Prime Minister Mrs. Indra Gandhi had once said that except for a microscopic minority the whole of India was backward. She desired that all our efforts should be to ensure the rights and privileges guaranteed to all sections of the people.

A commission headed by Shri B.P. Mandal to investigate into the conditions of backward classes was constituted by the President in 1981. The Mandal Report had recommended the "Perpetration of the caste system in determining the socially and educationally backward classes"[69] instead of economic condition. The commission observed that apart from the Scheduled Castes and Scheduled Tribes, there were 3743 backward castes and classes who constitute fifty-two per cent of India's total population. It is on account of this perpetuity of the caste system that the Union and State Governments are reluctant to accept the recommendation. The truth of the matter is that you cannot eat the cake and have it too. If a casteless and classless society is endearing, we have to shun the fanciful device of treating caste with an evil design to perpetuate it on the principle of "divide and rule". We have to look back to the results achieved by our past efforts only to find that slow pace of progress in the field of welfare of the backward classes is caused by our hasty attempts, incoherent and inconsistent, more to win the favour and laurels than a well-concerted all-pronged attack on the curse of backwardness. The result have been that the higher income brackets and the top crust within the weaker sections have syphoned off all the facilities in the name of backward classes, creating a class within a class, without filtering down those facilities to the bulk of the under-privileged and widening the agonizing gap between the hortative hopes and human dupes vis-a-vis that serf-like sector of the Indian society, the backward classes.

Article 17

Article 17 of the Indian Constitution making provision for removing the taint of untouchability from the Indian soil is a landmark in the constitutional history of India, not because the beam of uptouchability from the eyes of the nation has been removed, but because of its bold proclamation, in the fundamental law of the land, of the abolition of untouchability and making its practice a penal offence. The bleeding wound is sought to be healed by the balm of the constitutional provision. Sir Ivor Jennings has critically noted this step as a bad taste on the part of the framers of the Constitution because, he feels, that social evils should be fought at the social level through social reform, and not through the Constitution which incorporates the fundamental law of the nation. So that as it may, it is, undoubtedly, a Charter of Liberty for the one-fifth of the nation's population suffering from the pangs of the age-old curse of untouchability. It opens a way for their deliverance from perpetual subjugation and despondence from perpetual humiliation and disgrace. If the Constitution reflects the social, economic and political aspirations of the nation, the fathers of the Constitution have aptly incorporated that social aspiration of the nation, wishing to atone for its crimes towards humanity, to redeem a debt which was centuries overdue and to expiate for the sin it had been guilty of for ages, as a justiciable right in the most sacred law of the nation. Long before the dawn of freedom numerous social thinkers and reformers had awakened the nation towards the proliferating evils emanating on the social horizon by this sepsis of untouchability. Mahatma Gandhi, the Father of the Nation, had exhorted the nation to remove the taint of untouchability and had launched the biggest religious reform movement in India, if not in the world, involving, as it did, the well-being of nearly sixty million human beings living in serfdom. Thus, the great socio-religious movement had already presaged the constitution-making on the threshfold of "Swaraj" and it was in the fitness of things that the death-blow was dealt to the monster by declaring it a crime against humanity and a justiciable right to rid the Hindu society of its curse with the quickest dispatch. Thus Article 17 is a remedy against injustice, inequality and enforced disability. It proclaims :

> "Untouchability" is abolished and its practice in any form is forbidden. The enforcement of any disability arising out of "untouchability" shall be an offence punishable in accordance with law".[70]

But untouchability is nowhere defined in the Constitution, nor in the various Acts pertaining to it, Mahatma Gandhi "put it in the forefront of the Congress programme in the conviction that unless the Hindus were prepared to wipe out this stain they could not regard themselves as fit for Swaraj. But he was confident that the sin the Caste Hindus were guilty of for ages cannot be expiated by mere removal of physical untouchability" As he said :

> "The removal of untouchability means the removal of all distinctions of superiority and inferiority attached to birth."[71]

When a correspondent pointed out that the evil of untouchability lay in our peculiar social system exclusively based on the principle of heredity and the evil, therefore, cannot end without an end to the caste idea, Gandhi wrote, "Does untochability in the case of a cobbler or scavenger attach to birth or occupation? If it attaches to birth it is hideous and must be rooted out; if it attaches to occupation it may be a sanitary rule of great importance. It is of universal application, A collier, whilst he is engaged in his work is practically an untouchable. He himself refuses to shake the hand extended to him and says, "I am too dirty". But his work finished, he takes his bath, changes his dress and very properly mixes with the highest in the land, Immediately, therefore, we remove the taint of birth, i.e. the idea of superiority and inferiority attaching to birth, we purify Varanashram. The scavenger's children may remain scavenger without being or feeling degraded and they will be no more considered untouchables than Brahmans. The fault does not, therefore, lie in recognizing the law of heredity and transmission of qualities from generation to generation, but it lies with the faulty conception of inequality."[72]

It will be evident from the above that Gandhi viewed untouchability as a mental attitude of the caste Hindus to believe and treat this suppressed class of the Hindus, "Harijans", as Bapu coined the word so dearly—"man of God"—as inferior to them and untouchable for them on the basis of their birth. An attempt was made in the Constitution Assembly to define the word "Untouchability" on an amendment moved by Shri Rohini Kumar Choudhary, which, *inter alia*, proposed to state that "Untouchability means any act committed in exercise of discrimination on grounds of religion, caste or lawful vocation of life".[73] The majority of members, however, felt that the term should be left to be determined by law. Shri K.M. Munshi replying to the debate said, "The word 'Untouchability' is put purposely within inverted commas in order to indicate that the union legislature when it defines 'Untouchability' will be able to deal with it in the sense in which it is normally understood."[74] As Dr. S.N. Banerjee said in the Constituent Assembly, Untouchability should be considered "not a disease but a symptom of a disease".[75]

Thus, the makers of the Constitution also felt that untouchability was a social stigma attached to certain classes of people, on the basis of their birth, and not on the basis of their occupation or vocation, and was surely symptomatic of a diseased mind. Article 17 envisages to remove this social stigma by preventing its manifestation in social behaviour born of a prejudiced mind and jaundiced vision. Its object is to uproot this scandalously disastrous and irrational social action from the activities of the nation. Justifying the inclusion of this Article in the Constitution, Dr. Ambedkar said : "This Assembly instead of leaving it to our Parliament or to a State Legislature to make the enforcement of any disability arising out of untouchability a crime, itself declares any such enforcement an offence punishable by law".[76]

In Devarajah *vs.* Padmanna case, the Mysore High Court held that the term is not to be understood in its literal sense and that, "Untouchability' in the Act refers to the social disabilities historically imposed on certain classes of people by reason of their birth in certain castes and would not include an instigation of social boycott by reason of the conduct of certain persons."[77]

While speaking on the Untouchability (Offence) Bill, 1955, the then Home Minister of India had categorically stated :

> "This cancer of untouchability has entered into the very vitals of our society. It is not only a blot on the Hindu religion but it has created intolerance, sectionalism, and fissiparous tendencies. Many of the evils that we find in our society today are traceable to this heinous monstrosity. It was really strange that Hindu with their sublime philosophy and their merciful kind-heartedness even towards insects should have been party to such an intolerable dwarfing of manhood. Yet untouchability has been there for centuries and we have now to atone for it. The idea of untouchability is entirely repugnant to the structure, spirit and provisions of the Constitution".[78]

The Untouchability (Offences) Act 1955, which was a supplementary measure to Article 17 of the Constitution, came into force in June, 1955. The Act prescribes punishment for the practice of untouchability, for the enforcement of any disability arising therefrom and for ancillary matters. It provides punishment for enforcing certain religious, social and other disabilities on the ground of "untouchability". The Act brings within its net whosoever even abets any offence under this Act and is a comprehensive measure which is being strengthened with the wide powers to the State to punish the offenders. Section 6 of the Act provides :

"Whoever on the ground of 'Untouchability' refuses to sell any goods or refuses to render any service to any person at the same time and place and on the same terms and conditions at or on which such goods are sold or services are rendered to other persons in the ordinary course of business, shall be punishable with imprisonment which may extend to six months or with fine which may extend to five hundred rupees or with both."[79]

Section 3 of the Act provides that whoever on the ground of 'Untouchability' prevents any person :

"(a) From entering any place of public worship which is open to other persons professing the same religion or belonging to the same religious denomination or any section thereof, as such person; or

(b) From worshiping or offering prayers or performing any religious service in any place of public worship, or bathing in, or using the waters of, any sacred tank, well, spring or watercourse, in the same manner and to the same extent as is permissible to other persons professing the same religion, or belonging to the same religious denomination on any section thereof, as such person, shall be punishable with imprisonment which may extend to six months, or with fine which may extend to five hundred rupees or with both."[80]

In Bengal, a cobbler is an untouchable but not a barber. In a case, one Pakhubhendari, a barber, refused to serve a cobbler, Banmali Das, on the ground of untouchability. The case came up before the Calcutta High Court. The defendant took the plea that the Bengal Hindu Social Disabilities Removal Act, 1948, was in violation of the constitutional provision of freedom of profession, trade or business. The High Court rejected this contention and held : "All it does is to prohibit him from discriminating between one Hindu and another in carrying out his duties as a barber. It does not deny any person equality before the law. It tends to make all persons equal in society and before the law and it cannot possibly be argued that this Act denies any person equal protection of the law."[81]

In P.S. Charya *vs.* State of Madras, the Madras High Court held that the Madras Temple Entry Authorization Act,

1947, as amended in 1949 was not repugnant to any provision of the Constitution. To prevent certain classes of Hindus, who were once called as depressed classes, from entering a public meeting was certainly to practise untouchability. What was provided in the Act of 1947 was merely the fulfilment of the directive given under Article 17 of the Constitution.[82]

However, the abolition of "Untouchability" under Article 17 does not mean that it also guarantees the right of access to use of private homes and property. The private owner of a place or object cannot be presumed to have violated Article 17 or the Untouchability (Offences) Act, 1955. The citizens have an equal right to enjoy the public facilities offered in public institutions or public places. Any discrimination in the enjoyment of this right may constitute an offence under the Act provided it is based on the practice of untouchability and relates to public institutions, public places or public facilities. The word "Untouchability" lacks precision since it has neither been defined in the Constitution or in the Act. Legally it means untouchability on grounds of descent, caste, race or religion. The words "in any form" may cover all facets of the practice of untouchability but not all places where it may take place. It relates only to public places or institutions.

In spite of these constitutional and several legal provisions India cannot claim to have uprooted the evils of untouchability which has formed a sepsis on our body politic. As a matter of fact, legislation is fragile vehicle of social reform and social reform is primarily achieved by active public awakening and cooperation. It needs sincere efforts, not only on the part of law-makers, but also a sustained constructive efforts on the part of the general public. In the 19th Report for the year 1969-70, the Commissioner for Scheduled Castes and Scheduled Tribes recommended a complete change in the minds of the people which alone could solve the problem of the down-trodden people of these communities. The 20th Report of the Commissioner reveals some interesting facts and states that the unsatisfactory progress was mainly attributable to the lack of proper implementation of the various welfare measures undertaken for their development. The basic reason of this deplorable state is, the report mentioned :

"First, general lack of sense of urgency on the part of those responsible for the implementation of the schemes, secondly inefficient financial provisions for the welfare schemes, due to low priority accorded to them in the various Five Year Plans, and, thirdly, lack of people's participation in the implementation of the schemes, particularly due to a lukewarm attitude in that respect on the part of the political parties and want of revolutionary urge and zeal on the part of social workers."[83] Indeed, it is the bounden duty of the Government to devise ways and means to solicit active support of the public leaders, social reformers and people in general, and to impart training to the spirit and mind of the youngsters so that a social order is created in which the taint of untouchbility vanishes from the land of Gandhi.

Article 18

The resolution regarding the aims and objects moved by Pandit Jawahar Lal Nehru, in the Constituent Assembly contained the firm resolve to proclaim India as an Independent Sovereign Republic and to draw up for her future governance a constitution... "Wherein shall be guaranteed and secured to all people of India, justice, social, economic and political, equality of status and of opportunity before the law : freedom of trought, expression, belief, faith, worship, vocation, association and action, subject to law and public morality.[84]" "This order of precedence of social justice in the aims and objects Resolution as well as in the Preambled objectives of the Constitution is not just accidental. It implies the intense faith of the framers of the Constitution that social justice has to precede in importance to justice in the economic and political field, i.e. they visualized it fully well that justice in society, in the realm of law, social status and opportunity is pre-conditioned to other forms of justice. Even in the matter of Fundamental Rights, social justice reads the rights in other fields, and the order of priority given to social justice reflects the intense concern of the makers of the Constitution for the achievement of the same, because justice in the social field is sine qua non for the achievement and stability of justice in other walks of life. What is noteworthy is the concern for social justice. Social justice must precede an egalitarian order. Article 18 of the Constitution is based on the idea of a social revolution which will ensure a sense of oneness amongst the millions of Indian citizens by preventing practices designed to fillip the feeling of inherent superiority amongst the privileged few. The Article aims at "preventing the power to confer title being abused for corrupting the public life of the country."[85] During the British rule, these methods and practices for creating differences and divisions among the people were intentionally devised. The conferring of decorative titles with an avowed purpose of creating a class of favourites and bootlickers for the administration, in fact, paid great dividends to the British Empire. The British rulers followed their policy of "divide and rule" by the masked trickery, conferring fastidious honours and frivolous titles to persons who showed an inkling to the Empire and which multiplied the obedience and support of the latter to the Government. A calculated drive to create such henchmen in every nook and corner of the public life in India become a vital policy of the British Government to create a hiatus between the various sections of the society, which was already devastatingly bifurcated into "haves" and "have-nots". Flattery and support to the British rulers was the only yardstick for bestowing on these people honours and titles of nobility like Sir, Khan Bahadur, Rai Bahadur, Rao Sahib, Devan Bahadur, etc. These privileged persons had formed a class of their own and were quite antagonistic to the national movement and cruelly apathetic to the freedom fighters languishing in British jails.

With the dawn of freedom, the framers of the Constitution, conscious of its chasmy impact on social inequality, thought it meet to impose a bar on such conduct of the State in free India, and included this right in the justiciable part of the basic rights of the citizens, i.e. Part III of the Constitution. All Indians have been finally guaranteed the equality of status in the social field, by banning the practice of conferring honorary titles of nobility by the State in Article 18 of the Constitution. The total prohibition of conferment of title in the Draft and prohibition of conferring 'hereditary titles' in the Report can be compared with the provision that finally emerged in the form of Article 18.

However, it is obvious that the various clauses of the Article are preventive measures, aimed at preventing the recurrence of any artificial barrier to social equality. The State, as defined in Article 12, cannot confer any title on a citizen, which is not a military or academic distinction, under clause (1) of Article 18. This prohibition is applicable only to the State. However, titles conferring academic distinctions on individuals by the universities and other academic institutions under the State as well as military titles indicating gallantry and heroic deeds on the part of recipients, by the State, can be conferred. Clauses (2) to (4) are related with foreign States. Clause (2) absolutely prohibits to a citizen of India from accepting, such prohibited titles from any foreign State. This exclusive, prohibition under Clause (2) is a salutary check to reduce intensity of a citizen's loyalty to his motherland and is a wholesome practice to make the citizens wholly Indian in outlook, thought and action. Again, Clause (3) stipulates that the non-citizens who hold any office of profit or trust under the State can accept such titles from any foreign State only after the prior consent of the President of India is secured. And Clause (4) makes a provision that no citizen or non-citizen, who holds any office of profit or trust under the State can obtain or receive or accept any presents, remuneration or office of any kind from any foreign State without first obtaining the consent of the President of India for the said purpose. Thus, while Clause (2) absolutely bars any citizen from receiving such artificial decorative titles from foreign States, Clauses (3) imposes conditional restriction to only those non-citizens who hold any office of profit or trust in the State, as defined in Article 12, as they can so receive only after prior sanction of the President of India is obtained : whereas, Clause (4), applicable to both citizens and non-citizens who hold any office of profit or trust under the State, puts a conditional bar to receive or accept any present, emolument or office from or under any foreign State only after the prior consent of the President of India is obtained for the said purpose. Clauses (3) and (4) are thus designed to secure loyalty from persons in the service of the State, whether citizen or non-citizen, and to shut out all foreign influence in the governance end administration of the nation.

But curiously enough, soon after the enforcement of the Constitution, the Government of India introduced in 1954 some State decorations to persons having record of distinguished public service in any field including services rendered by Government servants. Any person rendering exceptional service in the advancement of arts, literature and science or any public service of the highest order can be awarded Bharat Ratna, while Padma Vibhushan, Padma Bhushan and Padma Shri are three decoratory awards in order of merit, which can be awarded to persons with a record of distinguished public service in any field by the State. Holders of the decoratory award of Bharat Ratna are given the ninth place in the National Warrant of Precedence. The Government notification introducing these awards specifically mentions that such decorations will not be used as appendage to the names of the recipients. It is on this ground that supporters of State decoration claim that the same is beyond the coverage of the word "title" and, therefore, outside the purview of Article 18 of the Constitution. Critics, on the other hand, regard it as a violation of the spirit, if not the latter, of the Constitution. "The critics gain strength on this point from the fact that decorations are divided into several classes, superior and inferior, and that holders of the Bharat Ratna have been assigned a place in the Warrant of Precedence (9th place, i.e. just below the Cabinet Minister of the Union), which is usually meant for indicating the rank of the different dignitaries and high officials of the State, in the interests of discipline in the administration... The result is the creation of a rank of persons on the basis of Government recognition, in the same way as the conferment of nobility would have."[86] Apart from the legality of the Award, one way or the other, it cannot be denied that the institution of the Award runs counter to the spirit of democracy, be lies the hortative hopes of the people and the endearing objective of the Fathers of the Constitution to put an end to this man-made, superficial social inequality. Though the legal implication of this 'Award' is not clearly settled yet, it is most likely that persons in an identical position do obtain a legal right against the State and can sue the State for discrimination on an unreasonable basis and on the prohibited ground under Article 18(1) of the

Constitution for conference of a social privilege, prohibited under the Constitution, to a person, thus depriving any or all the other citizens equality before the law. If a special privilege is bestowed on a person, the others are deprived of it without there being a rational ground, and thus it divests the latter of equality before the law and seems violative of Article 14. This is more so because, like Article 14, Article 18 "is a self-executing provision end does not envisage legislation to implement".[87]

It, however, depends finally upon the discretion and further interpretation of the Article by the Court. If the court does not hold an affirmative view on this question, "some of the provisions in Part III would become non-justiciable like the Directive Principles of State Policy included in Part IV and the result would be contrary to the scheme underlying the Constitution".[88]

It is to be noted that the prohibition in this connection in USA, Germeny, Japan and Ireland is only against the conferment of the titles of nobility and the original intention of the makers of the Indian Constitution, reflected during debates in the Constituent Assembly, had also been to abolish only the hereditary titles. Speaking on Article 12 of the Draft Constitution Shri Masani said : "It may be possible for the Union to honour some of its citizens who distinguished themselves in several walks of life like science and the arts, with other kinds of honours not amounting to titles; but the idea of a man putting something before or after his name as an award for service rendered will not be possible in a free India."[89]

Replying to the debate, Sri Prakash observed : "I should like to make it plain that this clause does not prohibit even the State from bestowing a proper honour. A title is something that hangs to one's name. I understand it is a British innovation. Other States also honour their citizens for good work but those citizens do not necessarily hang their titles to their names as people in Britain or British governed parts of the world do. That is all this clause seeks to do. If the State wants to honour a citizen, if a citizen has done particularly good work, then there are a thousand ways in which the State can honour the citizen. If the people want to honour a leader then they can also honour him; but we want to abolish this corroding, corrupting practice which makes an individual go about currying favour with authority to get particular distinctions."[90] But by professing abolition of titles, perhaps, the framer did not express their intention in unequivocal terms. The result is that since 1954, the Union Government has been awarding such titles lavishly on person selected on frivolous grounds, which are, in fact, not merit-recognizing but class-creating awards. The holders of the awards have really formed a class within class and are freely using these as appendages to their names and on letter-pads. The prevalent practice of conferring these awards breeds patronage, sprawns nepotism, smacks of favouritism and feeds on discrimination and creates social inequality. There is no preventive measure available in Constitution and no penal action can be taken against persons or the State violating the provisions of Article 18. Dr Ambedker stated in the Constituent Assembly that Parliament might, while enacting the citizenship law disqualify such persons from citizenship, but the Citizenship Act 1955 did not contain any such provision. As Dr. Ambedkar said :

> "The non-acceptance of titles is a condition of continued citizenship : it is not a right : it is a duty imposed upon the individual that if he continues to be the citizen of this country, then he must abide by certain conditions. One of the conditions is that he must not accept a title because it would be open for Parliament, when it provides by law, as to what should be done to persons who violate the provisions of the Article... one of the penalties may be that he may lose the right of citizenship."[91]

However, on its very appearance, the Article seems to be only "a prescription or prohibition observable and enforceable by the persons and bodies concerned only as a moral obligations."[92] Unlike Article 17, it does not prescribe legislative enactment to punish the offender of the provision. Though Article 35(A) (II) authorizes Parliament to make laws for prescribing punishment for these acts declared to be offences under Part III of the Constitution, it can be of no avail, for Article 18 does not declare any act to be offensive. It may be that an employee under the State can be dismissed from his job if he committs any breach of the provisions, but in respect of other persons action can hardly be contemplated. Further, the Article had nothing to do with the existing titles, privileges and immunities of the rulers of the former princely States of British India, which were actually safeguarded to them under Articles 352 and 291 of the Constitution. It is a matter of great relief that the then Prime Minister of India, Mrs. Indira Gandhi, took steps for the abrogation of those absolute arrangements under the Constitution by taking steps for the enactment of the Constitution (Twenty-sixth Amendment) Act, 1971, which repealed those obnoxious provisions.

Sir Ivor Jennings, on the other hand, evaluating the importance of Article 18, has expresed the view that these restrictions on public officers might have, as well, been imposed by administrative regulations. To quote him :

> "The rule in Article 18, incorrectly summarized by the marginal note as abolition of title, that no title, not being a military or academic distinction, shall be conferred by the State, is apparently part of the 'right to Equality'. It seems to be no breach of the right to equality if Sir John Brown becomes Dr. John Brown, or General John Brown, or Pandit John Brown or Mr. Justice Brown or Rotarian John Brown or even Sri John Brown. M.S.F., or if he rolls round in a gold-plated car or loads his wife with jewellery and silk saris, but if, like the present writer, he becomes an impecunious Knight, the Right to Equality is broken. In whom is this right vested? It cannot be in Sir John Brown, it is neither in rem nor in personam, neither corporal nor incorporal... it is, in fact, not a right at all, but a restriction on the executive and legislative power."[93]

Even if, for the sake of argument, it is admitted that the Article does not create any right, it is nonetheless essential that this archaic system should end in free India so that this vestige of feudalism is uprooted. In a democratic republic vested interest must not be allowed to grow as a class affecting the nascent growth of the country. In 1970, an attempt was initiated by Shri J.B. Kriplani, in the Lok Sabha, to do away with this practice of conferring awards. He had pointed out that this constitutional provision had been circumvented by an executive order of the Government using the word "awards" instead of "titles". The very system has been institutionalized and the spirit behind the government policy initiating these decorations has come to an end. Acharaya Kriplani strongly criticized the Government for its abject failure to ensure that only merit and talent are selected for such awards. He cited the case of Rituick Ghattak, a West Bengal artist, who had abused Mahatma Gandhi, as one such conferee. Indeed, the process of selection includes state's recommendations for its quota and also consideration of certain recommendations of professionals from unofficial bodies. "Communal, regional and linguistic ratios have to be maintained. Politics, arts, sports, science, administration and social service have to be evenly balanced. The result has sometimes been a hotch-potch of personalities. Parochialism, Vanity and current political fashion have caused a further misuse of State honours."[94] In fact, persons of integrity have, at times, refused this honour, which, they felt, stood devalued and frustrated the very purpose for which honours were introduced. Man like J.B. Kriplani, Sucheta Kripalani, Maulana Abdul Kalam Azad, Chelpathi Rau, Khushwant Singh and others have refused to be decorated with such awards. Misuse of the awards has also been exemplified in the case of Dr. N.S. Jain, a noted Delhi eye surgeon, who has undergone life imprisonment for his involvement in a sex scandal and murder of his own wife, and who has been granted Presidential pardon. Though the Bill of Acharya Kripalani was finally rejected by the Lok Sabha, the idea behind it had gained ground and when the Janata Party came to power at the Centre, these awards were abolished in 1977. Just after assuming the office, the Prime Minister, Shri Morarji Desai stated : "We had the question examined whether the institution of civil awards, namely, Bharat Ratna and Padma awards, was in conformity with Article 18 of the Constitution. The Attorney-General of India was consulted on this matter and his advice was that after "A harmonious interpretation of the word 'title' in Clause (1) of Article 18 as well as Clauses (2) and (3) thereof the Bharat Ratna and Padma awards would fall within the prohibition of grant of titles and would in his view be contrary not only to the letter, but also of the spirit of Article 18 (1)".[95]

The Janata Government accepted the advice and accordingly discontinued the awards but these were re-introduced by Mrs. Gandhi, when she came to power again in 1980. If the practice is to be continued, however, a restriction on the number of recipients and a more rational basis for selection is the urgent need.

REFERENCES

1. *Nationalism*, R.N. Tagore (Mac Millan) pp. 123-24.
2. Grammer of Politics, Harold Laski, p. 176.
3. *Independence and After*, J.L. Nehru (1940) p. 28.
4. Joshi *vs.* State of Bombay (1955) 1. SCR. 1215.
5. AIR. 1953 Madhya Bharat 147.
6. C.A.D. Nov. 29, 1948, pp. 650-51.
7. AIR 1952 Cal 61.
8. AIR 1951 Sc. 226.
9. *Ibid.*
10. (1954) SCR. 930.
11. AIR 1951 Bombay 285.
12. AIR 1953 Bom. 311.
13. (1985) 4 SCC. 197.
14. AIR 1953 Sc. 384.
15. AIR 1954 Mad 67.
16. AIR 1951 Pun 344.
17. AIR 1955 H.P. 9.
18. AIR. 1955 Sc. 334.
19. (1984) 3 SCC 654.
20. (1985) 3 SCC. 22.
21. AIR 1960 Sc. 1208.
22. Commentary on the Constitution of India, D.D.Basu, 1961, Vol. I, p. 463.
23. C.A.D., Nov. 29, 1948, p. 661.
24. *Ibid.*
25. Untouchability (Offences) Act, 1955 : Section 2(e).
26. *Ibid.*
27. AIR 1958 Mad. 282.
28. D.D.Basu, *op.cit.,* p. 516.
29. Untouchability (Offences) Act, *op.cit.*, Section 4(I) IV.
30. *Ibid.*, (V).
31. *Ibid.*, 2(d).
32. D.D.Basu, *op.cit.,* p. 518.
33. *Ibid.*
34. C.A.D.; Nov. 29, 1948. p. 662.
35. *Ibid.*

36. (1960), 64 C.W.N. 348 (355).
37. AIR 1952 Cal. 822.
38. AIR 1953 Bom. 34 (461).
39. AIR 1954 Sc. 321.
40. AIR 1955 Assam 1980.
41. *The Times of India*, April 25, 1985.
42. *Ibid.*
43. *Ibid.*
44. *Ibid.*
45. AIR 1951 Sc. 226.
46. Suppeme Court on Ammendments of Fundamental Rights in Indian Constitution. N.A. Palkhiwala (1973) p. 470.
47. AIR 1951 Sc. 229.
48. AIR 1951 Mad. 21.
49. AIR 1976 Sc. 1904.
50. AIR 1960 Mysore. 338.
51. AIR. 1975 Sc. 563
52. *Ibid.*
53. (1975) 2 SCR. 761.
54. AIR 1981 Sc. 1009.
55. AIR 1963 Sc. 649.
56. *Ibid.*
57. The Constitution of India (1980), Pub. Div. Govt. of India, p. 217.
58. AIR 1963 Sc. 649.
59. *Ibid.*
60. *Ibid.*
61. *Ibid.*
62. AIR 1963 Sc. 1823.
63. AIR 1968 Sc. 1012 and AIR 1968 Sc. 1379.
64. AIR 1971 Sc. 2303.
65. C.A.D., Nov. 29, 1948, pp. 661-66.
66. AIR 1976 Sc. 2383.
67. *Ibid.*
68. *Ibid.*
69. *The Hindustan Times*, April 28, 1983.
70. The Constitution of India (1980) p. 9.
71. The Bleeding Wond : M.K. Gandhi (1936), p. 35.
72. *Ibid.* pp. 77-78.
73. C.A.D, April 28, 1947, Vol. 3. p. 395.
74. *Ibid.*
75. *Ibid.*, p. 403.
76. *Ibid.*, Nov. 29, 1948, p. 661.
77. AIR 1958 Mysore 84.
78. (Quted in) Constitutional Govt. of India : M.V. Pylee (1965) p. 215.
79. Untouchability (Offences) Act, 1955, Section 6.

80. *Ibid.,* Section 3.
81. AIR 1951 Cal 167.
82. AIR 1956 Mad 541.
83. Report of the Comissioner for Scheduled Castes and Scheduled Tribes, 1970, Vol. II, p.167.
84. C.A.D.Dec, 13, 1946 : Vol.1. No.5. p. 57.
85. D.D.Basu, *op.cit.,* p. 540.
86. D.L.Basu, *op.cit.*, p. 542.
87. *Ibid.*
88. *Ibid.*
89. C.A.D. April 29, 1947, Vol. III, No. 2.
90. *Ibid.*
91. *Ibid.* p.709.
92. The Constitution of India : Raghavacharya, p. 57.
93. Some Characteristics of Indian Constitution, Ivor Jennings (1953), p. 18.
94. *The Hindustan Times*, Nov. 22, 1970.
95. *The Indian Nation*, July 14, 1977.

CHAPTER 5

EQUALITY OF OPPORTUNITY

(a) The Background

The equality of opportunity provided in Article 16 is an instance of application of the general principle of equality in the field of employment by the State. It was, indeed, by providing equal opportunity to all, even to the lowest and the poorest in the land, that a true democracy could thrive. Mahatma Gandhi, the Father of the Nation, had categorically stated : "My notion of democracy is that under it the weakest should have the same opportunity as the strongest."[1]

Jawaharlal Nehru, the architect of modern India, had visualized, long before independence, that without economic freedom, there could be no real freedom. He once said that "to call a starving man free is to mock him".[2] His future plan for independent India envisaged that any "economic programme must aim at the removal of all economic inequalities and an equitable distribution of wealth".[3] Nehru fundamentally believed that social justice coupled with economic equality must be ensured to the masses and the existing class structure must be changed. Towards 1937, he had written :

> "The form of government is after all a means to an end; even freedom itself is a means, the end being human well-being, human growth, the ending of poverty and disease and suffering, and the opportunity for everyone to live

the "good life" physically and mentally."[4] Further, replying to a criticism, he said; "No one has said... that all men are physically or mentally equal, or that all nations are similarly situated. What has been said, and what is admitted by the great majority of intelligent men, is that all human beings should have an equality of opportunity. The present capitalist system does not and cannot in the nature of things provide this equality of opportunity."[5]

Similar view have been expressed by some modern thinkers, Laski has said :

> "The survival of political democracy today is, all over the world, definitely impossible unless it can conquer the central citadel of economic power. There cannot, in a word be democracy unless there is socialism."[6]

Nehru had foretold this : "If we survey the world today, we find that capitalism, having solved the problem of production, helplessly faces the allied problem of distribution and is unable to solve it. It was not in the nature of the capitalist system to deal satisfactorily with distribution and production alone makes the world top-heavy and unbalanced. To find a solution for distributing wealth and purchasing power evenly is to put an end to the basic inequalities of the capitalist system and to replace capitalism itself by a more scientific system... communists and socialists point with confidence to the way of socialism and they are an over-growing power for they have science and logic on their side."[7] And answering the question "Whither India," he had retorted :

> "Surely to the great human goal of social and economic equality, to the ending of all exploitation of nation by nation and class by class, to national freedom within the framework of international cooperative socialist world federation."[8]

After the realisation of his cherished dream of Swaraj, Nehru, moving his resolution on the aims and objects, which were the fundamentals commonly held and accepted by the people, said : "The Resolution that I am placing before you defines our aims, describes an outline of the plan and points the way which we are going to tread."[9] And one of the points embedded was to draw up a constitution, "wherein shall be guaranteed and secured to all the people of India justice, social, economic and political; equality of status and of opportunity, and before the law... and wherein adequate safeguards shall be provided for minorities, backward and tribal areas and depressed and other backward classes."[10]

Speaking on the Resolution, Sir V.I. Munshiswami Pillai (Madras, General) had said : "the sixty millions of untouchables form the backbone of Hinduism and I am sure that in your deliberations in framing the Constitution you will see that all the disabilities of the Harijans are taken note of and remedied in a manner that they may enjoy equal privileges in this great country."[11] And Mr. M.R. Masani (Bombay, General) had said :

"The Resolution also provides for equality of opportunity. Equality of opportunity, Sir, presupposes equal facilities in education and in the development of talent that is latent in each one of us. Today, among our masses a fund of latent talent exists which has no chance to come out and contribute to our national good. Equality of opportunity certainly assumes that every child in this country, every boy and girl, will get an equal opportunity to develop those faculties which he or she possesses in order to contribute to the common good."[12]

Prof. N.G. Ranga (Madras, General), speaking on the Resolution, ably pointed out the wretched conditions of the depressed and emphatically recommended concrete measures to make them stand as equal partners with the rest of the community in building a strong and united India. He had said "Millions and millions of out countrymen are not able to take advantage of the various liberties that we have laid down here, the various privileges, that, we say, are being thrown open for everyone to enjoy. They are not educated. Economically, they are oppressed and suppressed also, and socially, they are backward and downtrodden. For all these people so many more things have to be done, may be for sometime to come, before they came to enjoy these rights. They need props. They need a ladder by which they can reach on to the stage when it will be possible for them to come to appreciates the value of the rights that we are placing before them and enjoy them."[13] And replying to the debate, Nehru had said :

> "The first task of this Assembly is to free India through a new constitution, to feed the starving people and clothe the naked masses, and to give to every Indian fullest opportunity to develop himself according to his capacity. If we cannot solve this problem soon, all our paper constitutions will become useless and purposeless."[14]

Nehru had, long before freedom, visualized this basic urge of the people, when he wrote : "The whole basis and urge of the national movement came from a desire for economic betterment, to throw off the burdens that crushed the masses and to end the exploitation of the Indian people.... the exploited and suffering masses must carry on the struggle for their drill-sergeant is hunger. Swaraj or freedom from exploitation for them is not a fine paper constitution or a problem of the hereafter. It is a question of the here and now, of immediate relief."[15]

The framers of the Constitution, assembled in the Constituent Assembly, were well aware of the task of immediate relief to the downtrodden, the hungry and the depressed masses. The Advisory Committee, appointed by the resolution of the Assembly of January 24, 1947, in its interim report on the subject of fundamental rights had provided in Clause (5) for equality of opportunity. The Draft of the new constitution, prepared by the Drafting Committee appointed by the resolution of the Constituent Assembly of August 29, 1947 contained this right of equality of opportunity in matters of public employment in Article 10. At the final stage Article 10 of the Draft Constitution was numbered as Article 16 of the Constitution, as adopted and enacted by the Constituent Assembly on November 26, 1949. We have discussed in detail the implications of Articles 14 and 15 in the preceding two chapters. Whereas Article 14 ensures that all shall be treated equally, Article 15 is a concentrated application of equality of treatment in the social field and Article 16 is a specific application of equality of treatment in the field of employment, thus paving the way for economic justice.

In fact, Articles 14 to 16 form part of a constitutional code of guarantee of equality, in fulfilment of the longcherished ideal of the national leaders preambled in the Constitution, and they supplement each other. This code illustrates the multi-faceted character of the central concept of equality enunciated in Article 14, which declares the proposition of equality in its bald universality, Article 15 which prevents discrimination in treatment and Article 16 which provides equal opportunity of employment under the State are only an incident of guarantee of equality under Article 14. Whereas Article 14 confers right to treatment as an equal, embedded in the idea of universal brotherhood advocated by the Father of the Nation, which is the right only to be treated with same respect and concern as any other human being. Articles 15 and 16, which elaborate the right to equal treatment, i.e. the right to receive the same distribution of burden or benefit, are only incidental and derivable from the mainspring of equality contained in Article 14 of the Constitution, and the former two Articles have only enabled the latter to remain a projector with a view to adopting it to the grim realities permeating the nation's social, economic, cultural and political perspectives. Thus the multifaceted trait of this code of equality makes it possible to facilely serve every segment of the body-politic and set the parameters for the principled solution of social disabilities.

The most important point regarding this Article is that the absolutely universal provision of equality of opportunity by throwing open all public jobs to all citizens of India in Clause (1) is hedged with other clauses ameliorative of the ingrained inequalities in the social fabric and imbedded to imbrue the abysmal economic inequality. Secondly, the general provision of Clause (1) is specificated as non-discrimination in bequest of the right to equality for public employment, irrespective of religion, race, caste, sex, place of birth, descent, residence or any of them. It, ostensibly means that discrimination on grounds other than prohibited in Clause (2) can be made within the bounds of reason.

It is to be noted that "residence" as a ground of prohibition, which found place in Clause (2) finally, was neither mentioned in the Interim Report on the Fundamental Rights of the Advisory Committee, nor in the Draft Constitution. The "residence" as a ground prohibiting discrimination, in Clause (2) and a new clause excepting those public jobs which the Parliament may declare to be reserved to "residence" of a State unit, numbered as Clause (3), were inserted in Article

15 of the Constitution and adopted in its final form by the Constituent Assembly through an amendment based on the motion of Yaspat Roy Kapoor and in consideration of the views expressed by K.M. Munshi and Alladi Krishna Swami Aiyar. The argument on the motion ensued with heat and light, passion and reason and there was much 'behind-the-scene' activity and protracted negotiations. Mr. Kapoor observed that his object was to ensure that "every citizen of the country, wherever he might be living, should have an equal opportunity of employment under the State... anywhere in the country : and that, there being only one citizenship of the whole country it should carry with it the unfettered right and privilege of employment in any part and in every nook and corner of this country".[16] The motion was finally accepted as a sort of compromise between those that wanted to curb provincialism, which had ominously begun to raise its ugly head, and those that wanted to prevent "birds of passage without any roots" from getting jobs in any State unit. While accepting the motion, Dr. Ambedkar significantly made it clear :

> "It is the feeling of many persons in this House that, since we have established a common citizenship throughout India... It is only a concomitant thing that residence should not be required for holding a particular post in a parties State because, in so far as you make residence a qualification, you are really subtracting from the value of a common citizenship which we have established by this Constitution. Therefore, in my judgement, the argument that residence should not be a qualification to hold appointments under the State is a perfectly valid and perfectly sound argument. At the same time, it must be realized that you can allow people who are flying from one province to another, from one State to another, as mere birds of passage without any roots, without any connection with that particular province, just to come, apply for posts and, so to say, take the plums and walk away. Therefore some limitation is necessary."[17]
> Describing the practice of laying down residential qualification already established in various provinces. Dr. Ambedkar continued, "while it might be desirable to fix

a period as a qualifying test, that qualifying test should be uniform throughout India. Consequently, if that object is to be achieved, viz. that the qualifying residential period should be uniform, that object can be achieved only by giving the power to Parliament and not giving it to the local units, whether Provinces or States... That is the underlying purpose of this amendment putting down residence as a qualification."[18]

Another interesting event followed with the amendment moved by Somanath Lahiri in the Constituent Assembly to the effect that "political creed" should be added as another ground prohibiting discrimination. Replying to the motion Sardar Valabhbhai Patel said : "I think it an absurd idea to provide for non-discrimination as regards a political creed. Political creed may be of any kind. There may be some political creeds highly objectionable. Some may not be deserving of discrimination, but may actually be deserving of suppression altogether."[19] It is interesting to recall in this connection that the Motilal Nehru Committee set up by the All Parties Conference in early 1928 to recommend a model constitution had enunciated one of the fundamental rights as follows :

"(XIII) No person shall by reason of his religion, caste or creed be prejudiced in any way in regard to public employment, office of power or honour and the exercise of any trade or calling."[20] The 45th session of the AICC at Karachi held in March, 1931, also adopted Resolution No. 15 containing the abovesaid item in its declaration on Fundamental Rights in Swaraj.[21] In 1937, the AICC had reiterated this right in its Fundamental Rights Resolution :

"(IV) All citizens are equal before law, irrespective of religion, race, creed or sex."[22]

The "creed" as a ground of non-discrimination, which was professed by the Congress categorically for a decade, was of no import and omitted, thus enabling the State to exclude anti-social and unwanted political elements, without obvious constitutional barrier.

Having gleaned the views of some national leaders and

the objectives of the framers of the Constitution, it is meet to our study that the dynamics and dialectics of socio-economic justice, in the context of political freedom enshrined in Part III of the Constitution calculated to guarantee the equality of oportunity to all, even to the lowliest of the low, the limping brackets of the social order emanating from the feudal-colonial nightmarish era of history, which has been the cynosure of judicial scrutiny from time to time, should be closely followed in the light of some leading cases, to evolve the meaning given to it and observe the purpose it has served.

(b) Judicial Interpretation of Clause (1)

The term "employment" or "appointment" used in Clause (1) has been adjudged to be of wide import and covers not only the appointment or employment of a person, but also his promotion, service conditions and even termination of service. In Sukh Nandan *vs.* State of Bihar (AIR 1957, Pat 517) it has been held that "appointment" and "employment" have different connotations. The former postulates the existence of a relationship of master and servant, employer and employees, and always indicates an office, while the latter does not imply the relationship of this kind and may not also relate to an office. However, it has been established by the Supreme Court in General Manager *vs.* Rangachari Case (AIR 1962 SC 36) that both the terms have the same meaning so far as Article 16 is concerned. Similarly, in G.D. Rama Rao *vs.* Andhra Pradesh the Supreme Court held that the term "Office" under the State should be given "its natural meaning, which means all offices under the State".[23]

It has also been ruled by the Supreme Court that the words "appointment or employment" used in Clause (1) of Article 16 guarantees "an equal opportunity to all citizens to apply for employment under State"[24] and it "confers a right of equality not only for applying for a post but also for considering that application on merit".[25] However, it does not confer on the applicant "any right to be appointed to the post for which he applies".[26] In High Court, Calcutta *vs.* Anil Kumar, the Supreme Court held that "the fact that the High Court made its choice in a particular way cannot be said to amount to discrimination against the plaintiff as equal opportunity contemplated by Article 16 (1) does not mean getting the particular post for which a number of persons have been considered... so long as the plaintiff, along with others under consideration, had been given his chance, it cannot be said that he had not had equal opportunity along with others, who may have been selected in preference to him. When the number of posts to be filled is less than the number of persons under consideration for those posts, it would be a case of many being called and few being chosen".[27]

However, equality of opportunity of employment under Article 16 (1) postulates equality between equals only, and does not confer any guarantee of absolute equality for all classes of persons. It admits of reasonable classification having nexus to the purpose behind. In Banarsi Das *vs.* State of Uttar Pradesh, the classification with regard to the appointment of Patwaris was upheld by the Supreme Court holding that : "the Government were within their rights to lay down qualifications for the new service and were entitled to exclude those who had exhibited a lack of proper discipline and hence Article 16(1) was not violated."[28]

The Supreme Court has ruled that equality of opportunity is guaranteed to all citizens in all matters relating to employment which includes appointment, promotion, salary, increments, leave, pension and other conditions of service, but does not prohibit prescription of reasonable rules for selection.

But in Union of India *vs.* R.G. Kashikar (1986) the Supreme Court held that "the denial of the benefit of revision of pay scales to the instructors on the ground that the National Fitness Corps was in transitional state and the proposal to transfer the services of the instructors was pending, was per se discriminatory and violative of Articles 14 and 16. The Central Government employees could not be classified as those who work on Central Government activities and those who work on State Government activities. Such classification would be without any rational and reasonable basis."[29] The Court, therefore, ruled :

> "Such a classification or differentiation of the instructors under the scheme as a class of Central Government

> employees for depriving them of the benefits in "matters relating to employment" which expression includes matters relating to salary, periodical increments, leave, gratuity, pension, age of superannuation, etc..., although they continued to remain Central Government employees, till the date of absorption, was per se discriminatory and violative of Articles 14 and 16 of the Constitution".[30]

In Smt. Poona Mal *vs.* Union of India (1985) the Supreme Court has specifically held the pension to an employee as a right arising out of his duties. The Court observed :

> "Pension is not merely a statutory right but it is the fulfilment of a constitutional promise in as much as it partakes of the character of public assistance in cases of unemployment, old-age, disablement, or similar other cases of undeserved want. Relevant rules merely make effective the constitutional mandate. Pension is a right not a bounty or gratuitous payment. The payment of pension does not depend on the discretion of the government but is governed by the relevant rules and anyone entitled to pension under the rules can claim it as a matter of right. Where the government servant rendered service, to compensate which a family pension scheme is devised, the widow and the dependent minors would equally be entitled to family pension as a matter of right."[31]

Thus, the pension is a constitutional mandate to the government emanating from directive principles and a right to the employees and his family arising out of the performance of duties by the government servant.

In the matter of confirmation of service, in the case B.S. Yadav *vs.* State of Haryana (1981) the Supreme Court has held :

> "The fairness which Articles 14 and 16 postulate is that if a promotee is otherwise fit for confirmation and a vacancy falling within the quota of promotees is available in which he can be confirmed, his confirmation ought not to be postponed until a direct recruit, whether yet appointed or not, completes his period of probation and thereupon becomes eligible for confirmation. The adoption

of this principle in the matter of confirmation will not, in practice, give any undue advantage to the promotees."[32]

Similarly, in State of U.P. *vs.* Ram Gopal Shukla (1981), the U.P. promotion by selection in consultation with the Public Service Commission (Procedure) Rules 1970 and the amendments made in 1972 was challenged as arbitrary and discriminatory. The Supreme Court ruled :

> "There appears to be no rational basis for such a departure from the ordinary operation of the 1970 Rules which envisaged the preparation of a new list every year and for singling out of one particular list for according perfect treatment to the persons whose names were contained therein. The classification in this case, therefore, cannot be said to be a reasonable classification based on intelligible differentia having a nexus to the object sought to be achieved.

"Further, though the rules regulating the conditions of service are within the executive power of State or its legislative powers under the provisions of Article 309, such rules have to be reasonable, fair and not grossly unjust, if they are to survive the test of Articles 14 and 16 of the Constitution. A rule which contemplates that unless the list of 300 persons in exhausted no other person can be selected obviously is unjust and it deprives other persons in the same situation of the opportunity of being considered for promotion."[33]

In State of Jammu and Kashmir *vs.* Triloki Nath Khosla, the Supreme Court has ruled that "equality being a dynamic concept with flexible import, the pragmatic doctrine of classification and equal treatment to all who fall within each class must be read into Articles 14 to 16, but care has to be taken to see that classification is not pushed to such an extent as to make the protective wall of equality raised by the trinity cave in and collapse."[34] The court held that the State may make rules guided by realities just as the legislature "is free of recognize degrees of harm and it may confine its restrictions to those classes of cases where the need is deemed to be the clearest".[35]

Earlier, in State of Mysore *vs.* V.P. Narasingha Rao also,

the Supreme Court had held that "there is no denial of equality of opportunity unless the person who complains of discrimination is equality situated with the person or persons who are alleged to have been favoured. Article 16(1) does not bar a reasonable classification of employees or reasonable test for their selection."[36]

But where a test of selection is based on unreasonableness, the court has struck down such rules. In State of Maharashtra *vs.* Raj Kumar (1982), the Supreme Court made the following observation : "We have gone through the rules framed by the Government and adopted by the Public Service Commission and we find that the rules framed suffer from clear and serious constitutional infirmities... In the first place, the object of the rule was to take officers who had full knowledge of rural life, its problems, aptitudes, working of the people in villages and the suitability of working as officers in the rural areas so as to be materially useful and in order to make a constructive contribution to the upliftment of rural life. In order to achieve this purpose a rule was made that a candidate coming from rural areas will be a rural candidate and he must have passed SSC Examination, which is held from a village or town having only a "C" type Municipality. This rule however, when translated, into action does not seem to fulfil or carryout the object because as the Rule stands, any person who may not have lived in a village at all can appear at SSC. Examination from a village and yet become eligible for selection in the competitive examination. Thus, there is no nexus between the classification made (assuming for the purpose of this case that the classification is unreasonable) and the object which is sought to be achieved as a result of which the rule is clearly violative of Articles 14 and 16 of the Constitution of India."[37] Further, the court held :

> "In such a situation there was absolutely no occasion for making an express provision for giving weightage which would virtually convert merit into demerit and demerit into merit and would be per se violative of Article 14 of the Constitution as being an impermissible classification. The rules of the weightage as applied in this case is manifestly unreasonable and wholly arbitrary and cannot be sustained'.[38]

"The rule also provides the viva voce Board would put relevant questions to judge suitability of candidates for working in rural areas and to test whether or not they have sufficient knowledge of rural problems, and this no doubt amounts to a sufficient safeguard to ascertain the ability of the candidate regarding his knowledge about the affairs of the village."[39] The Court, therefore, observed :

In the State of Kerala *vs.* Thomas N.M., Chief Justice A..N. Roy has epitomized the position in a few paras :

"Articles 14, 15 and 16 form part of a string of constitutionally guaranteed rights. These rights supplement each other. Article 16, which ensures to all citizens equality of opportunity in matters relating to employment is an incident of guarantee of equality in Article 14. Both Articles 14 and 16 (1) permit reasonable classification having a nexus to the object to be achieved.

"Discrimination is the essence of classification. Classification is, therefore, to be founded on substantial differences which distinguish persons grouped together from those left out of the groups and such differential attributes must bear a just and rational relation to the object sought to be achieved.

"Under Article 16(1) equality of opportunity means equality as between members of the same class of employees and not equality between members of separate, independent classes".

"The rule of parity is the equal treatment of equals in equal circumstances. The rule of differentiation is enacting laws differentiating between different persons or things in different circumstances. The circumstances which govern one set of persons or objects may not necessarily be the same as governing another set of persons or objects so that the question of unequal treatment does not really arise between persons governed by different conditions and different set of circumstances."

"A classification in order to be constitutional must rest upon distinctions that are substantial and not merely illusory. The test is whether it has a reasonable basis free from artificiality and arbitrariness embracing all and omitting none naturally falling into that category."[40]

Similarly, illuminating is the observation made by the Supreme Court on the multi-faceted traits of equality, comprising the string of Articles from 14 to 16 and standing as a bulwark against tyranny and discrimination. In E.P. Royappa *vs.* State of Tamil Nadu (1974), the Court observed thus :

> "Though enacted as a distinct and independent Fundamental Right because of its great importance as a principle ensuring equality of opportunity in public employment which is so vital to the building up of the new classless egalitarian society envisaged in the Constitution. Article 16 is only an instance of the application of the concept of equality enshrined in Article 14. In other words, Article 14 is the genus, while Article 16 is the species. Article 16 gives effect to the doctrine of equality in all matters relating to public employment. The basic principle which, therefore, informs Articles 14 to 16 is equality and inhibition against discrimination"[41]

Thus, equality under Article 16 could not have a different meaning and content from equality under Article 14. In this connection, we can visualize the similarity of conception when Mahatama Gandhi said :

> "Economic equality of my conception does not mean that everyone would literally have the same amount. It simply means that everybody should have enough for his or her needs. For instance, I require two shawls in winter, whereas my grandnephew Kanu Gandhi, who stays with me and is like my own son, does not require any warm clothing whatsoever. I require goat's milk, oranges and other fruit. Kanu can do with ordinary food. I envy Kanu, but there is no point in it. Kanu is a young man, whereas I am an old man of 76. The monthly expense of my food is far more than that of Kanu but that does not mean that there is economic inequality between us. The elephant needs a thousand times more food than the ant, but that is no indication of inequality. So, the real meaning of economic equality is : "To each according to his need." That is the definition of Marx. If a single man demanded as much as a man with wife and four children, that would be a violation of economic equality".[42]

> "Thus, we arrive at the constitutional truism that the State may classify, based upon substantial differentia, groups or classes and this process does not necessarily spell violation of Articles 14 to 16".[43]

The State is within the constitutional ambit if it frames necessary rules imposing reasonable conditions and prescribing necessary qualifications. It can, "lay down such prerequisite conditions for appointment as would be conducive to the maintenance of proper discipline amongst Government servants."[44] But such conditions must be available to all citizens and "must have reasonable relation to the suitability for a post".[45] "Knowledge of State language in the case of State service"[46] has been held to be a valid condition, as the test was for all candidates without discrimination. It was further justified on the ground that under Article 29 regional language and culture were to be encouraged. However, conditions borne out of regional considerations have been sometimes imposed, which were seemingly unjust. Conditions such as "graduates of a local university" or "only those need apply that have passed SSLC with Telugu as a language do not appear to be based on a rational consideration". "As it is, Article 16 has been an eyesore to many of the backward States, and there is a feeling of resentment, a psychological burden, that outsiders are thrust upon them by the Constitution. Consequently, they have been compelled—successfully also— to circumvent this provision by other means, especially by putting in a restricted educational and/or language qualification".[47]

However, in Sukha Nandan Thakur *vs.* State of Bihar the High Court has observed that "Article 15(1) is wider in scope than 16(2) because the former lays down general principles of equality of opportunity while the latter provides against discrimination on certain specific grounds. But this equality, not being a mathematical equality does not prevent an appointing authority from making selections from numerous candidates before makings appointments : only the selective test should not be arbitrary and must be based on some reasonable principle".[48]

The State is within its bounds to refuse to appoint a person to a post even after the inclusion of his name in the list of approved candidates. In K. Sadanadan *vs.* State of Kerala, the High Court upheld the right of the State

Government to refuse the appointment of the petitioner in case his character and antecedents were found doubtful and there was no violation of Article 16. The Court observed :

"The States Government is absolutely entitled to take the character and the antecedents of the petitioner into account. The qualification regarding character and antecedents had a reasonable basis in relation to the appointment".[49] But rejecting a candidate merely on the ground of political sufferer or political values has not been considered legitimate. The Supreme Court in the State of M.P. *vs.* Ramashankar Raghuvanshi has observed :

> "We do not have the slightest doubt that the whole business of seeking police reports, about the political faith, belief and association and the past political activity of a candidate for public employment is repugnant to the basic rights guaranteed by the Constitution... We think it offends the fundamental rights guaranteed by Articles 14 and 16 of the Constitution to deny employment to an individual because of his past political affinities, unless such affinities are considered likely to affect the integrity and efficiency of the individual's service."[50]

In Mervyn Continho *vs.* Collector of Custom, the Supreme Court held that there was no infringement of Article 16(1) in following the rotational system when there were two systems of recruitment.[51] But the Supreme Court, while examining Rule 9(2) of the Mysore Recruitment of Gazetted Probationers Rules (1959) which provided discretionary powers to the Government to appoint a candidate to a particular cadre for which it considered him more suitable, in the State of Mysore *vs.* S.G. Jayram, declared the above rule void and violative of Articles 14 and 15 (1) and observed that the Government under the cover of the impugned rule could exercise this unbridled power by assigning a Class I post to a less meritorious candidate and thereby unreasonably discriminate with other successful candidates and ignore their just claim for recruitment to the office under the State.[52]

Similarly, it has been held by the Supreme Court that no agreement or contract will offset the right accruing to a person under Article 16 (1). In M.V. Kurlakose *vs.* State of Kerala it maintained that the right of a person under agreement or award cannot be identified with rights under Article 16(1) of the Constitution.[53]

Thus, reasonable classification and formulation of rules and conditions of recruitment on a rational basis have been upheld as within the power of the State. It is also firmly established that Article 16 (1) covers the matter pertaining to promotion as well. Inequality or partisonality in providing opportunity for promotion is frowned at and has been declared violative of Article 16(1), though the court has held that Article 16(1) does not impose any restriction on the State "from laying conditions of efficiency or other qualifications for securing the best service, for being eligible for promotion".[54] It has been conclusively established that with rgard to promotion, which is nothing but appointment to thc higher grade, "all employees holding poets in the case grade shall be eligible for being considered on merits."[55]

However, it has been held that equality in promotion does not imply absolute equality, but only equality between members of the same class. In A.I.S.M. and A.S.M. *vs.* General Manager, Central Railway the Supreme Court observed : "Equality of promotion must mean equality as between members of the same class of employees, and not equality between members of separate and independent classes... That the rules of promotion of roadside Station Masters are not the same as those of guards does not mean that Article 16 has been violated."[56] The Supreme Court reiterated this position again in State of Punjab *vs.* Joginder Singh and observed, "if they were two distinct services, there was no question of inter se seniority between members of the two services nor of any comparison between the two in the matter of promotion".[57]

It has also been held that mere seniority does not confer any legal right to promotion and "there is no violation of Article 16(1) if a senior officer has been considered along with others but the Government has considered someone below him to be fit for the higher post".[58]

In the case of recruitment to a service from different sources, for the purpose of equivalence, the adjustment of seniority has been resorted to. In this process of adjustment of seniority between the two sources of recruits, a preferential treatment of one course to the other has also been held valid. In S.P. Jaishinghhani *vs.* Union of India (1967), the Supreme

Court observed that in case recruitment was made from two different sources, a preferential treatment of one in relation to the other for the purpose of adjustment or determination of seniority inter se can legitimately be sustained on the basis of a valid classification, if the difference between the two sources has a reasonable relation to the nature of the post to which the recruitment is made. In this case the Supreme Court upheld the provision contained in the seniority rules of the Income Tax Service, whereby a weightage was given to the promotees by providing that three years of outstanding work in class II will be treated as equivalent to two years of probation in Class I (Grade II) service.[59]

But in Narender Chadha *vs.* Union of India (1986), the Supreme Court held : "that when an officer has worked for a period for nearly fifteen to twenty years in a post and had never been reverted it cannot be held that the officer's continuous officiation was a mere temporary or local or stop gap arrangement even though the order of appointment may state so. In such circumstances the entire period of officiating has to be counted for seniority. Any other view would be violative of Articles 14 and 16(1) of the Constitution".[60]

Similarly, in N.K. Chauhan *vs.* State of Gujarat (1977) the Supreme Court had observed :

> "Seniority will depend on length of continuous officiating service and cannot be upset by later arrivals from the open market save to the extent to which any excess promotees may have to be pushed down."[61]

In the State of Jammu & Kashmir *vs.* Trilokinath Khosla, the J&K Engineering (Gazetted) Service Recruitment Rules, 1970, were impugned on the ground that they provided that only those Assistant Engineers who possessed Bachelor of Engineering degree or the qualification of AMIE would be eligible for promotion and the discrimination made between degree holders and diploma holders was arbitrary and capricious because academic or technical qualification should have been the basis of recruitment and of promotion.

It was held by the Supreme Court that unless the classification was unjust on the face of it, the burden was on the petitioner to set out facts necessary to sustain the plea of discrimination and to adduce cogent and convincing evidence to prove those facts, for there was a presumption that every factor which was relevant or material was taken into account in formulating the classification. Thus it was no part of the respondents' burden to justify the classification or to establish its constitutionality. "Formal education may not always produce excellence but a classification founded on variant educational qualifications is, for purposes of promotion to the post of Executive Engineer, to say the least, not unjust on the face of it and the onus, therefore, cannot shift from where it originally lay."[62]

Similarly, in the Registrar, High Court, Madhya Pradesh *vs.* B.S. Nigam it was held by the Supreme Court that equality of opportunity under Article 16(1) does not imply promotion to a post even without due experience. It observed, "where experience as Civil Judge, Class I, at least for a short period is a necessary qualification for promotion as Additional District and Sessions Judge, a Civil Judge, Class II, who on a number of occasions had been found unfit to be posted as civil judge, Class I, in comparison with others who were his junior in service, cannot, as soon as he is found fit to exercise the power of a Civil Judge, Class I, claim seniority over his Juniors earlier selected to exercise the power of Civil Judge, Class I, in the matter of promotion to the posts of Additional District and Sessions Judges. To decide his claim merely on the basis of entry into service would be a mockery of all cannons of justice and fair play."[63]

In the State of Gujrat *vs.* C.S. Desai, the Supreme Court held "that the direct recruits and promotees in Class II constituted two distinct groups or classes. This classification had a historical background and was based on intelligible differentia".[64] It was further observed that 'if the pre-selection service as officiating Deputy Engineer of direct recruits having such service is taken into account for the purpose of promotion, it would create two classes amongst the same group and result in discrimination against those direct recruits who had no such pre-selection service to their credit".[65]

Again, in Bishan Serup Gupta *vs.* Union of India (1975), the Supreme Court observed : "There is no question in this case of any discrimination being made in a service after officers of the two sources have been brought in one cadre. It is true that seniority is a vital element in the matter of promotion but that does not mean that allotment of seniority by rule, relative to recruitment, involves any classification for the purposes of promotion. The argument that the promotees and direct recruits become one class immediately on entry and, thereafter, there could be no classification between them does not disclose the correct approach to the problem of fixing inter se seniority between them. When recruits from two sources have come into a service it is essential to fix inter se seniority for a proper integration of the cadre. Therefore, it is really a case of adjustment of seniority between the recruits and does not amount to making a classification after their absorption in one service."[66]

Similarly, in R.R. Makashi *vs.* I.M. Menon (1982), the Supreme Court onserved :

> "When personel drawn from the different sources are being absorbed and integrated into a new department, it is primarily for the Government or the executive authority concerned to decide as a matter of policy how the equation of posts should be effected. The courts will not interfere with such a decision unless it is shown to be arbitrary, unreasonable or unfair, and if no manifest unfairness or unreasonableness is made out, the court will not sit in appeal and examine the propriety or wisdom of the principle of equation of posts adopted by the Government."[67]

The Court, therefore, held, 'in the instant case, in equating the post of Supply Inspector in the CFD (Controller of Food-grains Distribution) Bombay, which were to be merged with a new Bombay Rationing Office (BRO), with that of clerk with two years regular service in other government departments, no arbitrary or unreasonable treatment was involved".[68]

Thus, reasonable classification in the matters of promotion also has been held to be valid for the purpose of Article 16(1), Further it has also been held by the Supreme Court that qualification for a particular post can be a rational differentia even in the matter of promotion. In Subhash Chandra Jain *vs.* Delhi Electric Supply Undertaking, the court held that "DESU had the power to prescribe relevant qualification for promotion as junior stenographers,"[69] and it was directed by the court that the steno-typists passing the trade-test must be posted "in displacement of steno-typists who had not passed the trade-test but were functioning as junior stenographer".[70] The Supreme Court observed :

> "We see no difficulty in resolving the conflict and we discern a plain discrimination in the petitioner being denied the claim that he puts forward that if he passes the trade-test which is the qualification for junior stenographer's post, he should be posted in displacement of steno-typists who have not passed the trade-test, but are still functioning as junior stenographers. It is a well-established law that qualification for a particular post can be a rational differentia within the meaning of Article 16. It is equally clear that when a qualification has been prescribed for a post, that cannot be obliterated by posting those who do not have that qualification".[71]

Moreover, in S.L. Sachdeva *vs.* Union of India, Chief Justice Y.V. Chandrachud, delivering the judgement, held that, "Directions in the letter of the Director-General P&T dated 19-5-75 providing that the number of selection grade posts of head clerks, which will be available to the Upper Division Clerks drawn from the audit offices in the savings bank control and internal check organization would be determined on the basis of the existing strength, at any given time, of such clerks in the particular circle, is unreasonable and arbitrary.

"Apart from the injustice in specific cases where Upper Division Clerks drawn from the audit offices are attached to comparatively smaller circles, the classification made for the purpose of determining the promotional opportunities seems to us unreasonable and arbitrary... There is no reason thus why different tests should be prescribed for determining their respective promotional opportunities, and that too solely with reference to the source from which they are drawn. The test of educational qualifications can conceivably be an intelligible differentia bearing nexus with the object of ensuring greater efficiency in public services. But once a cadre is formed by recruiting persons drawn from different departments of the government, there would normally be no justification for discriminating between them by subjecting one class to more onerous terms in the matter of promotional chances. The impugned directives are, therefore, unconstitutional".[72]

Similarly, in G.S. Lamba *vs.* Union of India (1985), the Supreme Court observed :

> "Once the promotees were promoted regularly to substantive vacancies even if temporary, unless there was a chance of their demotion to the lower cadre, their continuous officiation confers on them an advantage of being senior to the latter recruits under Rule 21(4). By the enormous departure or by the power to relax, the quota rule was not adhered to, and so the rota Rule for inter se seniority as prescribed under Section 25(1) (ii) cannot be given effect to. In the absence of any other valid principle of seniority it is well established that the continuous officiation in the cadre, grade or service will provide a valid principle of seniority. The seniority lists having not been prepared on this principle are liable to be quashed and set aside".[73]

The termination of service of an employee is also covered by the guarantee of equality of opportunity under Article 16. An employee in the service of the State is safeguarded against arbitrary and discriminatory termination of services. The mere fact of termination of service, however, cannot make the act arbitrary, unless the petitioner proves candidly the discriminatory and arbitrary action of the authority. In the Union of India *vs.* Pandurang, the Supreme Court held that the termination of the petitioner on the ground that he has been detained under the law of Preventive Detention was valid and observed, "the service of an employee was terminated while employees junior to him were retained in service does not by itself prove unequal treatment".[74]

Similarly, in Champaklal *vs.* Union of India, the Supreme Court held that there is no discrimination " if the Government servants are classified into temporary and permanent servants and are, therefore, provided different modes of termination of service seperately, e.g. by service of a notice".[75] It was further held in this case that if a temporary employee is retrenched on account of abolition of one of several temporary posts requiring same qualifications and length of service and a junior to him is retained while he is retrenched, such retrenchment must be held to be arbitrary and violative of Article 16.[76] But, as it has been held by the Supreme Court in Satish Chandra Anand *vs.* Union of India, the discharge of a public servant serving on a contract basis for a temporary period cannot be treated as a case of dismissal under Article 311.[77]

In Balbir Singh Marware *vs.* State of Madhya Pradesh the Supreme Court held that retrenchment depends on the discretion of the authorities concerned and is not illegal unless there is clear infringement of any constitutional or legal right, but it was made clear that like appointment to an office certain selection and gradation of employees is imperative for purposes of retrenchment.[78]

However, the Supreme Court has always held that termination of the service of an employee must be based on rational grounds and must not be arbitrary. In Nepal Singh *vs.* State of Uttar Pradesh (1985), the court observed :

> "A fundamental implication in the guarantee of Articles 14 and 16 is that fair and just treatment will be accorded to all, whether individually or jointly as a class. When a government servant satisfies the court prima facie that an order terminating his service violates Articles 14 and 16, the competent authority must discharge the burden of showing that the power to terminate the services was exercised honestly and in good faith, on valid considerations, fairly and without discrimination."[79]

Similarly, in K.C. Joshi *vs.* Union of India (1985) the Supreme Court held :

> "If the termination of service is attempted to be sustained on the ground that the services of the incumbent were no more required, it will impel the court to inquire whether the post had been abolished or whether, while retaining his juniors, the inconvenient person was thrown out under the garb of his being surplus. Court has to examine how he became unsuitable".[80]

It ruled : "In the present case having regard to the several certificates obtained by the appellant from officers under whom he had worked certifying him to be sincere, hard working, dependable, well-conversant with his work, conscientious and of blameless character, as also the facts showing the ONGC's dislike and detestation for the appellant, trade unionist, who was also a protected workmen, it is clear that the charge of unsuitability is either cooked up or conjured up for a collateral purpose of doing away with the service of an active trade union worker who because of his activities became an eyesore. The appellant was thus victimized by the ONGC, a public sector undertaking. The discharge of the appelant was also violative of Articles 14 and 16 as his juniors were shown to have been retained in service and he had been picked up arbitrarily."[81] The Court further observed :

> "When the State action affects livelihood or attaches stigma, the punitive action can be taken after holding an inquiry according to the minimum principles of natural justice, which are an unbiased judge, and an opportunity to controvert the allegation and to clear oneself".[82]

In the circumstances, the termination of the service of the petitioner was declared illegal, invalid and unjustified. However, retrenchment on account of "unsatisfactory work and conduct" and "doubtful antecedents" has been held to be valid.[83] But, "arbitrary imposition of a ban"[84] or termination on the ground simply that "he belongs to another State or has a particular colour or height"[85] has been held to be arbitrary and void.

In the matter of superannuation, if the Government decides to extend the age of retirement, any discriminatory classification has been held to be void. In Andhra Pradesh, the age of superannuating was reduced from 58 to 55 by enacting Andhra Pradesh Public Employment (Regulation and Superannuating) Act (23 of 1984). However, on public agitation, realizing injustice caused, an ordinance was promulgated after some time, restoring the age of retirement to 58 years. But soon after restoration, an Amendment Act (3 of 1985) was passed that persons retired under the provision of the Act (23 of 1984) before the date of passing of the Ordinance shall be excluded from the benefit of the Ordinance. A case B. Prabhakar Rao *vs.* State of Andhra Prdesh (1986) came up before the Supreme Court. The court held that the action of the Government and provisions of the ordinance and A.P.P.E. (Amendment) Act (3 of 1985) denying a benefit to a class of Government employees were arbitrary and discriminatory. As the court lucidly put it :

> "Legislation to remedy wrongs ought not to exclude from their purview a few of the wronged persons unless the situation and the circumstances make the redressal of the wrong, in their case, either impossible or so detrimental to the public interest that the mischief of the remedy overweighs the mischief sought to be remedied.

"It is open to the court to give retrospectivity to a legislation to which the legislature plainly and expressly refused to give retrospectivity, because, unlike the United Kingdom, India has a written Constitution which confers justiciable fundamental rights, and so the very refusal to make an Act retrospective or the non-application of the Act with reference to a date or to an event that took place before the enactment may, by itself, create an impermissible classification justifying the striking down of the non-retrospectivity or non-application clause, as offending the fundamental right to equality before the law and the equal protection of the law".[86]

Compendiously, it can be said that the Supreme Court has taken up strict interpretation of laws to safeguard the interest of the employees, on the whole.

Clause (2)

Clause (2) of Article 16 is complementary to Clause (1) thereof in the sense that it helps to effectively enforce the general provisions of equality of opportunity provided in the latter. It rules out certain specific grounds of discrimination like religion, race, caste, sex, place of birth, descent and residence and stipulates that there can be no discrimination between citizens, only on one or more of these grounds. Thus, it is specific prohibition of discrimination and helps to give a meaning and content of Clause (1), ascertain its parameter and gives an inflection to it. The two clauses are conjugated together to give an effective reality to the right of equality of opportunity, and the other three clauses serve as a specific illustration of this right of equality of opportunity or the method of its application in some specific cases.

"The two new grounds of prohibited discrimination used in Clause (2) are "descent" and "residence'. And they are not used in Clause (2) of Article 15. We have already noted that their inclusion was an act of conciliation between the warring factions in the Constituent Assembly to ward off the danger of provincialism, and as a sort of appeasement to the protagonists, Clause (3) was inserted as a relief measure. These two words have been used not only to avoid discrimination between citizens in every nook and corner of the country but also to maintain a national character of services under the State in the interest of unity and integrity of the nation. The courts in India have effectively safeguarded this right to equality in the matter of public employment whenever it was denied to a citizen on grounds mentioned in Clause (2) of Article 16. Thus, in Dasarath Ram Rao *vs.* Andhra Pradesh, the Supreme Court held that descent was a forbidden ground of classification. The impugned Act provided that in the appointment of village Munsiffs the Collector should consider the case of heirs of the last incumbents of the office only. The court held it as a clear case of discrimination on the ground of descent only in as much as it stipulated that only persons who are heirs of the last incumbents to the office can be considered for that office, and none else."[87]

Likewise in Balkrishna Hegde *vs.* Shankar Hegde, the Mysore High Court ruled that Government offices at the village level are well within the meaning of "Office under the State", and, consequentally, the appointing authority should make recruitment without any regard for the principle of hereditary succession even for the offices in the village held by village officers, and held the rule stipulating such provision as violation of Article 16(2) on the ground of descent.[88]

Similarly, in Venkataramne *vs.* State of Madras, the petitioner was more qualified than some others recruited in the subordinate judicial service, but was not selected since the Communal Government order had fixed a quota for different castes and communities. The Supreme Court by its unanimous judgement held that the petitioner was not selected for appointment only because he was a Brahmin and this ineligibility created by the impugned Government order constituted a clear violation of his right under Clauses (1) and (2) of Article 16. Thus the Order, making discrimination on the ground of caste by making the distribution of offices amongst communities according to fixed ratios, was struck down.[89]

In considering the cases of discrimination in the matter of public employment, the Supreme Court has not only limited its judgement on the grounds of discrimination prohibited under Article 16(2), but has even gone beyond it, if the discrimination has seemed grossly unjust and palpably unreasonable. It may be recalled in this connection that Clause (1) of Article 16 has wider import and can cover every ground of discrimination other than those mentioned in Clause (2) of the Article. Not only that, even Article 14 can be invoked if the discrimination is patently unreasonable and flagrantly violative of natural justice. Thus, while in Bhaktavetsalam *vs.* A.P.P.S.C., the High Court held that advocates, for the purpose of recruitment of the State judiciary, must be practising advocates in the High Court of that State only,[90] the Supreme Court in Pendurangrao *vs.* A.P.P.S.C., a case of similar nature, maintained that although the advocates practiced in different High Courts, they belonged to the same class of advocates. It was, therefore, ruled that the classification between the same class of advocates merely on the ground of maintaining the efficiency of the State Judicial Service must be struck down as violative of Articles 14 and 16.[91]

In Janardhana *vs.* Union of India (1983) a case of such flagrant discrimination came up before the Supreme Court. The Court observed unanimously :

"We will have qualms of conscience if we do not draw attention to a very unjust, unfair, and inequitable situation having a demoralizing effect on public services probably ensuing from certain rules framed by the Government and the decisions of this court. Even where the recruitment to a service is from more than one source and a quota is fixed for each service, yet more often the appointing authority to meet its exigencies of service exceeds the quota from the easily available source of promotees because the procedure of making recruitment from the market by direct recruitment is long prolix and time-consuming. After the promotee is promoted, he continuously renders service and is neither found wanting nor inefficient and is discharging his duties to the satisfaction of all, a fresh recruit from the market years after a promotee was inducted in the service comes and challenges all the past recruitments made before he was born in service and some decisions, especially the ratio of Jaisinghani's case as interpreted in two B.S. Gupta's cases, give him an advantage to the extent of the promotee being preceded in seniority by a direct recruit who enters service long after the promotee was promoted and was rendering service when the direct recruit may be a schoolian or a college-going boy.... A mandamus issued in Jaisinghani's case led to a situation where promotees of the year 1962 had to yield place to direct recruits of 1965 and the position worsened thereafter.

Shorn of all service jurisprudence jargon, let us bluntly notice the situation that a primary school student when the promotee was a member of the service barged in and claimed and got seniority over the promotee. If this has not a demoralizing effect on service we fail to see what other inequitous approach would be more damaging.

It is, therefore, time to clearly initiate a proposition that a direct recruit who comes into service, after the promotee was already unconditionally and without reservation promoted and whose promotion is not shown to be invalid or illegal according to relavant statutory or non-statutory rules, should not be permitted by any principle of seniority to score a march over a promotee because that itself being arbitrary would be violative of Articles 14 and 16."[92]

The decision speaks volumes about the deepest concern of the highest court of justice on the land to mitigate injustice where the impugned rule or legislation is blatantly discriminating and arbitrary.

Similarly, in Indra Vadan N. Shah *vs.* State of Gujarat (1986), the Supreme Court declared "the provisions of rule 6(4) (i) read with 6(4) (iiia) of the Gujarat Judicial Service Recruitment Rules, 1961, irrational, arbitrary and unreasonable as there is no nexus to the object sought to be achieved by introducing the age restriction in regard to appointment of Assistant Judge by promotion from amongst members holding posts of civil judge (Junior Division) and those in the cadre of civil judge (Senior Division) whose names have been entered in the selection list. Though the post of Assistant Judge as well as the post of District Judge belong to the senior branch of Gujarat Judicial Service, yet in the higher cadre of District Judge no such age bar has been introduced."[93]

The Court further observed :

> "Articles 14 and 16 of the Constitution ensure that there should not be any discrimination in the matter of appointment in service, nor will there be any arbitrariness or unreasonableness in the rules of recruitment providing for appointment in the service either by promotion or by direct recruitment".[94] And held, "there is obviously no rationale nor any reasonableness for introduction of this age bar in regard to appointment by promotion to the post of an Assistant Judge. The rule is, therefore, arbitrary and it violates the salutary principles of equality and want of arbitrariness in the matter of public employment as guaranteed by Articles 14 and 16 of the Constitution".[95]

Finally, the nature of the Right to Equality of Opportunity s not in the nature of a property in private possession, and t must be shorn of any monopolistic nature. This has been succinctly put in the observation of the Supreme Court in State of Maharastra *vs.* Chandrabhan (1963).

"Public employment opportunity is national wealth in which all citizens are equally entitled to share and no class of people can monopolize public employment in the guise of efficiency' or other ground, but the right to equal opportunity to public employment cannot be treated as new form of private property with its attribute of competitive exploitation".[96]

Clause (3)

Clause (3) provides a leeway to discrimination on the ground of residence prohibited under Clause (2) of Article 16 and is a sort of specification of the method of application of the relevant ground under Clause (2). It illustrates permissible classification on the ground of residence. It points out the way in which the contemplated prohibition on the ground of residence" is to be applied in a particular case and empowers the Parliament, instead of the local legislature as heretofore, to make law, if necessary, specifying for a class or classes of employment or appointment to an office under the State Government or Union Territory any requirement as to residence within that State or Union Territory prior to such employment or appointment. In short, it exemplifies permissible classifi-cation on the basis of residential qualification. Soon after the enforcement of the Constitution, a States Reorganization Commission was set up. In 1955, the Commission in its report drew the attention of the Union Government towards the urgency of framing rules under Clause (3) and pointed out the dubious device adopted by some States of preferring the "sons of the soil" as against "birds of the passage" in their public employment. The Parliament, therefore, passed the Public Employment (Requirement as to Residence) Act, 1957 and annuled all State laws in force prescribing residential qualification for public employment in States or Union Territories. Under the Act, no one can stand disqualified merely on the ground that he is not the resident of a particular State. However, Section 3 of this Act empowers the Central Government to frame rules in respect of certain class or classes of employment under any State or Union Territory prescribing requirement as regards residence. The Act further provides that any condition of the knowledge of State language shall be illegal and void. These provisions have been made with a view to ensuring the unity of the country and achieve the goal of national integration.

The most important case under this clause was A.V.S. Narsinha Rao *vs.* State of Andhra Pradesh in which the State Government order of January 21, 1969, relieving all non-domiciled persons on and after November 1, 1956, from certain categories of posts reserved for the domiciles of Telangana under the Andhra Pradesh Public Employment (Requirement as to Residence) Rules, 1959, framed by the Union Government, was challenged. The case came up in appeal before the Supreme Court under Article 32 of the Constitution. The petitioners submitted that their Right to Equality in the matters of public employment was infringed on the ground of residence by the order of the State Government. The relevant Act of the Parliament, the Rules of 1959 made thereunder by the Union Government and the consequential order of the State Government were declared void. While delivering the judgement, Chief Justice Hidayatullah, observed :

> "The Constitution, as it stands, speaks of a whole State as the venue for residential qualification, and it is impossible to think that the Constituent Assembly was thinking of residence in districts, taluquas, cities, towns or villages. The fact that this clause is an exception and came as an amendment must dictate that no narrow construction upon the conception should be placed as indeed the debates in the Constituent Assembly also seem to indicate."[97]

Thus, the Supreme Court maintained in this case that there could be no discrimination on the ground of period of residence between residents of the same State. It held that Clause (3) of Article 16 provided only an exception to Rule of Equality under Clauses (1) and (2) with a view to respecting" local sentiments or to prevent inroads from more advanced States into less developed States".[98]

Soon after this judgement, a case V. Venkat Reddy *vs.* State of Andhra Pradesh came up before the High Court in which the validity of "Mulki Rules", which were declared by the Nizam of Hyderabad during pre-independence days, was challenged. The Full Bench of the High Court ruled that, "The Mulki Rules are not valid and operative after the formation of the State of Andhra Pradesh. In any event, they do not revive and cannot be deemed to be valid and operative in view of the decision of the Supreme Court in A.V. S. Narsimha Rao's case".[99]

The matter came up in appeal before the Supreme Court. The Court ruled that Sections 2 and 3 of the Public Employment (Requirement as to Residence) Act, 1957, contemplated an integrated scheme. It was held that once Section 3 became unconstitutional, Section 2 thereof which rejected the "Mulki Rules" was also to be held invalid. Therefore, the sole result was that, in law, there was no repeal at all of "Mulki Rules".[100] The judgement of the Supreme Court created a furore in the

State, and ultimately the Centre had to devise a six-point formula for preserving the unity and integrity of Andhra Pradesh, through which the Mulki Rules were done away with, and the district-wise residential qualification for the purpose of public employment introduced.

Clause (4)

The Clause (4) of Article 16 typifies permissible classifi-cation of citizens under Clause (1) of the article who on the ground of their intense socio-economic and educational backwardness, are declared as constituting a "backward class" by the State, and who are deemed to be unrepresented in the services of that State. It may be recalled that under Article 340 of the Constitution the President is empowered to appoint a commission to investigate into the conditions of backward classes and to ascertain a test of backwardness for application in different States. As we have noted earlier, the efforts so far in this direction have been abortive and, as an interim arrangement, the States have been asked to devise their own test formula in the meantime and go ahead with their plan for advancement of the backward classes in their States. This has given rise to a variety of tests in different States and has given rise to a lot of litigation. Further, under Articles 341 and 342, the President may, with respect to any State or Union Territory, by public notification, specify the castes, races or tribes or parts of or group within castes, races or tribes, and specify the tribes or tribal communities, which shall for the purpose of this Constitution be deemed to be Scheduled Castes and Scheduled Tribes respectively in relation to that State or Union Territory. And, above all, the socio-economic rights of the citizen enunciated in Part IV of the Constitution, which, though non-justiciable by their very nature, yet fundamental in the governance of the State, contain Article 46 which ensures that, while making laws, "the state shall promote with special care the educational and economic interest of the weaker section of the people, and in particular, of the Scheduled Castes and the Scheduled Tribes, and shall protect them from social injustice and all forms of exploitation".[101]

Thus, there are two sets of backward classes viz. firstly, those backwardmost classes of citizens, who have been declared by the President as Scheduled Castes and Scheduled Tribes under Articles 341 and 342 of the Constitution; and, secondly, "other backward classes as the President may, on receipt of the report of a commission appointed under Clause (1) of Article 340, by order specify...[102], These "other backward classes" are left to be determined by the States till touch time the President is enabled to act under Article 340.

This has, however, created a ticklish situation. As the material power is the key to socio-economic salvation, unless a uniform test is devised, the starving millions in different States will turn the test of backwardness formulated by different States on very varying considerations into a game of hide-and-seek, and the veracity of the observation made by Justice Iyer of the Supreme Court cannot be denied that "the employment market is distressingly a musical-chair business and when starvation faces men their sympathy for their far weaker brethren vanishes".[103] The term "backward classes of citizens" continues to remain a lawyer's paradise and is subjected to jugglery of words in the courts of justice. As a matter of fact, there is no precise and immutable yardstick to gauge the criteria in this regard, which leads to very various interpretation of this clause from time to time and the judges continue to wield wide discretion while applying it. Some members of the Constituent Assembly in the course of deliberations had already observed that in the absence of a clear definition, the term "backward classes of citizens" might be subjected to different interpretations and might lead to unwarranted litigations. Dr Ambedkar, however, allayed the misgivings :

> "If the local government included in this category of reservations such a large number of seats, I think one could very well go to the Federal Court and the Supreme Court and say that the reservation is of such a magnitude that the rule regarding equality of opportunity has been destroyed and the court will then come to the conclusion whether the local government or the State Government has acted in a reasonable and prudent manner."[104] Earlier when a question was put to the Chairman of the Drafting

> Committee as to what was a backward community, Dr. Ambedkar retorted : "A backward community is a community which is backward in the opinion of the Government".[105] As regards the quantum of reservation, Dr Ambedkar said : "A reservation of 70 per cent of the posts would be an abuse of the provision in Article 16(4) which was intended to authorize the reservation of a minority of seats".[106]

But this is only about the quantum of reservation. The expectation of Dr. Ambadkar that the Government will form a uniform opinion as to what constitutes backwardness is belied so far and the matter remains the bone of contention between the contending parties and is under fire. There are three other Articles of the Constitution which may be useful for understanding the intricacies of the problem of vagueness the word "backward" is beset with.

Article 340 making provision for appointment of a commission to investigate the conditions of backward classes reads :

> "340 (1) The President may by order appoint a commission consisting of such persons as he thinks fit to investigate the conditions of socially and educationally backward classes within the territory of India and the difficulties under which they labour and make recommendations as to the steps that should be taken by the Union or any State to remove such difficulties and to improve their condition and as to the grants that should be made for the purpose by the Union or any State and the conditions subject to which such grants should be made, and the order appointing such commission shall define the procedure to be followed by the Commission.
>
> (2) A commission so appointed shall investigate the matters referred to them and present to the President a report setting out the facts as found by them and making such recommendations as they think proper.
>
> (3)............"[107]

Besides Article 338, in Clause (1), provides for special officer for Scheduled Castes and Scheduled Tribes, to be appointed by the President, and in Clause (2) specifies the duty of the said commission. Clause (3) of Article 338 reads :

"338 (3). In this Article, reference to the Scheduled Castes and Scheduled Tribes shall be construed as including reference to such other backward classes as the President may on receipt of the report of the commission appointed under Clause (1) of Article 340, by order specify and also to the Anglo-Indian community".[108]

Finally, Article 335 provides :

"335, The claims of the members of the Scheduled Castes and Scheduled Tribes shall be taken into consideration, consistently, with the maintenance of efficiency of administration, in the making of appointments to services and posts in connection with the affairs of the Union or of a State".[109]

A perusal of the above-mentioned Articles leads us to believe that the term "backward class" includes within its meaning the term "Scheduled Castes and Scheduled Tribes" for all purpose, but not vice versa. The former is included in the latter as "other backward classes" only once, i.e. with its reference to Article 338, Thus the Constitution nowhere defines "backward classes" and it is left to the President, under the Constitution, to define and specify these classes. The President has been able to define and specify the Scheduled Castes and Scheduled Tribes, the backward most classes, within the territory of India under Articles 341 and 342, but is not enabled to define and specify "other backward classes" in pursuance of Article 340. Consequently, a stop-gap arrangement has been made by allowing States to formulate their own criteria to ascertain the "other backward classes of citizens" and this has endangered the unity and integrity of the country, engendered on unjust sharing in the loaves and fishes meant for the more acutely backwards, and engulfed the people in vacillations and vicissitudes. It is high time, therefore, that the government rises to the occasion to enable itself to devise a uniform test to ascertain "other backward classes" within the territory of India. As it is, the court is the only saviour against unfairness and arbitrary executive orders regarding the test and composition of backward classes in different States and the autophagous instinct of some castes unfairly declared as backward class by the State. Let us have a look at some important judicial pronouncements to be able to see more clearly the picture displayed by Clause 4 of Article 16 and adjudge how far the courts have been able to protect the interest of the social brackets consisting the backward classes. The first important case that came up before the Supreme Court with regard to Clause 4 was Venkat Ramana *vs.* State of Madras. The Madras Public Service Commission invited applications for 83 posts of District Munsiffs under the Subordinate Judicial Service. The notification of the Commission specified that the selection of candidates was to be made on the caste and communal basis as per rules prescribed under the Madras Communal Government Order. The caste-wise ratio was as follows : Harijan—19. Muslim—5, Christian—6, Backward Hindus—10, Non-Brahmin Hindu—32 and Brahmins—11. Thus the total number of vacancies were proposed to be filled on a caste and communal basis. The Supreme Court struck down the order as completely violative of Article 16(2) of the Constitution. Justice S. R. Das ruled that Article 16(4) does not enable to reserve posts on communal lines, and declared :

"Article 16(4) permits reservation in favour of backward classes and reservation in favour of other communities which cannot be regarded as backward is not sanctioned by Article 16(4) and such a reservation violates the guarantees contained in Article 16(1) and (2)". Dealing with the facts involved in the case, the court observed that the ineligibility of the petitioner "created by communal Government order does not appear to us to be sanctified by Clause (4) of Article 16 and it is an infringement of the fundamental rights guaranteed to the petitioner as an individual citizen under Article 16(1) and (2). The communal Government order, in our opinion, is repugnant to the provisions of Article 16, and is as such void and illegal. We, therefore, direct the respondents to consider and dispose of the petitioner's application for the post after taking it on file on its merits and without applying the rule of communal rotation". (Venkat Ramana *vs.* State of Madras)

Thus, the presumption that the Government can reserve the posts on caste and communal basis was shattered in the very first case that came up before the Court, when it held that there can be no reservation of posts for persons who do not belong to "backward class," under Clause (4) of Article 16.

The next important case was the General Manager, Southern Railways *vs.* Rangachari (1962). Two circulars issued by the Railway Board reserving some (promotional) selection posts in class III of the Railway Service in favour of the members of the Scheduled Castes and Scheduled Tribes were questioned in that case as offending Article 16. It was contended that Article 16(4) applied only to reservation of posts at the stage of initial appointment and not to promotional posts. This contention was finally rejected by the Supreme Court and it was held that Article 16(4) applied at the stage of initial appointment as well as at the stage of promotion by selection. It is also noteworthy that the Supreme Court pronounced, for the first time in its judgement, that Article 16(4) is in the nature of an exception to the Rule of Equality of Opportunity, and as such it relates only to appointment, and not to service conditions, like Clause 1 or 2. (General Manager Southern Railways *vs.* Rangachari, 1962)

In Devedasan *vs.* Union of India (1964), the Supreme Court conclusively observed that reservation for the backward communities should not interfere with the rights of other communities. The principle that the reserved quotas should not together exceed 50 per cent of the available vacancies in any one year was affirmed by the Supreme Court, as the reason for striking down a "carry-forward" rule which stipulated that for promotions in the Central Secretariat Service it will be permissible to carry forward the vacancies of the annual reserved quota for two successive years. However, in the instant case it was found that observance of the rule had resulted in 65 per cent of the vacancies of the year being filled by reserved quotas, current and carried forward. The "carry-forward" rule was held unconstitutional on the ground that each year of recruitment had to be considered as a distinct unit for applying the 50 per cent rule (upheld by the court/earlier in the Balaji case), for the satisfaction of Article 16(1). Seventeen-and-a-half per cent of the vacancies were to be reserved for the Scheduled Castes and Scheduled Tribes in any year. This carry-forward rule so operated in the instant case that out of 45 appointments, 29 were from amongst the Scheduled Castes and Scheduled Tribes. Justice Mudholkar, on behalf of the majority, while delivering the judgement, observed :

"We would like to emphasize that the guarantee contained in Article 16(1) is for ensuring equality of opportunity for all citizens relating to employment, and to appointment to any office under the State. This means that on every occasion for recruitment the State should see that all citizens are treated equally. The guarantee is to each individual citizen and, therefore, every citizen who is seeking employment or appointment to an office under the State is entitled to be afforded an opportunity for seeking such employment or appointment whenever it is intended to be filled. In order to effectuate the guarantee each year of recruitment will have to be considered by itself and the reservation for backward communities should not be so excessive as to create a monopoly or to disturb the legitimates claims of other communities". (Devadasan *vs.* Union of India 1964).

It is important to remember that the Court did not strike down the rule on any hypothetical consideration of its adverse effect in future or on the ground that it was inherently vicious. It was founded upon the actual working of the rule in practice, and the judgement indicated that the effect of such a rule would have to be watched from year to year.

In Bhaiyalal *vs.* Harikishan Singh (1965), the Supreme Court held that an inquiry whether the appellant belonged to the Bohar Caste, which was not recognized as a Scheduled Caste, or to the Chamar Caste, as declared by him, could not be permitted because of the provisions container in Article 341. No court can come to a finding that any caste or any tribe is a scheduled caste or a scheduled tribe, because under Article 341 a Notification to this effect is issued by the President only after an elaborate inquiry, and the motive behind the Notification is to provide protection to the members of these limping brackets of the society. Thus a court cannot sit in judgement on the policy of inclusion of any caste or group within the caste or any tribe or group within the tribe in the list of Scheduled Castes and Scheduled Tribes notified under Article 341. They are Scheduled Castes and Scheduled Tribes and not a caste within the ordinary meaning of caste. "The President notifies Scheduled Castes not with reference to any caste characteristics, but their abysmal backwardness, as in evident from the scheme of Part XVI. He appoints under Article 338 a special Officer whose duty is to investigate all matters relating to safeguards for the Scheduled Castes and Scheduled Tribes. The Constitution provides not merely for adequate representation of the Scheduled Castes and Scheduled Tribes to services and posts under the Union and States, but also provides for reservation of seats for them in the legislature.

A cursory study of the Article relating to the status and safeguards of the Scheduled Castes and Scheduled Tribes puts it beyond doubt that the Founding Fathers have assigned to them a special place and shown towards them special concern and charged the State with special mandates to redeem these handicapped human sectors from their grossly retarded situation,. Indeed, they are not merely backward, but are the backward most and cannot be equated with just any other caste in the Hindu fold". (Bhaiyalal *vs.* Harikishan Singh 1965).

In C.A. Rajendran *vs.* Union of India (1958) an official memorandum of the Union Government was impugned as discriminatory on the ground that it provided reservations for the Scheduled Castes and Scheduled Tribes only in Class III and IV services and deprived them of the benefit of such reservation at the time of appointment for Class I and II posts. The Supreme Court rejecting the contention observed that Article 16(4) did not guarantee any right to any citizen, nor did it impose any constitutional or legal obligation on the State to compulsorily make reservation for the backward classes at the initial stage of recruitment or at the stage of promotion. It only enables the State to make reservation for the backward classes and in consonance with Article 335. "the claims of the members of the Schedule Castes and Scheduled Tribes shall be taken into consideration, consistantly with the maintenance of efficiency of administration" while making appointments. Dismissing the petition, Justice V. Ramaswami observed :

> "Article 16(4) is an enabling provision and confers a discretionary power on the State to make a reservation of appointments in favour of the backward class of citizens which, in its opinion, is not adequately represented in the services of the State". (C.A. Rajendran *vs.* Union of India 1958).

In State of Punjab *vs.* Hiralal (1971), the Supreme Court reversed the decision of the High Court observing :

> "The extent of reservation to be made is primarily a matter for the State to decide. By this we do not mean to say that the decision of the State is not open to judicial review. The reservation must be only for the purpose of giving adequate representation in the services to the Scheduled Castes, Scheduled Tribes and Backward Classes". The court, further ruled : "There was no material before the High Court and there is no material before us from which we can conclude that the impugned order is violative of Article 16(1). Reservation of appointments under Article 16(4) cannot be struck down on hypothetical grounds or on imaginary possibilities. He who assails the reservation under that Article must satisfactorily establish that there has been a violation of Article 16(1)... The mere fact that the reservations made may give extensive benefits to some of the persons who have the benefits of reservation is bad. The length of the leaps provided depends upon the gap to be covered". (State of Punjab *vs.* Hiralal, 1971).

The reservation of posts under the State of Jammu and Kashmir in the ratio of 50 :40 :10 : for Muslims; Jammu Hindus and Kashmiri Hindus respectively was challenged as violative of Article 16(1) before the Supreme Court in Triloki Nath *vs.* State of Jammu and Kashmir (1969). While admitting the right of the State to make reservation for the Backward Classes, the court struck down the order as it maintained that the distribution of total number of posts for appointment on the basis of community or place of residence was not sanctioned by Article 16(4) and was against the constitutional guarantee set forth in Clauses (1) and (2) of Article 16.

Likewise, a case of similar nature arose in Janaki Prasad Parimoo *vs.* State of Jammu and Kashmir (1973), in which the Supreme Court observed :

"Mere educational backwardness or the social backwardness which makes a class of citizens backward is not enough. The class identified as backward class must be both educationally and socially backward... Backward classes must be comparable to the Scheduled Castes and Scheduled Tribes".

Thus a synonymity in educational and social conditions with the Scheduled Castes and Scheduled Tribes becomes the first imperative condition to a class of citizens to be adjudicated as "backward class".

Perhaps, the most important of the cases for interpretation of Article 16 that came up before the Supreme Court is State of Kerala *vs.* N.N. Thomas (1976), which was decided by a bench of seven judges. The important question to be determined was whether the rule which gave a longer period of exemption to members belonging to the Scheduled Castes and Scheduled Tribes than to others from passing certain departmental test was not violative of Article 16(1) of the Constitution. The Supreme Court upheld the rule as valid. While amplifying Article 16(4), the court observed :

> "The rule of equality within Articles 14 and 16 (1) will not be violated by a rule which will ensure equality of representation in the services for unrepresented classes after satisfying the basic needs of efficiency of administration. Article 16(2) rules out some basis of classification including race, caste, descent, place of birth, etc. Article 16(4) clarifies and explains that classification on the basis of backwardness does not fall within Article 16(2) and is legitimate for the purpose of Article 16(1). If preference shall be given to a particular under-represented community other than a backward class or under-represented States in All-India services, such a rule will contravene Article 16(2). A similar rule giving preference to an unrepresented backward community is valid and will not contravenes Articles 14, 16(1) and 16(2). Article 16(4) removes any doubt in this respect". The court further said :

> "The Constitution makes a classification of Scheduled Castes and Scheduled Tribes in numerous provisions and gives a mandate to the State to accord special or favoured treatment to them... The classification of employees belonging to the Scheduled Castes and Scheduled Tribes for allowing them an extended period of two years for passing the special tests for promotion is a just and reasonable classification having a rational nexus to the

object of providing equal opportunity for all citizens in matters relating to employment or appointment to public offices.

"Our Constitution aims at equality of status and of opportunity for all citizens including those who are socially, economically and educationally backward. The claims of members of backward classes require adequate representation in legislative and executive bodies. If members of Scheduled Castes and Tribe, who are said by this Court to be backward classes, can maintain minimum necessary requirement of administrative efficiency, not only representation but also preference may be given to them to enforce equality and to eliminate inequality. Articles 15(4) and 16(4) bring out the position of backward classes to merit equality." Special provisions are made for the advancement of backward classes and reservations of appointments and posts for them to secure adequate representation. These provisions will bring out the content of equality guaranteed by Articles 14, 15(1) and 16(1). The basic concept of equality is equality of opportunity for appointment. Preferential treatment for members of the Backward Classes with due regard to administrative efficiency alone can mean equality of opportunity for all citizens. Equality under Article 16 could not have a different content from equality under Article 14. Equality of opportunity for unequals can only mean aggravation of inequality. Equality of opportunity admits discrimination with reason and prohibits discrimination without reason. Discrimination with reasons means rational classification for differential treatment having nexus to the constitutionally permissible object, preferential representation for the Backward Classes in services with due regard to administrative efficiency is a permissible object and backward classes are a rational classification recognized by our Constitution". (State of Kerala *vs.* N.M. Thomas; 1976).

One important facet of this decision is that the rule propounded in General Manager *vs.* Rangachari case (1962) that Article 16(4) is in the nature of an exception to Article 16(1) was given a go-by and it was held, as we have seen, that differential treatment in standards of selection visualized by Article 16(4) is not an exception but within the scope of equality. It was a facet, an illustration, a method or application of Article 16(1).

In fact, for the members of a hierarchical society, equality of opportunity can make sense only if a strategy is evolved by which the dehumanized human sector, the underprivileged, are provided environmental facilities for a swift and steady development of their vast human potential. It was the proven social reality of depressed employment problem of some age-long depressed and suppressed segment of citizens of free India that coaxed the Founding Fathers of the Constitution to maintain that, in such a situation, mechanical equality is to perpetuate actual inequality, and, therefore, adopted and enacted many provisions to ameliorate the lot of the weaker sections of society and fight out this fell backwardness from the territory of India.

Yet another case challenging the promotion of the Scheduled Castes and Scheduled Tribes under Sub-rule (2a) of Rule 12 of the Central Secretariat Service Rules and Regulations of 1979 made thereunder came up for adjudication before the Supreme Court in S.S. Sharma *vs.* Union of India (1981) The Supreme Court held that the impugned Rules "cannot be said to contravene Articles 14, 15 and 16 of the Constitution on the ground that they result in two avenues of promotion for government servants belonging to the Scheduled Castes and Scheduled Tribes while a single avenue only of promotion is available to other government servants, especially when General Category vacancies have not remained unfilled for want of suitable candidates.

The two avenues of promotion spoken of in relation to government servants belonging to the Scheduled Castes and Scheduled Tribes consist, in one, the preparation of a list of officers falling within the field of selection both of the general category and members of the Scheduled Castes and Scheduled Tribes and their selection on the basis of principles laid down and, two, the selection of candidates of the Scheduled Castes and Scheduled Tribes consequent upon the limited departmental examination. It is to be remembered that resort to limited departmental examination is not simultaneous with the preparation of the list embodying the field of selection. The question of holding the examination arises only, as sub-rule (2a) of Rule 12 declares, when the reserved vacancies cannot be filled because eligible officers from the Scheduled Castes and Scheduled Tribes are not available through the original process, resort to the further process arises because of the constitutional mandate in favour of the Scheduled Castes and Scheduled Tribes, because reserved vacancies must be filled if that is possible". Thus, an alternative process of differentiation in fulfilment of the constitutional mandate in favour of the backward classes is anticipated and declared valid.

A landmark case that came up before the Supreme Court is recent time is ABSK. Sangh (Rly) *vs.* Union of India (1983) in which ten circulars of the Railway Board purporting to promotions to selection and non-selection posts of the Scheduled Castes and Scheduled Tribes in the Indian Railways were under fire. The court held the circulars valid and in conformity with Article 16(4). It ruled : "The fundamental right of equality of opportunity has to be read as justifying the categorization of the Scheduled Castes and Secheduled Tribes separately for the purpose of "adequate representation" in the services under the State. The object is constitutionally sanctioned in terms, as Articles 16(4) and 46 specificate. The classification is just and reasonable... one of the circulars sought to be quashed by the petitioners relates only to selection posts and has been expressly upheld in Rangachari's case (1962). The quantum of reservation is not excessive, the field of eligibility is not too unreasonable, the operation of the reservation is limited to selection posts and no... relaxation of qualifications is written into the circular except that the candidates of the Scheduled Castes and Scheduled Tribes communities "should be judged in a sympathetic manner". Moreover, administrative efficiency is secure because there is a direction "to give such staff additional training and coaching, tc bring them up to the standard of others. The rejection of the invalidatory contention of the petitioners is inevitable... All that we need say is that the Railway Board shall take care to issue instructions to see that in no year shall the Scheduled Caste and Scheduled Tribe candidates be actually appointed to substantially more than 50% per cent of the promotion posts... substantial excess will void the selection."

Manifestly, the implication of this judgement is not far-reaching in the sense that promotion to selection grade to the Scheduled Castes and Scheduled Tribes was already declared valid as early as in 1952 and in this judgement promotion to non-selection posts has been declared valid, with a well-established rider of not more than 50 per cent reservation in any one year laid down since 1962. But the issues involved in this case were of tremendous import. Let us specificate the important issues and the opinion pronounced thereon in the course of the judgement.

Firstly, one of the contentious issues to be decided was whether Article 16(1) insists on absolute equality or prompts realistic and rational classification of unequal classes and treatment of such classes differently. The observation was that "the State may classify, based upon substantial differentia groups or classes, and this process does not necessarily spell violation of Articles 14 to 16.

Another issue raised was whether the Scheduled Castes and Scheduled Tribes stand on a different footing from the rest of the Indian Community. The court held that it is not matter of speculation or investigation because the Constitution itself has recognized the direct socio-economic backward status of these species of humanity.

Thirdly, the contention whether the Scheduled Castes and Tribes are castes, within the scope of Article 16(2), and if so, does Article 16(4) have special provisions in their favour in the matter of promotion and allied matters, the court observed : "Even assuming that there is discrimination, Article 16(2) cannot be invoked unless it is predicated that the Scheduled Castes are castes. Terminological similarities are an illusory guide and we cannot go by verbal verisimilitude. It is very doubtful whether the expression castes will apply to the Scheduled Castes. At any rate the Scheduled Tribes are identified by their tribal denomination. A tribe cannot be equated with a caste. There are sufficient indications in the Constitution to suggest that the Scheduled Castes are not mere castes. They may be something less or something more and the time badge is not the fact that the members belong to a caste but the circumstance that they belong to an indescribably backward human group. Even assuming they are, classification, if permitted, will validate the differential rules for promotion".

Lastly, the reply to the issue, whether the directives under attack impair administrative efficiency to an extent that it is violative of Article 335 was : "Competitive skill is more relevant in higher posts, especially those where selection is made by competitive examinations. Lesser classes of posts, where promotion is secured mechanically by virtue of seniority except where the candidate is unfit, do not require a high degree of skill as in the case of selection posts. And if in Rangachari reservation has been valid in selection posts, such reservation in non-selection posts is an afortiori case." (A.B.S.K. Sangh (Rly) *vs.* Union of India; 1983).

In Soosai *vs.* Union of India (1986), the Constitution (Scheduled Caste) Order, 1950, was impugned on the basis that members of the Scheduled Caste adopting Christianity were deprived of the privileges of the Scheduled Caste. The Court ruled :

"The depressed classes of the Hindus and the Sikh community suffered from economic and social disabilities and cultural and educational backwardness in character and degree that the members of these castes in the two communities called for the protection of the constitutional provision relating to the Scheduled Caste.

The declaration incorporated in para 3 deeming them to be members of the Scheduled Caste was a declaration made for the purpose of the Constitution. It was a declaration enjoined by Clause (1) of Article 341 of the Constitution. To establish that para 3 of the Constitution (Scheduled Caste) Order, 1950, discriminates against Christian members of the enumerated castes it must be shown that they suffer from a comparable depth of social and economic disabilities and cultural and educational backwardness and similar level of degradation within the Christian community necessitating intervention by the State under the provisions of the Constitution. It is not sufficient to show that the same caste continues after conversion. It is necessary to establish further that the disabilities and handicaps suffered from such caste membership in the social order of its origin—Hinduism—continue in their oppressive severity in the new environment of a different religious community." (Soosai *vs.* Union of India 1986) The impugned Order was, therefore, upheld by the court.

In the stream of judicial decisions, we find a growing concern and realization to safeguard the guarantee of caste-free equality to every citizen, enshrined in our Constitution. The judiciary has expressed its utmost concern for Harijans-Girizans and other weaker sections of the society and acted as a bullwark against various onslaughts on the benign privileges conferred by the Founding Fathers in the form of constitutional mandate to the powers-that-be, in order to foster them as equals in the mainstream of social life. The fallout of this benevolent differentiation has been to blow upon the "backwardness" syndrome with a view to embrace this constitutional amulet to some politically dominant castes masquerading in the garb of backward castes. The judiciary has nipped in the bud this autophagous attempt on an escalating scale, and the only silver lining on the dark horizon of caste-riven nation is the conspicuous awareness of the highest court in the land to scan and weed out this unwholesome effort of simulation and set at naught the vested political design to make room for the roost and rule over its destiny, pushing back the patriotic prospect of a homogenized society and projecting instead a disintegrated and heterogeneous body politic, with an evil intent to fish in troubled waters. However, the constitutional provisions neither impose any legal obligation on the State nor confer any constitutional right on the backward classes to enforce the State to redeem such obligation. It is for the government itself to rise to the occasion to wipe out the "backward" stigma eclipsing the nation in an earnest attempt to firmly establish socio-economic equality with which political equality may pale into oblivion and political democracy, in a land essentially undemocratic may cave in. It is well to remember the broodings of our philosopher-president Dr. Sarvapalli Radhakrishnnan : "India must have a 'socio-economic' revol-ution designed not only to bring about the real satisfaction of the fundamental needs of the common man, but to go much deeper and bring about 'a fundamental change in the structure of Indian society". (Mahatma Gandhi, 100 years; 1968).

Justice is a costly game still, notwithstanding the doctrine of "Public Interest Litigation" propounded by the highest court in recent times. Ultimately, "the weaker sections of the society" will find a ray of hope in their democratically elected government which has striven to get the Constitutional mandate to solve the greatest riddle—a nation whose one-fifth of the habitation is in the limbo of stratification whose vision is fogged by the spectre of economic compulsions, whose soul is caught in the quagmire of the deprivation and whose mind is warped by political doctrinarianism, parochialism, nepotism, anarchism, and distressed by terrorism, to mention only a few evils eating into the vitals of the Bharat of our dreams. A solution has to be found. It is a question of the here and now, of instant relief.

Clause (5)

Clause (5) of Article 16 is, like Clauses (3) and (4), an instance of application of the principle of equality of opportunity in public employment in the sphere of religion which stands as impermissible classification in Article 16(1) and prohibited ground of discrimination in Article 16 (2). Thus, it is a specific and practical application of the main Clauses (1) and (2) of the right to equality of opportunity. Despite prohibition of discrimination on the ground of religion, it anticipates and makes provision for the removal of any anomalous situation that may arise in consequence of the framing of any laws by the State under Article 26(d) enunciating the fundamental right to freedom of religion. Article 26, providing freedom to manage religious affairs, subject to public order, morality and health, to every religious denomination or any section thereof, "guarantees the right, *inter alia*, to administer its movable and immovable property in accordance with law. Some of the religious or denominational institutions were already being administered under the laws made by the Government of India, and after the enforcement of the Constitution others also could have been required to be administered in accordance with the law of the Union Government. To ward off a delicate situation, the specific application of discrimination on religious grounds stipulated in Clause (5) has been permitted to the State so that in making provision for the administration of any religious or denominational institution under the law the State could provide that the members of the managing committees of those religious or denominational institutions being administered or being taken over under the laws of the State shall be constituted only of persons belonging to the said religion or denomination, by the State. This provision has been, thus, enshrined in the Constitution to ensure communal or religious amity and peace and with a view to a harmonious adaptation of Article 26(d) with Article 16(2) of the Constitution, in the context of the existing laws as well as the laws which the State might have to make in future for the administration of such religious or denominational institutions which may come under the exclusive control of the State. Thus the law providing particular denominational or religious qualification for the membership of the administrative body of any religious or denominational institution under the control of the State shall not be construed as denial of equality of opportunity to persons professing other religions or sects. The provisions is based on a rational ground because it will not be proper on the part of the State to appoint a Muslim as a member of the administrative body of any Hindu religious or denominational institution or the other way round, which may result in misunderstanding and antagonism between different religions or sects. However, this provision is meant only for those offices relating to religious institutions, which are under the control and management of the Government.

REFERCNCES

1. Democracy, Real and Deceptive, M.K. Gandhi (1961), p. 11.
2. Glimpses of World History, J.L. Nehru (1962), Vol.1, p. 239.
3. Bofore and After Independece, Nehru's Specehes, Ed. J.S. Bright Vol. III, p. 124.
4. Recent Essays and Writings, J.L. Nehru (1937), p. 7.
5. *Ibid.*, p. 32.
6. Grammar of Politics, H.J. Laski, Preface.
7. Recent Essays, *op.cit.*, p. 16.
8. *Ibid.* pp. 24-25.
9. C.A.D. Vol. I, No. 5, pp. 55-57
10. *Ibid.*
11. *Ibid.*, 43
12. *Ibid.*, p. 90.
13. *Ibid.*, Vol. II, No. 1, p. 263.
14. *Ibid.*, p. 297.
15. Recent Essays, *op.cit.*, p. 21.
16. C.A.D. No. 30, 1948, pp. 676-78.

17. *Ibid.* pp. 69C-701.
18. *Ibid.*
19. C.A.D. Vol. III. p. 416.
20. Supplementary Report of the Committee, p. 33.'
21. *Congress Ke Prastav*, Kanhaiya Lal (1937), p. 510.
22. Report of the General Secretary (I.N.C) 1938, p. 29.
23. AIR 1961, Sc. 564.
24. Krishna Chander *vs.* C.T. Organisation, AIR 1962 Sc. 602.
25. *Parliamentary Democracy in India*, K.V. Rao (1960), p. 159.
26. AIR 1962, Sc. 602.
27. AIR 1962, Sc. 1704.
28. AIR 1956, Sc. 520.
29. AIR Sc. 431.
30. *Ibid.*
31. (1985)3 SCC. 345.
32. AIR 1981 Sc. 561.
33. AIR 1981 Sc. 1041.
34. (1974) 1.SCR. 771.
35. *Ibid.*
36. (1968) I.SCR. 407.
37. AIR 1982 Sc. 1301.
38. *Ibid.*
39. *Ibid.*
40. AIR 1976 Sc. 490.
41. (1974) 2 (SCR) 348.
42. *Harijan* : March 31, 1946.
43. AIR 1981 Sc. 300
44. K. Sadanandan *vs.* State of Kerala, AIR 1963, Ker. 591.
45. Panduragaro *vs.* A.P.P.S.C. (1963), 1 SCR 707.
46. Rahunadha Rao *vs.* State of Orissa, AIR 1955, Ori. 113
47. K.V. Rao, *op.cit.,* p. 161.
48. AIR 1957, Pat. 617.
49. AIR 1963, Ker. 591.
50. AIR 1983, Sc. 376
51. AIR 1963, Sc. 202
52. AIR 1967, Sc 62.
53. AIR 1977, Sc. 1509.
54. Ram Sharan *vs.* D.I.C., AIR. 1964, Sc. 1559.
55. Kishori *Vs.* Union of India, AIR. 1962, Sc. 1704.
56. AIR 1960, Sc. 384.
57. AIR 1963, Sc. 913.
58. High Court vs Amal Kumar, AIR 1962 Sc. 1704.
59. AIR 1967, Sc. 1427.
60. AIR 1986, Sc. 638.
61. AIR 1977, Sc. 251.
62. AIR 1974, Sc. 1.
63. AIR 1973, Sc. 1271.
64. AIR 1974, Sc. 246

65. *Ibid.*
66. (1975) 1 SCR 104.
67. AIR 1982, Sc. 101.
68. AIR *Ibid.*
69. AIR 1981, Sc. 75.
70. *Ibid.*
71. *Ibid.*
72. AIR 1981, Sc. 414.
73. (1985) 2 SCC. 604.
74. AIR 1962, Sc. 630.
75. AIR 1964, Sc. 1854.
76. *Ibid.*
77. AIR. 1953, Sc. 250.
78. AIR 1955 Sc. 289.
79. (1985) 1. SCC. 56.
80. (1985) 3 SCC. 153.
81. *Ibid.*
82. *Ibid.*
83. AIR 1962, Sc. 630.
84. AIR 1962, Sc. 62.
85. AIR 1959, Sc. 315.
86. AIR 1986, Sc. 210.
87. AIR 1961, Sc. 564.
88. AIR 1962, Mysore 233.
89. AIR 1951, Sc. 229.
90. AIR 1936, Andhra 14.
91. AIR 1956, Sc. 268.
92. AIR 1963, Sc. 769.
93. AIR 1986, Sc. 1035
94. *Ibid.*
95. *Ibid.*
96. AIR 1983, Sc. 803
97. AIR 1970, Sc. 422
98. *Ibid.*
99. AIR 1972, Sc. 827
100. *Ibid.*
101. The Constitution of India (1980) : p. 27
102. *Ibid.* Article 338 (3), p. 216.
103. A.B.S.K. Sangh (Rly) *vs.* Unton of India, AIR 1981 Sc. 300.
104. C.A.D. Vol. VII. p. 702
105. *Ibid.*
106. *Ibid.* Vol. VIII. p.701.
107. The Constitution of India (1980), p. 217.
108. *Ibid.*, p. 216.
109. *Ibid.*, p. 214.

CHAPTER 6

RIGHT TO SOCIO-ECONOMIC JUSTICE

(a) The Background

Part IV of the Constitution, enumerating the Fundamental Directives is an engine of socio-economic reforms envisaged by the Founding Fathers. It is a programme of socio-economic reconstruction of the Indian society which had been battered and deprived its ancient glory of equality and fraternity during the long night of feudal-colonial rule. Keeping in mind the passions that lie burried in the hearts of the masses of the Indian people and the intent to fulfil them, a Resolution regarding the aims and objects was moved in the Constituent Assembly on December 13, 1946, which contained a solemn resolve to work out a Constitution for free India wherein shall be guaranteed and secured to all the people of India Justice—social, economic and political— and this resolve was centered round the only task of the nation-builders set by the Father's of the Nation to extricate the groaning masses out of the invidious morass of poverty, squalor and stupor.

(b) Role of Nehru

This task of the nation-builders was amply reflected as early as 1928, when addressing a political conference at Amritsar, Shri Jawahar Lal Nehru, then a young man, said :

> "What shall it profit the masses of this country, the peasantry, the landless labourers, the workers, the shop-keepers, the artisans, if every one of the offices held by Englishmen in India today is held by an Indian It may benefit them a little as they can bring more pressure to bear on them or prefer them to an alien government. But fundamentally the condition cannot improve until the social fabric is changed, and I think that the only effective change can be the foundation of a Democratic Socialistic State".[1]

Again, in the U.P. Political Conference, he said : We have so far laid stress on political independence. It is now time for you to take the lead again and declare what you mean by independence. We are told by some people that the Congress must not concern itself with matters other than political. But life cannot be divided up into compartments, not indeed can politics itself ignore the other functions of society... what manner of independence is it which results in starvation for many and the exploitation of millions? Independence must necessarily involve freedom from all exploitation and to bring this about you must attack everything in your society, which helps the exploiter... The problem before us is, therefore, two-fold—firstly, to chalk out an economic and social programme which will provide freedom for the masses and then to indicate the manner of creating sanctions to enforce our programme".[2] It was this tirade against the socio-economic injustice initiated by Nehru, the messiah of the youth, which compelled the AICC to bring the following resolution in May, 1929 :

> "In order to remove the poverty and the misery of the Indian people and to ameliorate the condition of the masses, it is essential to make revolutionary changes in the present economic and social structure of society and to remove the gross inequalities".[3]

And this vow of a socio-economic revolution epitomized the historic declaration of the Lahore Congress for the attainment of Poorna Swaraj, under the presidentship of Nehru in 1929 who gave a clarion call to the nation for political and social revolution in India. In August, 1946, the Congress formed the first National Government of India and in November of the same year the Congress session at Meerut, adopted a resolution defining the Congress concept of freedom :

"In the opinion of the Congress Swaraj cannot be real for the masses unless it makes possible the achievement of a society in which democracy extends from the political to the social and economic sphere, and in which there will be no opportunity for the privileged classes to exploit the bulk of the people nor for gross inequalities such as exist at present. Such a society would ensure individual liberty, equality of opportunity and the fullest scope for every citizen for the development of his personality".[4]

Together with Gandhi, Jawaharlal Nehru had played the most crucial role in the tortuous and continued struggle for India's freedom from the foreign yoke. The dominant purpose of Swaraj was to usher in an era of social justice for the teeming millions. His contribution to the building up of modern India remains unique and unmatched. Moving for the acceptance of the objective Resolution in the Constituent Assembly, Nehru had said :

"I hope that this Resolution will lead us to a Constitution on the lines suggested by this Resolution. I trust that the Constitution itself will lead us to the real freedom that we have clamoured for and that real freedom in turn will bring food to our starving people, clothing for them, housing for them and all manner of opportunities for progress".[5]

After the attainment of political freedom, when Nehru was assigned the role of shaping the destiny of the nation as the first Prime Minister of free India, he pursued the goals set in the Constitution to secure to the masses the social justice, which 'ipso facto' included economic justice. The subdued aspiration to redeem the pledge to dedicate himself to the service of the starving millions was reflected in his address to the Constituent Assembly on August 14, 1947. He said :

"Long years ago we made a tryst with destiny, and now the time comes when we shall redeem our pledge, not wholly or in full measure, but very substantially... The service of India means the service of the millions who suffer. It means the ending of poverty and ignorance and disease and inequality of opportunity. The ambition of the greatest man of the our generation has been to wipe every tear from every eye. That may be beyond us, but as long as there are tears and sufferings so long our work will not be over".[6] After the Declaration of Independence, the AICC met at New Delhi in November, 1947, and resolved : "Political independence having been achieved, the Congress must address itself to the next great task, namely, the establishment of real democracy in the country and a society based on social justice and equality. Such a society must provide every man and woman with equality of opportunity and freedom to work for the unfettered development of his or her personality. This can only be realized when democracy extends from the political to the social and economic spheres".[7]

The long subjugation of India had made her inherit an accumulation of vital problems on the eve of her freedom. The country lacked the basic necessities of life for her masses and was caught in a spiral of inflation and rising prices. Nehru felt that though there was no sudden solution to the problem, the solutions also cannot be delayed. He felt that the interest of the suffering masses must come first and every vested interest that comes in their way must yield to them. He was in favour of a rapid change in the land tenure system and promoting industrialization on a large but balanced scale. He also believed that though production must get the top priority, fair and equitable distribution was vital for any solution of the problem. On the Independence Day, in his message to the Press, he outlined the direction in which the country shall move and the perimeter of the endeavour, which he planned. It was "to bring freedom and opportunity to the common masses, to the peasants and workers of India; to fight and end poverty and ignorance and disease; to build up a prosperous democratic and progressive nation, and to create social, economic and political institutions which will ensure justice and fullness of life to every man and women"...[8]

Nehru's first concern was to get this country going and to stabilize the economic conditions. He aimed at increased production and equitable distribution with a view to improving the standard of living of the common people and put an end to poverty and unemployment. Enunciating the economic policy of his government in February 1948, Nehru said :

> "...As far as the Congress is concerned it accepted the principle of nationalization of defence and key industries about 17 years ago, and I believe such industries had to be nationalized at some time or other. But when you come down to giving effect to this, we have to think as to what to choose first, and how to do it without upsetting the present structure and without actually interfering with production. It is far better for the State to concentrate on certain specific vital new industries, rather than go about nationalizing the many old ones, though in the case of some specific vital industries of national importance that might be done".[9]

He felt the need to steer clear of extremes of economic ideologies and gave birth to the concept of a mixed economy, a middle path, a third alternative, which retains free markets, while extending the scope of public ownership and control of the vital and strategic material resources of the community. He expressed the viwes :

> "If we do not ultimately solve the basic problems of food, clothing, housing and so on, it will not matter whether we call ourselves capitalists, socialists, communists or anything else. If we fail to solve these problems, we shall be swept away and somebody else will come in and try to solve them".[10]

The Avadi session of the Congress in 1954, under his leadership, dropped its previous goal of "Cooperative Commonwealth" and instead adopted the new goal of "Socialistic Pattern of Society".

Commending the new resolution for adoptions by the Avadi Congress session, Nehru said :

> "At no stage in the history of the freedom struggle have we been thinking of more political freedom. All the time, we thought of the economic aspect. We thought of the workers and peasants, the underdog, the downtrodden and the disinherited in India. The freedom struggle gained its social and economic content and now the time has

come when we should march forward in this direction. We declared openly what we have often said, that the type of society will be in keeping with India's genius."[11]

Thus, Nehru emerged in the Congress forum as the champion of the downtrodden and an unswerving advocate of socio-economic justice for the masses. The Objective Resolution in the Constituent Assembly reflects, therefore, the cherished ambition of the Founding Fathers which contains equality as the underlying theme and a firm resolve to extricate the common man out of the morass of poverty, ignorance and disease.

Thus the Constitution for a free India was the outcome of untold sufferings and immense sacrifice of the masses of this country. It was, therefore, natural that the Founding Fathers wished it to be so framed as to promote the interests of the masses. As Mr. R. V. Dhulekar (U.P. General) said in the Constituent Assembly :

"Mahatma Gandhi had summarized the philosophy of human life into two words—truth and non-violence. These two, truth and non-violence, form the creed of the Congress and the resolution before the House is based on them. The resolution is the true expression of the sentiments, ambitions good intentions and objects of the people."[12] The Preamble denotes the confluence of these objective in the constitutional framework and presages the Gandhian belief of the inevitable supremacy of truth. The Preamble and the Directive Principles stand in the same irrevocable relation as truth and non-violence, inter se. The Preamble denotes the objects, the ends-in-view, and the Directive Principles the means to achieve those ends. The ends and means are as inseparable as truth and non-violence and they are convertible terms. The Preamble describes the lofty ideals which ignited the whole nation towards the goal of freedom from the foreign yoke. With the achievement of political freedom, liberty was granted, but the "Poorna Swaraj" would remain a mirage, unless liberty was murtured to bloom on the threshold of equality and fraternity. Gandhi believed that the end is beyond one's control, and it is only the means, which can be controlled. It is means that matter; we have to take care of the means. It was Sardar Patel who was allotted the task of caring for the means to ensure the attainment of socio-economic freedom for the masses.

It was the adept draftsmanship and astute statesmanship of the Iron-Man of India, Sardar Valabhbhai Patel, who as Chairman of the Advisory Committee on Fundamental Rights, submitted to the Constituent Assembly an integrated scheme of rights in two parts. Presenting his Report, Sardar Patel said :

> "There were two parts of the Report : One contained fundamental rights which were justiciable and the other part of the report referred to fundamental rights which were not justiciable but were directives more or less which would be useful for the governance of the country".[13] But as we shall presently see, these rights in both the parts are intertwined and most of the rights set in one part overlap some corresponding rights in the other part, and in unison they herald the dawn of political freedom and socio-economic justice. The fundamental principles of governance as drafted by the Advisory Committee, the corresponding Directive Principles of State Policy, laid down in the Draft Constitution and also as it finally emerged are given in Appendix D.

In the text of the Directive Principles we find some words of wide import. The meaning of the words "State" and "the State" used at different places in Parts III and IV were clarified by Dr. Ambedkar thus :

> "In this Constitution the word "State" has been used in different senses. It is used as the collective entity, either representing the Centre or the province, both of which in certain parts of the Constitution are spoken of as 'State'. The words 'the State' are used both in the collective sense as well as in the distributive sense".[14] Thus, "State" is used in the collective sense in Part III and the use of the word "the State" in Part IV implies the Government and the legislature of the Union and each of the States as well as local or other authorities including Village Panchayats, District or Local Boards etc., within the territory of India.

As to the justification of the word "Directives" Dr Ambedkar said :

> "It is not the intention to introduce in this part these principles as mere pious declarations. It is the intention of this Assembly that in future both the legislature and the executive should not merely pay lip-service to these principles enacted in this part, but that they should be made the basis of all executive and legislative action that may be taken hereafter in the matter of the governance of the country".[15]

Similarly, the word "strive" in Article 30 of the Draft Constitution has been purposely used to ward off any attempt at evasion of its responsibility by the State. Dr. Ambedkar said :

> "We have used it because our intention is that even when there are circumstances which prevent the government, or which stand in the way of the government giving effect to those Directive Principles, they shall, even under hard and unpropitious circumstances, always strive for the fulfilment of these Directives".[16]

(c) Nature of Directives

The Directive Principles contained in Articles 37 to 51 of the Constitution of India provide means of a socio-economic order which the Founding Fathers wanted ultimately to be ushered in. Freedom had merely ushered a twilight of hope to the helpless and demoralized people and political justice, providing equality of treatment in political sphere aimed at the elimination of political exploitation of all sorts, bestowed on them as 'Fundamental Rights under Part III of the Constitution, only enabled them to stand up and gather strength and confidence in themselves, assured of their individual freedom, and set themselves to the task of achievement of socio-economic justice, leading to the fulfilment of the long-cherished dream of the nation. Even in the course of debates in the Constituent Assembly we find that the only purpose behind the fundamental directives of Part IV was that the establishment of political democracy must be backed and buttressed by the establishment of a socio-economic democracy. The fundamental rights in Part III were endowed to the citizens to enable them to cast off the slouah of despondence and gird up their loins in the task of nation-building and the fundamental directives in Part IV were the tunes and the notes to give rise to the music of socio-economic justice reverberating in the social order with the active cooperation of a free people gifted with the political freedom and set to the task of nation-building. The directives, animating the spiritual content of the teachings of the Father of the Nation, are a programme of socio-economic reconstruction in the light of that eternal light. They are a set of constructive programmes, rephased by the Constituent Assembly, on the part of the Government, as the Congress had declined to flower into a Lok Sevak Sangh for the achievement of an economic democracy after the attainment of political independence and had instead decided to form the government of a political democracy. The Founding Fathers had, therefore, no option but to include those constructive programmes in the form of fundamental directives to the governments of the future. It indicates the leadership of the government to furbish a sound socio-economic order of the nation rooted in the political democracy and enlivening and invigorating the latter, by enlisting the active cooperation of the free people in the task of national reconstruction. When it was pointed out that the Draft does not convey any clear indication as to the economic nature of the social order, Dr. Ambedkar said :

> "We have left enough room for a people of different ways of thinking, with regard to the reaching of the ideal of economic democracy; to strive in their own way, to persuade the electorate that it is the best way of reaching economic democracy, the fullest opportunity to act in the way in which they want to act".[17] And Dr. Ambedkar sounded a prophetic note when he said : "What great value these Directive Principles possess will be realized better when the forces of right contrive to capture power".[18] This distant vision of Dr. Ambedker has come true to a word.

Right from the enforcement of the Republican Constitution, the shape of events was ominous to the rightists. The country bestrode forward towards democratization with the enforcement of the constitution and the democratic general election on the basis of universal adult franchise. During the period 1950-63 the country witnessed a rapid political growth along side the socio-economic growth that the government projected. The abolition of Zamindari, the measures of land reform and consolidation of holdings enacted by the States, the beginning of Five-year Plans with an intent to boost up agriculture and bring in a Green Revolution had a charismatic influence on the masses. With the growth of the Panchayati Raj institutions, the mass-base and the popular participation in the processes of governance became manifest. These, in turn, provided a favourable environment for a structured progress towards economic self-reliance tinged with social justice.

Alike Gandhi, Nehru always felt the pulse of the people and not only advocated speedy reforms but was equally anxious of the people's participation in his scheme of things. Analyzing the task ahead, he wrote :

> "India's overriding and most urgent task is to raise the standard of living of her people and in order to achieve this, to carry out structural and organizational reforms not only as speedily as possible but with maximum popular support and participation".[19]

It was, therefore, that though the forces of the right within the Congress Party continued to impede the progress, if not the processes set in motion, the unswerving socialistic faith in Nehru and the mass-base of his government compelled the rightists to withdraw honourably under the garb of the Kamaraj Plan in 1963, and his untiring effort to achieve freedom from poverty and distress for the masses continued almost smoothly.

But the problems of changing the feudal structure, the land tenure system and bringing social justice by narrowing down the yawning gap between the rich and the poor required not only palliatives in the form of legislative actions but also a strong and positive execution of the policies enunciated. Whatever the law may or may not provide, the welfare of a country depends upon the way in which it is administered. The administrative system designed for the colonial economy remained inadaptable for the welfare economy of a democratic country. Even Nehru, on May 3, 1958, at a meeting of the Parliamentary Party, complained against "what was happening in the country as a whole, a deterioration of our standards, a certain coarseness, a certain vulgarity coming into our public life. We are obviously getting less idealistic, in fact idealism was rather fading out and there was a certain communal feeling creeping in even among Congressmen. The atmosphere was getting murkier, heavier and more difficult for a sensitive person to breathe easily". And in the situation, he candidly admitted that he was "doing the work more as a robot or automation that with a deep sense of function".[20] And Nehru passed away in 1964 as a "prophet frustrated". The cause of such frustration lies in the failure to speedily implement the land distribution and tenancy reform, and give a proper shape to education and the administrative system in free India. "Had those steps been taken, democracy would have been accompanied by basic changes in society and the 1950s would not now appear more and more of a faded golden" age."[21]

(d) Role of Indira Gandhi

Smt. Indira Gandhi was sworn in as the third Prime Minister of India on January 24, 1966. While Nehru had proved his mettle through long years of service and sacrifice and the office of Prime Minister was only a de jure recognition of his status as the outstanding leader of his people, Smt. Gandhi had still to prove her capacity to successfully grapple with the problems the nation was beset with at the close of the Nehru era.

Apart from political upheavals, social tumult and growing impatience of the masses for socio-economic justice, the conditions of the economy had also begun to worsen right from 1965. An overall picture of the economic situation she had to face has been ably presented by R.H. Cassen :

> "In 1965 there began the series of calamities which struck like hammer-blows at the economy and at the principles and conduct of fifteen years of economic policy under planning. There was a brief but unpleasant conflict with Pakistan. The crop-year of 1965-66 suffered from acute drought and food production fell to the level of late 1950s necessitating heavy imports of food. Despite large volumes

> of aid the balance of payments was in a chronic crisis and India came under great pressure to devalue the rupee in June, 1966. It was politically traumatic as there was great debate about its advisability and the politicians of the day saw themselves and were seen by others to be submitting to the influence of the World Bank and IMF and other forces in the international community, particularly the views of the major aid giving countries. The devaluation, though necessary for long term rectification of structural problems in the country, was also badly timed—industrial recession and shortage of domestic agricultural products are not the conditions for profiting from reduced export prices and more expensive imports. The Aid India Consortium attempted to guarantee an aid package to see India through the devaluation, including an annual 900 million dollars of non-project aid. The package fell apart after the first year, particularly owing to American defections. The year 1966-67 was another year of severe drought; coming on top of that of previous year, when stocks were already depleted, it was a calamity of a magnitude unparallelled since Independence. Only a major inflow of food aid in those two years saved India from famines in which hundreds of thousand if not millions might have died".[22]

She possessed a bubbling spirit for going the socialist way and was enormously optimistic to tide over the wind.

Only after sixty days of assuming office, Mrs. Gandhi confidently asserted in March, 1966 :

> "Enormous as are the problems facing us, I feel certain that we shall come through this difficult, and almost unprecedented, period of storm and crisis with success".[23]

It was the strong confidence in the Indian people, inherited from her father that made her so optimistic. She based her strategy on the ideological line of the "socialistic pattern of society", the goal set out in the Avadi session of the Congress. The Ten Point (Economic) Programme devised by Nehru and accepted by the Congress for establishing in the country a socialist pattern of society to ensure that the growing contrast between the rich and the poor is erased became the basis of her economic programme. It included some radical measures like nationalization of insurance companies, social control of banks, restrictions on moncpolies, ceiling on urban property, State takeover of import and export trade, control of foodgrain distribution, land reforms, abolition of privy purses, etc. She was convinced that the speedy reforms in the socio-economic field was imperative for the removal of instability, tumult and disorder that the country was facing, and her impatience to quicken the pace of reform is reflected in the nature and content of the measures she initited in order to translate the political freedom into social and economic security, especially during the period 1969-75 during which she made great strides in the field of socio-economic justice. Talking to a journalist, she said :

> "We have to move faster; we can't afford not to, and certain people oppose this. But if we don't move faster, people are not prepared to wait for us. They'll try to take the solution into their own hands, to resolve matters in their own way. The people of this country today are more and more conscious of what they need and want".[24]

Explaining the causative factor behind this growing impatience, she said on another occasion :

> "To a large extent, progress itself is the cause of such a development. Because as a society marches on, makes progress, advances, people's expectations also rise along with it".[25]

She believed that real peace is unattainable in a democratic country without a ceaseless war against poverty, ignorance and disease. What was saddening to her was the broadening gap between profession and practice, between resolutions and performances. And this had to be removed. Poverty was the central problem and during the total period of 18 years that followed, she was all through restless and anxious to bridge the gap between promise and performance. Her main ideas and aims remained unchanged. Expressing her thoughts on India's problems, and the policies she wished to follow, Mrs. Gandhi said :

> "Poverty is indeed the central problem facing us and it

is by the way in which we set out to tackle it that we as a nation will be judged...

In economic development, as in other fields of national activity, there is a disconcerting gap between intention and action. To bridge this gap we should boldly adopt whatever far-reaching changes in administration may be found necessary. We must introduce new organizational patterns and modern tools and techniques of management and administration."[26]

Again, in a National Development Council meeting on May 30, 1972, she reiterated her views :

"The most important problem before all of us is the poverty of large sections of our people and the fact that in spite of several plans and many programmes on which a lot of money has been spent we have not made much dent on problems faced by the lowest strata of society".[27]

She strongly held the view that only the eradication of poverty, ignorance and disease could remove the growing instability and impatience of the common man. Her period of office, particularly from 1969 to 1975, is distinguished by her crusade against divisive forces and relentless efforts to infuse greater dynamism to her various social and economic programmes. The period from 1966 to 1968 was her testing time within which by her sheer tenacity and skill, she outflanked her adversaries forming a rightist camp. In the Banglore session of the AICC in July, 1969, she successfully won the final battle for radical economic reforms. Her note on economic policy and programme reflects her determination to set into motion the radical measures ordained to make freedom meaningful for the masses, which, *inter alia*, proposed the following :—

The Congress has always championed the cause of the weaker sections, minorities and underprivileged. This should continue to be the policy of the Congress :

(a) Impose ceiling on unproductive expenditure and conspicuous consumption of corporate bodies :

(b) Nationalized financial institutions should introduce a

change in the credit-worthiness criteria in their lending policies, so as to encourage professional and competent persons;

(c) Special efforts should be made to finance new entrepreneurs in less developed regions and a special fund should be provided for provision of assistance to backward regions;

(d) Expeditious appointment of Monopolies Commission manned by persons of integrity;

(e) Public sector projects should be given more autonomy and manned by young competent persons committed to the project;

(f) Special effort should be made to build up a cadre of public sector projects;

(g) The consumer industries should be reserved whenever possible for a development in the cooperative and small-scale sector and entry of big business should be banned in the manufactures of these projects;

(h) Special efforts should be made to encourage new talent to provide avenues of employment to the young and educated;

(i) Foreign capital should not be allowed to enter a field in which technical know-how is available;

(j) Heavy penalties should be imposed on those who indulge in restrictive trade practices."

(i) Agriculture

(a) Service cooperatives should be built up in rural areas;

(b) Special assistance should be provided to small agriculturists and farm cooperatives to enable them to take processing of agro-based and other industries;

(c) Special attention should be paid to the development of minor irrigation projects, etc.

(ii) Land Reforms

Land reform is no less important. If we do not act urgently, grave political and economic problems will arise. From time to time suggestions have been made to improve the lot of the tenant and of landless agricultural labourers :

1. Declare all tenancies as non-resumable;
2. Give the tenants the right to mortgage their interests in land for obtaining credit;
3. Place restrictions of sale of land by the Scheduled Castes and Scheduled Tribes and Backward Classes in favour of others;
4. Enforce ceiling on land holdings energetically;
5. Draw up a programme for distribution of Government Wasteland held by Panchayats;
6. Enact legislation to protect tenants, agricultural workers, from their house-sites...

A review of agricultural wages is also called for in the light of increased yields now obtaining. Minimum wages for agricultural labour have to be prescribed for each tract and enforced. This will enable landless labourers to participate in the fruits of the Green Revolution".[28]

(e) Resume of the Directives

The resolution adopted at the AICC laid down in categorical terms how the economic goal of the country is to be achieved. "There has been" the Resolution says, "a good deal of discussion in the Congress organization regarding the economic and social policy and the direction to be given to the economy to reach the socialist goal which the Congress has pledged to achieve".[29] The AICC welcomed the note of the Prime Minister. The resolution sounded a note of caution that it is necessary to set in motion social forces for making improvement in the standard of living at the millions who live at subsistence or lower than subsistence level and that the aspect of social justice does not get clouded. The resolution also called upon the Central and State Governments to take appropriate steps expeditiously to implement the various points, raised in the note of the Prime Minister. The note jotted down by the Prime Minister was only a restatement of the economic policy of the Congress adopted long ago, suggesting certain radical measures to intensify the efforts towards the social goal. She held the view that stability cannot be achieved unless we make considerable progress towards the goal, from which the country was lagging far behind. She said :

> "Stability cannot be and should not be equated with the perpetuation of status quo. Stability cannot be brought about if the present inequalities are allowed to remain or to grow. And unless we take note of the aspirations of the people and engineer change peacefully, we shall be overtaken by events and by far greater violence".[30]

It was her firm belief that social justice is not only compatible with economic growth, but is an essential condition for sustained and orderly growth. And guided by her unswerving conviction and unflinching devotion to serve the cause of the downtrodden, she ride roughshod on the political machinery of the nation, adopting radical measures on all fronts and expecting quick results. She desired that "our commitment to certain well-defined objectives of reform must be accompanied by an equally clear commitments to fulfilling them by a certain date".[31]

The first radical measure was adopted in July, 1969, when the Government of India took over 14 leading commercial banks with assets of 66.6 million dollars. The decision was taken with a view to accelerating the achievement of economic growth tinged with social justice, and aimed at (a) the removal of control by a few; (b) provision of adequate credit for agriculture and small industries; (c) giving a professional bent to bank management; (d) the encouragement of new classes of entrepreneurs; and (e) provision of adequate training and better conditions of service for the bank staff. It brought about a metamorphic change in the nature, concept and scope of banking business. Justifying her action, Mrs. Gandhi said :

> "We nationalized them in order to have a more rational credit policy and to ensure a faster rate of growth of our banking system... while banks will continue to meet genuine credit requirements of industry, Government will ensure that bank finance is not made available for speculation and it is not pre-empted in favour of a few industrial and trading firms".[32]

Mrs. Gandhi was also aware of the fact that the nationalization of banks, by itself, was not going to erase the growing

ization of banks, by itself, was not going to erase the growing disparity between the haves and the have-nots; but after the social control measure was put on the anvil and it did not click, she felt it was the only correct step. She asserted :

> "The nationalization of the fourteen big banks is evidence of our determination to bring a greater volume of resources within the area of social decision. It has affected a major change in our economic structure".[33]

The impact of the nationalization of banks was tremendous, "From that day onward, Mrs. Gandhi, the women, the unpopular one, the shy one, the awkward one, was besieged every day, by the poor; those who had never expected that any banks would lend money to them, those who had fatalistically accepted that like bullocks they would wait, heads down to the dusty wind, acceptors always, never makers of demands; and this woman, their prime Minister, had unyoked them, released them into fresh pastures. The small-scale industrialists, the peasants with or without land, these profitted and they knew it; 'Garibi Hatao', said Mrs. Gandhi, drive poverty away, and the poor of the land answered and applauded".[34]

The decision to nationalize the banks, the setting up of Monopolies Commission and the abolition of privy purses were widely welcomed throughout the country. In fact, the decision to abolish privy purses in September, 1970, was a momentous one, because the entrenched interests and the rightists' wind, called the syndicate, had girded up their loins and started a political battle, from which, in spite of initial reverses, Mrs. Gandhi emerged victorious. Reintroducing the proposal in the Lok-Sabha on December 2, 1971, in the form of the Constitution (25th Amendment) Bill, Mrs. Gandhi said :

> "There is a great deal of feeling in the country against inherited special status, against privileges unrelated to function or responsibility, against exemptions and facilities enjoyed without adequate reason. We have adopted a series of measures to remove such vested interests. Absentee landlords have been eliminated. The economic power of the merchant princes is being checked. It is but fair that the feudal princes also be asked to shed their special

privileges. A levelling process is at work in our society, a process which is abolishing divisions and class distinctions. The Bill represents the spirit of history".[35] While speaking on the purpose and rationale of the Bill on an earlier occasion, Mrs. Gandhi had said :

"This is a historic Bill for it represents an important step in the further democratization of our society. Naturally our mind goes back to the freedom struggle. One objective of that struggle was to free ourselves from foreign domination. The other which was no less important was to bring about an egalitarian society in which social divisions and disparities would be abolished. A special characteristic of our freedom movement was that it recognized no class distinction and sought to protect no privileges. We have not been able to establish a society of complete equality but we can claim that we are still engaged in this mighty endeavour".[36]

She was deeply committed to changing the conditions of living of millions of her people groaning under the weight of grinding poverty, the majority of whom were living much below the poverty line. She considered planning a vital instrument for the realization of the social objectives enunciated in the Constitution. Like her illustrious father, she was convinced of the vital role of the public sector in the economic set-up of the country and she looked forward to the progressive growth of the public sector with a view to imparting socio-economic justice to the downtrodden. She visualised a growing and dominant role for the public sector and wanted it to be able to influence and control the pace and direction for investment. The highest-ever amount of Rs. 15,982 crores was allotted to the public sector in the Fourth Five Year Plan (1969-74) as against a total outlay of Rs. 14,656 crores in the past three Plans. The Fourth Plan "aimed at raising the standard of living of the people through programmes which at the same time were designed to promote equality and social justice. The Plan laid particular emphasis on improving the conditions of the less privileged and weaker sections of society especially through the provision of employment and education. Efforts were also directed towards reduction of concentration and a wider diffusion of wealth, income and economic power."[37] She was convinced that the basic objective of a plan must be social justice and sought the cooperation of the people for its successful implementation. While accepting the indispensability of planning in the context of socio-economic reforms, Mrs. Gandhi said :

> "Our planning should result not only in an integrated process of increased production, but rational distribution of the added wealth. The overriding inspiration must be a burning sense of social justice. While increased production is of the utmost importance, it is equally important to remove, or reduce, and prevent the concentration of wealth and economic power. The benefits of development should accrue in increasing measure to the common man and the weaker sections of the society, so that the forces of production can be fully unleashed. A sense of involvement, of participation by the people as a whole, is vital for the success of any plan of rapid economic growth. This can be evoked only by securing social justice, by reducing disparities of income and wealth, and by redressing regional imbalances. A reorientation of socio-economic institutions in this spirit is accordingly the first necessity".[38]

The major objective of the Fifth Plan was self-reliance and eradication of poverty. Addressing a meeting of the National Development Council on September 24, 1976, Mrs. Gandhi said :

> "No Plan can ignore the deep-seated urges of our people for greater equality. The reduction of disparities of all kinds—social, economic and regional —must always remain one of the central objectives of our development planning".[39]

Mrs. Gandhi was deeply conscious of her task of socio-economic justice and her budgetary and fiscal policies were also oriented to relieve the burden of economic disparities, besides envisaging a prominent role to the public sector as the main means of attaining a socialistic society. She viewed socialism as the product of age-long experience and believed that in the fight against poverty, inequality and disparities of income and wealth, freedom was the firs stage while socialism was the second She utilized all measures at her command with this end in view. Speaking on her first Budget in 1970, she said :

> "The Budget aims at economic growth. But of what use is economic growth, if it is accompanied by increased social tensions and if it does not mitigate distributive injustices? The gain from economic growth should be shared by all sections of society. The increase in the Plan outlay by its own momentum will bring greater opportunities for gainful employment to the weaker sections of society".[40] Similarly, speaking on the Finance Bill she said :
>
> "The Bill gives concrete shape to the task of reconciling the need for augmented revenues for developmental purposes, with that of using the fiscal device for furthering distributive justice".[41]

She was equally concerned about the failure of the government to implement the land reform measures and was aware of the fact that the various disturbances brewing in the country side were the result of this failure to fulfil the commitment of the Congress made during the struggle for national liberation. She believed that the land reform was the most crucial test, which the country's political system must pass in order to survive. She gave vent to her deep concern for speedy implementation of land reform measures in her speech to the nation on August 15, 1970, when she said :

> "Some people have too much land whereas some have no land at all. This is not just. We have taken a few steps in this direction which has given relief to some people. It is our duty to see that the Acts which were passed with this end in view are immediately enforced. Whether this is done by the Central or the State government, implementation must be done honestly and effectively".[42] She believed that the real problem was not the formulation of objectives, but their implementation. It was not the policy that had failed but it was the failure on the part of the government to deliver the goods and act with the sincerity and seriousness required for the task". Exhorting the Chief Ministers of various States, she said :

millions of our people than land reforms. No other measure is remotely comparable in its power to transform their lives, to realize their latent energies and to give them not only economic betterment but hope in their future, confidence in themselves as human beings and, equally important, faith in our democratic processes".[43]

In the Chief Ministers' conference in September, 1970, she said :

"The land reform measures implemented have failed to match the legitimate expectations which were first fostered among the millions of cultivators during the national movement. We have yet to create an equitable tenurial system for the village poor. We have yet to devise a system for the distribution of credit and inputs which is not biased in favour of the affluent. In short, we have yet to create institutional conditions which would enable small farmers, tenants and landless labourers to share in the agricultural New Deal".[44]

In pursuance of her notes on economic policy, certain radical measures were taken on the agricultural front. A new ceiling on agricultural lands was fixed. Minimum wages for the agricultural labour on a zonal basis and a minimum amount of bonus of 8.33 per cent for industrial labour were also fixed. She believed that the development of agriculture depended on proper industrialization, and on the other hand, industry cannot flourish without agriculture. Hence she was in favour of a co-ordinated development in both the sectors.

She held the view that any decision on nationalization must fit in with the general scheme of priorities of the economy and should further the social objectives in view. Twenty-eight commercial banks had been finally nationalized; 106 general insurance companies were also taken over. The nationalization of coal industry with 226 coking coal mines including coke-oven plants also followed :

In July, 1975 she announced a 20 Point Programme for boosting her "Garibi Hatao" or "Drive Poverty Away" campaign. Unfortunately, the programme was not properly evaluated in her time as it got mixed up with the Emergency excesses.

Nevertheless, it is increasingly being realized that it was an important step to achieve the goals of socio-economic justice. In fact, she was so much concerned with the poverty-stricken masses that, along side the administrative, fiscal and legal measures to eradicate poverty, she did not hesitate to remove whatever impediments came in her way. She became the first Prime Minister of India who tried to fulfil the constitutional mandate in the form of the fundamental principles of governance and realized the full implications of the provisions under Part IV of the Constitution devised as a means for the achievement of the goal set by the Founding Fathers of the Constitution—the goal of a social revolution. She was also aware of the growing menace consequent to the concentration of economic power and material resources of the community in a few hands. Though she was not against private property, when it came in conflict with public purpose, she felt, the former must yield to the latter. For cutting the Gordian Knot of concentration of economic power, she brought an amendment to the Constitution which was enacted as the Constitution (25th Amendment) Act, 1971. A New Article 31 (C) was inserted by this amendment which gave primacy to the Directive Principle under Clauses (b) and (c) of Article 39 over Articles 13, 14, 19, and 31 of the Fundamental Rights. Thus, the entrenched interests in the national economy who took shelter behind the Fundamental Rights guaranteed to the individuals were laid bare and the constitutional impediments to the socio-economic justice were removed. The government had to step in as there was no effective force or in-built correctives in the economic system against the possible abuses flowing from the concentration of economic power, and the abuses had to be eroded and cleaned up to speed up socio-economic justice.

Even after her miraculous victory against the formidable combine of reactionary and feudal forces in early 1971, the rightists left no stone unturned to put obstructions in her progressive measures and halt the process of reform, but the indomitable spirit of socialism in Mrs. Gandhi, imbued by the Father of the Nation and her own father, goaded her to run headlong towards the goal despite the obstructionlists' tactics. She strongly felt : "Our people yearn for socialism, for the

She strongly felt : "Our people yearn for socialism, for the fight against poverty to be intensified, for inequality and disparities to be lessened." And she intensified the fight. In her bid to achieve a socialist State, she proposed suitable constitutional amendments with a view to releasing the forces of socio-economic justice which shall flow after the operation of the in-built constitutional mechanism, lying almost idle in the non-justiciable corner of the Constitution. The Constitution (42nd Amendment) Act, 1976, was enacted to give effect to her policies. It *inter alia* inserted the words "Socialist Secular" in the Preamble, Articles 39A 43A and 48A in the Directive Principles providing for equal justice and free legal aid, workers' participation in management and maintenance of ecological balance, and gave primacy to any or all of the Directive Principles over Articles 13, 14, 19 and 31 of the Fundamental Rights. Thus, the Fundamentalists, wont to oppose her progressive measures intended to bring socio-economic justice emanating form the Directive Principles, were deprived of the armoury of legal equality and civil rights guaranteed to the citizens for their individual development which were being used to countermand progressive measures for the sake of the development of the nation. She even helped the government during the Janata regime to remove the rights to property guaranteed as Fundamental Rights under Article 31 of the Constitution, and the individual's rights to property was thus out of harm's way.

Mrs. Gandhi was presiding over the destiny of the nation at a time when all classes, entrenched and sectional interests, were making incessant demands. She faced shortages and unemployment, drought and famine with undaunted valour. The war and the influx of refugees had shattered the country's economy and had encouraged corruption and vice at the governmental level. If she could not stem the tide of corruption and violence or strengthen the organizational structures so vital for the effective functioning of the Government, history will not blame her, because she played her part well, saved the integrity and unity of the nation and even laid down her life for the noble cause of a united and socialist India.

After we have had a good look of the policies adopted by the State in pursuance of the Directive Principles; now, we can proceed to have a glimpse of the judicial viewpoints on the issue, but before that it would not be out of place to have a bird's eye-view of the Directive Principles. Indicating their great value in defence of Article 29 of the Draft, Dr. Ambedkar said :

> "They lay down that our ideal is economic democracy. Our objective in framing the Constitution is really two-fold : (i) to lay down the form of parliamentary democracy, and (ii) to lay down that our ideal is economic democracy and also to prescribe that every government whatever it is in power, shall strive to bring about economic democracy".[45] As it finally emerged, Article 37 stipulates that though the provisions of Part IV shall not be cognizable by a court of law, the principles there in laid down shall be fundamental in the governance of the nation and it shall be the bounden duty of the State to apply those principles while making laws. This Article is a vita glass for visualizing the aspirations of the Founding Fathers for the future shape of the socio-economic transformation of the nation as provided for in the subsequent Articles.

After the preamble of the Directive Principles is laid down in Article 37, prefaces the establishment of a Welfare State with the plain and obvious purpose of bringing about betterment of the lot of the downtrodden in a smooth, steady and peaceful manner. It enjoins upon the State to strive to promote the welfare of the people by securing and protecting in an effective manner a social order in which justice—social, economic and political—shall inform all the institutions of national life. The State is further bequeathed the task to strive to minimize the gross inequalities in income, status, facilities and opportunities not only amongst individuals, but also amongst the groups or classes of individuals. Thus Article 38 incorporates a direction to the State to secure a social order for the promotion of general welfare of the people. It sets out in general terms the national objective and the subsequent ones delineate concrete measures as a follow-up action visualized by the Founding Fathers of the Constitution. In a way, social justice includes economic justice as well within its parameters. The concept of social justice includes within its bounds the objectives of removing all inequalities and of providing equal opportunities to all. Economic equality is a parapet on the social structure because the ultimate determinant of social iniquity is the degree of discrimination and poverty. "Poverty is self-perpetuating because the poorest communities are poorest in services which would eliminate it."[46]

Article 39 sets out an action plan for the realization of the social order and economic objectives enunciated in Article 38. Article 39A inserted by the 42nd Amendment ensures that the legal system operates to promote justice on a basis of equal opportunity and provides by schemes or suitable legislation for free legal aid, that opportunities for securing justice are not unavailable to any citizen by reason of economic or other disabilities.

Article 40 is a new clause, consequent to the Amendment of Article 31 of the Draft Constitution, moved by Shri K. Santhanam, for the establishment of Village Panchayats as the self-governing units, envisaging a village republic of Gandhian order.

Article 41 enjoins upon the State to make effective provision, within the limits of its economic capacity and development, for securing to all citizens the right to work, to education and to public assistance in case of unemployment and to other social security measures, and Article 42 obliges the State to provide for human conditions of work and for maternity relief.

Referring to these provisions, Shri H.V. Kamath said in the Constituent Assembly :

> If the provisions of these Articles are going to be seriously implemented and the Government will really and in earnest take action in accordance with the provisions of these articles, I have no doubt that they will provide a new charter, the charter of a new life for the exploited, disinherited and the underprivileged and they will provide the basis or the framework for the blue-print of economic and social democracy in our country."[47] But visualizing the establishment of a social democracy, he sounded a note of caution :
>
> "Social democracy to my mind means all men, one class; all men, one caste; and I hope we are moving towards

> the creation of a casteless and classless society which Mahatma Gandhi envisaged for the social order in India... Parliamentary democracy is not enough; unless you translate this political freedom, this parliamentary democracy into the life of the common man in economic and social terms this parliamentary democracy will not work and parliamentary democracy will be dead... Therefore, we should take heed betimes and try to establish in our country economic and social democracy".[48]

Article 43 provides that the State shall secure to all workers work, a living wage, a decent standard of life and full enjoyment of leisure and social and cultural opportunities and to promote cottage industries on individual or cooperative basis. It requires the State not only to ensure work for all who are willing and able to work. It at the same time calls for better working conditions including a living wage to ensure a decent living. But in the hiererchy of wages, the concept of living wage stands at the apex followed by a fair wage and minimum wage. The State, after five decades of freedom, has been able merely to legislate on minimum wages for workers in various vocations of life and some such legislations still remain to be implemented in practice, chiefly in the case of agricultural and domestic workers. Article 43A, inserted by the 42nd Amendment of the Constitution, prescribes suitable legislation to secure workers' participation in the management of industries or undertakings.

Article 44 enjoins upon the State to strive to secure a uniform civil code for all citizens, indicating the fond hope of the Founding Fathers to see the whole of India welded and united together as a single nation. It is well to recall that the only hindrance that comes in the way of a uniform civil code is the personal law of marriage and succession prevailing differently in different communities. Justifying the inclusion of this provision, Shri K.M. Munshi, member of the Drafting Committee, pointed out that the article was in consonance with the fundamental right to freedom of religion and not tyrannous to the minority or majority, but merely designed to unify and consolidate the nation by every means without interfering with the religious practices."

He further said : "If, however, the religious practices in the past have been so construed as to cover the whole field of life, we have reached a point where we must put our foot down and say that these matters are not religion, they are purely matters for secular legislation. It is not merely a question for minorities but also affects the majority. There are many among the Hindus who do not like a uniform civil code, because they take the same view as honourable Muslim Members who spoke last. The sooner we forget this isolationist outlook on life, the better it will be for the country. Religion must be restricted to spheres which legitimately appertain to religion, and the rest of life must be regulated, unified and modified in such a manner that we may evolve as early as possible a strong and consolidated nation. Our first problem and the most important problem is to produce national unity in this country...I hope our friends will not feel that this is an attempt to exercise a tyranny over a minority; it is much tyrannous to the majority.

"This attitude of mind perpetuated under the British Rule that personal law is part of religion has been fostered by the British, and by the British courts. We must, therefore, outgrow it."[49] Even after five decades of independence, the clarion call goes unheeded.

Article 45 contemplates that the State shall strive for free and compulsory education for all children until they attain the age of 14 years, within a period of ten years. The idea is clearly to engage all the children in educational institutions until they attain the prescribed age, which is buttressed by the provision of Article 24 of the Fundamental Rights which prohibits their employment in hazardous occupations until the age of 14. The child must be kept occupied in some institution. That is the main object of this Article. The goal is still eluding us.

Article 46 stipulates the provision that the State shall promote the educational and economic interest of the weaker sections of the society and protect them against exploitation and social injustice. The article exhibits the real Gandhian spirit. The great importance which the Founding Fathers attached to the protection, advancement and prevention of exploitation of the weaker sections, including the Scheduled Castes and Scheduled Tribes, may be gathered from the inter spersed provisions of the Constitution with the lucid intent that the exploitations of these limping brackets of the social order shall be extirpated with special care by the State. Besides, the Fundamental Rights under Articles 15(4) and 16(4) which enjoin upon the State to make special provision for reservation in Government posts and admissions to educational institutions, even the fundamental civil rights guaranteed by Article 19(1) (a) and (e), i.e. the right to move freely throughout the territory of India, and the right to reside and settle in any part of India are made expressly subject to reasonable restrictions aimed at protecting the interests of the Scheduled Castes and Scheduled Tribes. Articles 330 and 332 provide for reservation of seats for the Scheduled Castes and Scheduled Tribes in the House of the People and Legislative Assemblies of each State, respectively. Article 335 obligates the State to consider the claims of the Scheduled Castes and Scheduled Tribes consistently, with the maintenance of efficiency of administration, in the making of appointment to services and posts in connection with the affairs of the State. Article 340 empowers the President to appoint a commission to inquire and investigate the conditions of socially and educationally backward classes of citizens and, on the receipt of the report, to specify the backward classes. Articles 341 and 342 empower the President to specify the castes, races or tribes or parts or groups thereof as Scheduled Castes and Scheduled Tribes respectively. Article 244 and 244A make special provision for the administration and control of the Scheduled Areas and the Scheduled Tribe in any State by the application of the Fifth and Sixth Schedules. Article 346 in Clauses (24) and (25) defines Scheduled Castes and Scheduled Tribes. Article 275 declares the grants-in-aid of the revenues of a State, such capital and recurring sums as may be deemed necessary by the Union to meet the cost of development schemes for the promotion of the welfare of the Scheduled Tribes in such States as Charged Expenditure on the Consolidated Fund of India. The fundamental obligation imposed on the State under Article 46 enabled by the foregoing provisions referred to above, illustrates the multi-faceted character of the egalitarian concept of the Founding Fathers and portends the special care and duty of the State to take positive and effective measures for the promotion, protection and preservation of the interests and dignity of the weaker sections.

Article 47 obligates the State to regard the raising of the level of nutrition and the standard of living of citizens and the improvement of public health as among its primary duties. It also contemplates prohibition by the State of intoxicating drinks and of drugs, which are injurious to health. Shri B. Pattabhi Sitaramayya, justifying the insertion of prohibition in the Constitution, said :

> "We have included it as one of the Directives in our Constitution. It will be a great moral reform, the monetary equivalent of which may mean loss to the government of the provinces but the moral equivalent of it would be a great asset to the nation in future years."[50]

Article 48 enjoins upon the State to organize agriculture and animal husbandry on modern and scientific lines, and Article 48A, inserted by the 42nd Amendment, requires of the State to protect and improve the ecology of the nation and to safeguard the forests and wildlife.

Article 49 obligates the State to protect every monument or place or object of artistic or historic interest from spoilation disfigurement, removal, destruction, disposal or export as the case may be. The Article is designed to protect and preserve the ancient relics or monuments of national importance.

Article 50 enjoins upon the state to separate the judiciary from the executive in the public-services of the state. Speaking on the Article, Pandit Nehru had said :

> "I may say straight off that so far as the government is concerned, it is entirely in favour of the separation of judicial and executive functions. I may further say that the sooner it is brought about the better".[51] Article 51 stipulates that the State shall endeavor to promote international peace and security and settlement of international disputes by arbitration. The President of the Constituent Assembly, Dr. Rajendra Prasad, in his concluding speech, made a reference to this laudable article :
>
> "We have not provided for the good of our people only

but have laid down in our directive Principles that our State shall endeavour to promote material peace and security, maintain just and honourable relations between nations, foster respect for international laws and treaty obligations and encourage settlement of international disputes by arbitration. In a world torn with conflicts, in a world which even after the devastation of two world wars is still depending on armaments to establish peace and goodwill, we are destined to play a great part, if we prove true to the teachings of the Father of the Nation and give effect to this Directive Principle in the Constitution".[52]

We have broadly dealt with the mechanism of socio-economic transformation projected by the Founding Fathers of the Constitution. They are couched in general terms to allow for a certain measure of elasticity and scope for its development to meet the various exigencies during the onward march of the nation towards the goal of economic democracy. The political struggle ended with the declaration of independence, but a more arduous struggle in the social and economic sphere had to ensue. The member of the Constituent Assembly had very well visualized the potential dangers lurking behind a political freedom, without economic freedom of the masses, and also the awareness and consciousness of the masses of the inalienable rights of the socio-economic justice accruing to a free citizen crushed by years of poverty and deprivation. They were also aware of the problems which frustration arising out of belied hopes generates, and of the subterranean forces that it sets inmotion. Shri H.V. Kamath had sounded a note of caution :

"There are millions of people in India today who want to work, but do not get work. There are a few parasites who can work, but do not want to work. As Bernard Shaw has said, at the one end we have got man with appetites but no dinners; at the other we have men with dinners but no appetites. This social order is a house divided against itself. So long as this house divided continues, there will be no peace in the world; there will be no happiness in the world. We will have violent movements; we will have desperate man armed with

> bullets, armed with Bren-guns, trying to overthrow the social order. You cannot entirely blame them, you cannot find fault with them only; the fault lies also with those of us who want to perpetuate the exploiting social order".[53]

(f) Views of Founding Fathers

It is to preempt such an eventuality that the Founding Fathers of the Constitution have provided guidelines for waging the struggle against poverty and squalor, ignorance and superstition, and declared them of fundamental importance in the governance of the country, and a bounden duty of the State to apply them in making laws, for the steady realization of economic democracy which must lie at the root of a sound political democracy. "Great economic disparities are as much a menace to political democracy as are the forces of authoritarianism and dictatorship. A few islands of richness in a vast sea of poverty, some stray oasis of affluence in a vast desert of want and privation constitute dangerous irritants for the health and well-being of the nation. Such disparities generate social tensions, the threat of which few democratic societies can withstand".[54] The wishes, aspirations and interests of the common man can never be realized in the absence of economic equality by any political device whatsoever. Gandhi had advocated for the greatest good of all in "Swaraj" whose sum total shall be greater than the greatest good of any other society. Freedom was only a means to achieve this good life; and that freedom cannot be complete unless the political democracy is allowed to evolve, to grow into economic and social democracy. In December, 1954, the Parliament resolved to evolve a "Socialistic Pattern of Society" in the context of economic planning and the 42nd Amendment of the Constitution in 1976 added the word "socialist secular" in the Preamble, thus signifying the twilight of socialism in India. Several policies have been enunciated to safeguard the interests of the weaker sections of society. Thus the broad objectives of the economic policy became the achievement of a socialist pattern of society. The Second Plan stressed that the pattern of development and the lines along which economic activity is directed should be closely linked from the start to the basic objective, which the society has in view. Enumerating the social objectives in planning, the third Five-Year Plan states :

"The Directive Principles of State Policy in the Constitution have placed before the country the objectives of securing adequate means of livelihood and the right to work, to education and to public assistance in cases of unemployment, old age, sickness and disablement and in other cases of undeserved want. They have also affirmed that for realizing these goals, the ownership and control of the material resources of the country should be so distributed as to best subserve the common good and that the operation of the economic system should not result in the concentration of wealth and economic power in the hands of a few. The successive Five Year Plans which the country undertakes have to keep in view these basic considerations."[55] To asses as to how far planning has promoted the socio-economic transformation of the society by its efforts to ameliorate the lot of the weaker sections of the society, it will be appropriate to recall the efforts made in this direction through the various Plans. Whereas the Scheduled Castes and Scheduled Tribes only make for a quarter of the total population, merely 8.48 per cent of the total outlays during the six plans have been alotted for the welfare of the weaker sections of the society including other social welfare programmes. This is all that was required to prove the justification of the special measures to improve the economic conditions of the weaker sections of the society. The concept of socialistic pattern of society which the planners wanted to achieve remains a far cry. It is well to remember what Dr. Rajendra Prased, presiding over the Constituent Assembly, had said :

"After all, the Constitution like a machine, is a lifeless thing. It acquires life because of the men who control it and operate it, and India needs today nothing more than a set of honest men who will have the interest of the country before them."

"Mahatma Gandhi laid stress on the purity of the methods which had to be pursued for attaining our ends. Let us not forget that this teaching has an eternal value and was not intended only for the period of stress and struggle but has as much authority and value today as it ever had before. We have a tendency to blame others for everything that goes wrong and not to introspect and try to see if we have any share in it or not. It is much easier to scan one's own actions and motives if one is inclined to do so than to appraise correctly the actions and motives of others".[56]

Instead of feeling the pulse of the nation and do self-appraisal, a tendency has gown in recent years to blame the Constitution and inadequacy of the laws for all pitfalls, shortcomings and failures. It is also alleged that judicial verdicts act as a great deterrent and as a setback to all socio-economic progress of the nation; and the Fundamental Rights act as a great barrier to the realization of the goal set out in the Directive Principles of State Policy. "Experience, however, tells us that the desire to do away with the Bill of Rights is actuated not so much by a desire to remove hurdles in the way of socio-economic reforms as with a view to arming the persons in authority with more powers".[57] The elimination of basic rights and curtailment of civil liberties have always presaged dictatorship; absolute power has always corrupted absolutely. On the pretext of socio-economic changes, the balance of power between the organs of the government is sought to be disturbed, structural changes in the Constitution are sought for and unsavoury truths focussed in judicial verdicts are frowned at. One of the precious rights of the people, the right to property, has been annihilated from the realm of Fundamental Rights, apart from some major constitutional amendments purported to hasten economic emancipation of the downtrodden, but the depth of poverty goes on deepening incessantly and the gulf between the rich and the poor, the haves and the have-nots is getting wider and wider. While delivering the Patel Memorial Lectures justice H.R. Khanna had said :

"The commitment given to the posterity in Articles 39 and 41, although a period of more than quarter of a century has elapsed since the coming into force of this Constitution, has strong ring of irony. These articles pose a question for all those who have been in charge of the affairs of the State. The articles provide, with all the evidence of mounting unemploy-ment amongst the educated and not so well educated and even amongst persons holding high technical qualifications, enough material for indictment at the bar of history of all those entrusted with economic planning. They are answerable as to why the goals set out in the above articles are, if anything, more remote than they were at the time the Constitution was framed. A question also arises as to what we have done in concrete terms for providing assistance in old age, sickness and disablement, apart from making pious speeches and passing nobly worded resolutions".[58] Surely, we can tract out a plethora of legislation and uncountable resolutions twinkling hopes in the human hearts, whose fulfilment in concrete terms, has been dismal and negligible. The frustrations created have given rise to disorder and chaos in the social order and the confusion is worst confounded.

(g) Judicial Pronouncement

Let us spread the canvass and focus the searchlight of our inquiry on some important judicial decisions of the Supreme Court to evaluate the contention that the judiciary has undermined the process and slackened the pace of socio-economic transformation in its observance of constitutional mandate of protecting the Fundamental Rights of the citizens vis-a-vis the Directive Principles of State Policy.

Even while the right to property was a Fundamental Right in the Constitution, a case which came up before the Supreme Court under the heels of Zamindari Abolition Act was State of Bihar *vs.* Kameshwar Singh, in 1952 : The Act was upheld on the ground that the enactment was in pursuance of Article 39. In his judgement, Justice Mahajan emphasized the importance of the Directive Principles of State Policy, as follows :

> "Concentration of big blocks of land in the hands of a few individuals is contrary to the principle on which the Constitution of India is based. The purpose of the acquisition as contemplated by the impugned Act, therefore, is to do away with the concentration of big blocks of land and means of production in the hands of a few individuals and to so distribute the ownership and control of the material resources which come in the hands of the State as to subserve the common good as best as possible. It aims at destroying the inferiority complex in

> a large number of citizens of the State and giving them a status of equality with their former lords and prevents the accumulation of big tracts of land in the hands of a few individuals which is contrary to the expressed intentions of the Constitution".[59]

Justice S.R. Das, in his separate concurring judgement likewise observed :

> "Surely, it is to subserve the common good by bringing the land, which feeds and sustains the community and also produces wealth by its forest, mineral and other resources, under State ownership or control. This State ownership or control over land is a necessary preliminary step towards the implementation of the Directive Principles of State Policy and it cannot but be a public purpose".[60]

Thus, taking over the property with the object of public purpose was held just because the Act was in pursuance of the purposes enumerated in Article 39.

Similarly, in Golaknath *vs.* State of Punjab (1967), a landmark case in the history of the Supreme Court, which upheld the immutable nature of the Fundamental Rights, Chief Justice K. Subbarao, presiding over a bench of II judges, opined :

> "The Fundamental Rights and the Directive Principles of State Policy enshrined in the Constitution formed an 'integrated scheme' and was elastic enough to respond to the changing needs of the society".[61]

This conception of an "integrated scheme" of Parts III and IV formulated in the Golaknath case held good in later decisions as well, and, after the insertion of Article 31C, in the Constitution by the 25th Amendment of 1971 and its validation by the Supreme Court, as we shall presently see, the judicial outlook is oriented more towards the Directive Principles, if the objective is considered rational.

In another landmark case, Keshavanand Bharti *vs.* State of Kerala (1973), the Supreme Court has discussed in detail the significance of the Directive Principles of State Policy. In its historic judgement, the 'Right to Property' has been, for the first time, declared to be subservient to the common good. Justice A.N. Roy observed :

> "The Directive Principles are also fundamental. They can be effective if they are to prevail over the Fundamental Rights of a few in order to subserve the common good and not to allow the economic system to result to the common detriment. It is the duty of the State to promote common good... Consideration of social justice will include the relevant Directive Principles, particularly in Article 39(b) and (c)".[62]

Likewise Justice Reddy opined : "In order to further the directives, persons may be grouped in relation to property they own or hold or the economic power they possess, in payment of compensation at different rates to different classes of persons depending on the extent of the value of the property they own or possess, or in respect of classes of persons to whom the material resources of the country are distributed".[63] He further observed that "if full compensation is paid for the property taken in furtherance of the objectives under Article 39(b) and (c), the very objective sought to be implemented would fail... Any law which makes a reasonable classification to further the objectives of Article 39(b) and (c) would undoubtedly fulfil the requirements of Article 14. In fact, the availability of Article 14 in respect of laws under Article 31(c) would ensure 'distributive justice' or 'economic justice' which without it would be thwarted".[64]

Thus, we find the Supreme Court championing the principle of "distributive justice" and this idea of distributive justice has also been upheld in many other decisions.

In State of Kerala *vs.* Thomas (1976), the Supreme Court held the view :

> "The Directive Principles of State Policy, fundamental in the governance on the country, enjoin on the State the promotion with special care of the educational and economic interests of the weaker sections of the people, and, in particular, the Scheduled Castes and the Scheduled Tribes... and protect them from social injustice. To neglect this obligation is to play truant with Article 46".[65]

Again in A.B.S.K. Sangh *vs.* Union of India (1981), the Supreme Court held the view that the Directive Principles serve as a code of interpretation, and said :

"Because the Fundamental Rights are justiciable and the Directive Principles are not, it was assumed, in the beginning that the Fundamental Rights held a superior position under the Constitution than the Directive Principles, and that the latter were of secondary importance as compared with the Fundamental Rights. That way of thinking is of the past and has become obsolete. It is now universally recognized that the difference lies in this that the Fundamental Rights are primarily aimed at assuring political freedom to the citizens by protecting them against excessive State action while the Directive Principles are aimed at securing social and economic freedoms by appropriate State action. The Fundamental Rights are intended to foster the ideal of a political democracy and to prevent the establishment of authoritarian rule but they are of no value unless they can be enforced by resort to courts. The Directive Principles cannot in the very nature of things be enforced in a Court of Law. It is unimaginable that any court can compel a legislature to make a law. If the court can compel Parliament to make laws then parliamentary democracy would soon be reduced to an oligarchy of judges. It is in this sense that the Constitution says that the Directive Principles shall not be enforceable by courts. It does not mean that the Directive Principles are less important than the Fundamental Rights or that they are not binding on the various organs of the State. Article 37 of the Constitution emphatically States that the Directive Principles are nevertheless fundamental in the governance of the country and it shall be the duty of the State to apply these principles in making laws. It follows that it becomes the duty of the court to apply the Directive Principles in interpreting the Constitution and the laws. The Fundamental Rights should thus be interpreted in the light of the Directive Principles and the latter should, whenever and wherever possible, be read into the former. Every law attacked on the ground of infringement of a Fundamental Right should among other considerations, be examined to find if the law does not advance one or other of the Directive Principles or it it is not in discharge of some of the undoubted obligations of the State, constitutional or otherwise, towards its citizens or sections of its citizens, flowing out of the Preamble, the Directive Principles and other provisions of the Constitution".[66]

Similarly, in another landmark case, Minerva Mills Ltd. *vs.* Union of India (1980), wherein Section 4 of the Constitution (Forty-second Amendment) Act, 1976, giving primacy to the Directive Principles over the Fundamental Rights was, *inter alia*, impugned, the Supreme Court, while declaring Section 4 ultra vires and void, made a clear distinction between the Fundamental Rights and the Directive Principles which are an integrated and indivisible scheme of the Constitution. The Court, presided over by Chief Justice Y. V. Chandrachud, observed :

"There is no doubt that the courts have always attached very great importance to the preservation of human liberties, no less importance has been attached to some of the Directive Principles of State Policy enunciated in Part IV. The Indian Constitution is first and foremost a social document and the majority of its provisions are aimed at furthering the goals of social revolution by establishing the condition necessary of its achievement. Therefore import of the Directive Principles of State Policy in the scheme of our Constitution cannot ever be overemphasized. These principles project the high ideals, which the Constitution aims to achieve. In fact the Directive Principles are fundamental in the governance of the country and there is no scheme of public life where the delay can defeat justice with more telling effect than the one in which the common man seeks the realization of his aspirations. The promise of a better tomorrow must be fulfilled today, day after tomorrow it runs the risk of being conveniently forgotten. Indeed, so many tomorrows have come and gone without a leaf turning that today there is a lurking danger that people will work out their destiny through the compelled cult of their own 'dirty hands'. Words bandied about in marbled halls say much but fail to achieve as much".[67] Making a lucid distinction between the two Rights, the Court remarked :

"Parts III and IV are like two wheals of a chariot, one no less important than the other. You snap one and the other will loose its efficacy. They are like a twin formula for achieving the social revolution, which is the ideal, which the visionary founders of the Constitution set before themselves. Indian Constitution is founded on the bedrock of the balance between Parts III and IV. To give absolute primacy to one over the other is to disturb the harmony of the Constitution.

Just as the rights conferred by Part III would be without a radar and a compass if they were not geared to an ideal, in the same manner the attainment of the ideal set out in Part IV would become a pretence or tyranny if the price to be paid for achieving that ideal is human freedom. The goals set out in Part IV have, therefore, to be achieved without the abrogation of the means provided for by Part III. It is in this sense that Parts III and IV together constitute the core of our Constitution and combine to form its conscience".[68]

Even in Waman Rao *vs.* Union of India (1981), while pronouncing on the validity of Article 31C, the Supreme Court observed :

> "Article 31C of the Constitution, as it stood prior to its amendment by Section 4 of the Constitution 42nd Amendment) Act, 1976, is valid to the extent to which its constitutionality was upheld in the Keshavanand Bharati case. Article 31C is not like an unchartered sea. It gives protection to a defined and limited category of laws, which are passed for giving effect to the policy of the State towards securing the principles specified in Clause (b) or Clause (c) of Article 39. These clauses of Article 39 contain Directive Principles, which are vital to the well-being of the country and the welfare of its people. It is impossible to conceive that any law passed for such a purpose can at all violate Article 14 or Article 19. Article 31 is now out of harm's way. In fact, far from damaging the basic structure of the Constitution, laws passed truely and bona fide for giving effect to the Directive Principles in Clauses (b) and (a) of Article 39 will fortify that structure".[69]

The Court had so far held the view in the judgement of the two leading cases cited above that Section 4 of the

Constitution (42nd Amendment) Act, 1976, was ultra vires, and the position held in Keshavanand Bharati's case (1973) that Article 31C, inserted by the Constitution (25th Amendment) Act, 1971, as it stood at that time, was constitutionally valid. In other words, Article 31C which was originally devised as a protection to the laws giving effect to the policy of Clauses (b) and (c) of Article 39 against the Fundamental Rights under Articles 14, 19 and 31 continued to be intra vires, but the extension of this protective umbrellas to laws made for giving effect to all or any of the Directive Principles by Section 4 of the 42nd Amendment remained unacceptable after the judgement in the Minerva Mill's case in 1980.

However, in 1983, the Supreme Court reversed its earlier stand that the goal should be achieved without the abrogation of the means, and in Sanjeev Coke Manufacturing Co. *vs.* M/s. Bharat Cooking Coal Ltd. accorded legal validity of Section 4 of the Constitution (42nd Amendment) Act extending the protection of laws for giving effect to all or any of the Directive Principles intended to give primacy to the Directive Principles over the Fundamental Rights, and the observations to the contrary in the Minarva Mill's case were held obiter. The Supreme Court observed :

> "The dialects, the logic and the rationale involved in upholding the validity of Article 31C when it comfined its protection to laws enacted to further Article 39 (b) or Article 39 (c) should, uncompromisingly, lead to the same resolute conclusion that Article 31 (c) with its extended protection is also constitutionally valid".[70]

It will be, thus, observed that the court has given a clean chit to the state to proceed ahead with the goals enunciated by the Founding Fathers for the realization of a social and economic democracy as set out in Part IV of the Constitution even at the cost of overriding Article 14 and Article 19 of the Fundamental Rights under Part III of the Constitution.

The State of Madras *vs.* Champakam Dorairajen (AIR 1951 Sc. 226) was the first case which brought under the judicial focus the conflict between the Fundamental Rights and the Directive Principles of State Policy. The Supreme Court observed : "The chapters on Fundamental Rights is sacrosanct and is not liable to be abridged by any legislative or executive act, except to the extent provided in Part III. Hence, in case of conflict between the Directive Principles and the Fundamental Rights the former have to conform to and run as subsidiary to the chapter on the Fundamental Rights".[71] After the insertion of a new Article 31C by the Constitution (25th Amendment) Act, 1971, which came into force from April 28, 1972 the primacy given to the Directive Principles enunciated in Clauses (b) and (c) of Article 39 over Articles 14, 19 and 31 by the aforesaid constitutional amendment was upheld by the Supreme Court in Keshavanand Bharati case (1973). When the Constitution (42nd Amendment) Act, 1976, which came into force on January 3, 1977, under Section 4, substituted "all or any of the principles laid down in Part IV" for "the principles specified in Clause (b) or Clause (c) of Article 39" in Article 31C, the new provisions under Section 4 were challenged before the Supreme Court in the Minerva Mills case (1980) and the Waman Rao case (1981), and Section (4) was struck down in both the cases and Article 31C was held valid, as it originally stood. Thus the primacy of the Fundamental Rights under Articles 14, 19 and 31 gave way to Article 39 (b) and Article 39(c) of the Directive Principles after the 25th Amendment and the courts continued to give effect to the same. The primacy given to all or any of the Directive Principles over Article 14 and Article 19 (Article 31 having been repealed by the 44th Amendment with effect from June 20, 1979) of the Fundamental Rights by the 42nd Amendment Act, though turned down by the Supreme Court in the two consecutive judgement, was now held to be valid and constitutional in Sanjeev Coke Manufacturing Co. Ltd. *vs.* Bharat Coking Coal Ltd. (1983). The Supreme Court held in this case that the fulfilment of the requirement of Article 14 or Article 19 was not a condition precedent to the laws seeking the protection of the amended Article 31C (as amended by Section 4 of the Constitution 42nd Amendment Act). The Supreme Court made significant observations :

"It cannot be contended that any law seeking the protection of Article 31C must not be a law founded on discrimination. To make it a condition precedent that a law seeking the haven of Article 31C must be non-discriminatory or based on reasonable classification is to make Article 31C meaningless. If Article 14 is not offended, no one need give any immunity from any attack based on Article 14."

"The broad egalitarian principle of social and economic justice for all was implicit in every Directive Principle and therefore, a law designed to promote the Directive Principles, even if it came into conflict with the formalistic and doctrinaire view of equality before the law, would most certainly advance the broader egalitarian principle and the desirable constitutional goal of social and economic justice for all. If the law was aimed at the broader egalitarianism of the Directive Principles, Article 31C protected the law from needless, unending and rancorous debates on the question whether the law contravened Article 14's concept of equality before the law..."[72]

Thus, "Where Article 31C comes in Article 14 goes out".[73] The vail of secrosanctity given to the Fundamental Rights in the Champakam Dorairajan case (1951) is ripped off in the Sanjeev Coke Manufacturing case (1983), the doors for socio-economic justice contrived in the Directive Principles by the Founding Fathers have been thrown open and the string of Fundamental Rights of Articles 14, 19 and 31 is out of the harm's way. No constitutional barrier in the Fundamental Rights is now traceable for a plausible explanation for the dilly-dallying policy of the State since 1983 in the implementation of the Fundamental principles of governance and keeping the people on tenterhooks for the speedy realization of the cherished goal of socio-economic justices.

The Court has even gone to the extend of reading the Directive Principles into the Fundamental Rights and has upheld the principle laid down by the various Articles of Part IV. Thus in A.K. Roy *vs.* Union of India (1982) the Supreme Court upheld the principle of "equal pay for equal work" set forth in the Directive Principles and observed :

> "It is true that the principle of 'equal pay for equal work' is not expressly declared by our Constitution to be a Fundamental Right. But it certainly is a constitutional goal. Article 39 (d) of the Constitution proclaims equal pay for equal work for both man and woman as a Directive

Principle of State Policy. It means equal pay for equal work for everyone, and as between the sexes. The Directive Principles, as has been pointed out in some of the judgements of this court, have to be read into the Fundamental Rights as a matter of interpretation. To the vast majority of the people the equality clauses of the Constitution would mean nothing if they are unconcerned with the work they do and the pay they get. To them equality clauses will have some substance if equal work means equal pay.

"Construing Articles 14 and 16 in the light of the Preamble and Article 39 (d) we are of the view that the principle 'equal pay for equal work' is deducible from those Articles and may be properly applied".[74]

Likewise, in State of Tamil Nadu *vs.* Abu Kabur Bai (1984), the Supreme Court invoked the doctrine of harmonious interpretation of the Fundamental Rights and Directive Principles. The court observed :

"On a careful consideration of the legal and historical aspects of the Directive Principles and Fundamental Rights there appears to be complete unanimity of judicial opinion that although the Directive Principles are not enforceable yet the court should make a real attempt at harmonizing and reconciling the Directive Principles and Fundamental Rights and any collision between the two should be avoided as far as possible".[75]

Again, in L.P. Appelwar *vs.* State of Maharashtra (1985) the Supreme Court invoked the concept of "distributive justice". The Court observed :

"The concept of distributive justice in the sphere of law-making connotes, *inter alia*, the removal of economic inequalities and rectifying the injustice resulting from dealings or transactions between unequals in the society. All such laws may take the form of forced distribution of wealth as a means of achieving fair division of material resources among the members of society or there may be legislative control of unfair agreements. Distributive fairness can only be achieved by taxation or contractual regulation at some sacrifice in individual liberty".[76]

Again, in Indian Express Newspaper Pvt. Ltd. *vs.* Union of India (1985), the Supreme Court, upholding the classification of newspapers on the basis of their circulation for the purpose of levying customs duty, held :

> "There is nothing sinister in the object nor can it be said that the classification has no nexus with the object to be achieved. It is the duty of the State to encourage education through the medium of the Press under Article 41.[77]

Thus, it is clear that the laws made by the State are held to be valid if they are enacted with the *bona fide* intent and express purpose to proceed towards the goal set by the Directive Principles. But it is also true that in a democratic structure the *bona fide* or the rationale of a State action can be adjudged only by the independent judiciary, which cannot blindly toe the line set by the State like that of the totalitarian States. The court will have to intervene if there are complaints of invasion on the liberty or policical freedom of the citizens by any State action and to adjudge whether the object sought to be achieved is rational and just or whether the impugned law bears a nexus with the Directive Principles for which protection of Article 31C is sought. In some judicial decisions we find the Court defending some valuable right, enlarging the scope of the Fundamental Rights by a harmonious interpretation and invoking its inter-dependence with the Directive Principles. We have seen above how the court interpreted some Directive Principles to bring some valuable rights within the four corners of a fundamental right. In Olga Tallis *vs.* Bombay Municipal Corporation (1985), likewise, the Supreme Court interpreted the right to livelihood as an inherent connotation of the Fundamental Right to life, with the code of interpretation provided by the Directive Principles. The court observed :

> "The principle contained in Articles 39 (a) and 41 must be regarded as equally fundamental in the understanding and interpretation of the meaning and content of the Fundamental Rights. If there is an obligation upon the State to secure to the citizens an adequate means of livelihood and right to work, it would be sheer pedantry

to exclude the right to livelihood from the content of the right to life. Any person, who is deprived of his right to livelihood, except according to just and fair procedure established by law, can challenge the deprivation as offending the right to life under Article 21 of the Constitution."[78]

It has now achieved the unanimity of judicial decisions that the Directive Principles are as much a part of the Constitution, as is the Preamble, though like the latter the former is also not enforceable by the court in the sense that it cannot compel the Parliament to do what it does not think or like to do in the making of the laws. But nothing prohibits the court to adjudge any State action through the interpretation of these Directive Principles or the Preamble and the Court has always held that the Directive Principles obligate the State to take appropriate action in accordance with the guidelines enunciated in Part IV and all *bona fide* and rational action in pursuance of those objectives are valid. "Whether it is the Constitution that is expounded or the Constitutional validity of a statute that is considered, a cardinal rule is to look to the Preamble to the Constitution as the guiding light and to the Directive Principle of State Policy as the book of interpretation. The Preamble embodies and expresses the hopes and aspirations of the people. The Directive Principles set proximate goals. When it is the task of examining statutes against the Constitution, it is through these glasses that the Court must look, 'distant vision' or 'near vision".[79]

The Preamble promises justice, liberty and equality of status and of opportunity within the framework of a Sovereign, socialist, secular, democratic republic. On January 3, 1977 the 42nd Amendment proclaimed India as a Socialist Republic. The implication of the term "Socialist", which has now become the centre of the hopes and aspirations of the millions of masses, is clearly to set up a socialist welfare society in place of a feudal-exploitative society. The Founding Fathers had dreamt of a cooperative commonwealth and furnished ways and means for its establishment through the willing cooperation of the people in the programme of national reconstruction set forth in Chapter IV of the Constitution.

With the removal of foreign shackles, only the negative part of "Swaraj" had been achieved. Ages of exploitation had brought in squalor, lethargy, simulation and frustration which in turn made the picture of the nation dipped in poverty, ignorance and disease, more gloomy and frightening. The Directive Principles are laid down, as fundamental in the governance of the country and it is the duty of the State to apply these Principles to the making of the laws. A resolute determination of the State for the establishment of an economic democracy, with the willing cooperation of the people, followed by strong and calculated action programmes oriented towards the objectives, can alone avert a national disaster. It would be a sheer act of folly to presume that the government alone and by itself, without the willing and active cooperation of the people, would be able to deliver the goods and usher in economic democracy. Every citizen has his own part to play. The State and the people must play the game in a spirit of national service. We must close our ranks and face the common enemies of poverty, ignorance and disease with a missionary zeal. We have to play the game or perish in the holocaust engulfing the nation.

REFERENCES

1. Land Reform in India (quoted), H.D. Malviya (1954) p. 9.
2. *Ibid.,* p. 20.
3. *Ibid.,* p. 22
4. *Ibid.,* p. 77
5. Nehru : The First Sixty Years, Dorothy Norman (1965), Vol. II. p. 300.
6. *Ibid.*, 335.
7. Malviya, *op.cit.,* p. 78.
8. Norman, *op.cit.,* p. 340.
9. *Ibid.,* pp. 379-80.
10. J.L. Nehru Speeches, Vol. II, Pub. Div. p. 278.
11. Socialist ideology of Congress (quoted), H.D. Malviya (1966), p. 36.
12. C.A.D. II. 2; Jan, 21, 1947.
13. *Ibid.*, Vol. II Aug. 30, 1947.
14. *Ibid.,* VII. 9. Nov. 19, 1948.
15. *Ibid.*
16. *Ibid.*
17. *Ibid.*
18. *Ibid.,* Vol. VII. No-1. Nov. 4. 1948.
19. Normal; *op.cit.,* p. 540.
20. Whither Indian after Independence (quoted) : Premnath Bajaj (1970) pp. 169-70.
21. *J.L. Nehru : A Biography*, S. Gopal, 1984, Vol. III, p. 120
22. *India : Population, Economy Society;* R.H. Cassen (1978) pp. 213-14.
23. *Face to Face with Indira Gandhi;* R.K. Karanjia (1974); p.11.

24. Mrs. Gandhi, Dom Moraes (1980); p. 170.
25. *Times of India* : Exerpts from Interview with Fatma R. Zakaria, Nov. 25, 1984.
26. *Indira Priyadarshini,* Sheela (1966), p. 80.
27. The Years of Endeavour, Pub. Div. Govt. of India (1983), p. 403.
28. Indira Gandhi (quoted); T.N. Jha (1983), pp. 87-90.
29. Congress Bulletin, 1969.
30. The Years of Endeavour, Pub. Div. p. 256.
31. *Ibid.* p. 272.
32. *Ibid.* p. 38.
33. *Ibid.* p. 322.
34. Dom Maraes, *op.cit.*, p. 163.
35. The Years of Endeavour, *op.cit.*, p. 153.
36. *Ibid.*, p. 61
37. India, 1975, Pub. Div. Govt. of India, p. 263.
38. The Year of Endeavour, *op.cit.*, p. 320
39. T.N. Jha, *op.cit.*, p. 98.
40. The Years of Endeavour, *op.cit.*, p. 311.
41. *Ibid.*, p. 42.
42. *Ibid.*, p. 57.
43. *Ibid.*, p. 267.
44. *Ibid.*, p. 271.
45. C.A.D. VII. Nov 19, 1948.
46. Patel Memerial Lectures, Justice H.R. Khanna (1977).
47. C.A.D. VII.9. Nov. 19. 1948.
48. *Ibid.*
49. *Ibid.*, VII, II. Nov. 23, 1948.
50. *Ibid.*, XI.II. Nov. 25, 1949.
51. *Ibid.*, VII.II. Nov. 23, 1948.
52. *Ibid.*, XI.12. Nov. 26, 1949.
53. *Ibid.*, VII.9. Nov. 19, 1948.
54. H.R. Khanna, *op.cit.*
55. Third Five Year Plan, A Draft Outline, p. 3.
56. C.A.D., XI.12. Nov. 26, 1949.
57. H.R. Khanna, *op.cit.*
58. *Ibid.*
59. AIR 1952, Sc. 252.
60. *Ibid.*
61. AIR 1967, Sc 1643.
62. AIR 1973, Sc. 1461.
63. *Ibid.*
64. *Ibid.*
65. AIR 1976, Sc. 490.
66. AIR 1981, Sc. 300.
67. AIR 1980, Sc. 1789.
68. *Ibid.*
69. AIR 1981, Sc. 271.
70. AIR 1983, Sc. 239.
71. AIR 1951, Sc. 226.
72. AIR 1983, Sc. 239.
73. *Ibid.*
74. AIR 1982, Sc. 710.
75. AIR 1984, Sc. 226.
76. (1985) I. SCC. 479.
77. (1985) I. SCC. 641.
78. (1985) I. SCC. 545.
79. AIR 1986, Sc. 859. Atam Prakash *vs.* State of Haryana.

CHAPTER 7

CONCLUSION AND RECOMMENDATIONS

I. CONTENTS OF EQUALITY

Equality is a basic ingredient of democracy. In the words of Lipson, "Democracy differs most from other political system in the special importance it gives to the questions of philosophy."[1] Our quest into the evolution of the right to equality in the context of its ultimate incorporation in the Constitution of India naturally dovetails a bird's eye view of its moral and philoso-phical foundation, both in India and the West. This is more so because in modern times democracy was firmly grounded in the Western thought much before the Indians began to aspire for it. The Western ideas had, therefore, nourished and shaped the concept of this right to equality in India at least in the initial stage of its evolution.

The concept of equality implies both equality-as-justice and equality-as-sameness; the former promotes authentic diversity, professes equal opportunity to all and prescribes privileged differentiation; the latter stands for uniformity, treats all men alike and worthy of equal respect as human beings. In fact, while the former can be promoted by State action, the latter contains the ethical and philosophical foundation of equality and is dependent on the mental attitude of the individual. The spread of Christianity, the advent of natural law philosophers, the rise of utilitarians, libertarians and equalitarians in the Victorian era have all contributed to the growth of the egalitarian concept in the Western thought. These thinkers have differed over the precedence to be given to the various species and taken equality as the repudiation of certain disparities prevalent in the society, instead of others. The natural law philosophers maintain that all man-made inequalities came to the fore with the growth and spread of civilization. They, however, maintain that the universe being essentially materialistic, every phenomenon occurring therein including inequality, should be adjudged on the materialistic plane.

The idea of the eighteenth century thinkers influenced the champions of liberty and equality in France and America. It heralded a new age and it seemed men were going to act to get out of the abyss of misery created by their own wrongful actions in the past. However, in the new settlement named as the United States of America, the notion of equality, taken largely in the sense of equality-as-sameness, that developed in the country, resulted in the establishment of a social democracy, avowed to equal treatment and respect for the next man, whoever he may be in France it emerged in the form of a socialist democracy, occupied primarily with the problem of economic equality.While equality in the social democracy is adopted as a way of life, with its accent on equality-as-sameness, in socialist democracy, with its primary emphasis on equality-as-justice, it is more an enforcement of State Policy than a spontaneous force in social life.

Liberty and equality, are the warring twin, littered by democracy in the universe of human desire. The problems of equality veer round the emphasis on their respective doses, because we cannot have both full to the brim. The libertarians, in the Victorian era, were primarily concerned with the safeguard of individual liberty and their moralistic notion of equality-as-justice was contrived to further, and not hamper, the cause of liberty. They favoured equal opportunities to all, abolition of privileges and equality before the law as the desired doses of equality. But equality of opportunities not only presupposes equality before law and satisfaction of certain basic rights, but also the satisfaction of certain basic needs which can be met only by offering privileges to the underprivileged and handicapped. The equalitarians, therefore, claimed that the equal chance of developing to the full the latent qualities of an individual depended not only on the absence of disabilities alone but also on the presence of abilities. The liberterians parted company with the equalitarians on the question of giving privileges to the weakest and underprivileged because they thought it going too far and reckoned it an encroachment on liberty in the interest of more equality. When the fight between liberty and equality came to such a pass, democracy took up the cudgels and tried to steer midway between the two extremes and reach a point of equilibrium by devising welfare measures aimed to boost up equality awarding privileges to the underprivileged.

The socialists, on the other hand, like the liberals, stand on the other extreme, and give emphasis to equality over the considerations of liberty. For the purpose of equalizing opportunities, they take strongest measures for economic equality, in the sense of equalizing abilities, but the nature and content of the means adopted vary sharply with the democrats. The democrats accept only such formulas and means which are prone to strike a balance between liberty and equality, the socialists go ahead with the job of achieving economic equality even to the negation of liberty.

The socialists, of the Marxist brand, remove the problem of economic equality by abolishing at one stroke all private ownership of property, but in so doing they at once create a monopoly of power at the hands of bureaucracy which is another form of inequality. State ownership creates bureaucratic monopoly of political power, and economic power begins to be guided by the logic of the political power of the all-powerful State. In the democratic system the State keeps an eye on the economic power of the private owners; in the socialist system there is no machinery or system to keep an eye on the all-powerful State. The giant State cannot be resisted by citizens even if it divests them of all their precious rights and liberties because they have not the economic self-sufficiency to do so and act as a robot to fulfil the wishes of the mighty State. The result is great inequality of political power.

Thus, the various systems of Western political thought,

with their primary emphasis on equality-as-justice differ sharply, on the one hand, over the emphasis given to the one or the other of the twin desires of equality and liberty, and on the other, over the ways and means devised to achieve equality and the precedence given to the species of inequality to be eroded. The Western concept of equality, by and large, is grounded in the notion of equality-as-justice. Even the great champion of modern socialism, Prof. Laski, has emphatically repudiated the notion of equality-as-sameness and has emphasized the equality-as-justice.

II. CONCEPT OF EQUALITY : INDIAN *VS.* WESTERN

The concept of equality in ancient India stands in sharp contrast with the Western notion on the subject. This is because of the varying philosophical foundations of the two streams of thought.

Firstly, the Western emphasis is on matter. Everything depends on matter and is the resultant of matter. The whole universe is essentially materialistic and every phenomenon herein, including inequality causing human miseries, should be adjudged on the materialistic plane. The concept of equality that prevails in the ancient times in India was, on the other hand, primarily based on the spiritualistic notion of the oneness of all beings. Secondly, the philosophies underlying the two concepts differ with regard to the conception and place of individual being after death. The Western philosophies believe in automatic evolution of man and that nothing remains or reappears after death. This leads to a longing to enjoy the matter to the fullest extent in the present life without any apprehension past this life. The Indian concept of rebirth, retribution and transmigration of soul act as a salutary check on the inhuman actions and selfish ends.

Thirdly, the two systems differ as to the cosmological concept regarding the place of being in nature. The basic tenet of Hindu philosophy is that there is a speck of divinity in every being. It is accepted as a cardinal article of faith by every Indian, leading to certain social results of great import. This basic notion about the individual's cosmic life stands in sharp contradiction with the biological theory of evolution of the individual and cosmos which has pervaded the Western thought. This has also resulted in the ingrained disposition towards equality-as-sameness in the social fabric.

Lastly, one of the important differences between the two systems relates to the place of religion in the scientific scheme of thought. In the West, religion has always demanded faith in the blind adherence to the religious scriptures; in India, on the other hand, tenets of religion have always been tested on the touchstone of wisdom and under the focus of logic. The religion in India is the begetter of all knowledge and science, and thereby transfigurates every human activity.

Our quest of equality in the ancient India leads us to a humanitarian social atmosphere and a rational social order. This attitude of universal brotherhood imbued in the notion of equality-as-sameness abounds in the description of social life and thought in the scriptures of the time. Equality is more a way of thinking, a habit of thought; its removal on the physical plane is not enough because in the physical world the differences are bound to occur and recur. The scourge of inequality is born in the minds of men and it is to be banished from the mental cave.

The realization of the manifestation of the Supreme Self in all beings evolved into the concept of the fundamental equality of all beings in ancient India. Unless the society is helped to see this fundamental unity behind the massive manifoldness it cannot cast off its problem of growing inequality, only by adopting mundane measures. The material achievements are bound to be unequal according to the differing human qualities and capabilities and measures aimed at mitigating only the material causes of inequality are not of much avail in devising a permanent solution of the problem in the absence of the spiritualistic nation of fundamental oneness. The plant of equality in a society has to be rooted deep in the heart on the soil of knowledge. The spiritual and human knowledge which pervaded the Vedic thought was woven into the social and economic fabric of the nation by devising an educational system suitable for the purpose.

The social and economic structure of the ancient India also revolved round its social system of Varnashrama Dharma. This social division of individuals and their life-cycle, viz., the

Chaturvarna and Ashrama-Dharma was bound up with the function of the individual, and not with the birth or colour or status of the individual in society. The Varnashrama Dharma was the axis around which the social organization revolved in ancient India; the degeneration of the society and the inequalities and imbalance in the social order followed the deviation from the path of the accepted Dharma.

III. THE BIRTH OF A PRECOCIOUS NATIONALISM

Enslaved and ravaged by the colonial masters and deep sheathing in the abyss of inequality, deprivation and disease, India presented a picture of utter annihilation of its golden past and a total destruction of its ancient socio-economic structure. The urges to and aspirations of equality, giving rise to Indian nationalism, converged into a tidal way of the freedom movement under the unimpugnable leadership of Mahatma Gandhi, and the concept of equality that evolved in Modern India during the nineteenth and early twentieth centuries culminated in the notion of equality propounded and practised by Gandhi.

Gandhi viewed the activities of life as a compact whole which could not be divided into watertight compartments. Likewise, the three value concept of liberty, equality and humanism, which find a preeminent place in the Gandhian scheme, are interdependent and interrelated, and they constitute his synthetic ideal of socio-economic justice. "Swarajya" to Gandhi meant complete independence from the colonial rule and complete economic independence. The square of "Swarajya" was built on the four pillars of political independence, economic independence, moral elevation and social reform convolved on the solid foundation of Truth and Non-violence. It was not an imitation of Western democracies. He firmly believed that the external freedom that the people of a free country attain will be in exact proportion to the inward freedom to which they may have grown at a given moment. His concept of freedom is, thus, concomitant with social and moral values imbued in the individual beings.Gandhian Swarajya is the sum total of the Swarajya, of the individuals, wherein the individual is the supreme consideration.

He was in favour of the greatest good of all and believed that Swarajya could be ensured in a human society only by adhering to this principle. Such a society can be sustained only by complete self-sacrifice. The object of a human being should be the good of all with the weak being served first. This required a humanitarian outlook and due importance to spiritual pursuits. To Gandhi, equality is of soul and crusade against inequality has to be launched there. The problem of equality defies political solution. The equality in any society can be assured only by a proper training of body, mind and soul together of the individuals constituting the social fabric.

Apart from devising a system of education to serve the purpose, Gandhi also evolved the concept of bread-labour and Swadeshi. The theory of bread-labour was enunciated to instil a sense of respect for physical labour and extricate it from the stigma of inferiority attached to it. Though the idea of Swadeshi was innovated as a reaction to the Partition of Bengal in 1906, Gandhi gave a new orientation to the concept, imparting a multidimensional trait to it. Swadeshi was a law of life evolved to generate self-respect and self-dependence on the one hand and cast off inequalities and iniquitous distinctions on the other. In such a society equality is bound to permeate the social order. Thus, the traditional Indian concept of equality emanating from the notion of equality-as-sameness finds it full manifestation in the concept of equality conceived by Gandhi.

Gandhi not only propounded equality, but also formulated certain essential measures for its realization in the socio-economic order by devising an educational framework pulsating with the notion of equality-as-sameness, on the one hand, and evolving a constructive programme to erase the aberrations of the social order to be followed by the non-government agencies and voluntary organisations, based on the notion of equality-as-justice, on the other. The concept of trusteeship chalked out by him also convolved together with the notion of equality-as-justice. His idea of trusteeship was the most radical in approach, yet grounded in truth and non-violence. Gandhi believed that violence was the root cause of all iniquities. However, in case the capitalists failed to accept trusteeship he was in favour of coercion under the law. The trusteeship formula was designed as an ideal remedy for the eradication of economic inequality. The economic equality of his conception was a function of decentralization of industries and devaluation of power culminating in a self-sufficient village republic. He considered large scale industries and labour-saving machineries as breeders of violence and advised cautious approach to them, in case of necessity, under government control.

If, however, in spite of the efficacious measures, the malaise of inequality and socio-economic injustice occurs on the social horizon, he devised the method of Satyagrah or soul-force and non-violent non-cooperation as the infallible weapons to drive away all inequalities and injustices—social economic and political. Thus, Gandhi's vision of equality is a perfect blending of the two notions of equality attuned to his paramount principles of Truth and Non-violence, with, if need be, a minimum amount of coercion by the State.

Notwithstanding the notional differences, the concept of equality has evolved in the Western and Indian political thought within the perimeter of time and the obtaining socio-economic conditions. This evolution of the concept of equality in the social, economic and political spheres in decadent India moved the people to crave for equality. In the nineteenth century, some prominent social reformers, religious leaders and political thinkers raised their voice for socio-economic equality and amelioration in the living conditions of the people. Many religious leaders of the century started their movements for socio-religious reforms to drive away the age-old senseless social practices, corroding iniquities and invidious distinctions in the Hindu society and to bring out the nation from the morass of degradation and deprivation. By interpreting the humanistic and ethical tenets as the quintessence of religion and proclaiming inequality as the bane of human nature and a curse upon the mankind, they inspired and prodded the nation to jettison all iniquities in the social order, and usher in an era of equality, the doorway to freedom. The voice raised by the preceptors had a tremendous impact on the minds of the people and generated a spontaneous urge towards equality. It acted as a stepping stone for forging the unity of the nation and gave rise to a national awareness.

The impact of western education and the growing contact of the Indian intellectuals with the West had created in them an urge for equality and long overdue improvement in the socio-economic conditions. A deepening curiosity of the Westerners about the ancient wisdom of India also helped to foster a feeling of pride in the glorious heritage and led the people to wake up and come out from the state of despondence. The spread of Western education had given rise to a growing middle-class in the country united by a common language and faced with the common socio-economic problems. The national awakening had stirred the political consciousness of some intellectuals and as a resent political platforms were created at different places, which ultimately gave birth to the Indian National Congress in 1885.

Yet the Congress remained an organization of the intelligentsia who accepted, consciously or unconsciously, the inevitability of the British Empire and believed in its benevolence towards the people of India, They built up their own arguments in favour of the British Raj, and confined their activities to petition, prayer and protest against certain aberrations of the colonial rule, which seemed un-British to them. Though quite a few intellectuals began to grow suspect and examine the veracity of the British statements about our past and present conditions, still they continued to think and work within the framework of British ideology. These dissenting views and critical analysis of the British rule in India served a revolutionary purpose, provided a political and economic foundation to Indian nationalism and added fuel to the smouldering fire of patriotic spirit. The writings of Dadabhai, Romesh Dutt, Bankim Chandra and others played a revolutionary role in the development of our nationalist thought and the growing urge for equality was strengthened. Though the faith in the British version of the past history and the present economic condition of India began to dwindle the intellectuals continued to strive for social, economic and political reforms within the ambit of the British Raj, which they held to be ordained by providence for the good of India.

The beginning of the twentieth century brought into prominence on the Congress platform some extremists, notably Bal Gangadhar Tilak, Bipin Chandra Pal and Lala Lajpat Rai

Lal, Bal and Pal, as they were fondly called. These extremists aimed at the overthrow of the British Raj by violent means and declared that "Swarajya" was the birth-right of Indians. They also contrived measures to mobilize the masses and urged the nation to march ahead, by forging unity and shedding all iniquities, to wind up the British Raj and extricate themselves from the chain of age-long bondage. The moderates had held sway in the Indian National Congress, but after the secession of the extremists from the Congress as a sequel to the Surat split of 1907, certain changes in the political objectives of the party became inevitable. The Congress declared that the attainment by India of self-Government similar to that enjoyed by the self-governing Dominions of the British Empire was the goal of its political aspirations.

Yet it was not until the advent of Mahatma Gandhi on the political scene that the notion equality became the object of political debates. Gandhi started as a religious reformer, infused in truth and non-violence, to eradicate the social evils and the curse of inequalities and finding politics as the doorway to all socio-economic reforms walked on tiptoe. He became one with the masses, provided a mass-base and gave ethical orientation to politics and adorne politics with the quintessence of all religions— Truth and Non-violence. The concern for the common man became the primary object of Congress politics. The teeming millions were inflicted with poverty, ignorance and disease, but Gandhi knew they were the afflictions inflicted by a common virus—the virus of inequality. Gandhi was convinced that inequality was a radiative disease and it had been corroding the body politic. Unequality had, therefore, to be invaded on all fronts. The notion of equality emerged on the Congress forum, for the first time, in the resolution on fundamental rights adopted at the Bombay special session of the Indian National Congress, 1918. The scattered and random viewpoints on equality expressed by reformers, and intelligentsia in the 18th and 19th century, along with the tenets of our glorious cultural and religious heritage as also the thoughts of some Western thinkers like. Tolstoy, Thoreau and Ruskin, which had deeply influenced Gandhi, convolved to make a complete image of the Gandhian vision. Gandhi not only conceptualized the Indian viewpoints on equality, but also devised and experimented various measures for the eradication of all iniquities.

The political events of 1927 and 1928, the holding of All-Parties Conference, the drawing up of Dominion Constitution by that conference, and the dissenting voice of young Nehru and the ultimate rejection of the proposed constitution by the British Government paved the way for the adoption of the creed of complete Independence. In the course of the arduous journey towards equality it was finally realized in 1929, at the Lahore Congress, that equality shall remain a chimera without full freedom from alien control. The goal of complete Independence remained the guiding star of the national struggle until India became free in 1947. The cherished values of liberty, equality and fraternity as well as justice in the social, economic and political spheres of life were preamble in the Constitution as the objectives to be attained, and the deliberations of the Constituent Assembly reflect these fond hopes of the Founding Fathers. The Founding Fathers have also provided a built-in mechanism for the complete realization of these objectives, in Part III and IV of the Constitution, which together constitute the synthetic ideal of justice. It is manifest in the ideas expressed in the Constituent Assembly that a sincere adherence to the letter and spirit of the means provided is bound to give birth to a nation where justice shall inform all the spheres of national life and will make India a Sovereign Socialist Secular Democratic Republic.

IV. EQUALITY : THE FIRST CONCERN OF THE FOUNDING FATHERS

It was for the first time in the special session of Indian National Congress at Bombay in 1918 that a resolution urging upon the Government of India to include the Declaration of the Rights of the people of India as British citizens in the Statute to be passed by Parliament was passed. It declared that all Indian subjects of His Majesty are equal before the law, and there shall be no penal or administrative law in force in the Dominion, whether substantive or procedural, of a discriminative nature. The cherished goal of equality was enunciated long before the urge towards complete Independence. It was natural, therefore, that on the advent of freedom, equality should have been the first concern of the Founding Fathers of the Constitution while framing the Declaration of Fundamental Rights. The rights enumerated in Part III of the Constitution are the inalienable rights, which are most vital for the all-round development of the individual, which is a subject of supreme consideration in the Gandhian ideology.

Articles 14 to 16 form the code of equality, and Article 14 has been given a prominent place in the galaxy of Fundamental Rights. It is the harbinger of the Rule of law as against the rule of caprice of the colonial masters. It proclaims that all human beings shall be treated as equal in the eyes of the State and receive equal protection of the laws enforced by the State. It is in consonance with the Gandhian concept of the Supreme consideration of the individual, transcending even the bounds of nationality. The various facets of equality under Articles 14 to 16 are not only interwoven, but also overlap each other and even intertwine with other Fundamental Rights to inhibit injustice against any individual. But Article 14 stands aloft as the steering-wheel of the ship of justice, or, rather, the sun around which the other planets of Fundamental Rights revolve.

V. EQUALITY PROVISIONS AND JUDICIAL PRONOUNCEMENTS

The twin phrases constituting the legal equality under Article 14, viz. equality before the law, and equal protection of the laws, though seemingly identical, have different connotation, and their nature and scope have been subjected to a much closer scrutiny and elaborate interpretation by the highest court of the land, perhaps more than any other Article of the Constitution. A synoptic exposition of the pronouncements of the Supreme Court about the contents of the phrases is that while the former considers everyone equal before the law and proscribes any claim of special privilege or discrimination in the treatment of individuals, the latter postulates equal protection of like persons in like situations and circumstances and admits of rational classification. The two expressions take together establish what may be regarded as equality of legal status for all, based on the Gandhian principle of universal brotherhood. It forbid class legislation, but not reasonable classification by the State for the purpose of social and economic objectives of legislation.

The rule of differentiation was for the first time adopted in Chiranjit Lal Choudhary *vs.* Union of India, by the Supreme Court, wherein the Act providing for nationalization of Sholapur Spinning and Weaving Mills Ltd. was impugned on the ground of violation of Article 14. The Supreme Court upholding the validity of the Act observed :

> "The principle of equality did not mean that identically the same rules of law should be made applicable to all persons in spite of differences of circumstances and conditions; it meant only that there should be no discrimination between one person or another if, as regards the subject-matter of legislation, their position is the same."[2]

In Union of India *vs.* Tulsi Ram Patel, the Supreme Court, dealing with the object of Article 14, observed :

> What Article 14 forbids is discrimination by law, that is, treating persons similarly circumstanced differently and treating those not similarly circumstanced in the same way or, as has been pithily put, treating equals as unequals and unequals as equals".[3]

The meaning and content given to Article 14 in the various decisions of the Supreme Court also make it clear that equality, in the eyes of law connotes equal protection of all persons who are socially and economically equal, otherwise its universal application may perpetuate the curse of age-old inequalities and frustrate the very purpose of this Right. Article 14 is not designed to prevent legislatures to pass laws introducing reforms in some of the institutions only or objects having common characteristics or to particular areas only.

There may be an enactment relating to a single individual or object, if it is proved that on account of some specific reasons and purpose applicable to him and non-applicable to others, that single individual is a class in himself. Of late, the Supreme Court has begun to take a more liberal view on the vires of an enactment for giving shape to the lagislative policies of socio-economic reform and has refused to intervene in matters of State Policy. As the Supreme Court has succinctly put it :

"Scales of justice are not designed to weigh competing social and economic factors. In such matters legislative wisdom must prevail and judicial review must abstain".[4]

Equality before the law, in the opinion of the Supreme Court, connotes equality of status and the end of all privileges, signifying equal civil and political rights and equal access to public office or employment. On the other hand, equal protection of the laws forbids all individual discrimination, though it does not require identical treatment for all irrespective of regional differentiation; rather, it means that there should be no discrimination between persons situated similarly and under similar circumstances. It does not take away from a State the power of classifying persons for legitimate purpose.

In fact, upholding the rule of discrimination, the Supreme Court, in State of Bombay *vs.* Bulsara, while analyzing its meaning and scope, went to the extent of giving an important ruling that the presumption should always be in favour of the constitutionality of an enactment since it must be assumed that the legislature understands and correctly appreciates the needs of its own people; that the laws are enacted to deal with the problems manifested by experience and discriminations are based on rational grounds; that the varying needs of different classes of persons often require separate treatment; and that increase in inequality is not enough to strike down a classification. These presumptions can be rebutted by the appellant if it could be shown by him that there is no basis of classification at all and no difference peculiar to any individual or class, yet the law hits only a particular individual or class. If a law deals equally with the members of a well-defined class, it cannot be deemed to deny equal protection on the ground that it does not apply to other persons of a different class.

The Supreme Court further emphasized that the classification must be based on some real and substantive distinction bearing a nexus to the object sought to be achieved by the Act.

In K. Rajendran *vs.* State of Tamil Nadu, the Supreme Court held that any classification should satisfy two tests :

"(1) That there exists on intelligible differentia between those who are grouped together and those who are not included in the group, and (2) that there exists a reasonable nexus between the differentia and object for which classification is made".[5]

It has, from time to time, declared a number of measures unconstitutional and void because they were deemed unreasonable, arbitrary and discriminatory in the discharge of its constitutional mandate as protector of the Right to equality. In this connection Justice Bose in Kishan Singh *vs.* State of Rajasthan has observed :

> "Article 14 sets out an attitude of mind and a way of life, rather than a precise rule of law. The question of its application narrows down to a question of fact which must be determined, as each case arises, by the highest judges of the land, always keeping it in mind that the heart and core of democracy lie in the judicial process and the rule of law".[6]

Similarly, Justice Subba Rao, in connection with the rule of discrimination has opined :

> "The doctrine of classification is only a subsidiary rule evolved by Courts to give a practical content to the said doctrine (of equality before law). Overemphasis on the doctrine of classification may gradually and imperceptibly deprive Articles of its glorious content".[7]

In Meenakshi Mills Ltd. *vs.* A.V. Shastri and Budhan Choudhary *vs.* State of Bihar, the Supreme Court has viewed discrimination not only by a sustantive law, but by a rule of procedure also, as violative of Article 14. It has also been held that no subordinate legislation can escape the beacon light of justice emitted by Article 14. In the Indian Express Ltd. *vs.* Union of India, the Supreme Court held.

> "The subordinate legislation must yield to primary legislation. It may also be questioned on the ground that it is unreasonable, unreasonable not in the sense of not being reasonable but in the sense that it is manifestly arbitrary".[8]

It has also been held that violation of natural justice by the State shall be an arbitrary action and will attract the provisions of Article 14. In Satyavir Singh *vs.* Union of India the Supreme Court explained :

> "The principles of natural justice are not the creation of Article 14 of the Constitution. Article 14 is not the begetter of the principles of natural justice but is their constitutional guardian".[9]

Thus, Article 14 applies not only to discriminatory class legislation but also to all arbitrary and discriminatory action in the field of state activity. Even administrative orders, in exercise of executive power without making of laws, will attract the provision of Article 14, and if any impugned order suffers from arbitrariness or non-application of mind, the courts will definitely strike them down. Thus the principle of reasonableness and rationality which is legally and philosophically an essential ingredient of equality or non-arbitrariness is projected by Article 14. In K.P. Royappa *vs.* State of Tamil Nadu, the Supreme Court significantly observed :

> "Equality is antithetic to arbitrariness. In fact, equality and arbitrariness are sworn enemies; one belongs to the rule of law in a republic while the other to the whim and caprice of an absolute monarch".[10]

In State of Andhra Pradesh *vs.* Nalla Raja Reddy, the Supreme Court held.

> "Official arbitrariness is more subversive of the doctrine of equality than statutory discrimination. In respect of a statutory discrimination one knows where he stands, but the wand of official arbitrariness can be waved in all directions indiscriminately".[11]

No only have arbitrary acts, discriminatory laws and violations of natural justice been held to contravene Article 14, but even all actions or laws creating injustice have been held to be violative of Article 14.The right to equality emanates from the principle of equal justice. It signifies equal justice to all. The court has held the view that unless this right is assured to the downtrodden by the State, the right to equality cannot be endowed with a sense of reality and justice. The

Supreme Court has viewed Article 14 as providing an implied guarantee of equal justice and equal access to courts, and, on its part, has evolved the concept of Public Interest Litigation for vindication of this right on behalf of the downtrodden by interested persons or organizations.

The provision made in Part III of the Constitution for equality of social status is contained in Articles 15, 17 and 18. Article 15 is a specific application of the general rule against discrimination enunciated in Article 14 for protecting citizens only against discrimination on specific grounds of religion, race, caste, sex, place of birth or any of them. Whereas the first clause of Article 15 specifies various prohibitory grounds of discrimi-nation on which the State cannot discriminate between citizens for any purposes, the second clause restrains both the State and the individual from making discrimination against citizens on the prohibited grounds for the specific purpose of access to or use of public places or properties as enumerated in the clause, whosoever may be in control thereof. The third and fourth clauses enable the State to make special provision for women and children, and for the advancement of socially and educationally backward classes of citizens or for the Scheduled Castes and Scheduled Tribes, notwithstanding the rule stipulated in the first two clauses.

These benign provisions of the Constitution for the advancement of the weaker sections have been liberally interpreted by the highest court in India whenever a relevant matter has been brought up under judicial scrutiny. The court has held the view that as Article 15 is a specific application of the general rule of equality under Article 14, it admits of permissible classification. It has been held by several High Courts that introduction of a social reform by stages, territory-wise or community-wise, was not an unreasonable basis of classification. Similarly, it has been held that the classification of institutions, based on religion, with an object of better management of such institutions, cannot be deemed to be discriminatory or arbitrary. The analysis of various judicial decisions with regard to the ambit of Clauses (1) and (2) of Article 15, leads *inter alia* to the following conclusions :

(1) Only those discriminations that are based solely on the prohibited ground may attract the provisions of

Article 15; if it is in conjunction with some other ground, it may attract the provision of Article 14, but not of Article 15.

(2) Clause (1) of Article 15 relates to State only, whereas Clause (2) is related to both the State and individual actions.

(3) The provisions of Clause (1) are applicable only to State maintained institutions and not to State aided or affiliated institutions.

(4) The discrimination arising out of the personal law of religions cannot be held to be void.

(5) Residential qualification for admission in educational institutions are generally upheld. But recently, in Pradeep Jain *vs.* Union of India, the Supreme Court opined that the wholesale reservation of seats on the basis of domicile or residence or on the basis of institutional preference, excluding all students not satisfying the requirement irrespective of merit, was unconstitutional.

(6) Discrimination against woman on the ground of sex is not permissible.

(7) By providing against racial discrimination under clause (2), the Indian Constitution has provided a novel feature in that under Clause (2) both the State and private individuals are restrained from providing or effecting any discrimination against citizens. Thus, there can be no racial discrimination here in India against its citizens even by private individuals.

Clause (3) is a device of protective discrimination in the interest of women and children. Discriminations on the ground of sex in pursuance of Clause (3) have been held to be valid. In the Pratap Singh *vs.* Union of India case, the Supreme Court held that benign provision of the Hindu Succession Act in pursuance of Clause (3) of Article 15, which overrides Article 15 (1), is valid. Similarly, reservation of seats for women in educational institutions, special voting facilities for women, etc, have been held to be valid.

The purpose of Clause (4) is to bring Articles 15 and 29 in conformity with Articles 16(4), 45 and 340 so as to make it constitutional for the State to reserve seats in educational institutions for the advancement of socially and educationally backward classes of citizens or for the Scheduled Castes and Scheduled Tribes. It, thus, harmonises the fundamental rights of citizens with the claims of social good. But the concessions stipulated under Article 15(4) cannot be claimed by persons other than the backwards in terms of the Constitution. The backwardness relevant to Article 15(4) must be both social and educational, which arises, of course, ultimately and primarily due to poverty. It should, however be borne in mind that Article 15(4) does not empower the State to obliterate the fundamental right under Article 15(1), and the state cannot extend the reservation to such an extent as to nullify the guarantees of equality altogether.

Article 17 synchronizes with the framework of a social revolution set in the Constitution, for the realization of Gandhi's dream of an India free from the taint of untouchability. By forbidding the practice of untouchability, proclaiming it a penal offence and assigning this provision its rightful place in Part III of the Constitution containing the sacrosanct and basic rights of individuals, the curse of untouchability, which had cut through the roots of a fraternal bondage vital for the unity and integrity of the nation, is sought to be revoked. Article 17 is an unction to the bleeding wound of the nation.

The removal of untouchability, which was a blot on Hinduism, could alone have dissipated the greatest constraint in assuring the dignity of the individual and the unity of the nation. It was, therefore, in pursuance of the goal set by the Fathers of the Constitution that the provision of removal of untouchability was included as a Fundamental Right of individuals. Yet, untouchability is nowhere defined in the Constitution. However, in order to restrict the use of this word in broader ramification, the word "Untouchability" is put within inverted commas in Article 17 only to indicate that it will be dealt with by the State in the same sense in which it is normally used. It is an aberration of the Hindu social order being practised between the Hindus, inter se. It is this vile practice of the Hindus within their own rank that the word "untouchability" normally refers to; it is this form or branch of untouchability that is forbidden under the

Constitution; and it is the enforcement of any disability arising out of this form of untouchability that has been declared a penal offence. Untouchability was a social stigma in the Hindu social order only, attached to certain classes of people, on the basis of their birth. And it was the removal of this stigma that Mahatma Gandhi had fought for.

Thus, the term "untouchability" cannot be understood in its literal sense. It was, therefore, that in the Devarajan *vs.* Padmanna case, the Mysore High Court held that instigation of a social boycott would not denote untouchability. Pointing out the implication of the term, the Calcutta High Court, in the Benmali *vs.* Pakhu Bhandari case, held that "all it does is to prohibit him from discriminating between one Hindu and another in carrying out his duties as a barber."[12] The Madras High Court in P.S. Charya *vs.* State of Madras opined that to prevent certain classes of Hindu, who were called as depressed classes, from entering a public meeting was certainly to practise untouchability.

The Untouchability (Offences) Act, 1955, which was enacted as a supplementary measure to Article 17, came into force with effect from June, 1955. The Act prescribes punishment for the practice of untouchability, for the enforcement of any disability arising therefrom and for ancillary matters. It provides punishment for enforcing certain religious, social and other disabilities on the ground of "untouchability". However, the word "untouchability" lacks precision since it has neither been defined in the Constitution nor in the Act. Legally it means untouchability on grounds of descent, caste, race or religion. The words "in any form" may cover all facets of the practice of untouchability but not all places where it may take place. It relates only to public places or institutions.

Article 18 is another provision heralding an era of social revolution. It ensures the prevention of the feeling of inherent superiority inoculated by the conference of honorary titles, etc.... It takes away from the State the power to confer decorative and hereditary titles which were used to be abused for corrupting the public life of the country during the British days. The Constitution guarantees to all Indians an equality of status in the social field by banning the conference of honorary titles of nobility by the State under Clause (1) of

Article 18. Clauses (2) to (4) relate to foreign states; Clause (2) absolutely prohibits the acceptance of such titles from foreign States to a citizen; Clause (3) stipulates that a non-citizen holding office of profit or trust under the State can accept such titles with the consent of the President of India; and Clause (4) provides that no person holding any office under the State can receive any present, remuneration or office from any foreign State without the consent of the President of India.

However, the practice of conferring decorative awards on persons having a record of distinguished public service in any field is in vogue since 1954. The government of India has been awarding these decorations, but it has specifically provided that these decorations shall not be used as appendages to the names of the recipients. Misuse of these awards and the selection of awards have been the butt of protracted criticism from various corners, and at last the system was done away with during the Janata regime of Prime Minister Morarji Desai, but was reintroduced by Mrs. Gandhi when she came to power again in 1980.

Legality apart, it cannot be denied that the conference of such awards runs counter to the spirit of democracy. Though the provision has not been subjected to the searchlight of judicial review, as there has been no case-law on Article 18 as yet, it is most likely that persons in an identical position do obtain a legal right against the State and can sue the State for discrimination and deprivation of equality before the law.

The right to equality of opportunity provided to the citizens under Article 16 in the matter of appointment or employment under the State is an application of the general principle of equality in the field of public employment. The Article gives a concrete shape to the notion of democracy held by the Father of the Nation that under it the weakest should have the same opportunity as the strongest. It is a potent means in the economic programme of nation formulated by the Founding Fathers for the removal of economic inequalities for equitable distribution of wealth and for bridging the gulf between the haves and the have-nots. It ensures the masses social justice coupled with economic equality in an earnest effort to change the existing class structure. It is a fulfilment of the urges of the national movement, that arose from a desire for economic betterment, to throw off the burdens that crushed the common man and alleviate their sufferings.

Clause (1) of Article 16 has been adjudged to be of wide import and covers not only the appointment or employment of a person, but also his promotion, service conditions and even termination of service. Clause (2) is complementary to Clause (1) in the sense that it rules out certain specific grounds of discrimination like religion, race, caste, sex, place of birth and residence and stipulates that there can be no discrimination in the matter of public employment between citizens on any or all of the specified grounds alone. Clause (3) provides a leeway to discrimination on the ground of residence as prohibited under Clause (2). It specifies the method of application and illustrates permissible classification on the ground of residence. Likewise, Clause (4) of Article 16 is a specific application of the general principle of equality of opportunity which confers a discretionary power on the State to make a reservation of appointments in favour of the backward classes of citizens which, in its opinion, is not adequately represented in the services of the State.

In fact, equality under Article 16 could not have a different content from equality under Article 14. It, therefore, admits rational classification for differential treatment having nexus to the constitutionally permissible object. However, Article 16(4) permits reservation only for the backward classes and reservation for those classes or communities who are not backward under the terms of the Constitution cannot connote a permissible classification.

Thus, whereas Article 14 ensures that all shall be treated equally, Article 15 is a concentrated application of equality of treatment in the social field and Article 16 is a specific application of equality of treatment in the field of public employment, paving the way for socio-economic justice.

VI. PROVISIONS OF SOCIO-ECONOMIC JUSTICE AND ITS APPLICATION

Part IV of the Constitution is the harbinger of a social revolution and provides the real means to usher in a State with socio-economic justice. It is a step towards the concrete realization of "Ram Rajya" or "Swarajya" as Mahatma Gandhi put it. In fact, the provisions are enunciated in the form of constructive programme to be adopted by the State for the realization of the objectives of the Founding Fathers preambled in the Constitution, and for building a nation—sovereign, socialist, secular, democratic republic—endowing its citizens with liberty and fraternity and assuring the unity and integrity of the nation.

The efforts of the State towards the formulation of concrete measures for the fulfilment of the dream cherished in the Constitution are, on the whole laudable; the policy of proceeding towards socialism, as fondly professed during the national movement, has been preambled in the Fundamental Law of the land; the Directive Principles have been given primacy over the core of the Fundamental Rights under Articles 13, 14 and 19; the Right to property has been relegated to a lone corner of the Constitution; and most of the constitutional bottlenecks adversely affecting the speedy realization of socio-economic justice have been wiped out, but the dream is still a long distance away and the picture is getting murkier every day due to the failure of the programme on the level of implementation and infra-structural constraints.

In fact, the rights of liberty and equality are like two sides of the same coin—viewed from the angle of individual, it becomes freedom for the all-round development of the individual to contribute his mite to the establishment of his socio-economic freedom. But when the social aspect of these rights is stressed and analyzed into different parts, in terms of the social well-being, they become related to the masses and comprise equality between individuals, inter se. Inevitably, equal opportunities granted to individuals will tend to display unequal abilities and, therefore, along with identical equality of treatment, based on natural justice, there emerges the necessity of a scale or standard of proportionality in the application of equal opportunity. The gives rise to a difficult problem of deciding how and where to apply it. In a democratic society this scale of proportionalism is decided by the State, But it has to be just and rational, and this has to be decided by the judicial organ of the State. The balance between liberty and equality, between identical equality and proportional equality devised by the State, is to be adjudged by an independent judiciary in a federal set-up as was envisaged by the Founding Fathers.

In this connection, we can recall the judgement of the Supreme Court in the case challenging the Zamindary Abolition Act of Bihar, even before the First Amendment inserting Articles 31A and 31B in the right to property embraced in Article 31, wherein the Supreme Court had upheld the validity of the Act on the ground that it was a follow-up action by the State in pursuance of Article 39 which enjoins upon the State to provide for deconcentration of material resources and their distribution for the common good. Thus, at the very beginning we find the pronouncements of the highest judiciary attuned to the changing conditions of time and its concern for the defence of these rational measures which really are subservient to the socio-economic transformation of the nation. We have examined the role of judiciary in this connection wherein we have observed that by and large, the judiciary has, except in the Champakam case, wherein the Directive Principles have been judicially pronounced to be subservient to the Fundamental Rights, struck a fine balance between the two in case of a conflict and stressed the need of socio-economic transformation by strict adherence to the fundamental directives of the Constitution.

Turning towards the role the State is designed to play within the parameters of the Constitution, we cannot resist the temptation to recall the solemn warning of Dr. Ambedkar, Chairman of the Drafting Committee, in the course of his concluding speech in the Constituent Assembly :

> "We must make our political democracy a social democracy as well. Political democracy cannot last unless there lies at the base of it social democracy. What does social democracy mean? It means a way of life which recognizes liberty, equality and fraternity as the principles of life. These principles of liberty, equality and fraternity are not to be treated as separate items in a trinity. They form a union of trinity in the sense that to divorce one from the other is to defeat the very purpose of democracy.... we

must begin by acknowledging the fact that there is a complete absence of two things in Indian society. One of these is equality. On the social plane, we have in India a society based on the principle of graded inequality which means elevation for some and degradation for others. On the economic plane, we have a society in which there are some who have immense wealth as against many who live in abject poverty. On January 26, 1950, we are going to enter into a life of contradictions. In politics we will have equality and in social and economic life we will have inequality... How long shall we continue to live this life of contradictions? How long shall we continue to deny equality in our social and economic life? If we continue to deny it for long, we will do so only by putting our political democracy in peril. We must remove this contradiction at the earliest possible moment or else those who suffer from inequality will blow up the structure of political democracy which this assembly has so laboriously built up."[13] Pointing out that fraternity was the other thing absent in the Indian society, Dr. Ambedkar continued :

"The second thing we are wanting is recognition of the principle of fraternity. What does fraternity mean? Fraternity means a sense of common brotherhood of all Indians—if Indians be one people. It is the principle which gives unity and solidarity to social life.... I am of opinion that in believing that we are a nation, we are cherishing a great delusion. How can a people divided into several thousands of castes be a nation? The sooner we realize that we are not as yet a nation, in the social and psychological sense of the word, the better for us. For then only we shall realize the necessity of becoming a nation and seriously think of ways and means of realizing the goal.... These castes are anti-national. In the first place, because they bring about separation in social life. They are anti-national also because they generate jealousy and antipathy between caste and caste. But we must overcome all these difficulties if we wish to become a nation in reality. For fraternity can be a fact only where there is a nation. Without fraternity, equality and liberty will be no deeper than coats of paint."[14] The sincerity of the warning and the solemnity of the occasion are, in fact, our justification for quoting the warning at length. The contradictions and delusion referred to by Dr. Ambedkar were sought to be removed by enjoining upon the State to strictly adhere to the fundamental Directive Principles in the making of the laws and making these principles fundamental in the governance of the nation. The Sovereign Democratic Republic of India has been further qualified to be secular and socialist by enacting the Constitution (Forty second) Amendment Act, 1976 and the right to property as a fundamental right under Articles 19 and 31 has been obliterated by the Constitution (Forty fourth) Amendment Act, 1978, and has been relegated to an insignificant place as Article 309 A in Chapter IV of Part XII of the Constitution, and further, Article 31 C has been inserted by the Twenty fifth Amendment Act, 1971, to safeguard the laws enacted for giving effect to the Directives contained in Clauses (b) and (c) of Article 39.

Article 31C has been further amended to give primacy to any or all of the Directive Principles over Articles 13, 14 and 19 of the fundamental right and even the Directive Principles have been enlarged by adding Articles 39A, 43A, 48A, etc., through the Constitution (Forty second) Amendment Act. It is obvious, therefore, that the State has invested itself with all the necessary powers to efface the contradictions to which Dr. Ambadkar had made a pointed reference. The overriding consideration of space limits our scope of enquiry into the actual operation of the government policies in various fields. We may, nonetheless, turn our attention to one or two items where improvement was sought even during the freedom struggle, such as land reform. During the freedom struggle, Pandit Nehru once remarked :

> "The wind is blowing to the villages and to the mud huts where dwell our poverty srticken peasantry, and it is likely to become a hurricane if relief does not come to them soon. All our political problems and discussions are but the background for the outstanding and overwhelming problem of India—the land problem.[15]

The historic "Quit India" resolution on August 8, 1942, of the AICC had proclaimed that the Congress aims at the establishment of a government which would "promote the well-being and progress of workers in the fields and factories and elsewhere to whom essentially all power and authority must belong".[16]

When Gandhi was asked in 1942 about the programme for the improvement of the lot of the peasantry in free India he said :

> "The peasant would take the land. We would not have to tell them to take it. They would take it."[17] And on being asked whether the landlords shall be compensated, he retorted :
>
> "No, that would be fiscally impossible. You see, our gratitude to our millionaire friends does not prevent us from saying such things. The village would become a self-governing unit living its own life".[18]

Even in 1951, Prime Minister Nehru, presenting his report in the Bangalore session of the AICC, said :

> "As agriculture is the principal occupation of the great majority of our people, it must be the first concern of the State. The abolition of the zamindari system has been the first reform and this must be expedited. But it must be remembered that this by itself is no solution of the problem.There should be a diversion of a part of the agricultural population to other occupations. There should be a development of cottage and small scale industries. But essentially the problem of agriculture needs cooperative cultivation and the application of modern techniques".[19]

The AICC session at Agra in 1953 resolved that "the State Government should take immediate steps in regard to the collection of the requisite land data and the fixation of ceiling on land holdings, with a view to redistribute the land, as far as possible, among landless workers".[20]

The subsequent election manifestoes of the Congress have harped on the necessity of a ceiling on land and cooperative farming. The laws have been passed, but to no avail. Land, the base of India's economy, is still in a muddle, in spite of various Acts of the legislatures. The reason is not far to seek.

The profession has not been followed by practice, precepts have not been buttressed by example, and legislation has become an eye-wash and this has kept the people on the tenterhooks. The crux of the problem is that the bureaucracy, reared on the imperialist model, is insensitive to the urgency of the social regeneration and rejuvenation; it is reeking with corruption and self-aggrandizement unconcerned about problems the nation is beset with. Consequently, the problem of land remains unsolved even after fifty years of freedom.

The provision of the Directive Principles regarding economic justice is chiefly centered round Article 39 and they do not in any way commit the State to the collectivism or socialism on the Russian pattern. Indeed, the general intention of those principles embodied as fundamental directives is clearly to set up a "Socialist State" within the context of the socio-economic conditions of the nation. In fact, emphasis on small-scale organization, cooperative farming and development of village panchayat as a self-governing unit can easily lead to a Gandhian system of Village Republic. On December 21, 1954 the discussion on the economic situation led to a resolution in House of the People i.e. Lok Sabha, to the effect that the objective of our economic policy should be a socialistic pattern of society. But unfortunately, even after nine Five Year Plans, beginning with the first in April, 1951, the economic disparity between the haves and the have-nots is still sharp and becoming sharper and sharper.

VII. THE DYNAMICS OF STATE ACTION

The growth rate during the long spell of planning has been far from impressive. The long-term trend in the rate of growth of the economy has been around 3.5 per cent (GDP at factor cost between 1950-51 and 1984-85). It may be noted that during this period all the developing countries taken together have achieved a growthrate of 5.3 per cent per annum.

Even after the culmination of eight Five Year Plans, the overall achievement still remains tardy, as the following table will show :—

Indian Growth Performance[21]

Plan-period	Target (percent per annum)	Actual (percent perineum)
1. First Plan (1951-56)	2.1	3.61
2. Second Plan (1956-61)	4.5	4.27
3. Third Plan (1961-66)	5.6	2.84
4. Fourth Plan (1969-74)	5.7	3.30
5. Fifth Plan (1974-79)	4.4	4.80
6. Sixth Plan (1980-85)	5.2	5.66
7. Seventh Plan (1985-90)	5.0	6.01
8. Eighth Plan (1990-95)	5.6	6.78

Thus, the average growth rate comes to 4.66 per cent per annum in each plan period.

On the other hand, our rate of gross savings at 23.8 per cent at the end of 8th Plan is higher than most of the developing countries. The ratio of central and state taxes to gross domestic product (GDP) which was five-six per cent in the early fifties has been raised to above 17 per cent. Yet we are finding it increasingly difficult to secure the necessary resources for development, primarily because not only the savings are used quite unproductively, but also that they are used most extravagantly and inefficiently, and secondly, public expenditure besides causing wastage, has tended to outpace the growth of revenues due to a lack of clearly defined public expenditure policy. An economy that has scored the highest rate of savings amongst the developing countries and has yet secured a meagre rate of growth cannot be allowed to continue indefinitely, even after fifty years of gruelling experience. An economy whose industries and infrastructural facilities are still chronically overmanned cannot be expected to serve the purpose of socio-economic justice and cannot offer any recipe for eradication of unemployment.

An increase in the backlog of the unemployed from Plan to Plan is undoubtedly a matter of grave concern. This backlog was estimated to be not less than 14.5 million at the end of the Third Plan and has touched staggering heights. During the period 1967-74 there was a total of 39 million job-seekers.[22] Even during the 9th Plan, the labour force is projected to increase upto 52.4 million. In this connection it is well to remember the Gandhian challenge :

> "I would favour the use of the most elaborate machinery, if thereby India's pauperism and resulting idleness could be avoided. I have suggested hand-spinning as the only ready means of driving away penury and making famine of work and wealth impossible".[23] He had made it clear : "Mechanization is good when hands are too few for the work intended to be accomplished. It is an evil when there are more hands than required for work, as in the case of India".[24] Even after nearly fifty years of planning, the problem of unemployment remain an economic riddle and the relevance of Gandhi inevitably emerges as an alternative. Long ago, Gandhi had felt that the only hope for the poverty stricken people of the country was to avoid large-scale factory manufacture and to base our economic life on small-scale village industries. However, even while planning, the execution is more important than the framework and the outlay and, it is admitted, that the implementation has not only lagged behind but, due to inefficiency and corruption of those at the helm of execution, lack of devotion and zeal of the workers on the execution front and also the lack of warmth and cooperation of the people, it is recorded more on paper and has become a statistical jugglery of the past masters, peddling extremely specious arguments as the genuine stuff. The Directive Principles on economic equality still remain a far cry and even as regards the benefits accruing from an expanding economy, it is open to grave doubts whether they are being as widely distributed, territorially and economically as they might be if the implementations were better and people from the bottom were actively associated.

Indeed, it is the baneful flare for industrialism and technonomy that is fast leading the world to the brink of disaster. Apart from the growing ecological problems of the world, the stock of atomic weapons already piled up is sufficient to destroy the whole world twentysix times. The world is spending more than 100 trillion dollars on its armament, and the craze for technology has begun to take its toll as the Bhopal Gas tragedy and Chernovyl Atomic Plant accident. It is the system itself, in both capitalist and socialist countries, that needs to be scrapped or at least modified in the essential respects. Even in the West a fundamental revision of the basic values is being contemplated amongst the political theorists by advocating politics of limits. It is argued that "the earth's finite resources will not support an indefinite expansion of our industrial civilization along its present lines. The attempt to maintain the existing standard of living...will prove self-defesting, not only because it will produce ecological effects... but because it will widen the gap between rich and poor countries, generate more and more violent movements of insurrection and terrorism... and bring about a deterioration of the world's political climate as threatening as the deterioration of its physical climate...we need to impose limits not only on economic growth and technological development but on human pretensions and pride. Politics of limits entails the abandonment of the whole ideology of progress and the recovery and restatement of old religious insights, ones that stress the finitude of human powers and intelligence. Politics of limits has to rest on a new respect for tradition and for particular local, regional and national culture.[25]

Fifty years of trial of a system is enough to open a new vista of thinking on alternative measures. With all our planned economy, we have attained a percapita income of only Rs. 120 p.m. in 1979, whereas Kuwait, a small oil-exporting country, has reached a per capita income of Rs. 12,500 per month. Though the annual average rate of decline of the poverty ratio during the period from 1973-74 to 1993-94 has declined from 54.8 per cent to 36.0, the number of poor in the country has increased from 246 million to around 320 million, mainly due to the rise in population. According to an FAO (Food and Agriculture Organization) estimate nearly half of the total malnourished in the 85 developing countries in 1974-75 lived in India. The total malnourished in India 201 million were the largest any single country had".[26] Our planned economy is besieged with black economy running a parallel economy, as the following table will show :

Year	Size of black economy (Rs. in Crores)	Percentage of official G.N.P.
1967	3034.372	9.5
1978-79	46866.858	58.78

According to a recent International Monetary Fund report, black money of Indians in the Swiss banks alone, in December, 1985, is more than twenty thousand crores as against only ten thousand crores six years ago. By now it must have trebled nearly. The first offshoot of the black economy is the grave unreliability of statistics as the various transactional statistics of the black economy remain hidden in the womb of darkness and the genuine statistical data are based on specious presumptions. The corruption which thrives on black money in turn generates it. The ostensible display of wealth caused by the operation of the black economy only inflames and accentuates the hiatus between the classes. The black money rules the destiny of politicians and is fast becoming a crime money. In such a state of Indian economy, eradication of poverty is out of the question, erosion and elimination of the poor, the needy, the destitute can be the only natural consquence. And that is exactly what is being done by the National Planning Commission, preparing for the take off stage for the flight of the nation into the 21st century. Dr Rajni Kothari has beautifully put in the essence of a "two-nation" proposition in an illuminating and thought-provoking article "Flight into the 21st century."[27] "The new perspective has been aptly summarised by an arresting syndrome and mystique : of moving into the 21st century. It has four major characteristics. It is unambiguously futuristic with the intention of buying the past and to an extent the present (traditions, institutions, values). It is apolitical, based on the thought that much that is wrong around us is the outcome of politics, that it is politics that keeps us backward and makes us corrupt and compromising at every stage. It is technocratic, viewing technocracy as a substitue for politics marching ahead "scientifically" and unemotionally, with a no-nonsense attitude and an unquestioning faith in the inherently beneficial equality of modern techonology. It is managerial in which governance is seen as an essentially managerial task, and technical expertise takes the place of political competition between diverse social forces, and moralistic slogans, and populist rhetoric are sought to be replaced by hardheaded, cost-effective, depoliticized and modern managament.

"Together these four characteristics provide an altogether new impulse and thrust. It is an impulse that must of necessity divide the country into two—the scenario of two Indias in which the nation takes precedence over the people, the state over the social order, the thought of erecting a hard and efficient and homogeneous modern nation-state in the company of other "great powers" is found to be far more important than the democratic process that involves the mass of the people and respects the great diversity and heterogeneity in which they are anchored."[28]

This syndrome is of particular significance to India, which is still groaning under the weight of its grinding poverty. The technocrat's remedy is to bury the hatchet and build a new India of the 21st century. This importance of technology as a panacea of all misfortunes, as a solvent of all problems and the preparations afoot to build a technocratic State relegate to the background, behind the wall, the problems of the Welfare State or Gandhian Swaraj. It is fast moving to a state of mind and a mood of thinking that to worry all the time about the poor and the weaker sections and the unprivileged classes is what has kept this country weak and rudderless. What is required is to move forward into the 21st century with those who became capable of moving into it, and they say, if some 200 million could move into it, it will produce a powerful economy and help it emerge as a major world power, the rest could be thrown into the dustbin of history. This is all that is meant by the strong advocacy to move to "frontier technologies" to solve the basic problem of the people. In fact, the emphasis on socio-economic transformation of the nation to wipe off the tears from every eye has given way to the lust for becoming a super-power and a modern technocratic State. The colossal problems of social revolution cannot be solved by an emphasis on frontier technology and a simulation of the Western order. The immediats task of the nation-builders is freedom from hunger and deprivation, and it is no gainsaying that the industrial system based on the

Western model can deliver the goods. As the nation's beloved Prime Minister Pt. Jawahar Lal Nehru had declered on July 22, 1947.

> "There will be no full freedom in this country or in the world as long as a single human being is unfree. There will be no complete freedom as long as there is starvation, hunger, lack of clothing, lack of necessaries of life and lack of opportunities of growth for every single human being, man and woman and child, in this country. We aim at that. Let our country awake into that freedom."[29]

There are some Directive Principles which arc observed more in breach by the State than with any desire for their implementation. Take the example of prohibition. Since 1920, it has always been in the Congress programme and is also contained in the Directive Principles. Yet we find that even the laws ragarding prohibition of intoxicating drinks and drugs, which sometimes trickle through the legislatures, have been repealed on some pretext or the other. This has not only aggravated the poverty and miseries of the masses, but also subjected millions of men and women, labouring under the curse of intoxicants and narcotics, to untold suffering.

We speak glibly of economic freedom and social revolution and seem hardly to realize that these cannot be had unless the foundations for them are faithfully and firmly laid in the social and economic order. The Directive Principles, which embody the principles of their soild foundation, must be followed in letter and in spirit, if we want to bridge the gap between our profession and practice. It is of no avail blaming the Constitution and the form of governance for every prevalent ill and consequent misfortune. Everything depends upon the way the Constitution is worked in practice.

As Dr. B. Pattabhi Sitaramayya had said in the Constituent Assembly, a constitution "is a grammar of politics, it is compass to the political mariner. However good it may be, by itself it is inanimate, it is insensitive, and it cannot work by itself. It is of use to us only in the measure in which we are able to use it, because it has a tremendous reserve force, and everything depends on the manner in which we approach it, whether we observe the letter and ignore the spirit or whether we observe the letter and the spirit in equal measure.... It depends upon how we work it."[30]

VII. THE PANACEA

Legislation, Constitutional Amendments, paper schemes and extempore speeches from public platforms are no more of any use in solving the thorny problems of socio-economic in justice; they have become outmoded and unbelieveble. We cannot any longer indulge in the pastime of conjuring up an utopia. We have to live among the hard facts of reality. Gandhiji had said, "The hungry millions ask for one poem—Invigorating food."[31] Political democracy has to be buttressed by a firm establishment of socio-economic justice—it cannot thrive on the delusion of a techocratic State.

The Founding Fathers of the Constitution have set before the nation the objectives that had underlined all their efforts in the Preamble to the Constitution. For the achievement of these objectives, provisions have been made in Parts III and IV of the Constitution along with many ancillary provisions interspersed in the constitutional framework. The articles dealing with the socio-economic matters in Part III can be broadly classified under two heads. The first category consists of those articles which effect the socio-economic order indirectly and they are Articles 14, 16, 18, 19, 25, 26, 28, 29, 30, and 31. The framers of the Constitution, in the interest of the weaker sections of the nation, made it permissible to the State, under Clause (4) of Article 16, that if it found the representation of any backward class of citizens in the services of the State inadequate, it could make provision for reservation of appointments or posts in favour of them, keeping in view the efficiency of administration. The heterogeneous composition of the community is sought to be protected in the sphere of religion, language and culture through the various rights guaranteed by Articles 25 to 30, with an ultimate aim of protecting the minorities and achieve unity in the midst of diversity. According to Article 31 (now 300 A) the right to property is sought to be protected in accordance with law. These articles maintain the secular character of the State, and reflects the deep concern of the Founding Fathers for protecting the legitimate interests of the minorities. The second category consists of Articles 15, 17, 23, 24, 31A, 31B and 31C. Article 15 prohibits discrimination against citizens on enumerated grounds, Article 17 declares practice of untrouchability as an offence punishable in accordance with law, Articles 23 and 24 are designed to eliminate exploitation of men, women and children and 31A, 31B and 31C. which are latter insertions, are calculated to remove all hindrances in the way of the State to ameliorate the socio-economic condition of the nation in accordance with the directives under Part IV. The whole of the Directive Principles of State Policy are designed to speed up the socio-economic transformation of the nation in consonance with a Welfare State or Gandhian socialism.

But the Constitution alone is not sufficient to deliver the goods. Bemoaning the Constitution instead of our failures and misdeeds serves no purpose. On November 26, 1949, when the Constitution was being dedicated to the nation, the President of the Constituent Assembly, Dr. Rajendra Prasad had said :

> "Whatever the Constitution may or may not provide, the welfare of the country will depend upon the way in which the country is administered. That will depend upon the men who administer it. It is a trite saying that a country can have only the Government it deserves. If the people who are selected are capable and are men of character and integrity, they would be able to make the best even of a defective Constitution. If they are lacking in these the Constitution cannot help the country.[32]

We have to repose our faith in the vehicle for the onward progress of the nation towards a social revolution, which was the only problem before the Founding Fathers after the achievement of political independence. The objective and the means provided are in no way ungandhian; they are really an adaptation of the Gandhian views in the context of a free India. But when emphasis shifts from the achievement of socio-economic justice as the first task of the nation-builder to the lure of becoming a super power and a technocratic State in the mad race of power politics, it is futile to curse one or the other provision of the sacred Constitution under the cloak of an all powerful bureaucracy designed on the pattern set by the colonial masters. We must stop fiddling while the nation is burning. A whole generation has gone by, yet no salvation is in sight. The remedies administered to extricate the nation from the socio-economic maladise have proved worse than the disease, mainly because the prescriptions were "foreign" not indigenous or "Swadeshi" and also because the apparatus remained uncleansed and polluted in the debris of centuries of subjugation.

If we have not deviated from the path set by the Founding Fathers, if we have not denounced the motto of the greatest good of all envisaged by the Father of the Nation, and, above all, if we really aspire for the unity and integrity of the nation of nations, we can no longer keep in the forefront of our action programme, a blind imitation of industrial and technocratic civilization. Our immediate task must be a solution to the socio-economic transformation of the nation in pursuance of the fundamental directives set forth in the Constitution. A national debate must ensue on the relevance of Gandhian thought and its adaptation in the context of modern India. Let us ponder over how the Constitution has been denuded of the Gandhian essence in its application and has been prostituted in a fatal attempt to simulate the industrialism of the West.

Firstly, the universal adult franchise was insisted on by Gandhi, in the teeth of opposition from Nehru and Patel, because of his view that a political party would have to woe the masses, resulting in a political education of the masses. But alas! the electoral process has indirectly helped introduction of black money in the battle of ballot and the caravan of hirelings, boothgrabbers and criminals have all shattered the dream of the Mahatma. The selection of candidates, the undemocratic gestures of the political parties and their composition have given a death-blow to the political education of the masses. Politics has become a game of scoundrels and the helpless masses have only a small role to play.

Secondly, Article 45 enjoins upon the State to promote with special care the educational and economic interests of the weaker sections of the people and protect them against social injustice and all forms of exploitation. In addition Articles 15(4), 16 (4), 23, 24, 338, 340 etc, are designed to serve the same purpose. But this can never be achieved for a fraction of the population only while the rest of the socio-economic structure remains in a static condition. In order to achieve this end, the State will have to build up a socio-economic system free from all forms of exploitation. Only then the full fruits of the provisions made in the Constitution can be enjoyed by the limping brackets of the society. But the State has failed to remove all forms of exploitation and provide gainful employment to all, so we find only a rat-race even for a loaf of bread. This despite the provisions made for the weaker sections, leading to caste rivalry, and the benign discrimination of helping out the weaker sections in the matter of employment or appointment under the State has led to a backwardness syndrome to embrace which has induced many politically powerful castes disguised as backward classes encouraging ascendancy of caste in the political game. Each caste and community begins a political bargain for bigger bites of the scarcely available educational-cum-employment cake; and thereby, instead of a casteless egalitarian society, a caste-based socio-political framework had emerged with all its deleterious consequences on the unity and integrity of the nation.

Even after several legislations, like the protection of Civil Rights Act, 1976, and the Untouchability Offences Act, 1955, no appreciable improvement in the economic and social disabilities of the weaker sections is visible. As the report of the Commissioner for Scheduled Castes and Scheduled Tribes for the year 1977-78 states :

"No one who is familiar with the social climate prevailing in the rural areas would advance the argument that untouchability has declined in real terms... Even when large-scale acts of physical violence were committed against members of the Scheduled Castes, the provisions of the Act were not brought into force".[33] Even the draft Sixth Five Year Plan refers to the prevalence of poverty and inequality as having remained virtually unchanged in the case of these weaker sections. The difficulty is that it requires a social movement, a training of the mind and soul and an awakening of the consciousness for which law is a poor substitute.

Thirdly, the reservation of seats for the Scheduled Castes and Tribes in the Lower Houses of Parliament and the State Legislatures has been provided under Articles 330 and 332 respectively. This was designed to uplift the backward classes, on the one hand, and, on the other, create native elites from amongst them who would not only champion the just cause of the community but also participate in the mainstream of the nation in building the social and economic structure anew. The reservations were originally subjected to a time-limit of 10 years, thereby indicating that the arrangement cannot be permanent, but it continues through several extensions by way of amendments to the Constitution. After the Scheduled Castes and Scheduled Tribes (Amendment) Act, 1976, their respective population has become 16.48 per cent and 8.08 per cent of the total population according to 1991 census. Accordingly they have 84 and 41 seats in the Lok Sabha and 620 and 302 in the various Vidhan Sabhas respectively. Yet, it is generally accepted that these legislators are less articulate and independent than others and an analysis of their demands will show that they are much more inclined towards the well-off and pay scant attention to the *dalit* and *shoshit* masses of their community, which unfortunately is in accordance with the general political trend in the country. The upper caste strategy has been to co-opt the dominant ones from the advanced backward communities, which may suit both. Consequently, the reservation has failed to effectively benefit the weaker sections and has remained only a strategem in the political armoury.

Fourthly, the system of Panchayat Raj introduced in India presents a sordid imitation and lip-service to the ideas envisaged by Mahatma Gandhi. He had firmly believed that independence must begin at the bottom where every village will be a republic or panchayat having full powers. But the framers of the Constitution paid no heed to the cherished dream of Gandhi. The idea was not even mooted in the beginning except that the President of the Constituent Assembly, Dr. Rajendra Prasad, referred the matter for deep consideration. The idea of independence beginning at the bottom was talked out and a semblance of a village panchayat was added in the Draft Constitution only by way of amendment move by Shri K. Senthanam. It was accepted that at the stage of consideration of the Draft Constitution, it was not practical to form a system of governance beginning from the bottom, i.e. village republic, according to the constitutional adviser, Shri B. N. Rau. However, the organization of village panchayat as a unit of self-government was entrusted to the State, by adding Article 31A in the Draft Constitution, which forms part of the Directive Principles of State Policy as Article 40 of the Constitution of India. But the picture of village panchayat as constituted under the laws of most of the States is so distorted and twisted by the bureaucracy of the States in the making of laws on Panchyati Raj that instead of a self-governing unit, it has been rendered an officer-governing colony, and it is no wonder that when the task of rural development is entrusted to such panchayats they produce curious results.

Lastly, as we have noted earlier, the people's participation in any development activity is essential for converting the process of socio-economic development into a silent revolution. This would be highly beneficial not only in that it will educate the people and train their spirit, but would have soothing effect on the agitated minds and lessen the risk of a bloody revolution. Moreover, governmental agency is quite unsuited and unequal to the task. All through his life, Gandhi had held the view that work at the social and economic front should be, as far as possible, taken over by institutions of a voluntary character. It was, therefore, that he had advised the dissolution of the Congress and its flowering as Lok Sevak Sangh. He had firmly held the view that there should be a chain of voluntary organizations run democratically in the sphere of economic and social life of the messes. He had envisaged the revival of village as the centre of all activities. In the hierarchy of such institutions there would remain in the end institutions at the highest range, which, of necessity, were to be centralized and these should be under the control of the government. These institutions were expected to run under ideal conditions and for socialistic purposes. Even in his concept of basic education, the basis of self-support was induced to keep the system free of governmental control. But in the State built up in free India we have seen the gradual erosion of such voluntary organization, and a conscious or unconscious tendency of all institutions of voluntary character to flower and flourish at the behest of the powers-that-be. They have come to depend more and more on governmental assistance, and, consequently, their activities are turning more and more away from the public gaze, and little effort is made towards the marshalling of public cooperation. The result is that these institutions have lost their public character and are the first to rely on governmental help and subsidy.

Thus, even the different Gandhian ideas, which found favour with the constitution makers, have failed to yield the desire result, chiefly because the basic postulates have been put aside, and also because there has been no sincere and unflinching devotion to the execution of the ideas which are far more important than the mere enunciation of "pious wishes" in the non-justiciable corner of the Constitution. It is the spirit behind the ideas, which is lacking; the ideas are dead, a corpse, because the spirit behind has left.

It is a naive and dangerous thinking that the government alone can tackle all the problems in the socio-economic field. It is necessary that voluntary agencies born and working on Gandhian lines should receive spontaneous response from the people. But this is possible only when the government wholeheartedly imbibes this spirit and begins to give due consideration to such organization. The action/programme on the socio-economic front should, in the first instance, be chalked out by the voluntary agencies of dedicated and honest workers. It is a pity that the lethargy, sloth and idleness of the masses, generated during the long serfdom, still continue after five decades of freedom. The problem calls for salutary and appropriate policies of the State in conjunction with a large engagement commitment of non-governmental agencies. An all-parties forum can serve as an effective vehicle for reform, restoration and rejuvenation of established and reputed institutions set up on Gandhian lines and also for creating the infrastructure for newer ones, with public cooperation and support.

The constitutional mandates for the improvement of the socially and educationally backward classes are misconstrued and serve only as a vehicle of political preservation. To this end, it is necessary that the President should be enabled to act under Article 340 and specify the castes, or parts or groups of castes who are on par with the scheduled castes and scheduled tribes in the matter of backwardness both socially and educationally. Caste, ipso facto, is not a class in a secular State. Any emphasis on caste in the matter of distribution of power and pelf in the social order should be discouraged. The bogey of caste is raised because the term "backward class" remains undefined. It is also necessary that individuals or sections or groups of backward class, who have achieved a recognized social and economic status, should be deleted from the list of the Backward Classes.

Further, in addition to the present encouragement given to inter-dining and inter-marriage between the forward class and the backward class, provision should also be made, and necessary inducements through voluntary agencies given, for inter-dining and inter-marriage in the backward classes inter se.

Education is the corner-stone of any civilized society and is the beacon-light of its rich and varied culture. India has never lagged behind, so instead of emulating the Western pattern of education, it is necessary for the survival of the society that an education system based on Indian values should be re-established discarding all the baneful tenets of the Western education. The greats crisis of the present Indian education, it is generally agreed, is the crisis of character that it generates. The Ministry of Human Resource Development should centrally guide and shape anew the whole educational system strictly based on the wisdom of India, devoid of any tinge of Westernism. The values which we cherish should be clearly enunciated and educational institutions should be so shaped that they also develop the values of head and heart from the very childhood. It is tragic that though all political leaders in the five decades of freedom have been crying hoarse to revolutionize the present educational system, nothing tangible has been done so far. As Sardar Patel once said : "Everyone admits that the educational system is deficient and outmoded, but so great is our degradation that no one is meagre to change it. No courage is left in us. A revolution is badly wanted in this field".[34] The decrepit system is serving as a bonanza for rootless politicians, galore these days. It has also become their hunting ground for entrapping booth-grabbers and slogan-shouters and fire-arms wielders to serve the selfish interest of the rootless scoundrels, who can no more beguile the masses. The art of fear-menship is becoming the potent weapon of politicians and their role as people's representative is at its nadir. It is now universally agreed that liberty and equality, and fraternity which sustain freedom meet at least once in equilibrium and that is on the common ground of education. Madison wrote, as early as 1822 :

> "A popular government, without popular information or the means of acquiring it, is but a prologue to a Farce or a Tragedy, or perhaps both. Knowledge will forever govern ignorance, and a people who mean to be their own governors must arm themselves with the power which knowledge gives".[35]

Even Professor Gunnar Myrdal has laid great stress upon the importance of education in the eradication of poverty and a socio-economic transformation of the economically backward countries.

Improvement in the educational status will, ipso facto, lead to an increase in the social as well as economic status. "Amartya Sen has demonstrated very good economic reasons for putting one's children through college : the average income increase is many times the cost of the education to the parent that is, there is a large income differential between those who have the B.A. and other degrees and those who don't".[36] What is, therefore, required for a long-term remedial measure for the completion of a social revolution is a sound educational system on the lines of Gandhian thinking, aimed at inculcating values, and shaping the body, mind and soul of the student. And this should be devised on a priority basis. The education should be the prime concern of a bewildered society trying to extricate itself from the colonial and feudal socio-economic order. The liberty and equality, sought for since the founding of the Republic, will wither away unless we effect a proper compromise between them which is possible only through a sound Indian education policy oriented to shape the character and inculcate the values of life in the posterity. To reemphasize, only a revolution in the education system can be the harbinger of any social revolution dreamt of by the Founding Fathers of the Constitution who have provided the means in Parts III and IV of the Constitution as an integrated scheme. The problems that beset the egalitarian revolution in the socio-economic field in India are vitally linked with the problems that bedevil the educational system. A multi pronged attack on the maladies afflicting the educational system will also erode the very cause of the problem, and cut off the very vitals of the monster of inequality. Freedom in the physical world cannot thrive for long without physical equality and the latter cannot be achieved and sustained without mental equality. A sound system of education based on the ancient heritage and culture rooted in the soil is, therefore, the only guarantee for the mental equality in the physical world. Our Constitution is a master piece, acclaimed all the world over. It is no fault of the rafter if one is blind to it. But surely the solution lies in scrupulous adherence to the letter and spirit of the Constitution. The solution lies in the making of an individual deserving and fit to be administered under a sound and just system devised by the Founding Fathers. The making of a supreme individual is the only solution.

Nehru, the architect of Modern India, only a few days before his passing away on **May 25, 1964**, had written :

> "Socialism has become rather a vague word, with many meanings attached to it. In the modern world with its dynamism and its tremendous technological progress, it is clear that this concept of socialism itself undergoes a change, and yet its fundamental principles remain. In India, it is important for us to profit by modern technical processes and increase our production both in agriculture and industry. But, in doing so, we must not forget that the essential objective to be aimed at is the quality of the individual and the concept of *Dharma* underlying it".[37]

Let this vision inspire our efforts at national reconstruction on the machinery bequeathed to us and let our social life be fashioned on the principles underlying the philosophical outlook imbued in India's people by the Father of the Nation.

This survey of the means adopted and the end in view will lead us to an irresistible conclusion that means cannot be divorced from the end which we seek to attain. However, hard we may try to avoid it with all the cunning sagacity at our command, realization of the goal will be in exact proportion to the quality of the means. "It we take care of the means, we are bound to reach the end sooner or later. When once we have grasped this point, final victory is beyond question. As the means so the end."[38]

REFERENCES

1. *The Democratic Civilizations*; L. Lipson (1964), p. 217.
2. (1950) 3 SCR 869.
3. (1985) 3 SCC 398.
4. AIR 1983 Sc. 239.
5. AIR 1982 Sc. 1107.
6. AIR 1955 Sc. 795.
7. (1963) 2 SCR 353.
8. AIR 1986 Sc. 515.
9. AIR 1986 Sc. 555.
10. (1974) 2 SCR 348.
11. (1967) 3 SCR 28.
12. AIR 1951 Cal. 167.
13. CAD Vol. XI No. 11, Nov. 25, 1949.
14. *Ibid.*
15. *Land Reforms in India* : H.D. Malviya (1954), p. 55.
16. *Ibid.*, p. 70.
17. *Ibid.*, p. 71.
18. *Ibid.*
19. *Ibid.*, P. 91.
20. *Ibid.*, p. 95.
21. Nabhi's Ninth Five-Year Plan, p. 60.
22. *The Times of India* (Editorial) Dec. 8, 1983.
23. Socialism, M.K. Gandhi, p. 90.
24. Socialism and Gandhism (quoted) Ashok Mehta (1935), p. 20.
25. *The Hindustan Times,* Jan. 7, 1987, Article The Politics of Limits; Christopher Lasch, Harvard University.
26. *The Times of India, op. cit.*
27. *The Times of India,* April 27, 1986.
28. *Ibid.*
29. (Quoted) (1995) 1. SCC 26.
30. CAD Vol. XI. No. 11, Nov. 25, 1949.
31. Modern Indian Political Tradition; (Ed.) K.P. Karunakaran; p. 337.
32. CAD, XI, 12, Nov. 26, 1949.
33. *The Times of India*; May 3, 1980.
34. Sardar Patel, Rebel andleader; B.K. Ahluwalia (1981); p. 172.
35. Liberty *vs.* Equality; W.F. Russell (1936); p. 107.
36. *Economic and Political Weekly*, Annual Number Feb. 1972; Article—"Education and Inequality" Satish Sabreval.
37. India Needs Gandhi; Shriman Narayan; p. 78.
38. Selections from Gandhi; (Ed) N.K. Bose; p. 14.

APPENDIX– A

ALL PARTIES CONFERENCE 1928

THE RECOMMENDATIONS (CONSTITUTIONAL STATUS OF INDIA)

Fundamental Rights

4. (i) All powers of government and all authority, legislative, executive and judicial, are derived from the people and the same shall be exercised in the commonwealth of India through the organizations established by or under and in due process of this Constitution.

(ii) No person shall be deprived of his liberty nor shall his dwelling or property be entered, sequestered or cofiscated, save in accordance with law. All titles to private and personal property lawfully acquired and enjoyed at the establishment of the commonwealth are hereby guaranteed.

(iii) Freedom of conscience and the free profession and practice of religion are, subject to public order or morality, hereby guaranteed to every person.

(iv) The right of free expression of opinion, as well as the right to assemble peacefully and without arms, and to form associations or unions, i.e. hereby guaranteed for purposes not opposed to public order or morality.

(v) All citizens in the commonwealth of India have the right to free elementary education without any distinction of caste or creed in the matter of admission to any educational institution, maintained or aided by the State, and such right shall be enforceable as soon as due arrangements shall have been made by competent authority. Provided that adequate provision shall be made by the State for imparting public instruction in primary schools to the children of members of minorities of considerable strength in the population through the medium of their own language and in such script as is in vogue among them.

Explanation :— This provision will not prevent the State from making the teaching of the language of the commonwealth obligatory in the said schools.

(vi) All citizens are equal before the law and possess equal civic rights.

(vii) There shall be no penal law whether substantive or procedural of a discriminative nature.

(viii) No person shall be punished for any act which was not punishable under the law at the time it was committed.

(ix) No corporal punishment or other punishment involving torture of any kind shall be lawful.

(x) Every citizen shall have the right to a write of habeas corpus. Such right may be suspended in case of war or rebellion by an Act of the central legislature, or, if the legistautre is not in session, by the Governor-General-in-Council, and in such case he shall report the suspension to the legislature, at the earliest possible opportunity for such action as it may deem fit.

(xi) There shall be no State religion for the commonwealth of India or for any province in the commonwealth, nor shall the State either directly or indirectly endow any religion, or give any preference or impose any disability on account of religious belief or religious status.

(xii) No person attending any school receiving state aid or other public money shall by compelled to attend the religious instruction that may be given in the school.

(xiii) No person shall by reason of his religion, caste or creed be prejuidiced in any way in record to public employment, office of power or honour and the exercise of any trade or calling.

(xiv) All citizens have an equal right of access to, and use, of public roads, public wells and all other places of public resort.

(xv) Freedom of combination and association for the maintenance and improvement of labour and economic conditions is guaranteed to everyone and of all occupations. All agreements and measures tending to obstruct or restrict such freedom is illegal.

(xvi) No breach of contract of services or abetment thereof shall be made a criminal offence.

(xvii) Parliament shall make suitable laws for the maintenance of health and fitness for work of all citizens, securing of a living wage for every worker, the protection of motherhood, welfare of children and the economic consequences of old age, infirmity and unemployment and parliament shall also make laws to ensure fair rent and fixity and permanence of tenures to agricultural tenants.

(xviii) Every citizen shall have the right to keep and bear arms in accordance with the regulations made in that behalf.

(xix) Men and women shall have equal rights as citizens.

Notes : Notwithstanding anything to the contrary in article (iv) the Sikhs are entitled to carry Kripans.

(Supplementary Report., pp. 32-33)

APPENDIX- B

THE FUNDAMENTAL RIGHTS RESOLUTION

AT THE 45TH CONGRESS AT KARACHI, 1931

(Vide Resolution XV)

This Congress is of opinion that to enable the masses to appreciate what Swaraj, as conceived by the Congress, will mean to them, it is desirable to state the position of the Congress in a manner easily understood by them. In order to end the exploitation of the masses, political freedom must include real economic freedom of the starving millions. The Congress, therefore, declares that any Constitution which may be agreed to on its behalf should provide, or enable the Swaraj Government to provide, for the following :

I. Fundamental Rights of the People, including :

1. Freedom of association and combination;
2. Freedom of speech and of the press;
3. Freedom of conscience and the free profession and practice of religion subject to public order and morality;
4. Protection of the culture, language and scripts of the minorities ;
5. Equal rights and obligations of all citizens, without any discrimination on account of sex;

6. No disability to attach to any citizen by reason of his or her religion, caste or creed or sex in regard to public employment, office of power or honour and in the exercise of any trade or calling;
7. Equal rights to all citizens in regard to public roads, wells, schools and other places of public resort;
8. Right to keep and bear arms in accordance with regulations and reservations made in that behalf; and
9. No person shall be deprived of his liberty nor shall his dwelling or property be entered, sequestered or confiscated, save in accordance with law.

(Quoted : Land Reform in India, H.D. Malviya. p.27)

II. The Karachi Congress Resolution on Fundamental Rights and Economic Programme as varied by the All India Congress Committee in its Bombay meeting in August, 1931, runs as follows :—

This Congress is of opinion that to enable the masses to appreciate what "Swaraj" as conceived by the Congress, will mean to them, it is desirable to state the position of the Congress in a manner easily understood by them. In order to end the exploitation of the masses, political freedom must include real economic freedom of the starving millions. The Congress therefore declares that any Constitution which may be agreed to on its behalf should provide, or enable the Swaraj Government to provide the following :

FUNDAMENTAL RIGHTS AND DUTIES

1. (i) Every citizen of India has the right of free expression of opinion, the right of free association and combination, and the right to assemble peacefully and without arms, for a purpose not opposed to law or morality.

(ii) Every citizen shall enjoy freedom of conscience and the right freely to profess and practice his religion, subject to public order and morality.

(iii) The culture, language and script of the minorities and of the different linguistic areas shall be protected.

(iv) All citizens are equal before the law, irrespective of religion, caste, creed or sex.

(v) No disability attaches to any citizen by reason of his or her religion, caste, creed or sex, in regard to public employment, office of power or honour, and in the exercise of any trade or calling.

(vi) All citizens have equal rights and duties in regard to wells, tanks, roads, schools and places of public resort, maintained out of State or local funds, or dedicated by private persons for the use of the general public.

(vii) Every citizen has the right to keep and bear arms, in accordance with regulations and reservations made in that behalf.

(viii) No person shall be deprived of his liberty, nor shall his dwelling or property be entered, sequestered, or confiscated, save in accordance with law.

(ix) The State shall observe neutrality in regard to all religion.

(x) The franchise shall be on the basis of universal adult suffrage.

(xi) The State shall provide for free and compulsory primary education.

(xii) The State shall confer no titles.

(xiii) There shall be no capital punishment.

(xiv) Every citizen is free to move throughout India and to stay and settle in any part therof, to acquire property and to follow any trade or calling, and to be treated equally with regard to legal prosecution or protection in all part of India.

LABOUR

2. (a) The organisation of economic life must conform to the principle of justice, so that it may secure a decent standard of living.

(b) The State shall safeguard the interests of industrial workers and shall secure for them, by suitable legislation and other ways, a living wage, healthy conditions of work, limited hours of labour, suitable machinery for the settlement of disputes between employees and workman, and protection against the economic consequences of old age, sickness and unemployment.

3. Labour to be freed of serfdom and conditions bordering on serfdom.
4. Protection of women workers, and especially, adequate provision for leave during maternity period.
5. Children of school-going age shall not be employed in mines and factories.
6. Peasants and workers shall have the right to form unions to protect their interest.

TAXATION AND EXPENDITURE

7. The system of land tenure and revenue and rent shall be reformed and an equitable adjustment made of the burden on agricultural land immediately giving relief to the smaller peasantry, by a substantial reduction of agicultural rent and revenue now paid by them, and in case uneconomic holdings, exempting them from rent, so long as necessary, with such relief as may be just and necessary to holders of small estates affected by such exemption or reduction in rent, and to the same end, imposing a graded tax on net incomes from land above a reasonable minimum.
8. Death duties on a graduated scale shall be levied on property above a fixed minimum.
9. There shall be a drastic reduction of military expenditure so as to bring it down to at least one half of the present scale.
10. Expenditure and salaries in civil departments shall be largely reduced. No servant of the State, other than specially employed experts and the like, shall be paid above a certain fixed figure, which should not ordinarily exceed Rs. 500 per month.
11. No duty shall be levied on salt manufactured in India.
12. The State shall protect indigenous cloth; and for this purpose pursue the policy of exclusion of foreign cloth and foreign yarn from the country and adopt such other measures as may be found necessary. The State

shall also protect other indigenous industries, when necessary, against foreign competition.

13. Intoxicating drinks and drugs shall be totally prohibited, except for medicinal purposes.
14. Currency and exchange shall be regulated in the national interest.
15. The State shall own or control key industries and services, mineral resources, railways, waterways, shipping and other means of public transport.
16. Relief of agricultural indebtedness and control of usury—direct and indirect.
17. The State shall provide for the military training of citizens so as to organize a means of national defence apart from the regular military forces.

APPENDIX –C

EXCERPTS FROM ADVISORY COMMITTEE REPORT

I. RIGHT TO EQUALITY

4. (1) The State shall make no discrimination against any citizen on grounds of religion, race, caste or sex.

   (2) There shall be no discrimination against any citizen on any ground of religion race, caste or sex in regard to :—

   (a) access to trading establishments including public restaurants and hotels,

   (b) the use of wells, tanks, roads and places of public resort maintained wholly or partly out of public funds or dedicated to the use of the general public.

Provided that nothing contained in this clause, shall prevent separate provision being made for women and children.

5. There shall be equality of opportunity for all citizens in matter of public employment and in the exercise of carrying on of any occupation, trade, business or profession.

Nothing herein contained shall prevent the State from making provision for reservation in favour of classes who, in the opinion of the State, are not adequately represented in the public services.

No citizen shall on grounds only of religion, race, caste, sex, descent, place of birth or any of them be ineligible for public office or be prohibited from acquiring, holding or disposing of property or exercising or carrying on any occupation, trade, business or profession within the Union.

Nothing herein contained shall prevent a law being made prescribing that the incumbent of an offices to manage, administer or superintendent the affairs of a religious or denominational institution or the member of the governing body thereof shall be a member of that particular religion or denomination.

6. "Untouchability" in any form is abolished and the imposition of any disability on that account shall be an offence.
7. No heritable title shall be conferred by the Union.

No citizen of the Union and no person holding any office of profit or trust under the State shall, without the consent of the Union government, accept any present, emoluments, office, or title of any kind from any foreign State.

II. RIGHT TO EQUALITY (FROM DRAFT CONSTITUTION)

9. (1) The State shall not discriminate against any citizen on grounds only of religion, race, caste, sex or any of them.

In particular, no citizen shall, on grounds only of religion, race caste, sex or any of them, be subject to any disability, restriction or condition with regard to :

(a) access to shops, public restaurants, hotels and places of public entertainment, or

(b) the use of wells, tanks, roads and places of public resort maintained wholly or partly out of the revenues of the State or dedicated to the use of the general public.

(2) Nothing in the article shall prevent the States from making any special provision for women and children.

10. (1) There shall be equality of opportunity for all citizens in matters of employment under the State.

(2) Nothing in this article shall prevent the State from making any provision for the reservation of appointments or post in favour of any backward class of citizens who, in the opinion of the State are not adequately represented in services under the State.

(3) Nothing in this article shall effect the operation of any law which provides that the incumbent of an office in connection with the affairs of any religious or denominational institution or any member of the governing body thereof shall be a person professing a particular religion or belonging to a particular denomination.

11. "Untouchability" is abolished and its practice in any form is forbidden. The enforcement of any disability arising out of "Untouchability" shall be an offence punishable in accordance with law.

12. (1) No title shall be conferred by the State.

(2) No citizen of India shall accept any title from any foreign State.

(3) No person holding any office of profit or trust under the State shall, 'Without the consent of the President accept any present, emolument, title or office of any kind from or under any foreign State.

13.(1) Subject to the other provisions of this article all citizens shall have the right :

(a) to freedom of speech and expressions;

(b) to assemble peaceably and without arms;

(c) to form association or unions;

(d) to move freely throughout the territory of India;

(e) to reside and settle in any part of the territory of India;

(f) to acquire, hold and dispose of property; and

(g) to practice any profession, or to carry on any occupation, trade or business.

(2) Nothing in sub-clause (a) of Clause (1) of this article shall affect the operation of any existing law, or prevent the State from making any laws relating to libel,

slander, defamation, sedition or any other matter which offends against decency or morality or undermines the authority or foundation of the State.

(3) Nothing in sub-clause (b) of the said clause shall affect the operation of any existing law, or prevent the State from making any law, imposing in the interests of public order restrictions in the exercise of right conferred by the said sub-clause.

(4) Nothing in sub-clauses (c) of the said clause shall affect the operation of any existing law, or prevent the State from making any law, imposing, in the interest of the general public, restrictions on the exercise of the right conferred by the said Sub-clause.

(5) Nothing in sub-clauses (d), (e) and (f) of the said clause shall affect the operation of any existing law, or prevent the State from making any law, imposing restrictions on the exercise of any of the rights conferred by the said sub-clauses either in the interests of the general public or "for the protection of the interests of any aboriginal tribe."

(6) Nothing in sub-clauses (g) of the said clause shall affect the operation of any existing law, or prevent the State from making any law, imposing in the interests of public order, morality or health, restrictions on the exercise of the right conferred by said sub-clause and in particular prescribing, or empowering any authority to prescribe, the professional or technical qualifications necessary for practising any profession or carrying on any occupation, trade or business.

14 (1) No person shall be convicted of any offence except for violation of a law in force at the time of the commission of the act charged as on offence, nor subjected to a penalty greater than that which might have been inflicted under the law at the time of the commission of the offence.

(2) No person shall be punished for the same offence more than once.

(3) No person accused of any offence shall be compelled to be a witness himself.

15. No person shall be deprived of his life or personal liberty except according to procedure established by law, nor shall any person be denied equality before the law or the equal protection of the laws within the territory of India.

16. Subject to the provisions of Article 244 of this Constitution and of any law made by Parliament, trade commerce and intercourse throughout the territory of India shall be free.

17. (1) Traffic in human beings and begar and other similar forms of forced labour are prohibited and any contravention of this provision shall be an offence punishable in accordance with law.

(2) Nothing in this article shall prevent the State from imposing compulsory service for public purposes. In imposing such service the State shall not make any discrimination on the ground of race, religion, caste or class.

18. No child below the age of fourteen years shall be employed to work in any factory or mine or engaged in any other hazardous employment.

III. RIGHT TO EQUALITY

14. The State shall not deny to any person equality before the law or the equal protection of the laws within the territory of India.

15. (1) The State shall not discriminate against any citizen on grounds only of religion, race, caste, sex, place of birth or any of them.

(2) No citizen shall, on grounds only of religion, race, caste, sex, place of birth or any of them, be subject to any disability, liability, restriction or condition with regard to—

(a) access to shops, public restaurants, hotels and places of public entertainment; or

(b) the use of wells, tanks, bathing ghats, roads and places of public resort maintained wholly or partly out of State funds or dedicated to the use of the general public.

(3) Nothing in this article shall prevent the State from making any special provision for women and children.

[1][(4) Nothing in this article or in Clause (2) of Article 29 shall prevent the State from making any special provision for the advancement of any socially and educationally backward classes of citizens or for the Scheduled Castes and the Scheduled Tribes.]

16. (1) There shall be equality of opportunity for all citizens in matters relating to employment or appointment to any office under the State.

(2) No citizen shall on grounds only of religion, race, caste, sex, descent, place of birth, residence or any of them, be ineligible for, or discriminated against in respect of, any employment or office under the State.

[2](3) Nothing in this article shall prevent Parliament from making any law prescribing, in regard to a class or classes of employment or appointment to an offices [3](Under the Government of or any local or other authority within, a State or Union territory any requirement as to residence within that State or Union territory) prior to such employment or appointment.

(4) Nothing in this article shall prevent the State from making any provision for the reservation of appointment or posts in favour of any backward class of citizens which, in the opinion of the State, is not adequately represented in the services under the State.

(5) Nothing in this article shall effect the operation of any law which provides that the incumbent of an office in connection with the affairs of any religious or donominational institution or any member of the governing body thereof shall be a person professing a particular religion or belonging to a particular denomination.

17. "Untouchability" is abolished and its practice in any form in forbidden. The enforcement of any disability arising out of "Untouchability" shall be an offence punishable in accordance with law.

18. (1) No title, not being a military or academic distinction, shall be conferred by the State.

(2) No citizen of India shall accept any title from any foreign State.

(3) No person who is not a citizen of India shall while he holds any office of profit or trust under the State, accept without the consent of the President any title from any foreign State.

(4) No person holding any office of profit or trust under the State shall without the consent of the President, accept any present emolument, or office of any kind from or under any foreign State.

REFERENCES

1. Added by then Constitution (First Amendment) Act, 1951, s. 2. In its application to the State of Jammu and Kashmir, reference to Scheduled Tribes in cl. (4) of Art. 15, shall be omitted.
2. In Clause (3) of Art. 16, the reference to the State shall be construed as not including a reference to the State of Jammu and Kashmir.
3. Subs. by the Constitution (Seventh Amendment) Act, 1956, s. 29 and Sch. for "Under any State specified in the First Schedule or any local or other authority within its territory, any requirement as to residence within that State

APPENDIX–D

FUNDAMENTAL PRINCIPLES OF GOVERNANCE (ADVISORY COMMITTEE REPORT)

1. The principles of policy set forth in this part are intended for the guidance of the State, while these principles are not congnizable by any court, they are nevertheless fundamental in the governance of the country and their application in the making of laws shall be the duty of the State.
2. The State shall strive to promote the welfare of the whole people by securing and protecting as effectively as it may be a social order in which justice, social, economic and political shall inform all the institutions of national life.
3. The State shall in particular, direct its policy towards securing :
   (a) that the ownership and control of material resources of an adequete means of livalihood :
   (b) that the ownership and control of material resources of the community are so distributed as best to subserve the common good;
   (c) that the operation of free competition shall not be allowed to result in the concentration of

ownership and control of essential commodities in a few individuals to the common detriment;

(d) that there shall be equal pay for equal work for both men and women;

(e) that the strength and health of workers, men and women, and the tender age of children shall not be abused and that citizens shall not be forced by economic necessity to enter avocations unsuited to their age and strength;

(f) that childhood and youth are protected against exploitation and against moral and material abandonment.

4. The State shall, within the limits of its economic capacity and development, make effective provision for securing the right to work, to education and to public assistance in case of unemployment, old age, sickness, disablement and other cases of undeserved wants.
5. The State shall make provision for securing just and human conditions of work and for maternity relief for women.
6. The State shall endeavour to secure, by suitable legislation, economic organization and in other ways, to all workers, industrial or otherwise, work, a living wage, conditions of work securing a descent standard of life and full enjoyment of leisure and social and cultural opportunities.
7. The State shall endeavour to secure for the citizens, a uniform civil code.
8. Every citizen is entitled to free primary education, and it shall be the duty of the State to provide within a period of 10 years, from the commencement of this Constitution for free and compulsory primary education for all children until they complete the age of 14 years.
9. The State shall promote with special care the educational and economic interests of the weaker section of the schedule caste and aboriginal tribes, and shall protect them from social injustice and all forms of exploitation.

10. The State shall regard the raising of the level of nutrition and the standard of living of its people and the improvement of public health as among its primary duties.
11. It shall be the obligation of the State to protect every monument or place or object of artistic or historic interest, declared by the law of the Union to be of national importance, from spoliation, destruction, removal, disposal as far as may be, and to preserve and maintain them according to the law.
12. The State shall promote international peace and security by the prescription of open, just and hounourable relations between nations, by the firm establishment of the understandings of International law as the actual rule of conduct among governments and by the maintenance of justice and the scrupulous respect for treaty obligation in the dealings of organized people with one another.

II. DIRECTIVE PRINCIPLES OF STATE POLICY (DRAFT CONSTITUTION)

PART IV

28. In this Part unless the context otherwise requires, "The State" has the same meaning as in Part III of this Constitution.
29. The provisions contained in this Part shall not be enforceable by any court, but the principles therein laid down are nevertheless fundamental in the government of the country and it shall be duty of the State to apply these principles in making laws.
30 The State shall strive to promote the welfare of the people by securing and protecting as effectively as it may a social order in which justice, social, economic and political, shall inform all the institutions of the national life.
31. The State shall, in particular, direct its policy towards securing—
    (a) That the citizens, men and women equally, have the right to an adequate means of livelihood;

(b) That the ownership and control of the material resources of the community are so distributed as best to subserve the common good;

(c) that the operation of the economic system does not result in the concentration of wealth and means of production to the common detriment;

(d) that there is equal pay for equal work for both men and women;

(e) that the strength and health of workers, men and women and the tender age of children are not abused and that citizens are not forced by economic necessity to enter avocations unsuited to their age of strength; and

(f) that childhood and youth are protected against exploitation and against moral and material abandonment.

32. The State shall, within the limits of its economic capacity and development, make effective provision for securing the right to work, to education and to public assistance in case of unemployment, old age sickness, disablement, and other cases of undeserved want.

33. The State shall make provision of securing just and human conditions of work and for maternity relief.

34. The State shall endeavour to secure, by suitable legislation or economic organization or in any other way, to all workers, industrial or otherwise, work, a living wage, conditions of work ensuring a decent standard of life and full enjoyment of leisure and social and cultural opportunities.

35. The State shall endeavour to secure for the citizens a uniform civil code throughout the territory of India.

36. Every citizen is entitled to free primary education and the State shall endeavour to provide, within a period of ten years from the commencement of this Constitution, for free and compulsory education for all children until they complete the age of fourteen years.

37. The State shall promote with special care the educational and economic interests of the weaker section of the people, and in particular, of the

Scheduled Castes and the Scheduled tribes, and shall protect them from social injustice and all forms of exploitation.

38. The State shall regard the raising of the level of nutrition and standard of living of its people and the improvement of public health as among its primary duties.

39. It shall be the obligation of the State to protect every monument or place or object of artistic or historic interest, declared by Parliament by law to be of national importance, from spoilation destruction removal, disposal or export, as the case may be and to preserve and maintain according to law made by Parliament all such monuments or places or objects.

40. The State shall promote international peace and security by the prescription of open, just and honourable relations between nations, by the firm establishment of the understandings of international law as the actual rule of conduct among governments and by the maintenance of justice and respect for treaty obligations in the dealings of organized people with one another.

III. DIRECTIVE PRINCIPLES OF STATE POLICY

(Constitution of India as on 1st April, 1986)

36. In this Part; unless the context otherwise requires, "the State" has the same meaning as in Part III.

37. The provisions contained in this part shall not be enforceable by any court, but the principles therein laid down are nevertheless fundamental in the governance of the country and it shall be the duty of the State to apply these principles in making laws.

38. [1][(i)] The State shall strive to promote the welfare of the people by securing and protecting as effectively as it may a social order in which justice, social, economic and political shall inform all the institutions of the national life.

[2][(2) The State shall, in particular, strive to minimize the inequalities in income, and endeavour to eliminate inequalities in status, facilities and

opportunities, not only amongst individuals but also amongst group of people residing in different areas or engaged in different vocations.]

39. The State shall, in particular, direct its policy towards securing :

(a) that the citizens, men and women equally have the right to an adequate means of livelihood;

(b) that the worship and control of the material resources of the community are so distributed as best to subserve the common good;

(c) that the operation of the economic system does not result in the concentration of wealth and means of production to the common detriment;

(d) that there is equal pay for equal work for both men and women;

(e) that the health and strength of workers, men and women, and the tender age of children are not abused and that citizens are not forced by economic necessity to enter avocations unsuited to their age or strength;

[3][(f) that children are given opportunities and facilities to develop in a healthy manner and in conditions of freedom and dignity and that childhood and youth are protected against exploitation and against moral and material abandonment.]

[4][39A. The State shall secure that the operation of the legal system promotes justice, on a basis of equal opportunity, and shall, in particular, provide free legal aid, by suitable legislation or schemes or in any other way, to ensure that opportunities for securing justice are not denied to any citizen by reason of economic or other disabilities.]

40. The State shall take steps to organize village panchayats and endow them with such powers and authority as may be necessary to enable them to function as units of self-government.

41. The State shall, within the limit of its economic capacity and development, make effective provision for securing the right to work, to education and to

public assistance in cases of unemployment, old age, sickness and disablement, and in other cases of undeserved want.

42. The State shall make provision for security just and humane conditions of work and for maternity relief.

43. The State shall endeavour to secure by suitable legislation or economic organization or in any other way, to all workers, agricultural, industrial or otherwise work, a living wage, conditions of work assuring a decent standard of life and full enjoyment of liesure and social and cultural opportunities and, in particular, the State shall endeavour to promote cottage industries on an individual or co-operative basis in rural areas.

[5][43A. The State shall take steps, by suitable legislation or in any other way, to secure the participation of workers in the management of undertakings, establishment or other organizations engaged in any industries.]

44. The State shall endeavour to secure for the citizens a uniform civil code throughout the territory of India.

45. The State shall endeavour to provide, within a period of ten years from the commencement of this Constitution, for free and compulsory education for all children until they complete the age of fourteen years.

46. The State shall promote with special care the educational and economic interest of the weaker section of the people, and in particular, of the Scheduled Castes and Scheduled Tribes and shall protect them from social injustice and all forms of exploitation.

47. The State shall regard the raising of the level of nutrition and the standard of living of its people and the improvement of public health as among its primary duties and, in particular, the State shall endeavour to bring about prohibition of the consumption except for medicinal purpose of intoxicating drinks and of drugs which are injurious to health.

48. The State shall endeavour to organise agriculture and animal husbandry on modern and scientific lines and shall, in particular, take steps for preserving and

improving the breeds, and prohibiting the slaughter of cows and calves and other milch and draught cattle.

[6][48A. The State shall endeavour to protect and improve the environment and to safeguard the forests and the wild life of the country.]

49. It shall be the obligation of the State to protect every monument or place or object of artistic or historic interests.[7] (declared by or under law made by Parliament) to be of national importance, from spoilation, disfigurement, destruction, removal, disposal or export as the case may be.

50. The State shall take steps to separate the judiciary from the executive in the public service of the State.

51. The State shall endeavour to :

(a) promote international peace and security;

(b) maintain just and honourable relations between nations;

(c) foster respect for international law and treaty obligations in the dealings of organized people with one another; and

(d) encourage settlement of international disputes by arbitration.

REFERENCES

1. Art. 30 renumbered as Cl. (1) thereof the Constitution (forty Amendment) Act, 1978, s. 9 (w.e.f. 20-6-1979).
2. Ins. by s. 9. *Ibid.*, (w.e.f. 20.6.1979).
3. Subs. by the constitution (forty-second Amendment) Act, 1976, s. 7. for cl (f). w.e.f. 3.1.1977).
4. Ins. by s. 8. *Ibid.*, (w.e.f. 3.1.1977).
5. Ins. by Constitution (forty second Amendment) Act, 1976, s. 9 (w.e.f. 3.1.1977).
6. Ins. by the Constitution (forty-second Amendment) Act, 1976, S.10 (w.e.f 3.1.1977).
7. Subs. by the Constituion Act, 1956, s, 27, for declared by Parliament by law.

BIBLIOGRAPHY

PRIMARY SOURCES

Documents, Reports, etc.

Government of India Act, 1935.

Draft Constitution of India (1948).

(Prepared by the Drafting Committee dated 21st Feb., 1948)

The Constitution of India (modified upto 1st July, 1960).

The Constitution of India (modified upto 15th Jan, 1980).

The Constitution of India (modified upto 1st April, 1986).

All Parties Conference, 1928 : Report of the Nehru Committee appointed by the conference to determine the Principles of the Constitution of India.

All Parties Conference, 1928 : Supplementary Report of the Committee.

India in 1921-22 : Report by L.F. Rushbrook Williams, Director, Central Bureau of Information, Govt. of India.

India in 1924-25 : Report by L.F. Rushbrook Williams.

Constitution Assembly Debates : Official Reports, 12 Vols.

Report of the General Secretary I.N.C. : J.B. Kriplani, 1938.

Report of the Law Commission of India (Govt. of India Press) 48th Report 1972.

Report of the Commissioner for the S.C. and S.T. : 1970, Vol. II.

Charter of the United Nations, 1945.

Declaration of Human Rights, 1948.

The First Five Year Plan.
Second Five Year Plan, 1956.
Third Five Year Plan, A draft out line June, 1960.
Fourth Five Year Plan, 1969-74 (Summary of the Draft July, 1969).
Fifth Five Year Plan, 1974-79 (A draft out line).
Sixth Five Year Plan, 1980-85 (A draft out line).
Supreme Court Reports, 1950-86.
Supreme Court Cases, 1950-86.
All India Reporter, 1950-86.
Allahabad Law Journal.
Untouchability (Offences) Act, 1955.
Bihar Harijan (Removal of Civil Disabilities) Act, 1949.
Report on Currency and Finance, Reserve Bank of India, 1958-59, 59-60.
India-1975 (Pub. Div. Govt. of India).
Congress Election Manifesto, 1936.

Books

Laski, Harold—A Grammar of Politics.
Locke, John—Some Thoughts Concerning Education.
Linscott and Commins (Ed.). The Political Philosophers.
Sills, David, L., (Ed.) Encyclopedia of the Social Sciences Vol. V (1968).
Taittriya Upanishad.
Atharvaveda.
The Rg Veda-2 Vols. (tr.) Griffith, R.T.H. (1896).
Shukla Yajurveda.
Ishopanishad.
Valmiki Ramayan.
Chandogya Upanishad.
Bose, N.K. (Ed.) Selections from Gandhi.
Gandhi, M.K., Dawn of Freedom.
Gandhi, M.K., The Bleeding Wound.
Gandhi, M.K., Autobiography.
Gandhi, M.K., Socialism of My Conception.

Gandhi, M.K., Truth is God.
Gandhi, M.K., Democracy : Real and Deceptive.
Gandhi, M.K., To the Students.
Gandhi, M.K., Basic Education.
Gandhi, M.K., The Problem of Education.
Gandhi, M.K., Constructive Programme.
Gandhi, M.K., All Men are Brothers.
Gandhi, M.K., Communism and Communists.
Gandhi, M.K., Sarvodaya.
Gandhi, M.K., My Religion.
Nehru, J.L., Glimpses of World History, Vol. I and II.
Bright, J.S., (Ed) Selected Writings of J.L. Nehru (1916-50).
Nehru, J.L., Independence and After.
Nehru, J.L., Recent Essays and Writings.
Nehru, J.L., Autobiography.
Karunakaran, K.P. (Ed.), Modern Indian Political Tradition.
Oppenheim, F., International Encyclopaedia of Social Science Vol.V, (1972).
Vivekanand Swamy—Caste, Culture and Socialism.

Newspapers, Periodicals, etc.

The Indian Express.
The Times of India
The Hindustan Times.
The Indian Nation.
Harijan—published and edited by Gandhiji.
Young India published and edited by Gandhiji.
The Modern Review.
The American Review.
The Mainstream.
Economic and Political Weekly.
Socialist Thought and Practice (No. 34) A Yogoslav Journal.
The Federalist (No. 79) Ed. Hamilton.
Illustrated Weekly of India.
Indian Journal of Political Sciences.
Congress Bulletin, 1969.

Speeches, Lectures, etc.

Complete Works of Swami Vivekanand—Vol. I, III, IV and VI.

The Political Writings of Thomas Jefferson, Ed. E. Dumbauld (1966).

J.L. Nehru's Speeches, Pub. Div. Govt. of India, Vols. I, II, III.

Before and After Indepencence : Nehru's speeches—Ed. J. S. Bright, Vol. III.

Congress Ke Prastav, Ed. Kannaiya Lal.

Nehru : The First Sixty Years, Ed. Devothy Norman, Vol. II.

The Years of Endeavour, Speeches of Mrs. Gandhi, Pub. Div. Govt. of India.

SECONDARY SOURCES

Books

Aguilar, Cavarria. O.L. (Ed.) Traditional India.

Ahluwalia, B.K., Sardar Patel, Rebel and Leader.

Ahluwalia, B.K., Facets of Gandhi.

Aiyer, Alladi, K., The Constitution and Fundamental Rights (1955).

Altekar, A.S., Education in ancient India.

Appadorai, A., Documents on Political Thought in Modern India, Vol. I (1973).

Austin, Granville, The Indian Constitution, Corner Stone of a Nation (1974).

Bajaj, Premnath, Whither India after Independence (1970).

Bandyopadhyaya, J., Social and Political Thought of Gandhi.

Basham, A.L., The Wonder that was India (1954).

Basu, D.D., Commentary on the Constitution of India (1961) Vol. I.

Basu, D.D., Shorter Constitution of India (1970).

Bose, Anima, Dimensions of Peace and Non-Violence (1987).

Bose, N.K., Gandhi's Theory of Trusteeship.

Bose, N.K., Gandhism and Modern India.

Bose, N.K., My days with Gandhi (1953).

Bose, N.K., Studies in Gandhism (1959).

Bose, Wemai Sadhan–Indira Gandhi on Herself and Her times (1987).

Bowles, Chester, The Making of a Just Society.

Brecher, Michael, Nehru : A Political Biography (1959).

Brown, Herris, The Challenge of Man's Future.

Cassen, R.H., India : Population, Economy, Society (1978).

Chatterjee, Chinmoy, Vedantic Education.

Chaturvedi, Giridhar Sharma, Vedic Vigyan Aur Bhartiya Sanskriti (1960).

Chaturvedi, R.G., Natural and Social Justice (1970).

Chopra, Pran (Ed.), The Sage in Revolt.

Corwin, Edward. S., The Constitution of U.S.A.

Das, Durga, India from Curzon to Nehru, and After (1969).

Das, G.N., Concept of Equality in the Eye of law (1959).

Das, M.N., The Political Philosophy of J.L. Nehru (1961).

Desai, Mahadeo, The diary of Mahadeva Desai.

Dicey, A.V., Law of the Constitution.

Emerson and Haber, Political civil Rights in the U.S. (1958).

Gadgil, D.R., Some Observations on the draft Constitution.

Gajendragadkar, P.B., Law liberty and Social Justice (1965).

Gajendragadkar, P.B., The Constitution of India, its philosophy and Basic Postulates.

Ganguli, B.N., Concept of Equality (1979).

Gopal, S., J.L. Nehru : A Biography (1984) Vols. I to III.

Imam, M., The Indian Supreme Court and the Constitution (1970).

Jennings, Ivor, Some Characteristics of Indian Constitution.

Jennings, Ivor, The Law and the Constitution.

Jha, T.N., Indira Gandhi (1983).

Joshi, S.N., The Constitution of India (1950).

Josyer, G.R., Sanskrit Civilization.

Karanjia, R.K., Face to face with Indira Gandhi (1974).

Karanjia, R.K., The Philosophy of Mr. Nehru (1966).

Karunakaran, K.P., The Phenomenon of Nehru (1979).

Keith, A.B., The Constitutional History of India.
Khanna, H.R., Constitution and Socio-economic changes, Patel Memorial Lectures, 1977.
Kotnala, M.C., Raja Ram Mohan Roy and Indian Awakening (1975).
Kripalani, J.B., Gandhian Thought (1962).
Krishnamurti, V.G., Salute the Mahatma.
Lakoff, Sanfore, A. Equality in Political Philosophy.
Lal, Kanwar, Good Bye, Mr. Gandhi.
Lal, Pyare, Mahatma Gandhi, the Last Phase, Vols. I and II.
Lewis, M.D., Gandhi.
Lipson, L., The Democratic Civilizations (1964).
Lokhande, G.S., Bhim Rao Ramji Ambedkar.
Macdonell, History of Sanskrit Literature.
Mackenzie, J.S., Outlines of Social Philosophy (1952).
Malviya, H.D., Land Reforms in India (1954).
Malviya, H.D., Socialist Ideology of Congress (1966).
Mathur, J.S., (Ed.) Economic Thought of Mahatma Gandhi (1958).
Mayo, Henry B., The Democratic Theory (1967).
Mehta, Ashok, Socialism and Gandhism.
Mookerjee, Girja, Nehru, the Humanist (1972).
Moraes, Dom, Mrs. Gandhi (1980).
Munshi, K.M., Indian Constitutional Document.
Munshi, K.M., Pilgrimage to Freedom.
Narayan, Shriman, Indira Needs Gandhi.
Nath, Kedar, Indian Polity at the Cross Roads.
National Council on Asian Affairs, Gandhi's Reflections on Democracy, Philadelphia, U.S.A.
Nikam, W.K., Gandhi's Discovery of religion, 1963.
Ojha, Jagatguru Vaibhavam.
Ojha, Madhusudan, Maharsi Kul Vaibhavam (R.O.R.I. Jaipur).
Ojha, Madhusudan, Mannwantari Nirdharah.
Ojha, Madhusudan, Puranotapatti Prasangah.
Ojha, Panchabhoot Samiksha.
Palkhiwala, W.A., Supreme Court of Amendments of Fundamental Rights in Indian Constitution (1973).

Pandey, R.B. Hindu Samskaras (1969).
Panikkar, K.M., Essential Features of Indian Culture.
Piggott, Stuert, Prehistoric India (1961).
Pylee, M.V., Constitutional Government of India (1963).
Radhakrishnan, S. (Ed.), Mahatama Gandhi : 100 Years (1968).
Raghavacharya, N.R., The Constitution of India (1951).
Raj Gopalachari, C., Upanishads.
Raj Kumar, N.V., Development in the Congress Constitution.
Raja Ram and Iqbal Singh, Changing of India (1939).
Ram Krishna Mission, The Indian Scheme of Life.
Rao, K.V., Parliamentary Democracy in India.
Rao, V.K.R.V., Gandhian Alternative to Western Socialism.
Rau, B.N., Indian's Constitution in the Making.
Rivett, Kenneth, Economic Thought of Mahatma Gandhi (1959).
Rudolph, Susanneh, Education and Politics in India.
Russel, William F., Liberty vs. Equality (1936).
Saiyuddin, K.G., Significance of Gandhi as a Man and Thinker.
Sarkar, Bandna, Towards Trusteeship (1974).
Sartori, F., Democratic Theory.
Sen, Amartya, On Economic Inequality (1973).
Setalvad, M.C., The Indian Constitution (1967).
Sethi, J.D., Gandhi To-day.
Sethi and Bhandari, Plato and Aristotle (3rd. ed.).
Sharma, D.S., Hinduism through the Ages (1961).
Sharma, M.P., The Concept of Equality in the Indian Constitution (1983).
Sharma, S.R., Our Human Heritage (1964).
Sheela, Indira Priyadarshini (1966).
Shetty, K.P.K., Fundamental Rights and Socio-Economic Justice in the Indian Constitution.
Shukla, C., Gandhi's View of Life.
Singh, Gurumukh Nihal, Land Marks in Indian Constitutional and National Development, Vol. I.
Singh, V.B., From Naoroji to Nehru (1975).
Sinha, M.P., Contemporary Relevance of Gandhi.
Sinha, Sachchidanand, Some eminent Indian Contemporaries (1976).

Sitarammaya, Pattabhi, The History of the Indian National Congress, Vols. I, II. (1969)

Stokes, Eric : The Englion Utilitarians and India (1959).

Tagore, R.N., Nationalism.

Tawney, R.H., Eauality.

Tendulkar, D.G., Mahatma Vol I. to VIII.

Tope, T.K., The Constitution of India (1971).

Vepa, Ram. K., New Technology–A Gandhian concept (1975).

Verma, V.P., The Political Philosophy of Mahatma Gandhi (1965).

Vivekanand, Swamy, Dharma Rahasya.

Vivekanand, Swamy, Hinduism (1968).

Wills, Edward, Constitutional Limitations.

INDEX

Adam, John, 8
Adam Smith, 8
Adivasis, 55
Adult education, 55
Advance technology, 63
Agricultural labourers, 84
Agricultural new deal, 281, 288
Ahimsa, 21, 41, 64, 74
All-India Congress Committee (AICC), 104, 280, 282, 340, 341
All Parties Conference, 325, recommendations, 360-62
Ambedkar, B.R., 115, 14, 127, 182, 185, 196, 197, 202, 210, 221, 248, 249, 274, 275, 291, 338, 339, 340
American Rockefeller, 34
Ancient concept, 18-30
Angreziat (English ways and Culture), 111
Annie Besant, 88
Anti Christian, 8
Aristotle, 130
Arnold, Mathew, 6
Arya Samaj, 8, 88
Atharva Veda, 28
Authoritarianism, 298
Auxiliary Medical Corps (AMC), 155
Awards, misuse of, 212
Azad, Maulana Abul Kalam, 212

Backward classes, state give assistance to, 193-95
Bacon, Francis, 8
Banerjee, Purnima, 114
Banerjee, Surendra Nath, 92, 97, 201
Bangalore Session, 341
Bankruptcy, 57
Banking Companies (Acquisition and transfer of undertakings), Act, 146
Barnard Shah, 297
Basu, D.D., 183
Bengal Hindu Social Disabilities Removal Act, 203
Bentham, Jermey, 6
Bhagwati, P.N. (Chief Justice, Supreme Court), 145, 160, 161, 162, 190
Bharat Ratna, 208, 212
Bhopal Gas tragedy, 345
Bill of Rights, 9
Bodily organs, 49
Bombay Prevention of Hindu Bigamous Marriages Act, 174
Bose, Anand Mohan, 92
Brahmacharya, 21
Brahmanical philosophy, 87, 88, 89
Brhamo Samaj, 87, 88, 89
Brailsford, Henry, 54
Brajeshwar Prasad, 120
Bread-labour, 45-47
  principle of, 80
British Jails, freedom fighters languishing in, 206
British Parliament, 86
British Raj, 92, 323, 324
Buddhist philosophy, 20
Bureaucracy, 17, 75
Burke, Edmund, 86

Capitalism, 107, 217
Caste-ridden society, 167
Challenges, 31, 87, 243
Chandrachud, Y.V. (Chief Justice) 132, 236-37, 305

Charkha, 35, 63, 64, 64
Charkha Sangh, 57
Chatterjee, Bankim Chandra, 94
Chelpathi Rau, 212
Chernovyl Atomic Plant accident, 345
Christianity, 3, 87, 188, 190-93
Civil Disobedience Movement, 103
Co-education, 186
Collectivism, 46
Coking Coal Mines (Nationalization) Act, 147
Commission of Inquiry Act, 144
Common ownership, 16
Communal rotation, 251
Communal Unity, 55
Comte, August, 86
Congress Election manifesto, 105
Constituent Assembly, 112, 114, 118, 120, 125, 127, 169, 172, 182, 185, 200, 201, 209, 219, 221, 222, 223, 248, 292, 297
  resolution of, 267-69
Constitution of India, seventh schedule of, 174
Constitution (Forty second) Amendment Act, 340
Constitution, scheduled caste orders, 189
Constitutional prohibitions, 182
Constructive programme, 53-58, 275, 321
Consumerism, 66
Contract Labour (Regulation and Abolition) Act, 163
Corruption, 290, 346
Cow service (*Goseva*), 55
Criticism, 119

Das, S.R. (Justice), 156, 251, 302
  judgement, 188-89
Decentralization, 64
Declaration of Right, 9-11
Democracy, 52, 315
Democratic conception, 14
Desai, Morarji, 212, 335
Deshmukh, P.S., 114
Devi Prasad, 36, 37
Dharma, 22, 120
Dictatorship, 298
Differences, 3-4, 11-12, 18-19
Directive Principle of State Policy, 300, 301, 302, 305-10
  draft constitution, 377-82
Discrimination, 14, 51, 132-35, 138-40, 143, 167, 200, 220, 229-33, 239-40, 241-43, 328-36
  cases of, 242-43
  prohibition of, 168-69, 180-81, 263-64
Disparities, 4, 11, 38, 46, 290, 316
Divorced Muslim Wife, 187
Domiciles, posts reserved for, 245
Dominion Constitution, 325
Draft Constitution, 115, 117, 118, 125, 126, 168, 219, 280, 292, 294, 353-55
Dutt, Ramesh Chandra, 94

East India Company, 81, 82
Economic backwardness, 197-98
Economic democracy, 113
Economic equality, 14, 15, 55, 58-70, 73-74, 76, 91-92, 97, 107, 167
  problem of, 17, 316-18
Economic freedom, 216
Economic independence, 43
Economic inequality, 39
  eradication of, 322-34
  removal of, 335-36
Economic exploitation, 75
Education, 47-53
  defective, existing system of, 47-48
  development oriented system, 52

system of, 27, 29, 356-58
fundamentals of, 49-50
Educationally backwardness, 193-96
Egalitarians vi, 9, 31, 316-317
Emergency excesses, 289-90
Employment, 169
equality of, 220, 225-30
English education, 83, 91
Equal protection clause, 140-42, 156-57
Equal Remuneration Act, 164
Equal universal sufferage, 14
Equality, 38-39
advocates of, 9
conception of, 10, 19, 30, 318-20
demands for, 13
Gandhian prescription of, viii
income, 46
notion of, 14, 316
principle of, 77
problems of, 9, 24, 321
protagonists of, 60
provisions, 326-36
victorian conception, 7
Equality-as-Justice, 1, 2, 12, 16, 315, 321
Equality-as-Sameness, 1, 2, 12, 16, 315, 319, 321
Equality of opportunity,
fundamental rights of, 25, 259-60
guarantee of, 237
judicial interpretation, 223-260
principles of, 230-32, 263-64
provision of, 240-42
rights to, 244
rule of, 252-53
Equality of promotion, 232-34
Exploitation, 16, 35, 60, 65, 66, 69-70, 107, 167, 217-19, 294, 350, 352
Five Year Plans, 276, 342
Flagrantly hostile discrimination, 146
Food and Agriculture Organisation (FAO), 345
Founding Fathers, 114-120, 275
views of, 298-300
Fourth Five Year Plans, 285
Franklin, Benjamin, 8
Fraternity, 39
social ethics of, 89
French egalitarions, 85
French revolution, vi, 3, 11, 40
Frustration, 48
Fundamental Principles of Governance, 375-77
Fundamental Rights, 103, 125-30, 131, 175, 186, 195, 205, 221-22, 301-310, 337
declaration of, 326-27
resolution of, 104-106, 363-67
Gadgil, N.V., 118
Gajendragadkar (Justice), 143, 194
Gandhi, Mahatma, v, vi, 8, 31, 32-38, 41-44, 46, 49, 50-52, 106, 114-17, 168, 200, 212, 229, 299, 320, 324, 334, 337
assassination of, 51
education scheme, 51
Modern industrialised societies, 59, 60
repugnance of machines, 68
social and political thought, 38-40
socio-economic model, 39
vision of Rama Rajya, 56
vision of self-sufficient village, 110-112
Gandhian,
bread-labour, 45-47
challenges, 344
concept of, 30-76
education, 47-53
constructive programme,

55-56, 275, 321
economic equality, 58-70
equality, 38-39
humanism, 37-38
non-violence, 39-42
philosophy, 44
satyagraha, 44-45
spirit, viii
swadeshi, 42-44
swaraj, 32-37
trusteeship, 32-37
value system, 37-38
untouchability, 53-58
Garibi Hatao, 288
Geographical situation, classification based on, 152-53
Ghose, Aurobindo, 99
Gokhale, Gopal Krishna, 96, 97, 100
Good old savages, 9
Government servant, pension of, 225-26
Green revolution, 276
Gujarat Judicial service recruitment rules, 243-44

Handicapped, 13
Hanumanthaiya, K., 116
Harijans, 201
disabilities of, 218
exclusively for, 176
Hazard Paul, 8
Helvetins, 6
Hidayatullah (Chief Justice), 245
Hill and Uttarakhand, reservation for, 191
Hind Swaraj, 35, 36
Hindu civilisation, 20, 22, 23
Hindu Succession Act, 177
Hindu women, plight of, 177
Hindustani Talimi Sangh, 57
Hinduism, 53
Hobbes, 7, 10
Home Rule, 99
Human body, departments of, 29
Humanism, 37-38
Humanitarian social atmos-phere, 23-28

Income Tax Investigation Commission, 150
India's future economic constitution, 61-62
Indian Association, 92
Indian concept, evolution of, 18-20
Indian Constitution, v, 129
Indian Income Tax Act, 149
Indian Growth performance, 343
Indian National Congress, 93, 97, 98, 102, 323, 324, 325
Indian Nationalism, 232
Indian Rockefeller, 34
Indian social revolution, 90
Indira Gandhi, vii, 45, 198, 211, 213, 277, 278, 283, 284, 286, 290
Indira Priyadarshini, 109
Industrial revolution, 12, 13, 85, 101
Industrialisation, 35, 59, 67, 69, 97, 110
Industries, decentralisation of, 66-67
Inequality, 89
age old problems of, 94
conception of, 201
development of, 4
problems of, 4, 21
Inegalitarian rule, 13
Injustice, tyranny of, 167
Institutional variation, 3
Intellectual labour, 46
Inter-marriages, 356
International Monitary Fund (IMF), 278, 346
Ishwar Bhakti, 21

Jagmohan Lt. Governor of Delhi, 137

Jammu & Kashmir, reservation of posts, 285
Janata Party, 212
Jayaprakash Narayan, 40
Jefferson, Thomas, 9
Jennings, Sir Ivor, 130, 159, 199, 211
Jermy Bentham, 83, 86
Jesus Christ, 22, 46
Judicial interpretation, 127-135, 169-200, 223-264
  Article 15(1), 169-80
  Article 15(2), 184-85
  Article 15(3), 185-87
  Article 15(4), 187-98
  Article 17, 199-205
  Article 18, 205-210
  Clause (1), 223-44
  Clause (2), 240-44
  Clause (3), 244-47
  Clause (4), 247-62
  Clause (5), 263-64
Judicial pronouncement, viii, 301-312, 326-36
Kalelkar Commission, 198
Kamath, H.V., 115, 120, 292, 297
Kamraj plan, 276
Kapoor, Yaspat Roy, 119, 221
Karachi, 103
Karachi Congress Resolution, 364
Karma, 19
Kisan, 155
Kisan-Mazdoor Buddhijivi Kalekar Raj, 117
Khadi movement, 55, 58, 62
Khanna, H.R. (Justice), 301
Khushwant Singh, 346
Kripalani, J.B., 211, 212
Kshatriyas, 24, 30

Labour-Saving machinery, 68
Lahiri, Somnath, 222
Lahore Session, 106
Lala Lajpat Rai, 89, 99, 323
Land Reforms, 281
  implementation of, 287-88
Laski, 2, 167, 217
Legal status, equaltiy of, 124-150
Lenin, 40
Liberal democracy, 101
Liberal political ideas, 30
Liberalisation, 162
Liberation, national movement, 124
Local Areas of Consumption Act, 150
Locke, John, 4, 7, 8, 10
Lok Sevak Sangh, 124, 275, 354
Lord Acton, 11
Lord Bentick, 84, 98
Lord Cornwallis, 83
Lord Curzon, 98
Lord Hastings, 83
Lucknow Session, 97

Mac Arthar, Douglas, 41
Madras Communal Government Order, 291
Madras General Sales Tax Act, 149
Madras Hindu (Bigamy Prevention and Divorce) Act, 174
Madras Temple Entry Authorization Act, 203
Magne, Charle, 41
Maitra, Pandit Laksmikant, 117
Malviya, H.D., 364
Malviya, Madan Mohan, 97
Mandal report, 198
Mantras, 22
Marshall, C.J., 148
Marx, 15, 16
Masani, M. R., 218
Modern education, 70
Modernization, 85
Moksha, 54

Money Circulating Schemes (Banning Act), 146
Motilal Nehru Committee, 222
Mukherjee (Justice), 143
Mulki Rules, 246-47
Muniswamy Pillai, V.R., 114
Munshi, K.M., 201, 221, 293
Muslim Personal Low, 187
Myrdal Gunnar, 357

Nagpur Session, 99
Naoroji, Dadabhai, 84, 95, 96, 97
Napolean, 41
National Planning Committee, 63, 346
National Warrant of Precedence, 208
Nationalization of Bank, 284, 288, 289
Nayee Talim, 51
Nehru, Jawahar Lal, 35, 104, 106, 110, 125, 168, 205, 216, 218, 277, 340, 348, 358
Neo-vedantism, 85
Niyam, 21
Non-Cooperation programme, 56
Non-exploitation, 46
Non-violence, 39-42
Non-violent non-cooperation, 71
  principle of, 77
  revolution, 53, 73
  society, 40
  swaraj, 76

Objective resolution, 111-12, 183
Open revolt, 10
Opportunity, equality of, 216-260
Other Backward classes, 250-51

Padma Bhushan, 208
Padma Shri, 208
Padma Vibhushan, 208
Paine, Thomas, 8
Pal, Biban Chandra, 94, 99, 323
Panchayati Raj, 72, 115, 353
  institution, 276
Partition of Bengal, 98, 321
Patel, Sardar Vallabhbhai, 125, 222, 356
Patriotism, 88
Philosophic foundation, 18-23
Pillai, V.I. Munshiswamy, 218
Place of Public resort, 184, 185
Planning Commission, 59
Pole Star, 100
Political agitation, 99
Political aspiration, 89
Political democracy, 399
Political defferences, 44
Political equality, 41
Political exploitation, 274
Police power, classification based on, 148-52
Purna Swaraj, 34, 53, 93, 166
Poverty, 59, 110, 278, 279
  eradication of, 280-81
Precocious nationalism, 320-30
Prevention of Corruption Act, 143
Privy Purses, abolition of, 284
Prohibition against discrimination, 55, 169, 171-79, 181, 237, 241
Prohibit racial segregation, 181
Promotion opportunities, 236-37
Prosecution, procedure of, 133
Protection of equal Law, 140
Protective discrimination, 172-73, 185, 332
Public employment, 335-36
  opportunity, 244-45
Public Interest Litigation (PIL), 160-64, 331
  judgement, 163
Public servant, termination of, 238-39

Public Service Commission (Procedure) Rules, 226-28
Punjab Police Manual, 140
Punjab Pre-emption Act, 144
Punjab University, 178
Purusha-Shakti, 29
Pyarelal, 70, 74

Quit India movement, 108
  resolution, 340

Radhakrishna, S., 112, 262
Rajendra Prasad, 112, 299, 350, 353
Rajiv Gandhi, vii
Rajmannar, P.V., (Chief Justice), 175
Ramakrishna Mission, 87
Ramaswami, V. (Justice), 284
Ram-Rajya, 32, 33
Ranade, Mahadeva Govind, 96, 97
Ranga, M.G., 114, 117, 218
Recruitment system, 231
Republican Constitution, 275
Reservation, 179, 353
  quantum of, 299
Reservation of seats in Medical Colleges, 190-92
Reservation of seats for women in Colleges, 178, 186
Rights to equality, 125-36, 159-62, 368-69, 372-74
  from Draft Constitution, 369-72
Round Table Conference, 75
Rousseau, 5, 6, 7, 10
Rowlett Act, 100, 102
Roy, A.N. (Chief Justice) 191, 228, 302
Roy, Raja Ram Mohun, 83, 84, 85, 91

Sadavrata, 64
Santhanam, K., 119
Sardar Hukum Singh, 114
Sarvodaya, 32, 33, 34
Sati, abolition of, 82
Satyagraha, 44-45
Satya yuga, 29
Saxena, S.L., 115
Schumakar, E.F., 59, 65
Scheduled Castes and Scheduled Tribes,
  challenges promotion of, 258-60
  educational institutions for, 333
  reservation of, 250-55, 295
Service Recruitment Rules, 233
Seth, Damodar Swarup, 120
Shastri, Patanjali (Chief Justice), 131, 145
Sinha, Sachchidananda, 95
Sixth Five Year Plan, 352
Social Backwardness, 197-98
Social reforms movement, 84
Social status, equality of, 14, 96, 167-200
Socialism, 46, 109
Socio-economic Justice, 320-22
  nature of directives, 275-77
  provision of, 336-42
  right to, 267-300
  judicial pronouncement, 301-12
  role of Indira Gandhi, 277-81
  role of Nehru, 268-75
Socio-economic reform, 89
Socio-economic structure, 28-30
Special legal procedure, classification based on, 153-60
Spinning wheel, 62-66
Subha Rao (Chief Justice), 131, 159, 302, 329
Subordinate discrimination, 159
Subordinate Legislation 134-35
Sucheta Kripalani, 212

Sudras, 24
Supreme Court, 131, 134, 148, 150, 152, 154, 218, 230-40, 245
  Judgement, 138
  pronouncement of, 326-27, 53
Swadeshi, v, vii, 42-44, 64, 95, 101, 321, 357
  movement, 94
  policy of, 99
  spirit, vi, 43
Swaraj, vi, 32, 37, 39, 42, 47, 48, 55, 57, 58, 63, 66, 70, 71, 76, 77, 95, 96, 99, 102, 200, 217, 219, 298, 364
Swarajya, 125, 320, 324, 337
Swami Vivekananda, 31, 89, 90, 101

Tagore, Dwarkanath, 83
Tagore, Rabindranath, 167
Talimi Sangh, 57
Tamil Nadu Abolition of Posts of Part-time Villages Officers Act, 157
Tandolkar (Justice), 144
Tandan, Purushottam Das, 113
Taxation, 366-67
  classification based on, 149-50
Taxation of income (Investigation Commission Act), 149
Technological determination, 70
Ten point economic programme, 278
Terrorism, 345
Theosophical Society, 87-88
Tihar Jail, 140
Tilak, Bal Gangadhar, 99, 322
Tolstay, 324
Town Planning Scheme, 154
Tripathi, V.D., 113
Trusteeship, 71, 73, 74, 77, 321
20-Point Programme, 288

Unemployment, 59, 63, 67, 104, 110
Unless education, 48
Untouchability, 33, 53, 58, 172
  abolition of, 199-200
  eradication of, 96
  ground of, 200-205
  removal of, 54, 200, 333-35
Untouchability (Offences) Act, 182, 184, 202, 334, 352
Upanishadic thinkers, 25-26
Uttarakhand, 190

Vaishyas, 24
Vanprastha, 27
Varnashram, 201
Varnashram Dharms, 28
  social system of, 319, 320
Vedic literature, 28
Venkatramiah, E.S., (Justice), 137
Videshi spirit, vi, viii,
Village industry, 35, 55, 65, 68
Village Panchayats, 72, 95, 119, 185, 292
Village uplift movement, 110
Voltaire, 8, 10

West Bengal Foodgrains (Movement Control) Order, 173
Western democracies, 19, 320
White-collar Jobs, 48
Women, liberation of, 172
  reservation of seats for, 175-78
World Bank, 218
World War II, 124

Yama, 21
Yawning gap, vi

Zamindari Abolition Act, 301, 338